Robin Kelley O'Connor
Alistair Robertson
LOUIS LATOUR
Marvin R. Shanken
LF Bouchard
Rodney D. Strong
James Trezise
Mike Stephens
John L. Meis
Louis P. Martini

Gary Jordan

Kevin Arnold

A. J. ... Johann Krige

Greg May

Jeff Clarke

Kerry Brady   Roquel ...

Ch. Wijl   Theo Haart

ZACCAGNA

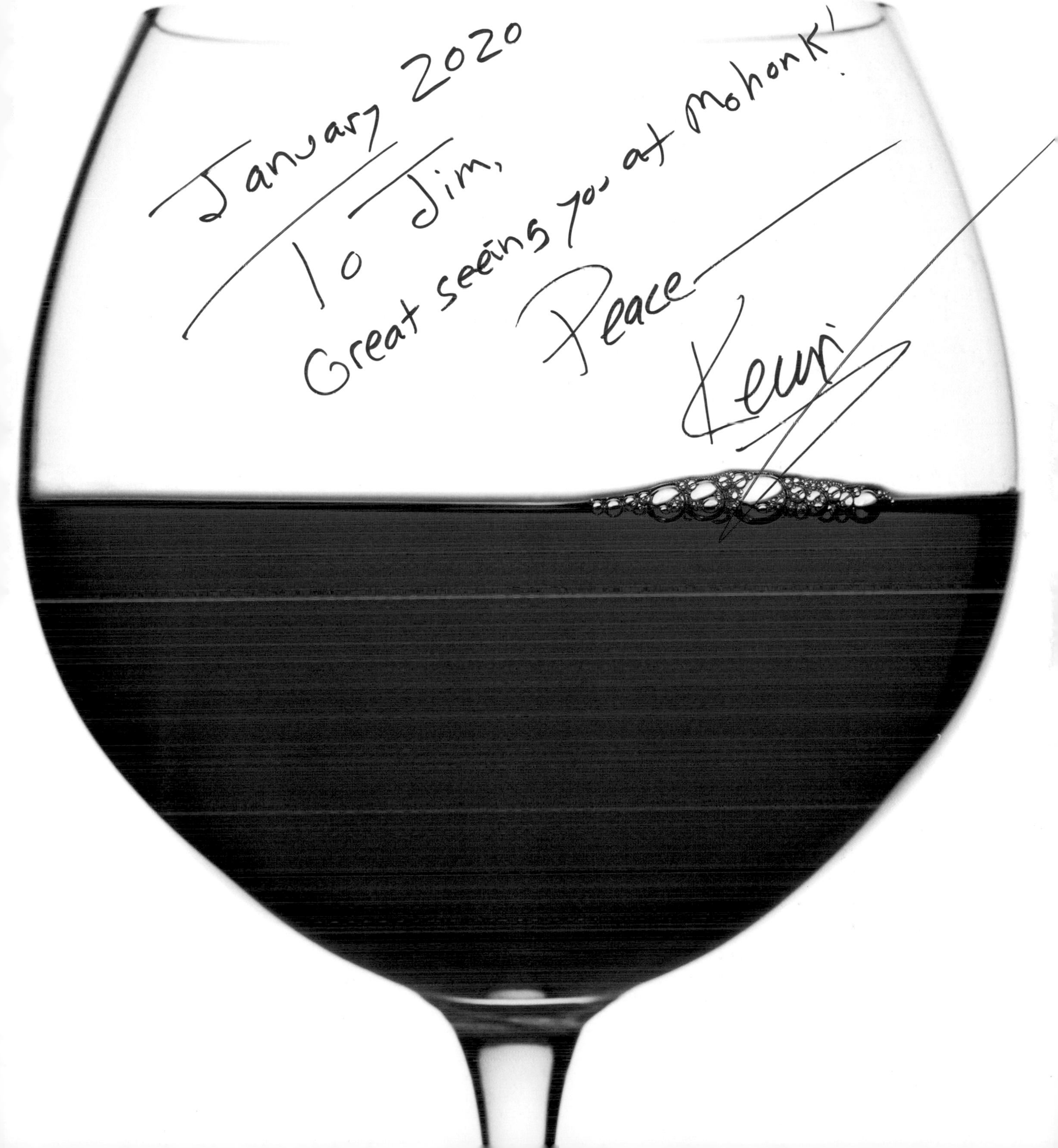
January 2020
To Jim,
Great seeing you at Mohonk!
Peace
Kevin

KEVIN ZRALY

· · · · · · · · · ·

WINDOWS ON THE WORLD COMPLETE WINE COURSE

·REVISED, UPDATED & EXPANDED·
2019 EDITION

· · · · · · · · · · ·

STERLING EPICURE
New York

Grape growers, winemakers, and wine friends throughout the world
have contributed their expertise and enthusiasm to this project. The signatures on the endpapers
come from some of the people whose help has proved invaluable to me.

STERLING EPICURE
New York

An Imprint of Sterling Publishing Co., Inc.
1166 Avenue of the Americas
New York, NY 10036

ISBN 978-1-4549-3046-4
978-1-4351-6881-7 (signed edition)

Distributed in Canada by Sterling Publishing Co., Inc.
c/o Canadian Manda Group, 664 Annette Street
Toronto, Ontario, M6S 2C8, Canada
Distributed in the United Kingdom by GMC Distribution Services
Castle Place, 166 High Street, Lewes, East Sussex, BN7 1XU, United Kingdom
Distributed in Australia by NewSouth Books
University of New South Wales, Sydney, NSW 2052, Australia

For information about custom editions, special sales, and premium and corporate purchases,
please contact Sterling Special Sales at 800-805-5489 or specialsales@sterlingpublishing.com.

Manufactured in Canada

2 4 6 8 10 9 7 5 3

sterlingpublishing.com
kevinzraly.com

Interior design by Ashley Prine
For image credits, see page 405

DEDICATION

This book is called *Windows on the World Complete Wine Course* for a reason. Windows on the World was the restaurant atop One World Trade Center in New York City. I worked there from the day it opened in 1976 and for the next 25 years—until September 11, 2001. I continue to title this book with the name of the restaurant to continue its legacy.

I dedicate this edition to all those who worked at Windows on the World, celebrated their birthdays, anniversaries, or bar mitzvahs there, dined there, or just had a glass of wine at the bar.

The Windows on the World Wine School continued uninterrupted for forty years. After the World Trade Center terrorist bombing in 1993 and even after its destruction in 2001, I continued the school at the Marriott Marquis Hotel in Times Square. In fall 2016, the Windows on the World Wine School ended its forty-year run. I am pleased to say that I never missed a class or stopped teaching one because of terrorism. I also dedicate this edition to the more than 20,000 students who took the class and learned to enjoy the taste of a great glass of wine.

I continue teaching advanced wine classes and master classes at Sherry-Lehmann Wines & Spirits on Park Avenue in New York City.

CONTENTS

FOR MORE INFORMATION, INCLUDING LINKS TO VIDEOS
AND PRONUNCIATIONS, VISIT KEVINZRALY.COM.

INTRODUCTION

AFTER 45 YEARS of teaching wine classes, I want to look back in time to describe my wine journey and why I wrote this book. I can say honestly that I am still having fun on this amazing adventure.

At age 25, I accepted the position of cellar master at Windows on the World, the restaurant opening at the top of One World Trade Center. I had the responsibility of selecting, ordering, and selling all the restaurant's wine. There I was, a kid in a candy store with carte blanche and only one mandate: create the biggest and best wine list New York City had ever seen. So I did. Within five years of opening, Windows on the World became the number-one dollar-volume restaurant, with more wine sold than any other restaurant in the world.

Wine had been my passion since my college days, when, at age 19, I landed a job as a waiter to earn some beer money. As fate had it, the restaurant received a four-star rating from *New York Times* restaurant critic Craig Claiborne, and the owner asked me to take over bartending duties. (At the time, the legal drinking age in New York was 18.) I began studying beer, distilled spirits, and wine, learning whatever I could as fast as I could. Then I tasted my first glass of great wine, and that was it. From that moment, wine became my passion, and I quickly switched from Budweiser to Burgundy!

Studying wine isn't merely learning about a beverage but also understanding the history, language, culture, and traditions of the people and countries where each wine is made. Wine is a complicated subject, one that reinvents itself every year with a new vintage. That wines constantly change makes for fascinating, lifelong study.

Over the next five years, I read as many wine books as I could find, attended wine tastings, and traveled to wineries in New York, California, and Europe. I taught my first class when I was 20 and, later, a two-credit wine course while I was still a college student.

All this helped when I interviewed for the job at Windows on the World. In fall 1976, the Windows on the World Wine School began. I had to decide which textbook to use. Unfortunately, most wine books available at the time were encyclopedic and too advanced for my students. So I started with my own handouts for each class. I also had a friend record a year of the wine school. After each class, she gave me a transcript of what I taught, including the students' questions. Those handouts and the transcripts eventually became the basis for this book, which I used in the Wine School since the book first was published in 1985. That it has sold more than three million copies since then is overwhelming!

As Shakespeare masterfully said, "Brevity is the soul of wit." In college, one of my favorite authors was George Orwell. In the essay "Rules of Communication," he writes: "Use simple language, simple expressions, and simple style." William Strunk Jr. and E. B. White continue that thought in *The Elements of Style*: "A sentence should contain no unnecessary words, a paragraph no unnecessary sentences." In updating this book, I followed that advice, and it continues to work well for my students and readers. The format has stayed very much the same for more than thirty years. To emphasize specific points and supplement the information in the text, I added sidebars. I love statistics, so I have included facts and figures as well as anecdotes, personal commentary, and quotes in the margins to reinforce the ideas in the main text. All these tools make learning about wine easy and fun.

Faced with the opportunity to revise, my approach over the years has been to add only up-to-date, useful information. Less is more.

In researching "The Greater World of Wine" chapter this past year, I tasted thousands of wines. Some were good, some not so good, and others outstanding, especially in the $20–$30 range. By constantly tasting wine, I learn new things every day. The journey continues.

THE STORY OF WINDOWS ON THE WORLD

Windows on the World opened its elevator doors for the first time on April 12, 1976, as a private luncheon club. The press had been writing about its opening for months, speculating whether the whole project—both the restaurant and the World Trade Center complex itself—could succeed. Never before had anyone attempted a project this large. It was designed not only to be the tallest building in the world, but it also was going to be one of the largest urban centers ever built, feeding more than 50,000 office workers and more than 150,000 commuters who would pass through the complex on their way to and from work every day.

All eyes fixed on Joe Baum, the man in charge of food services for the complex and mastermind behind the Windows on the World restaurant. Everyone wanted to see and feel and touch what Joe Baum had been working on for the previous six years. After all, Joe had created some of New York's most successful landmark restaurants, including the Four Seasons, la Fonda del Sol, and the Forum of the Twelve Caesars.

Baum's family owned a resort in New York's Saratoga Springs, so Joe grew up in the hospitality world. Shortly after graduating from the Cornell University School of Hotel Administration, he took a job with a major restaurant operator, Restaurant Associates (R.A.). While working at R.A., he developed a reputation: He became known in the industry as a maverick, genius, and pitbull—usually all at the same time. His innovative approach often landed him in trouble, and in the late '60s, Joe left R.A. to form his own consulting company. In 1970, he signed a contract with the Port Authority of New York and New Jersey to design and manage all the restaurant and food-service areas of the World Trade Center.

Joe and his associates conceived and organized 22 restaurants throughout the complex. They planned restaurants with names such as Eat & Drink, the Big Kitchen, and the Market Bar and Dining Room and included everything from Coffee Express, where commuters could grab a cup of coffee and a bagel while in transit, to Windows on the World. With almost 200,000 people working or passing through every day, the WTC became a city unto itself.

"To me, Windows on the World will always be about Joe Baum, who knew the significance of establishing an urban oasis atop the tallest towers in New York City. With its exciting architecture and its culinary and wine programs easily accessible to everyone, Windows satisfied the many appetites of body and soul."

—TONY ZAZULA, owner, Commerce Restaurant, New York City

Joe Baum

North View

SOUTH · New York Harbor

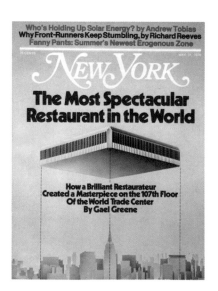

Who's Holding Up Solar Energy? by Andrew Tobias
Why Front-Runners Keep Stumbling, by Richard Reeves
Fanny Pants: Summer's Newest Erogenous Zone

NEW YORK

The Most Spectacular Restaurant in the World

How a Brilliant Restaurateur Created a Masterpiece on the 107th Floor Of the World Trade Center By Gael Greene

Joe had grandiose ideas for the restaurant on top of the World Trade Center—ideas that cost a lot of money. In the early '70s, New York City was in a severe fiscal crisis. Many New Yorkers opposed building the World Trade Center in the first place, and building anything extravagant meant facing intense scrutiny.

With the backing of the Port Authority, more than $17 million went into developing Windows on the World. The main focus was the 107th floor of One World Trade Center, divided into five parts: the Restaurant (seating nearly 300 guests); the City Lights Bar; Hors d'Oeuvrerie, which served everything except the main course; The Cellar in the Sky, a glass-enclosed working wine cellar that seated just 36 guests and served a seven-course, five-wine, one-seating dinner; and six private banquet rooms capable of seating more than 300 people. Altogether, Windows on the World spanned one acre, 107 stories up in the sky.

Joe Baum was a master contractor. He hired the best culinary talent available. He asked food author James Beard and chef Jacques Pépin to help develop the menus, Warren Platner to design the restaurant, and Milton Glaser to design the graphics—all the best in the business.

Joe asked me to handle the wine for Windows on the World and hired me as the cellar master. Friends warned me against leaving my job as a wine salesman to work at Windows, giving me three reasons not to take the job:

1. In 1976, no one went downtown after 6 PM.
2. Rooftop restaurants weren't considered quality operations.
3. Joe Baum had a reputation for being difficult.

On all three counts, it just wasn't so. I knew it was going to be a great restaurant and job when I asked Joe about creating the wine list. He said: "It's very simple. I want you to create the biggest and the best wine list that New York has ever seen, and don't worry about how much it costs!" There I was, a 25-year-old kid in a candy store—only it sold wine!

In May 1976, the cover of *New York* magazine read: "The Most Spectacular Restaurant in the World—How a Brilliant Restaurateur Created a Masterpiece on the 107th Floor of the World Trade Center." Some of the superlatives from that article by the illustrious Gael Greene included: "a miracle," "a masterpiece," "a dream," and "almost unreal." It went on, "Windows on the World is a triumph!" "No other sky-high restaurant quite prepares you for the astonishment of the horizon . . . like a luxury liner sailing through the blue skies," "Everything to hate and fear is invisible." This was the best article ever written about Windows on the World, and it

Teaching the Wine School in the early 1980s

A Windows on the World business card with Milton Glaser's memorable design

appeared *before* the public opening! We thought it couldn't get any better, but we were wrong. The best was yet to come.

The World Trade Center and Windows on the World became symbols of the financial turnaround of New York City, and their completion played a key role in the revitalization of Lower Manhattan. The year that Windows on the World opened, 1976, was also the bicentennial of America. From the 107th floor, imagine an unobstructed view of the spectacularly refurbished Statue of Liberty and all of New York Harbor with its flotilla of tall ships. What a sight! Seeing the bicentennial fireworks from Windows became the hottest ticket in the world.

On that memorable July Fourth evening, I went alone to the top of One World Trade Center (the broadcast antennae and barriers not yet erected) and watched all the fireworks displays within a 60-mile radius. *Life doesn't get much better than this*, I remember thinking. I was serving wine to kings, queens, presidents, sports heroes, and movie stars. During the next five years, I met every celebrity I had ever heard of or read about.

Windows on the World was an instant success and booked up months in advance. What made it so great? Was it the 60-second elevator ride? The menu concept? The youthful, energetic staff? The extensive and outrageously low-priced wine list? The most spectacular view in the world?

For me, it was all of the above.

The first five years of Windows on the World were nonstop. Always full for lunch and dinner, it was the restaurant destination of choice for

"On July 4, 1976, Windows on the World was filled with celebrities for the bicentennial fireworks display. I was given the very pleasant task of escorting Princess Grace of Monaco. As we watched the extravaganza over the Statue of Liberty, Princess Grace held my hand very tightly because the fireworks made her somewhat nervous. I asked if the moment reminded her of To Catch a Thief *and her very famous, very passionate scene with Cary Grant, set to the backdrop of fireworks. She was astounded I knew the film and the scene. So I told her that, if she wanted to watch the film again, she could that night because it was being shown at 11:30, on Channel Two."*

—MELVIN FREEMAN, page,
Windows on the World,
1976–1993 and 1996–2001

"Even more than high school and college, my 'education' at Windows on the World University has stood me well in tackling the challenges of the world at large."

—MICHAEL SKURNIK, assistant cellar master,
Windows on the World, 1977–1978;
now president, Michael Skurnik Wines Ltd

everyone, well, in the world. Combined with all the other World Trade Center restaurants, it proved so successful in the first five years (generating close to $50 million in revenue in 1980 alone) that a ballroom on the 106th floor joined the ranks in 1981. The demand for such a large space was overwhelming; prior to construction, very little banquet space was available to the public in downtown Manhattan. Again, the World Trade Center complex was playing a vital role in both the community and the economic redevelopment of the area.

In 1985, this book, *Windows on the World Complete Wine Course*, made its debut, putting the Wine School in print for the first time.

The first terrorist attack on the World Trade Center took place on February 26, 1993, at 12:18 pm. Six people were killed, including one of our employees who worked in the receiving department in the basement. Andrea Robinson, cellar master at the time, escorted all our guests down 107 flights of stairs to safety.

Windows on the World shut down after the bombing, leaving more than 400 food-service people without jobs. Within six months, I was the last on the payroll, and the restaurant lay dormant from February 1993, until June 1996. I was one of the few people allowed to enter after the 1993 bombing. It was a very lonely time.

In the Cellar in the Sky

An early brochure from the Windows on the World Wine School

The Port Authority knew that the restaurant was going to be closed but wanted to continue the Wine School. It had operated continuously since the restaurant opened in 1976. The school started with a small group of ten lunch-club members in 1976. Members invited their friends, who then invited *their* friends. Soon the friends of club members outnumbered the club members. Still, the class list kept growing. In 1980, we opened the school to the public. More than 20,000 students attended those classes.

"Windows was silent when I ran the wine school, but I relished its solitude. I roamed its floors, inspected its rooms, absorbed all that was left frozen in time. Like Jack Nicholson in The Shining, *I could sense the energy it embodied, feel its buzz, envision its diners, find myself immersed in the dream. But unlike Jack's, my visions embodied warmth and peace. The space lived and breathed even when empty and will continue to do so in our hearts."*
—REBECCA CHAPPA,
Wine School coordinator, 1994–1995;
owner, Wine by the Class
and Tannin Management

Although the restaurant closed from 1993 until 1996, I continued teaching the classes in three different locations in the World Trade Center complex. I'm proud that the school remained open during those difficult years; it kept the memory of the restaurant alive and became a symbol to everyone of its eventual return.

In late 1993, the Port Authority began looking for a new operator. Again, requests for proposals went out, and this time more than 30 restaurant operators expressed interest in taking over Windows on the World. A review committee examined each proposal and made recommendations. They narrowed it down to three entries: Alan Stillman, owner of Smith & Wollensky, the Post House, the Manhattan Ocean Club, Park Avenue Café, and Cité; Warner LeRoy of Tavern on the Green, Maxwell's Plum, and later the Russian Tea Room; and Joe Baum, original creator of Windows on the World, then operating the Rainbow Room.

The Port Authority awarded the contract to Joe Baum, and the renaissance of Windows on the World began. Both Andrea Robinson and I came back: she to develop the wine list and beverage program, and I to continue the Wine School. In all, the staff totaled more than 400 employees and represented more than 25 nationalities.

The names of many of the old spaces changed as part of the renovation: The old City Lights Bar and the Hors d'Oeuvrerie became the Greatest Bar on Earth. The Cellar in the Sky took up a new location overlooking the Statue of Liberty. The banquet rooms expanded.

The reopening of Windows on the World in June 1996, twenty years almost to the month after its first opening, happened because of Joe Baum's kinetic energy, joie de vivre, and theatrical hoopla. The celebrities came back, the paparazzi gathered in full force, the view was better than ever, and the wines had aged gracefully over the previous three years. It felt almost like 1976 all over again.

Within a year of reopening, management decided to make Windows on the World the ultimate American-style food and wine experience. The most important change was hiring Michael Lomonaco, former executive chef of the '21' Club, to oversee all culinary operations as the Windows chef. He was the first American-born chef to run the kitchen.

Under Lomonaco's leadership, Windows on the World received two stars from the The New York Times, three stars from Crains, a 22 in Zagat, and ranked in the top listing in Wine Spectator for overall dining. Over the next three years, Windows on the World remained a premier destination

Overlooking the East River and the Brooklyn Bridge, this picture was taken from the 107th floor of One World Trade Center

"What I remember most about Windows on the World is the employee cafeteria. It was in that room that friends congregated to eat, talk, and enjoy the view of the three bridges below us. It was here where laughter and happiness prevailed. Windows was my family in New York, my world that I loved so dearly."
—INEZ HOLDERNESS, beverage manager, Windows on the World, 1999–2001; owner, On the Square Restaurant & Wine Store, Tarboro, North Carolina

"Most people saw only the crowds of people and felt the energy of a busy restaurant complex when they came to Windows. We were lucky enough to experience the peace and beauty that surrounded us every day, long after the crowds had gone home. My favorite times occurred long after service was over, when I could turn off all the lights in the dining room and sit with a glass of wine to enjoy the beauty of the city stretched out before me."
—MELISSA TRUMBULL, restaurant manager, Windows on the World, 1997–2001; director, Ian Schrager's Royalton Restaurant

"Windows on the World reopening in 1996 was the launchpad for my career in wine. Working with Kevin and overseeing the award-winning wine list he created have given me tasteful (pun intended) memories to last a lifetime . . . 1989 Coche-Dury Corton Charlemagne, 1989 Comte de Vogue Musigny Blanc and 1975 Joseph Phelps 'Eisele Vineyard' Cabernet Sauvignon to name but a few!"
—RALPH HERSOM, cellar master, Windows on the World, 1996-1997; category manager of wine / beer /spirits, Hannaford Supermarkets

Michael Lomonaco

An early menu from Windows on the World

"When I reflect on the 22 years I spent at Windows on the World, no singular event immediately comes to mind but rather a series of images: the faces of children pressed up against the windows, the sun setting over the Statue of Liberty, and the laughter and joy of thousands of guests who created a lifetime of cherished memories."

—JULES ROINNEL,
director, the World Trade Center Club, 1979–2001

for corporate meetings, weddings, anniversaries, birthdays, and bar mitzvahs, often hosting parties of 10 to 1,200 people.

The Greatest Bar on Earth took on a life all its own. Under its old guise, the Bar closed at 10 PM. The new bar began attracting a younger, more vibrant international crowd that danced 'til the wee hours to the city's hottest bands and DJs. The Greatest Bar on Earth became a downtown late-night destination. Windows had learned to change with the times.

The Cellar in the Sky had been an integral part of the old Windows on the World, but by 1996 restaurants around the country were doing food and wine pairings as well. It was time to replace the Cellar with something new: a restaurant called Wild Blue. At Wild Blue—a restaurant within a restaurant—Michael and his chefs showcased their culinary skills. Wild Blue received four stars from *Crains*, a 25 in *Zagat*, a spot in the top-ten list of New York restaurants in *Wine Spectator*, and a rating as one of New York's best by *Esquire*.

Windows was the best it could be on September 10, 2001. It was producing more than $37 million in revenue and was the number-one dollar volume restaurant in the country. Of that $37 million, $5 million came from the sale of wines from among our 1,400 different selections. We were enthusiastic about our future and were preparing excitedly for our 25th anniversary celebration the following month, with the opening of the new wine cellar.

But on Tuesday, September 11, 2001, the world changed. What began as a beautiful, pristine September morning ended in a dark nightmare of death and destruction. Exactly 72 coworkers, one security officer, and seven construction workers who were building the new wine cellar died in the worst terrorist attack in American history.

For me, the loss remains incomprehensible. The World Trade Center complex was my New York City. It was a neighborhood. I shopped there. I stayed at the Marriott with my family. My dentist and my bank were there. I lost my home and community of 25 years, a community I helped build and watched grow. Windows on the World no longer exists, but the reflections of those windows will remain with me forever.

After September 11, 2001, I took every memento I had of the restaurant and shared all of it with the New York Public Library as part of a tribute they were holding to the greatest restaurants of the world. Now that the 9/11 Memorial has opened, it seems appropriate to share photos, menus, and memories of this very special restaurant once again. It's my way of honoring the legacy and keeping alive the memory of Windows on the World.

"I was in the 'Skybox' room overlooking The Greatest Bar on Earth Monday night September 10th. I was hosting my class called 'Spirits in the Skybox,' a name that has haunting implications. When we finished, my co-host and head bartender, George Delgado, and I invited a few friends and some members of the press to join us for a quick drink in the bar. I usually have cocktails, but this time we ordered Champagne. There was no particular celebration; the group just seemed to click, so we had several more bottles of Champagne and food. A DJ named Jennifer began spinning records. Someone in our group knew her, so we stayed and ended the evening dancing. I awoke Tuesday morning to the horror of the terrorist attack that finished off that medium-sized city called the World Trade Center. I will cherish the gift I was given of that last spontaneous celebration in the late Joe Baum's majestic Windows on the World. We were unknowingly lifting our Champagne glasses that night in farewell to all those friends and colleagues we would lose the following day."

—DALE DEGROFF,
master mixologist, Windows on the World, 1996–2001; author, kingcocktail.com

The World Trade Center Plaza in the 1980s. Minoru Yamasaki served as designer and lead architect of the World Trade Center. Fritz Koenig's bronze sculpture "The Sphere" stood in the plaza between the two towers. It was not destroyed and recently returned to Liberty Park, next to the 9/11 Memorial.

THE WINE REVOLUTION: 1970-2019

"May you live in interesting times."

In 1970, when I began my journey in wine, I studied French wines and a little German wine. Those were the only quality wines being made. Then it started to happen: California began to produce outstanding wines, especially Cabernet Sauvignon from the Napa Valley. Next, not in any specific order, Cabernet Sauvignon from Chile, Malbec from Argentina, Merlot from Washington State, Shiraz from Australia, Pinot Noir from Oregon, Sauvignon Blanc from New Zealand, Riesling from New York, and more came into the quality category. The resurgence of great wines from Italy and Spain also added to the wine revolution. Wine has become a global community, and today is the golden age for wine in the world.

Here are the changes since 1970 that have altered the course of viticulture and winemaking significantly. Wherever possible throughout the book, I have included sidebars comparing wine statistics from 1970 to now.

VITICULTURE AND WINEMAKING

Wine quality has improved enormously over the last five decades, more than at any other time in the history of winemaking. Vast strides have occurred in the science and technology, growers have readapted back-to-the-earth farming techniques, and widespread planting of international grapes has taken place, all of which have led to wine's rise in popularity throughout the world.

Here are some of the specific changes in high-quaity viticulture and winemaking that I have witnessed.

- More attention paid to individual vineyards, clonal selection, and trellis systems
- More care taken to match grape varieties with specific sites
- Vine density (number of vines planted per acre) has increased dramatically, which has allowed viticulturists to produce better grapes.
- Sustainability has become king: Grape growers are using fewer herbicides and pesticides, and many are going organic. There are more than 500 producers of biodynamic wines, including elite wineries such as Araujo, Benziger, Castello dei Rampolla, Chapoutier, Château Pontet-Canet, Domaine Leflaive, Domaine Leroy, Grgich Hills, J. Phelps, Quintessa, and Zind Humbrecht.
- Climate change: Between 1960 and 1969, grape harvesting in Burgundy, France, on average began on September 27. From 2000 to 2018, grape harvesting began closer to the first week of September. To help offset the effects of a shorter growing season, some viticulturists plant grapes vertically rather than horizontally to avoid excess sun.
- Winemakers increasingly are using natural rather than laboratory yeasts.
- Even though alcohol levels have reached historic highs, most quality winemakers have adjusted their techniques to keep all components of a wine in balance.
- Oak used far more judiciously
- Far less filtering of wine, leading to a more complex and natural taste
- Chaptalization (adding sugar) now rarely used

THE WINE REGIONS OF THE WORLD

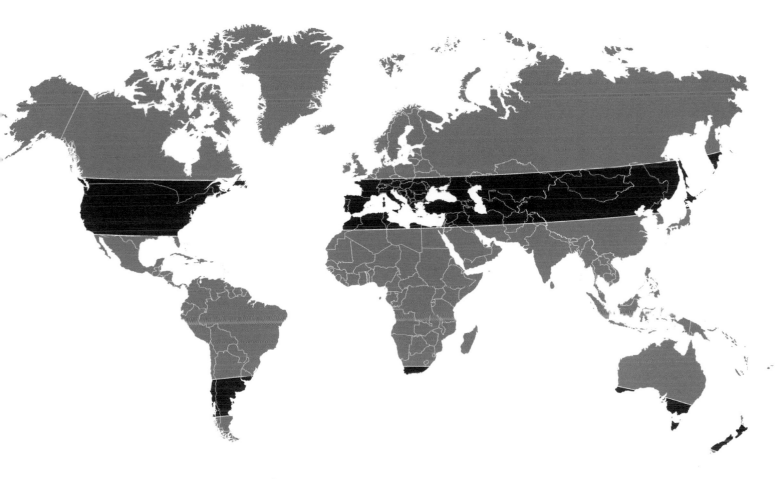

- Winemakers in California have been creating it for years, but the general public is hearing more about wine infused with marijuana. No doubt a few bottles will be on hand to celebrate the 50th anniversary of Woodstock!

- Screw caps gradually are replacing corks on more than just inexpensive wines: Screw caps seal 75 percent of Australian and more than 90 percent of New Zealand wines, but 70 percent of all wine stoppers in the world still are made of cork.

- The European Union has standardized basic wine labeling rules for member nations, and countries exporting to the EU (and worldwide) are following their regulations. For example, one law states that if a grape name appears on the label, the wine must contain a minimum of 85 percent of that grape.

- Wine consumption in America has increased more than 60 percent over the last 20 years.

THE BUSINESS OF WINE

Besides the tremendous elevation in wine quality, the wine business has benefited greatly from the global planting of *Vitis vinifera* grapes. Cabernet Sauvignon, Merlot, Pinot Noir, Chardonnay, Sauvignon Blanc, Riesling, and other familiar grapes now grow throughout the world, making it easier for you to buy unfamiliar wines with the expectation that you will be getting a wine familiar in style and of a fairly consistent quality.

Here are a few of the most significant advances in the business of wine:

- 2018 marked the 85th anniversary of the repeal of Prohibition (page 60).

- When I began my study of wine in 1970, Europe was by far the number-one producer of wine in the world, with 78 percent of total marketshare. In 2018, Europe dropped to 67 percent, and America increased to nearly 20 percent of worldwide wine production.

- When I started studying wine, America had only a few hundred wineries. Today there are almost 10,000, and wine is produced in all 50 states!

- Wine has enjoyed the largest growth rate of all alcoholic beverages since 2001.

- In 2005, the U.S. Supreme Court approved the interstate shipping of wine directly to consumers, causing most states to rewrite their wine laws. FedEx and UPS are delivering wine directly to consumers, which is now legal in many states.

- Celebrity branding is big, including football players (Drew Bledsoe, Mike Ditka, John Elway, John Madden, Joe Montana, Charles Woodson, Peyton Manning!), baseball stars (Tom Seaver), race-car drivers (Jeff Gordon, Mario Andretti), politicians (Nancy Pelosi), actors (Drew Barrymore, Kate Hudson, Angelina Jolie, Brad Pitt), and musicians (Bob Dylan, Dave Matthews, Zac Brown, John Legend, Sting). Celebrity wine sales exceeded $50 million in 2018.

- American wine names are becoming more creative, for example: The 7 Deadly Zins, The Big Easy, Cono Sur, Fat Bastard, Gnarly Head, Kick Ass Red, Killer Juice, Mad Housewife, Marilyn Merlot, Ménage à Trois, Message in a Bottle, Mommy's Time Out, Pandora's Amphora, Pinot Evil, and Red Truck.

- The quality of American wine lists has never been better. Although some restaurants have created "monster" lists for promotional purposes, others list only the best wines in each category. You can find wine lists in diners all across America now! Shake Shack has an extraordinary wine list.

- According to Silicon Valley Bank, fine wine sales—bottles priced at $20 or more—are expected to grow about 14 percent in 2018.

- The average price of a standard bottle of wine sold in a retail store in America is $10 a bottle. The price-quality relationship is the best it has ever been for the consumer.

- Costco sells more than $2 billion in wine annually, making it the largest retailer of wine in America. In 2010, Costco spent more than $22 million to help change Washington State's laws from state control to privatization of wine sales.

- Wine in a box is becoming more popular, especially among California jug wine producers, to reduce greenhouse emissions and lower carbon footprints by not having to ship glass. According to Nielsen, the value share of 3-liter boxes grew 94 percent from 2010 to 2015.

- Wine in cans is becoming more popular as well, especially in sports stadiums. Wines in cans include: Francis Ford Coppola Sofia, Infinite Monkey, and Underwood.

- Exports of American wine went from almost nothing in 1970 to more than $1.7 billion today!

- China has become the fifth largest wine consumer in the world and is expected to become the second largest wine consumer by 2020, after only the USA. The Chinese are drinking primarily red (their lucky color), and they are the largest consumer of red wine and the number-one importer of Bordeaux in the world.

- China now has more than 200 wineries. Château Lafite Rothschild released their first vintage of Domaine de Penglai, from Eastern China, in 2018, and the 2013 Ao Yun Shangri-La Cabernet Sauvignon (Yunnan Province) wine is selling for $300 in America!

- Thanks to the Internet, anyone can become a wine critic or ask the critics questions on eRobertParker.com, Wine Spectator's blog index, or Dr. Vino, to name a few.

- Want to own a vineyard? According to Silicon Valley Bank, 30 percent of U.S. wineries will be for sale in the next 5 years.

WINE CONSUMERS

GALLONS PER PERSON PER YEAR		
BEVERAGE	1970	2017
BEER	30.6	26.9
COFFEE	33.4	18.5
MILK	31.2	23.0
SOFT DRINKS	20.8	38.5
WINE	1.3	3.14

Better quality, familiar varietals, and expert marketing have given consumers worldwide some of the best wines ever produced at some of the most reasonable prices. Today you have a better selection of wine at all price points than ever before, and it promises to get even better in the future!

Here are some wine consumer highlights of the last forty years:

• In France, Spain, and Italy, wine consumption has dropped more than 50 percent since 1970.

• In 2012, America became the largest wine market in the world. In 2016, sales hit $39.8 billion, and imports crested $20.2 billion, pushing total wine sales to $60 billion. Sales the next year exceeded $62 billion. Americans are drinking more and better wine than ever before.

• 2017 was the 25th consecutive year of growth in American wine consumption. In 2016, it reached a record of 949 million gallons, an increase of more than 682 million gallons since 1970. Per capita wine consumption increased from 1.31 gallons in 1970 to 3.14 gallons in 2017.

• In 2017, Goldman Sachs downgraded beer and liquor and upgraded wine.

• Revenue for direct-to-consumer wines exceeds $2 billion, but interstate shipping continues to pose a problem for wine retailers in America.

• Transparency of wine prices worldwide has made it better for the consumer. Internet sites such as wine-searcher.com will give you the price of a wine around the world.

• Wine lovers are turning increasingly to auctions. Worldwide auction sales totaled $337 million in 2013, compared with $33 million in 1994. American auction sales in 2017 hit more than $168 million, and Internet auction sales exceeded $39.9 million.

• In 2018, Auction Napa Valley raised $13.6 million, bringing their total given to the Napa Valley community since 1980 to $180 million. The Naples Winter Wine Festival has raised more than $176 million since it began in 2001, with $15.26 million raised in 2018.

• Fraudulent wines have become more prevalent. Recently, a "wine collector" was found guilty of fraud for selling counterfeit wine. (Recommended reading: *The Billionaire's Vinegar*.)

• Since his first review in 1978, American wine critic Robert M. Parker Jr. has become an international icon with his 100-point scoring method. In 2014, he sold the *Wine Advocate* to three investors from Singapore but continues to write about California wine.

• The best châteaux of Bordeaux have been priced out of reach for the average consumer. From the great vintage of 2015, some of the top Bordeaux are selling for as much as $3,000 a bottle! China's passion for Bordeaux wines is increasing these prices.

WINE CONSUMERS BY GENDER

Female
57%

Male
43%

- The Millennial generation—born between 1981 and 1996, of legal drinking age as of 2017, and 79 million people strong—has shown the largest percentage increase in wine consumption over Generation X (born between 1965 and 1980, 44 million people) and Baby Boomers (born between 1945 and 1965, 75 million people).

- According to the *Journal of Wine Economics*, liberals drink more alcohol—and the numbers have increased considerably since the 2016 elections!

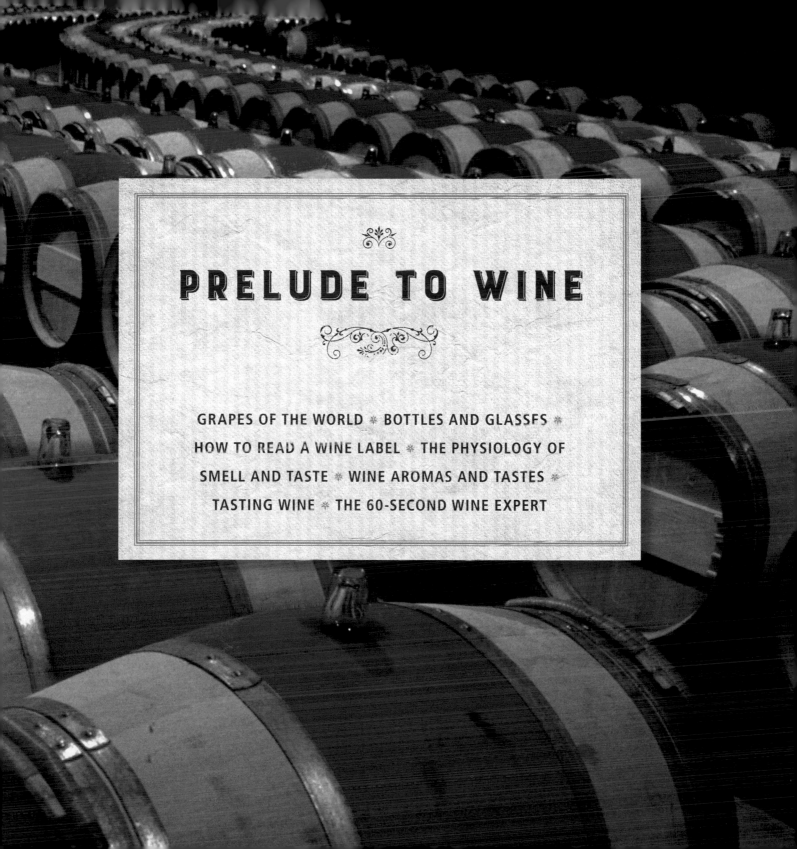

PRELUDE TO WINE

GRAPES OF THE WORLD ✳ BOTTLES AND GLASSES ✳
HOW TO READ A WINE LABEL ✳ THE PHYSIOLOGY OF
SMELL AND TASTE ✳ WINE AROMAS AND TASTES ✳
TASTING WINE ✳ THE 60-SECOND WINE EXPERT

Hundreds of different red-wine grapes are planted throughout the world. **CALIFORNIA ALONE GROWS MORE THAN 30 DIFFERENT RED-WINE GRAPE VARIETIES.**

OTHER RED GRAPES	
GRAPES	WHERE THEY GROW BEST
Agiorgitiko	Greece
Blaufränkisch	Austria
Barbera	Italy; California
Cariñena	Spain
Carménère	Chile
Cinsault	Rhône Valley
Concord	America
Cabernet Franc	Loire Valley and Bordeaux
Dolcetto	Italy
Grenache / Garnacha	Rhône Valley, Spain
Kadarka	Hungary
Kékfrankos	Hungary
Malbec	Bordeaux and Cahors, Argentina
Monastrell	Spain
Nerello Mascalese	Sicily
Nero d'Avola	Sicily
Petite Syrah	California
Pinot Meunier	Champagne
Portugieser	Hungary
St. Laurent	Austria
Xinomavro	Greece

GRAPES OF THE WORLD

S TUDENTS MOST FREQUENTLY ask what will help them most in learning about wine. The answer is to understand the major grape varieties and where they grow in the world.

RED GRAPES

Let's start with the three major grapes you need to know to understand red wine. Here are the major red-wine grapes, ranked from lightest to most full-bodied. This chart and the one on the next page will give you an idea of the styles of the wines and also a feeling for gradations of color, weight, tannin, and ageability.

GRAPES	BEST REGIONS	COLOR	BODY	TANNINS	AGEABILITY
		Lighter	*Light*	*Low*	*Drink young*
GAMAY	BEAUJOLAIS, FRANCE				
PINOT NOIR	BURGUNDY, FRANCE; CHAMPAGNE, FRANCE; CALIFORNIA; OREGON				
TEMPRANILLO	RIOJA, SPAIN				
SANGIOVESE	TUSCANY, ITALY				
MERLOT	BORDEAUX, FRANCE; NAPA, CALIFORNIA				
ZINFANDEL	CALIFORNIA				
CABERNET SAUVIGNON	BORDEAUX, FRANCE; NAPA, CALIFORNIA; CHILE				
NEBBIOLO	PIEDMONT, ITALY				
SYRAH / SHIRAZ	RHÔNE VALLEY, FRANCE; AUSTRALIA; CALIFORNIA				
		Deeper	*Full*	*High*	*Wine to age*

There are more than 1,300 different wine grapes in the world, but the majority of wine is made from fewer than 20 grapes.

WHITE GRAPES

More than 90 percent of all quality white wine comes from these three grapes, listed here from lightest style to fullest:

Riesling   Sauvignon Blanc   Chardonnay

World-class white wine also comes from other grapes, but knowing these three makes for a good start.

GRAPES	BEST REGIONS	COLOR	BODY	TANNINS	AGEABILITY
		Lighter	Light	Low	Drink young
RIESLING	GERMANY; ALSACE FRANCE; NEW YORK; WASHINGTON				
SAUVIGNON BLANC	BORDEAUX, FRANCE; LOIRE VALLEY, FRANCE; NEW ZEALAND; CALIFORNIA (FUMÉ BLANC)				
CHARDONNAY	BURGUNDY, FRANCE; CHAMPAGNE, FRANCE; CALIFORNIA; AUSTRALIA				
		Deeper	Full	High	Wine to age

Other countries grow world-class Rieslings, Sauvignon Blancs, and Chardonnays, but in general the above regions specialize in wines made from these grapes.

Given all the variables that go into making the many different styles of wine, putting these charts together proved extremely challenging. Exceptions to the rules always exist, just as other countries and wine regions not listed here produce world-class wine from some of the grapes shown. You'll discover this for yourself if you do your homework and taste a lot of different wines. Good luck!

OTHER WHITE GRAPES

GRAPES	WHERE THEY GROW BEST
Albariño	Spain
Assyrtiko	Greece
Chenin Blanc	Loire Valley, California
Furmint	Hungary
Gewürztraminer, Pinot Blanc, Pinot Gris	Alsace, France
Hárslevelü	Hungary
Grüner Veltliner	Austria
Macabeo	Spain
Moschofilero	Greece
Olaszrizling	Hungary
Pinot Grigio (Pinot Gris)	Italy; California; Oregon; Alsace, France
Roditis	Greece
Sémillon	Bordeaux (Sauternes), Australia
Szürkebarát	Hungary
Torrontés Riojano	Argentina
Trebbiano	Italy
Verdejo	Spain
Vidal	Canada, New York
Viognier	Rhône Valley, California

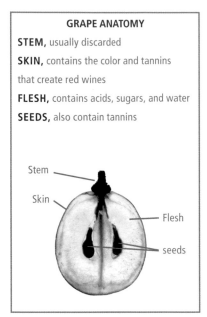

VITIS is Latin for vine.
VINUM is Latin for wine.

A SAMPLING OF GRAPES BY SPECIES:

Vitis vinifera	Chardonnay
	Cabernet Sauvignon
Vitis labrusca	Concord
	Catawba
Hybrids	Seyval Blanc
	Baco Noir

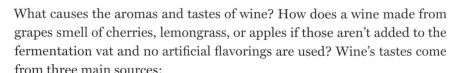

WINE AROMAS AND TASTES

What causes the aromas and tastes of wine? How does a wine made from grapes smell of cherries, lemongrass, or apples if those aren't added to the fermentation vat and no artificial flavorings are used? Wine's tastes come from three main sources:

Grapes   Fermentation   Maturation and Aging

The biology and chemistry of each of these sources give us the aroma compounds that we associate with different foods, spices, or minerals—and the main tastes of wine: sweet, sour, sometimes bitter. These aroma compounds are often the same as those in cherries, lemongrass, or apples, but they form due to the complicated biology of grapes, the metabolic action of yeast, or the many other chemical interactions of the winemaking and aging processes.

Following the winemaking process from grape to bottle will give us a chance to see how tastes form in our wine.

TASTES FROM GRAPES

The major wine grapes come from *Vitis vinifera*, which includes many different varieties of grapes—both red and white. However, other grapes are also used for winemaking. The most important native grape species in America is *Vitis labrusca*, which grows widely in New York as well as other East Coast and Midwestern states. Hybrids cross *Vitis vinifera* and native American grape species, such as *Vitis labrusca*.

The grape variety has a huge influence on wine taste. Varietal character—the usual or expected aroma and taste of a particular grape—is an important concept in winemaking, and each type of grape has typical characteristics. For example, black grapes with thick skins tend to produce wines high in tannin, which equates to bitterness and astringency when a wine is young. Riesling grapes tend to produce wines high in acidity (sourness and tartness), and Muscat grapes produce highly aromatic wines that smell of orange flowers. Many different aspects of varietal character come through in the wine. One of the winemaker's challenges is either to preserve or to tame the distinctive qualities of grapes to create a well-balanced wine.

RED GRAPE VARIETY	GRAPE TASTES
CABERNET SAUVIGNON	CASSIS (BLACK CURRANT), BLACKBERRY, VIOLETS
GARNACHA / GRENACHE	CHERRY, RASPBERRY, SPICY
MERLOT	BLACKBERRY, BLACK OLIVE, PLUM
NEBBIOLO	PLUM, RASPBERRY, TRUFFLE, ACIDITY
PINOT NOIR	PERFUMED, RASPBERRY, RED CHERRY, ACIDITY
SANGIOVESE	BLACK CHERRY, BLACKBERRY, VIOLET, SPICE
SYRAH / SHIRAZ	SPICY, BLACK FRUIT, BLUEBERRY
TEMPRANILLO	FRUITY, CHERRY
ZINFANDEL	SPICY, RIPE BERRY, CHERRY
WHITE GRAPE VARIETY	GRAPE TASTES
CHARDONNAY	APPLE, MELON, PEAR
RIESLING	MINERALITY, CITRUS, TROPICAL FRUIT, ACIDITY
SAUVIGNON BLANC	TOMATO STALK, CUT GRASS, GRAPEFRUIT, CITRUS, AROMATIC

Planting of vineyards for winemaking **BEGAN MORE THAN 8,000 YEARS AGO** near the Black Sea in places such as Georgia.

Winemakers say that **WINEMAKING BEGINS IN THE VINEYARD** with the growing of the grapes.

Vines are planted during their dormant periods, usually in the months of April and May. Most **VINES WILL CONTINUE TO PRODUCE GOOD-QUALITY GRAPES FOR 40 YEARS** or more.

A vine usually doesn't produce grapes suitable for winemaking **UNTIL THE THIRD YEAR.**

VINEYARD PRODUCTION:

5 bottles of wine produced annually from 1 grapevine

720 bottles of wine from a ton of grapes

5,500 bottles of wine produced annually from 1 acre of grapevines

(*Napa Valley Vintners*)

The "very French notion of terroir looks at all the natural conditions which influence the biology of the vinestock and thus the composition of the grape itself. The terroir is the coming together of the climate, the soil, and the landscape. It is the combination of an infinite number of factors: temperatures by night and by day, rainfall distribution, hours of sunlight, slope and drainage, to name but a few. All these factors react with each other to form, in part of the vineyard, what French wine growers call a terroir."

—BRUNO PRATS, former proprietor of Château Cos d'Estournel

LOCATION

It matters where grapes grow. Grapes are agricultural products that require specific growing conditions. Just as you wouldn't grow oranges in Maine, so you wouldn't try to grow grapes at the North Pole. Vines have limitations. Some of these limitations are the growing season, number of days of sunlight, angle of the sun, average temperature, and rainfall. Soil is of primary concern, and adequate drainage is a requisite. The right amount of sun ripens the grapes properly to give them their sugar.

Many grape varieties produce better wines when planted in certain locations. For example, most red grapes need a longer growing season than white grapes, so red grapes usually are planted in warmer locations. In colder northern regions—Germany and northern France, for instance—most vineyards are planted with white grapes. In the warmer regions of Italy, Spain, Portugal, and California's Napa Valley, red grapes thrive.

TERROIR

The concept of terroir can be difficult to grasp because it isn't scientific. It's the "somewhereness" of a particular region or vineyard, including the soil composition and geography; sunlight, weather, and climate; rainfall; plant life of the area; and many other elements. Many winemakers believe that terroir has an impact on the taste of wine, and the effects on grape quality from certain aspects of terroir, such as sunlight and soil drainage, are measurable.

The "taste" of soil One aspect of terroir widely believed to carry through into the finished wine is soil type. In general terms, this taste can be described as "minerality." Certain wine regions are famous for the apparent effect of their soil on the wines they produce. German Rieslings may taste of the slate in which they grow; likewise, in Burgundy the Chardonnay grapes, which grow in limestone, may feature aromas of gunflint or wet river pebbles. Grapevines don't absorb soil through their roots, and they take in only trace amounts of minerals available in any soil, making it more likely that minerality results from some other aspect of terroir or regional winemaking processes. Still, proponents of terroir swear by the taste of the land in wine. The mystery deepens when you consider that a sea brine aroma may manifest in Muscadet, grown at the mouth of the Loire River in France, near the Atlantic Ocean.

The taste of nearby plants On the other hand, the aromas of regional plants in wine likely come from the plants themselves. Eucalyptus aroma in wine has been shown in some cases to come from the transfer of eucalyptus oil from nearby trees to the grapes. The aroma of garrigue, the scrubby mixture of evergreen plants and herbs such as rosemary and wild thyme that grows in the southern Rhône Valley and around the Mediterranean, may find its way into wine in the same way. (Many wine tasters and critics use the expression of a wine smelling of dried herbs and spices.)

HARVEST

Grapes are picked when they reach the proper sugar / acid ratio for the style of wine the vintner wants to produce. Go to a vineyard in June and taste one of the small green grapes. Your mouth will pucker because the grape is so tart and acidic. Return to the same vineyard—even to that same vine—in September or October, and the grapes will taste sweet. All those months of sun have given sugar to the grape as a result of photosynthesis.

WEATHER

Weather can interfere with the quality of the harvest as well as its quantity. In the spring, as vines emerge from dormancy, a sudden frost may stop the flowering, thereby reducing yields. Even a strong windstorm can affect grapes adversely at this crucial time.

Not enough rain, too much rain, or rain at the wrong time also can wreak havoc. Rain just before the harvest will swell the grapes with water, diluting the juice and making thin, watery wines. Lack of rain will affect the wine's balance by creating a more powerful and concentrated wine but a smaller crop. A severe drop in temperature may affect vines even outside the growing season. But growers have countermeasures. They employ some of these while the grapes are on the vine; others are part of the winemaking process.

Randall Grahm, owner of Bonny Doon Vineyard in California, performed an admittedly crude **EXPERIMENT IN MINERALITY**: "We simply took interesting rocks, washed them very well, smashed them up, and immersed them in a barrel of wine for a certain period." The result? Changes in the texture of the wine, more intense aroma, and greater complexity.

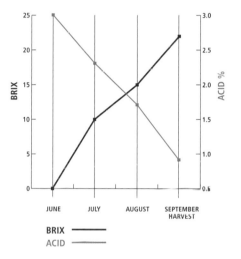

SEASONS IN THE SOUTHERN HEMISPHERE—which includes Australia, New Zealand, Chile, Argentina, and South Africa—are reversed.

It takes an average of **100 DAYS** between a vine's flowering and the harvest.

BRIX: the winemaker's measure of sugar in grapes.

PROBLEM	RESULTS IN	SOLUTIONS
FROST	REDUCED YIELD	WIND MACHINES, SPRINKLER SYSTEMS, FLAMING HEATERS
NOT ENOUGH SUN	UNDERRIPE, GREEN HERBAL, VEGETAL CHARACTER, HIGH ACID, LOW SUGAR	CHAPTALIZATION
TOO MUCH SUN	OVERRIPE, HIGH-ALCOHOL, PRUNE CHARACTER	AMELIORATION (THE ADDITION OF WATER)
TOO MUCH RAIN	THIN, WATERY WINES	PRAY FOR DRIER WEATHER!
MILDEW	ROT	SPRAY WITH COPPER SULFATE
DROUGHT	SCORCHED GRAPES	IRRIGATE OR PRAY FOR RAIN
HIGH ALCOHOL	CHANGE IN THE BALANCE OF THE COMPONENTS	DE-ALCOHOLIZE
HIGH ACIDITY	SOUR, TART WINE	DE-ACIDIFY
PHYLLOXERA	DEAD VINES	GRAFT VINES ONTO RESISTANT ROOTSTOCK

1989 In Bordeaux, it rained during the harvest of eight of the next ten vintages, affecting picking dates, yields, and the quality of the wine.

1991 April frost in Bordeaux destroyed more than half of the year's grape harvest

STORM STORIES

2001 A rainy September made for the wettest Champagne harvest since 1873.

2002 Spring frost damaged 80 percent of that year's Champagne grapes. A September hailstorm totally destroyed some of the best vineyards in Piedmont, Italy. Otherwise poor weather conditions in Tuscany resulted in no production of Chianti Classico Reserva.

2003 The historic and deadly heat wave in Europe changed the balance of the traditional style of wines produced in most regions. In New York State, the winter of 2003–04 was one of the coldest in 50 years. The result: a major decrease in wine production, with some vineyards losing more than 50 percent of their crop for the 2004 vintage.

2004 Burgundy suffered major hailstorms in July and August that damaged or destroyed at least 40 percent of the grapes.

2007 Hailstorms in Mendoza, Argentina, from December to February dramatically reduced yields. One in Alsace, France, that June destroyed entire vineyards.

2008 A spring frost—the worst since the early 1970s—damaged vineyards all over California. That same year, everything under the sun hit Australia: the worst drought ever, scorching heat in South Australia, and record-breaking rain and major flooding in the Hunter Valley.

2010 An earthquake in Chile devastated that year's vintage.

2012 Hurricane Sandy ravaged the East Coast and flooded many wine storage warehouses. Many people lost entire wine cellars.

2013 Hail, heavy rain, windstorms, and cold weather raged across France. The worst damage happened in Burgundy, Champagne, and Bordeaux, resulting in the smallest harvest in 40 years.

2014 California experienced the worst drought in more than 100 years. On the East Coast, frigid temperatures had a negative effect on the 2014 harvest. Hailstorms in Bordeaux, Champagne, the Rhône, and Burgundy caused heavy losses.

2016 Frost in Burgundy was the worst in 30 years. El Niño weather caused Argentina's worst harvest since 1957.

2017 Worldwide production of wine fell to its lowest level in half a century. Northern California suffered the worst wine disaster of the year, but other countries and regions had their own problems.

In January and February, Chile suffered devastating wildfires, with more than 100 vineyards damaged or destroyed. Century-old vines perished. Chile's president called it "the worst forestry disaster in our history."

Historic spring frosts, hail storms, and summer heat prevailed throughout France. The April frosts were the worst since 1991. Growers had the smallest crop since the 1940s, which suffered hail damage, spring frost, and drought. Many Bordeaux chateaux in Graves, St-Émilion, and Pomerol lost their entire crop. In Chablis and Champagne, frost caused major damage and extensive loss. All of this after a very short 2016 harvest also due to severe weather.

TO SEE THE DAMAGE that hail can cause to vines and grapes, watch the documentary *A Year in Burgundy*.

In the Douro region of Portugal, home of the great Port wines, draught caused growers to have the earliest harvest ever, beginning at the end of August. Spain had the same hot and humid drought conditions, which reduced their harvest by half, especially in regions such as Ribera del Duero.

Italians called 2017 the "Year of Lucifer." Daytime summer temperatures hovered between 90 and 100°F, while a drought raged throughout the country that will affect future wine production. The 2017 Italian harvest was the smallest in more than 50 years.

Dozens of wildfires burned in Oregon and Washington in July but fortunately didn't affect any vineyards, except for smoke.

A heat wave struck the North Coast and Napa Valley in September. Many days had high temperatures of more than 100°F. The following month, the Northern California Firestorm hit, obliterating 250,000 acres of vines and killing 42 people. It destroyed 8,000 structures, including more than a dozen wineries. Hundreds more wineries sustained property damage. By the time the fires started, 90 percent of all vineyards had picked their grapes already. Some wineries could lose all or part of their 2017 vintage, however, because they lost power, which cut electricity to temperature controls in fermentation tanks and caused the wine to spoil. Smoke taint, ashes, and burned buds from the fires also could affect the 2018 harvest. Only time will tell.

What's next? Ecological studies have shown that, over the next twenty years, some wine regions in Europe will become too hot for the grapes growing there now to survive. Even today, some workers are picking grapes while wearing bathing suits—unlike in the past, when they wore coats, hats, and gloves. No more August vacations!

RIPENESS

The concept of vintage—as in "2009 was a great vintage in Bordeaux"—involves all the weather and other events in the vineyard during the growing season, but in the end it comes back to the ripeness of the grapes at harvest. Were the grapes picked at the perfect moment in their development, when acidity, sugars, and flavors had peaked? Did this happen before the first killing frost and before a heavy rain that could dilute the juice or cause rot?

When grapes are ripe, they contain higher sugar levels, which generally translate to higher alcohol at fermentation and fuller body in the finished wine. The aromas and tastes of ripe grapes also are developed fully for greater richness and complexity in the wine. Green (unripe) grapes may result in wine with high acidity that's out of balance with the wine's other flavors and with high tannin from grape skins not yet fully developed. The winemaker also may have trouble achieving an acceptable level of alcohol from fermentation. Measures can be taken in the winery to correct these problems, but often it's not possible to undo the effects of green grapes completely.

VINE AGE

Older grapevines produce fewer bunches of grapes that tend to have smaller berries and concentrated flavors—a greater intensity of aroma and taste that translates into the wine made from these grapes.

PHYLLOXERA

A grape louse, phylloxera is one of the grapevine's worst enemies because it eventually kills the entire plant. An epidemic infestation in the 1870s came close to destroying *all* the vineyards of Europe. Luckily, the roots of native American vines have a natural immunity to this louse. After this discovery, all European vines were pulled up and grafted onto phylloxera-resistant American rootstocks.

Although the words "old vines" or "vieilles vignes" on a wine label aren't regulated legally, most winemakers agree that vines must be at least **35 YEARS OLD** to qualify.

Grapevines can grow and produce limited quantities of fruit for **MORE THAN 100 YEARS**. The Champagne house Bollinger still harvests vines planted in the mid-1800s.

One of the few countries to **ESCAPE PHYLLOXERA** is Chile. Chilean wine producers imported their vines from France in the 1860s, before phylloxera attacked the French vineyards.

In the early 1980s, phylloxera became a problem in the vineyards of California. Vineyard owners had to to replant their vines at a cost of $15,000 to $25,000 per acre, costing the California wine industry **MORE THAN $1 BILLION**.

NOBLE ROT

For almost all wines, rot is undesirable and can prove disastrous. But a few of the world's finest sweet wines couldn't be made without the presence of *Botrytis cinerea*, or "noble rot." The classic sweet wines of French Sauternes, German Beerenauslese and Trockenbeerenauslese, and Hungarian Tokay all have a distinctive honeyed flavor due to the presence of this type of rot. This mold punctures the grape skin, allowing water to dissipate and increasing the concentration of the sugar and acid. Wines made from grapes with noble rot also have an intensity of taste not found in conventionally harvested wines. The rot affects grape bunches gradually, so growers have the option of picking when grapes are affected only partially or waiting for a thorough onset. This means it's possible to taste only slight *Botrytis* in a wine or to have the full impact.

TASTES FROM FERMENTATION

Fermentation is the process by which grape juice turns into wine. The simple formula for fermentation is:

Sugar + Yeast = Alcohol + Carbon Dioxide

The fermentation process begins when the grapes are crushed and ends when all of the sugar has converted to alcohol or the alcohol level has reached around 15 percent, the point at which the alcohol kills off the yeast. Through photosynthesis, sugar occurs naturally in the ripe grape. Yeast also occurs naturally as the white bloom on the grape skin. Today's winemakers don't always use this natural yeast, however. Laboratories have isolated more strains of yeast, each strain contributing something unique to the style of the wine.

Carbon dioxide dissipates into the air, except in Champagne and other sparkling wines, in which this gas is retained through a special process that we'll discuss in Class Eleven.

The winemaking process, in which yeast consumes sugars in the grape must and produces alcohol and carbon dioxide, is also crucial to creating aromas and tastes in wine. Depending on the temperature of the fermentation, it may take less than a week (for red wines) or a few weeks or even months (for white and sweet wines). The temperature—hot fermentation or cold fermentation—also affects tastes created.

Many other factors come into play in creating taste, such as whether the wine ferments in stainless steel tanks (which, being inert, impart no aroma)

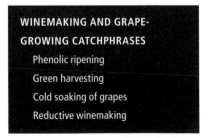

WINEMAKING AND GRAPE-GROWING CATCHPHRASES
Phenolic ripening
Green harvesting
Cold soaking of grapes
Reductive winemaking

TYPICAL ALCOHOL CONTENT	
LOW	
German Riesling	8–12.5%
MEDIUM	
Prosecco	11–12%
Champagne	12%
Most white wines	11.5–13.5%
Most red wine	12–14.5%
HIGH	
California Cabernet Sauvignon	13.5–15%
Sherry	15–22%
Port	20%

For wines sold in America, the alcohol percentage listed on the label is allowed a **MARGIN OF 1.5 PERCENT ABOVE OR BELOW THE PERCENTAGE STATED**, up to 14 percent. A wine labeled 13.5 percent alcohol could be as low as 12 percent or as high as 15 percent.

MOG: Material Other than Grapes. **MUST**: the juice and skin mixture that comes from the grapes.

Pressing white grape must is a delicate process usually done with **HIGH-TECH EQUIPMENT TO PREVENT A FORCEFUL PRESSING** that will extract bitter tannins from the skins and seeds.

or oak vats (which may add a slight oak flavor and tannin to the wine) as well as the type of yeast the winemaker uses for fermentation.

ALCOHOL CONTENT, FLAVORS, AND BODY

The more alcohol in a wine, the more body (weight) it will have. Riper grapes at harvest contain more natural sugar, which gives the yeast more to ferment into alcohol.

Sparkling wine
8–12% alcohol

Table wine
8–15% alcohol

Fortified wine
17–22% alcohol

"Extract"—the total solid material present in the liquid of wine—also contributes to body. Extract includes tannins, proteins, and other microscopic solids and can increase with maceration (see page 15) before or after fermentation and by not filtering the wine. Residual sugar remaining in the wine after fermentation is also part of the extract and contributes greatly to body. Sweet wines, for example, usually have more body than dry wines.

THE FERMENTATION PROCESS

Grapes come in from the vineyards, ideally packed carefully in small crates so they don't get crushed and begin fermentation before their time. For great wine, workers hand-sort the fruit on a conveyor belt to remove sticks, leaves, stones, and other MOG.

The winemaker must decide whether to destem the grapes. White grapes almost always go through the destemming machine. For red wine, leaving some or all of the stems intact will add tannin when the juice, skins, and stems soak together. The grapes also may go through a crusher, which breaks the berries.

After the grapes are sorted, destemmed, and possibly crushed, red and white wines follow different paths, primarily due to the grape skins. All grape skins contain flavor compounds essential to the success of the wine. But skins and seeds also contain tannin, which can cause bitterness and astringency in young wines. Past a certain point, tannin is undesirable in white wines. For this reason, after crushing, the white grape must usually is pressed immediately to separate the juice for fermentation.

Some types of white grapes may be allowed to soak for a certain time with the skins, a process called skin contact. This technique allows varietal aromas and tastes—those specific to the grape variety—to be extracted from the skins and creates a richer flavor in the wine.

RED GRAPES AND WHITE WINE

The color of wine comes primarily from the grape skins. By removing the skins immediately after picking, no color transfers to the wine, and it will be white. In the Champagne region of France, many of the grapes are red, yet most of the resulting wine is white. California's White Zinfandel wine comes from red Zinfandel grapes.

MACERATION

Unlike white skins and juice, which are separated before fermentation, the must of black grapes goes directly to the fermentation vats. There, it may undergo maceration, or soaking, to extract aromas, tannins, and color from the skins. Maceration increases aroma intensity and the wine's mouthfeel— the weight and texture of the wine in your mouth. The winemaker may choose to macerate the must before and/or after fermentation.

CARBONIC MACERATION

Beaujolais, from Burgundy, France, has a particularly light and fruity taste, with an aroma of freshly crushed strawberries or red raspberries. This comes from a process called carbonic maceration, in which the grape berries, left whole, undergo a type of internal fermentation, without the assistance of yeast. Eventually, normal fermentation takes place, but the initial, whole-berry fermentation gives the wines a brighter color and that distinctive tutti-frutti.

ADDING SUGAR

In regions where the law allows it, winemakers sometimes add sugar to wine before fermentation. The process is called chaptalization (after Jean-Antoine

"Wine makes daily living easier, less hurried, with fewer tensions and more tolerance."

BENJAMIN FRANKLIN

Some of the natural sugars in ripe grapes remain undigested by yeast after fermentation. This is called the **RESIDUAL SUGAR** in the wine, or RS. A wine with no RS or RS below a certain legal level is a "dry" wine.

The European Union rules that a wine labeled **"DRY"** can have up to 4 grams of sugar per liter. A wine labeled **"SWEET"** can have 45 grams per liter.

Chaptal, a proponent of the practice in the early 1800s), and it enables the yeast to generate more alcohol in the final wine. The added sugar compensates for grapes that don't have enough of their own natural sugars to produce a wine of sufficient alcohol—basically to compensate for underripe grapes. Chaptalization doesn't result in a sweet wine because all of the sugars convert into alcohol.

DOES THE YEAST HAVE A TASTE?

Yeast does have a taste, as you know if you've ever smelled or eaten freshly baked bread. In winemaking, the yeast always has some impact on the taste of the finished wine, but whether it's detectable depends on choices made by the winemaker. A sure way to create a yeasty aroma in wine is lees contact.

Lees are the dead yeast cells and other solids that settle to the bottom of the wine after fermentation. When fermentation takes place in barrels, white wine often ages in the barrels with the lees for up to a year after fermentation has ended. This lees contact gives the wine a rich mouthfeel and a brioche or bread-roll aroma—the same effect that yeast has in Champagne making. Stirring the lees in the barrels, a process called *bâtonnage*, can increase their influence.

TANNIN

Tannin is a natural preservative and one of the many components that give wine its longevity. It comes from the skins, pits, and stems of the grapes. Think of tannins as "astringent." Especially in young wines, tannin can make the wine taste bitter. Tannin is not a taste, however—it's a tactile sensation. Red wines generally have a higher level of tannin than whites because red grapes usually ferment with their skins. Tannin also comes from wood, such as the oak barrels in which some wines ferment or age.

Tannin is also found in strong tea. What can you add to tea to make it less astringent? Milk—the fat and proteins in milk soften the tannins. So it is with a highly tannic wine. If you take another milk by-product, such as cheese, and have it with wine, it softens the tannin and makes the wine more appealing. Have a beef dish or one served with a cream sauce and a young, tannic red wine to enjoy this phenomenon for yourself.

Sur lie, a French term, inidcates when a wine has **AGED WITH ITS SEDIMENT**, such as dead yeast cells and grape skins and seeds.

Naturally occuring wild yeast floats through in vineyards all over the world, and many wineries ferment using only the yeast present on the grape skins at harvest. **SOME WINEMAKERS USE CULTURED YEAST**, however, which can give a more predictable flavor.

THREE HIGH-TANNIN GRAPES

Nebbiolo

Cabernet Sauvignon

Syrah / Shiraz

WALNUTS also contain tannin.

Pharaoh Tutankhamen, who died in 1327 B.C., apparently preferred the taste of red wine, according to scientists who found **ANCIENT RESIDUES OF RED-WINE COMPOUNDS** (tannins) in jars in his tomb.

FIVE HIGH-ACID GRAPES

Riesling (white)

Chenin Blanc (white)

Nebbiolo (red)

Sangiovese (red)

Pinot Noir (red)

AS SUGAR LEVELS INCREASE, perceived acidity decreases.

ACIDITY

All wine has a certain amount of acidity. White wines generally have more perceived acidity than reds, though winemakers try to balance the fruit and acid. An overly acidic wine tastes tart or sour. Acidity is a very important component in the aging of wines.

MALOLACTIC FERMENTATION

Malolactic fermentation ("malo" for short) takes place after the alcoholic fermentation and any lees contact. Almost all red wines undergo malo for increased stability after bottling, but winemakers use it very selectively for whites.

Grapes have a high level of tart malic acid at harvest, the same acidity as in green apples. For most red wines and some whites, the winemaker will allow lactic bacteria naturally present to start a malolactic fermentation and convert some of that puckery malic acid into softer lactic acid. Vintners avoid malo for

In general, the **LIGHTER THE COLOR**, the more perceived acidity.

The word *malic* comes from the **LATIN WORD FOR APPLE**, *malum*.

most white wines, except for some Chardonnays, because tart acidity is often desirable and because malo tends to give wines a buttery flavor. If you've ever had a rich, buttery California Chardonnay, you've tasted the effects of malo.

TASTES FROM MATURATION AND AGING

Barrels have been used to ferment, mature, and ship wine for thousands of years. Early in the history of barrel use, winemakers discovered that different kinds of barrels, or even different sizes, used for varying amounts of time imparted certain flavors to wine. These flavors range from woody or cedar to vanilla or coconut, depending on the source of the barrels and how they were made.

Relatively recent alternatives to barrels, such as cement vats or stainless steel tanks, allow wines to remain free of oak tastes for a bright, fruity effect. Most wines have no oak aging, and it's up to the winemaker to determine the type and amount of oak influence in wine.

"I like to think about the life of wine, how it is a living thing. I like to think about what was going on the year the grapes were growing. How the sun was shining, if it rained. I like to think about all the people who tended and picked the grapes. And if it's an old wine, how many of them must be dead by now. I like how wine continues to evolve, like if I opened a bottle of wine today it would taste different than if I'd opened it on any other day because a bottle of wine is actually alive. And it's constantly evolving and gaining complexity, that is until it peaks, like your '61. And then it begins its steady inevitable decline."

—MAYA, from the movie *Sideways* (2004)

RED GRAPE VARIETY	WINEMAKING AND AGING TASTES
CABERNET SAUVIGNON	PENCIL SHAVINGS, TOAST, TOBACCO, DEAD LEAF
GARNACHA / GRENACHE	CONCENTRATIONS, EXTRACTION
MERLOT	PENCIL SHAVINGS, TOAST
NEBBIOLO	STRONG TEA, NUTMEG, GAMEY
PINOT NOIR	SMOKY, EARTHY
SANGIOVESE	CEDAR, PLUM, VANILLA
SYRAH / SHIRAZ	TOASTY, VANILLA, COFFEE
TEMPRANILLO	OAK (AMERICAN), TOBACCO
ZINFANDEL	SAVORY, TAR, CHOCOLATE
WHITE GRAPE VARIETY	WINEMAKING AND AGING TASTES
CHARDONNAY	VANILLA, TOAST, BUTTERSCOTCH
RIESLING	STEELY, GREEN APPLES, GASOLINE
SAUVIGNON BLANC	COCONUT, SMOKY, VANILLA

Large barrels vs. small Barrels range in size from 1,000- or 1,200-liter giants down to fewer than 100 liters. The larger the barrel, the lower the ratio of barrel surface area to liquid volume, meaning that less of the wine will make direct contact with the inner surface of the barrel. The largest barrels have little if any flavor impact on the wine. The barrel size most recognizable to consumers is the 225-liter barrique used in Bordeaux.

Oak flavor The wood cells inside the barrel impart their tastes and tannins when they come into contact with the alcohol in wine, adding an oak taste. New barrels impart more taste. As barrels are used again and again, the wine leaches much of the flavor and tannin from the cells, leaving the barrel "neutral." Not only flavor and tannin come from barrels, however—they also allow more oxygen contact with the wine. Barrels used in their first three years to impart flavor may be kept for many more simply to give wines a very slow oxidation. Winemakers often age a percentage of a given wine in new barrels and the rest in neutral barrels, then blend the two wines to achieve the desired style.

Toast When barrels are made, coopers hold them over a heat source (fire) that makes the wood pliable and easier to bend. It also toasts the wood. The more the flame chars the interior, the more of a barrier exists between the cells of the oak and the wine. This means less tannin and wood flavor will leach into the wine. But the toasting process imparts tastes of its own. Winemakers can order barrels with different degrees of toast depending on what flavors they want. Light toast gives few tastes of its own but still allows the wine access to heavy tannin from the oak cells. Medium toast often gives the wine a vanilla or caramel taste. Heavy toast can taste like cloves, cinnamon, smoke, or coffee.

American, French, or Eastern European oak Oak for barrels comes from all over America and Europe. American oak barrels are less expensive, but European oak adds a different intensity and flavor to the wine. Winemakers source barrels according to what taste and tannin profile they want for the wine. Differences in taste derive from the different species of oak, different grains of the wood, and variations in barrel making.

"UNFILTERED" WINE

After any barrel aging and before bottling, wine may be filtered to remove stray yeast cells or bacteria, microscopic bits of grape material, and other

---

Alternatives that may be used **TO ACHIEVE A BASIC OAK EFFECT** in less expensive wines: oak sticks or barrel staves, oak pellets, chips, powder, and even oak extract.

The flavor that a barrel gives a wine is different depending on **WHERE THE BARREL CAME FROM.** America, France, and Slavonia (Croatia) all make barrels that give a wine distinct but different flavors.

French barriques cost up to $1,200 each, while American oak barrels of the same size **COST ROUGHLY HALF.** A barrique holds 225 liters (60 gallons).

potentially unstable solids. The winemaker can give the wine a light filtration or a heavier one. Heavy filtration can strip out so much of the solid matter that the wine loses texture and taste. Some winemakers and consumers believe that wine should remain unfiltered, in its more natural state, for a fuller, truer taste experience. Unfiltered wine may appear slightly less clear than filtered wine and have fuller body and richer mouthfeel, a more intense taste, and even some sediment (dregs) on the bottom of the bottle.

VINTAGE

A vintage indicates the year the grapes were harvested, so every year is a vintage year. A vintage chart reflects the weather conditions for various years. Better weather usually results in a better rating for the vintage and therefore a higher likelihood that the wine will age well.

ARE ALL WINES MEANT TO BE AGED?

No. It's a common misconception that all wines improve with age. More than 90 percent of all wines in the world are made to be consumed within one year, and less than 1 percent of the world's wines are made to be aged for more than five years. Wines change with age. Some get better, but most don't. The good news is that the 1 percent represents more than 350 million bottles of wine from every vintage!

AGING AND THE TASTE OF RED WINE

Wine is like a living organism, always changing from the moment it comes into being. Even bottled, it ages due to the effects of oxygen and reactions

Roman scientist Pliny the Elder made the first known reference to a specific vintage, rating wines of 121 B.C. **"OF THE HIGHEST EXCELLENCE."**

2005, 2010, and 2015 were great vintages in **EVERY MAJOR WINE REGION ON EARTH!**

Around 90 percent of wine bought in America is consumed **WITHIN 24 HOURS OF PURCHASE**.

"The truth of wine aging is that it is unknown, unstudied, poorly understood, and poorly predicted!"

—ZELMA LONG,
American winemaker

**MY FAVORITE WINES
FOR LONG AGING:**

REDS:

Bordeaux

Barolo or Barbaresco

Napa Cabernet Sauvignon

Rhône Valley (Syrah / Grenache)

Vintage Port

WHITES:

Burgundy from the Côte de
Beaune

Chenin Blanc (Vouvray) from the Loire
Valley

German Riesling (Auslese or above)

Tokay from Hungary

Bordeaux (Sauternes)

---

that cause tannins to drop to the bottom of the bottle as grainy sediment, new tastes to develop, and color to change from opaque to transluscent.

As tannins become sediment, the tannin in the wine itself decreases, so the wine tastes softer, with more fruit, tannin, and acid balance. When wine is young, its fruit flavors are fresh; as it ages, the fruit may taste dried (dried cherries, prunes, dates), and the wine may develop vegetal aromas (mushrooms, canned peas, asparagus). Oxygen also makes itself known in the form of a gradual browning of the wine's color and a gradual nutty flavor.

WHAT MAKES A WINE LAST MORE THAN FIVE YEARS?

The color and the grape Red wines, because of their tannin content, generally will age longer than whites. Certain red grapes, such as Cabernet Sauvignon, tend to have more tannin than, say, Pinot Noir.

The vineyard Certain locations have optimal conditions for growing grapes, including slope of the land, soil, weather, and drainage. All of these factors contribute to producing a great wine that will taste better after aging.

The vintage The better the weather conditions, the more likely the wines from that vintage will have a better balance of fruits, acids, and tannins and therefore have the potential to age longer.

Vinification The longer the wine remains in contact with its skins during fermentation (maceration) and if it ferments and / or ages in oak, the more of the natural preservative tannin it will have, which can help it age longer. These are just two examples of how winemaking can affect the aging of wine.

Storage conditions Even the best-made wines in the world won't age well if stored improperly. Best storage conditions: 55°F and 75 percent relative humidity.

BAD TASTES

Successful winemaking depends on the cooperation of certain microorganisms and the good behavior of others. Occasionally, things go wrong. Here are the five most common wine faults or flaws and how they taste.

Corked wine This isn't bits of cork floating in the glass. "Corked" describes a musty aroma in wine caused by the organic compound called trichloroanisole (TCA). Many theories explain how TCA affects the cork, but we know that, when TCA in the cork comes into contact with wine in the bottle, it causes a smell similar to wet or mildewed cardboard. This can range in strength from almost undetectable—when it merely dulls the flavor of the wine—to a strong reek that you can smell from across the room.

There's no remedy for corked wine. Because it causes huge losses in the wine industry each year, many winemakers are switching to screw-cap closures instead of natural cork.

Oxidation Just as a cut apple oxidizes when exposed to air, grape juice undergoes a transformation through contact with oxygen. Oxygen begins its interaction with grape juice the moment the grapes are harvested and brought to the winery, and much of winemaking is about carefully protecting the wine from oxygen. Many winemakers, depending on the style of wine they produce, allow controlled oxidation to add an additional layer of taste in their wine. Accidental overexposure to oxygen results in browning of the wine and a nutty, sherrylike flavor.

Sulfur Sulfur dioxide is a natural antioxidant, preservative, and disinfectant used by most winemakers at various stages of the winemaking process to prevent unwanted oxidation of the grape juice and to inhibit the action of bacteria or wild yeast. If the level of sulfur in the finished wine isn't monitored carefully, you'll know by the smell (burnt matches) that sulfur was overused. If there's any hint of sulfur dioxide in the wine, that's a flaw.

Brett If you've ever tasted a wine with an aroma of a barnyard—more specifically: sweaty saddle or sweaty horse—you've tasted Brett. Brett is short for *Brettanomyces*, a wild yeast that may grow in the winery, particularly on equipment or in barrels not carefully cleaned, and it will infect wine that comes into contact with it. For some, Brett isn't all that bad: Many tasters think it adds a desirable complexity to the taste of wine when present at low levels.

Volatile acidity All wines have a certain level of desirable volatile acidity, (VA), but VA becomes a fault when the *Acetobacter* bacterium—used to create vinegar—goes to work. *Acetobacter* creates excess acetic acid in wine, which in high concentrations causes the wine to smell like vinegar.

TCA is present not only in wine but causes **MUSTY ODORS** in some packaged food products as well.

To identify the flavor of oxidation in wine, **THINK OF SHERRY,** which is intentionally oxidized during winemaking.

Winemakers can avoid adding sulfur during winemaking, but all wines contain a small amount because **YEAST PRODUCES SULFUR** during fermentation.

Sulfur is a **COMMON PRESERVATIVE** in foods such as dried fruit.

——— **FURTHER READING** ———
The Art and Science of Wine by James Halliday
From Vines to Wine by Jeff Cox
The Vintner's Apprentice by Eric Miller

BOTTLES AND GLASSES

BOTTLES

SIZES AND NAMES

NAME	BOTTLE RATIO	VOLUME
SPLIT	¼	187.5 ML
DEMI / HALF	½	375 ML
STANDARD	1	750 ML
MAGNUM	2	1.5 L
JEROBOAM	4	3 L
REHOBOAM	6	4.5 L
SALMANAZAR	12	9 L
BALTHAZAR	16	12 L
NEBUCHADNEZZAR	20	15 L
MELCHIOR	24	18 L

SHAPES AND WINES

The shape of a bottle can tell you at a glance what kind of wine it likely contains, but the **COLOR ALSO CAN HELP.** Certain German white wines usually come in brown bottles, while others come in green.

From the Jeroboam up, wine bottle sizes take their names from kings in the Old Testament.

Riesling
Flute-style

Cabernet Sauvignon, Merlot
Squared shoulders

Chardonnay, Pinot Noir
Sloping shoulders

Champagne, sparkling wine
Sloping shoulders, thicker glass

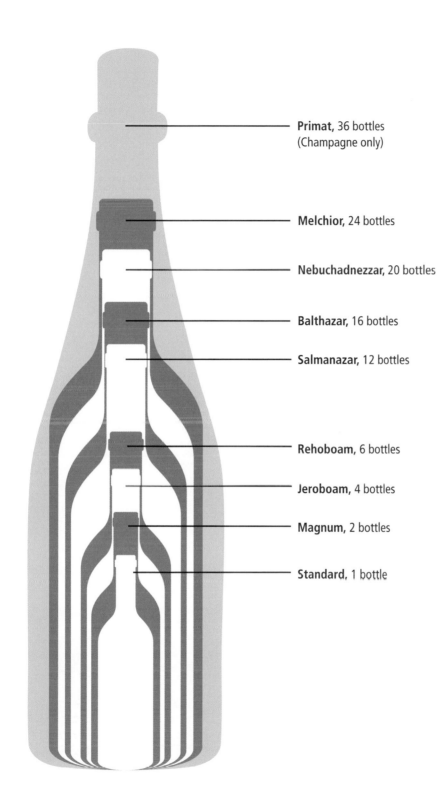

Primat, 36 bottles
(Champagne only)

Melchior, 24 bottles

Nebuchadnezzar, 20 bottles

Balthazar, 16 bottles

Salmanazar, 12 bottles

Rehoboam, 6 bottles

Jeroboam, 4 bottles

Magnum, 2 bottles

Standard, 1 bottle

36 BILLION BOTTLES are produced every year, and 31.4 billion are bought and sold.

Which size bottle do many collectors **PREFER FOR AGING** their wines? See page 345.

Demi / Half

Split

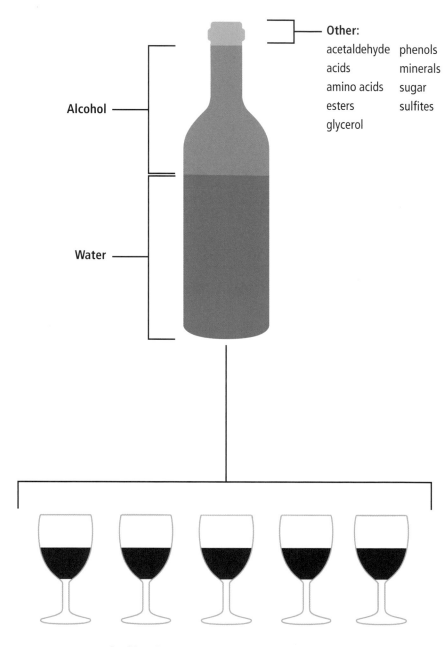

CONTENTS OF A BOTTLE OF WINE

Other:

acetaldehyde	phenols
acids	minerals
amino acids	sugar
esters	sulfites
glycerol	

Alcohol

Water

A bottle of wine (750 ml) contains 600–800 grapes (2.4 pounds) and on average contains **86 PERCENT WATER**.

A standard 225-liter barrel of wine contains **240 BOTTLES**.

1 standard bottle (750 ml) = 5 glasses (5 ounces / 150 ml)

GLASSES

WINE GLASSES AND WINE STYLES

Bold Red
Example: Cabernet Sauvignon

Light Red
Example: Pinot Noir

Sweet Red
Example: Port

Bold White
Example: Chardonnay

Delicate White
Example:
Sauvignon Blanc

Flute
Example: sparkling

Sweet White
Example: Sauternes

These are just some of the specialized glasses that glassmakers have created for various styles of wine. An **ALL-PURPOSE 10–12 OUNCE** wine glass is perfectly appropriate for all still wines.

"Wine is the most healthful and most hygienic of beverages."

—LOUIS PASTEUR

NEW WORLD VS. OLD WORLD
Wines from America, Argentina, Australia, Chile, New Zealand, and South Africa usually list the grape variety on the label. French, Italian, and Spanish wines usually list the region, village, or vineyard where the wine was made—but not the grape.

As you will see, wines can be labeled and named by region, varietal, or proprietary name, and different rules apply in different countries. See "How to Buy a German Wine," on page 271, for a different example.

HOW TO READ A WINE LABEL

Labels tell you everything you need to know about the wine—and more. Here are some quick tips you can use when you scan the shelves at your favorite retailer. The Rudd label below will serve as an example.

COUNTRY America
STATE California
COUNTY Sonoma
WINE REGION (AVA) Russian River Valley
VINEYARD Bacigalupi
WINERY Rudd
GRAPE Chardonnay
VINTAGE 2006

The most important piece of information on the label is the producer's name. In this case, the producer is Rudd.

This label shows that the wine comes from the Chardonnay grape. For American wines, if the grape variety appears on the label, a minimum of 75 percent of the wine must come from that grape variety.

If the wine bears a vintage date, 95 percent of the grapes must have harvested that year.

If the wine is designated "California," then 100 percent of the grapes must have grown in California.

If the label designates a certain federally recognized viticultural area (AVA), such as the Russian River Valley (as on our sample label), then at least 85 percent of the grapes used to make that wine must have grown in that location.

The alcohol content is given in percentages. Usually, the higher the percentage of alcohol, the "fuller" the wine will taste.

"Produced and bottled by" means that at least 75 percent of the wine was fermented by the winery named on the label.

Some labels will tell you the exact varietal breakdown of the wine, the sugar content of the grapes when picked, or the amount of residual sugar (to indicate how sweet or dry the wine is).

THE PHYSIOLOGY OF SMELL AND TASTE

BY KEVIN ZRALY AND WENDY DUBIT

One of the most wonderful things about wine is its ability to bring us to our senses. All of our senses factor into the enjoyment of wine, but none does so as powerfully or pleasurably as olfaction, our sense of smell. Happily, most wine tasters regularly experience what evolving scientific understanding also proves: the importance of smell and its impact on everything from learning and loving to aging and health.

Our love of wine and fascination with olfaction brought Wendy and me together to write this chapter. We hope you enjoy it with a good glass of wine, great memories in mind, and more in the making.

A LETTER FROM KEVIN

The sense of smell has always fascinated me. The sweet aroma of chamomile tea brewing on the kitchen woodstove dominates my earliest memories of my grandfather's farm. I grew up in a small town not far from New York City in a house surrounded by a forest of clean, fragrant pines. That memory no doubt led me to build a new house smack in the middle of a pine forest later in life.

When I was a child, I practically lived at the local swimming pool, and I smelled of chlorine all summer long. Even as an adult, I find the smell and taste of hot buttered popcorn contributes enormously to how much I enjoy a movie. Of course not everything smells like roses or summons sweet memories. We once had a gingko tree in our front yard that shed foul, nasty-smelling fruit once a year.

As a teenager with skyrocketing hormones, I doused myself in English Leather cologne. To this day, opening a bottle immediately transports me back to the fun-filled days of my youth. I'm not sure why, but I stopped wearing cologne when I truly began to smell wine. Is it coincidence, or is it smell?

Scent critic Chandler Burr rated the top ten best-smelling cities in the world. My hometown, **PLEASANTVILLE, NEW YORK, CAME IN SECOND!**

Nor will I ever forget the smell of downtown New York City following the September 11th terrorist attacks. It lingered for months. Even a year later, a sudden whiff caught me by surprise. Almost 20 years later, its mephitic cloud still hovers in my mind, a smell indelibly etched in my memory.

The smells of wine—earth, grapes, the wine itself—seduced me as a young adult; 40 years later I remain in their thrall. The sexy musk of freshly plowed earth, the fragrant balm of grapes fermenting right after harvest, and the lusty bouquet of new Beaujolais still intoxicate me. An old red wine with hints of tobacco, mushrooms, fallen leaves, and the damp-earth smell of my wine cellar still invigorate.

Just as the smell of cooking garlic whets my appetite and the smell of the seashore calms my nerves, so the smell of crisp autumn air reminds me that the harvest is happening and my favorite time of year has come to its end.

Smell is critical to the preservation of life and one of our most primitive senses. Yet we humans, having radically reshaped our relationship with the natural world, often take our sense of smell for granted. I continue to examine how smell and taste figure in my life. I hope that you will enjoy exploring the fascinating mysteries of olfaction in this chapter and that it will enrich your daily life and intensify your enjoyment of wine.

A LETTER FROM WENDY

I've always lived fully attuned to each of the five senses, but I've followed my nose most. Doing so has brought me nearly everywhere I want to be—most notably to the wine industry.

From as far back as age eight, I implicitly linked my sense of smell to my love of learning. If my mind tired during studies, I might peel a tangerine or sit nearer a lilac bush or linden tree. By high school, I used this technique more explicitly and began adding color and music for optimal learning and sensory experiences. Concepts and their applications became linked to and triggered by shades and scents of citrus and pine, strands of Vivaldi and Chopin. What I lacked in photographic memory, I usually could compensate for by engaging and summoning my senses.

As a teen, I was invited to the "openings" of my parent's dinner parties, where my dad, who delighted in all things Burgundy and Bordeaux, offered me a small pour of wine and asked for my olfactory impressions. I'll always remember the evening I discovered a marriage of river rocks, wet leather

WENDY DUBIT, founder of the Senses Bureau (www.thesensesbureau.com) and Vergant Media (vergant.com), served as editor in chief of *Friends of Wine* and *Wine Enthusiast* magazines before starting a number of media entities ranging from record labels to television series. She continues to write and speak on wine, food, and lifestyle and to lead tastings worldwide, including Wine Workout, which uses tasting wine as a way to strengthen the senses, memory, and mind.

from the underside of a saddle, hay flecked with wildflowers, and golden apples in a single pour.

"Ah," Dad said, nodding in encouragement, "Puligny-Montrachet."

The name itself was as delightfully poetic to my ear as the wine had been to my nose and mouth. Even though those youthful days were rich with honest smells—kitchen, backyard, woods, stream, farm—I'll always remember being most awed by the abundant and complex smells I found in a single glass of wine. A glass of great wine encompasses an entire world of smell, layer upon layer of riches.

Since those early dinner parties, Puligny-Montrachet has become one of my favorite wines and a symbol of the enduring bond between Dad and me. The last time I saw him was in a hospital—decades later—and I'll always cherish the evening he asked for a glass of it. Surely he knew that the orderlies wouldn't bring a bottle with his dinner, so I talked to him about the wine. I described its beguiling white Burgundian blend of minerals, acidity, crisp fruit, and toasted oak. I recalled our trips to the Côte de Nuits and the Côte de Beaune, detailing the particular pleasures of each bottle of wine we'd brought home. As I was talking, my father became increasingly relaxed. By the time I finished, he was utterly calm, with a dramatically improved oxygenation level.

"Thank you," he said, bowing his head. "I just wanted to hear it in your words."

Wine is both training ground and playground for all five of our senses, our memory, and our intellect. Consequently, our enjoyment and understanding of the full wine-tasting experience improve dramatically if we observe, smell, taste, feel, analyze, and remember more carefully. Good wine demands that we stop and savor each taste to allow its rich, sensuous story to unfold more completely. Every wine deserves the attention of all five senses. But smell, with its ability to evoke memory and feeling, matters most.

HOW WE SMELL

With each inhalation, we gather essential information about the world around us—its delights, opportunities, and dangers. We can shut our eyes, close our mouths, withdraw our touch, and cover our ears, but the nose, with notable exceptions, is always working, alerting us to potential danger and possible pleasure.

Our sense of smell also enhances learning, evokes memory, promotes healing, cements desire, and inspires us to action. It's so important to the preservation and sustenance of life that the instantaneous information it gathers bypasses the thalamus, which processes other senses, and moves directly to the limbic system.

The limbic system controls our emotions, emotional responses, moods, motivations, and our pain and pleasure sensations, and it's where we analyze olfactory stimuli. It plays its role in the formation of memory by integrating emotional states with stored memories of physical sensations, such as smells, creating our most important and primitive form of learning: working memory. We remember smell differently than we recall sight, sound, taste, or touch because we may respond to smell the same way we respond to emotion: an increased heart rate, enhanced sensitivity, and faster breathing. This emotional connection gives smell the power to stimulate memory so strongly and explains why a single smell can transport us instantly back to a particular time and place.

OLFACTORY
BULB

LIMBIC
SYSTEM

In 2004, Columbia University professor Richard Axel and Fred Hutchinson Cancer Research Center professor Linda Buck received the Nobel Prize in Medicine for their breakthrough discoveries in olfaction. Axel and Buck discovered a large family of genes in the cells of the epithelium, or lining, of the upper part of the nose controlling production of unique protein receptors, called olfactory receptors.

Olfactory receptors specialize in recognizing and then attaching themselves to thousands of specific molecules of incoming odorants. Once attached, the trapped molecules convert to electrical signals. These signals relay to neurons in the olfactory bulbs (one in each nasal cavity) before traveling along the olfactory nerve to the primary olfactory cortex, part of the brain's limbic system, for analysis and response. By the time the electrical

The **OLDEST PART OF THE HUMAN BRAIN** is the olfactory region.

As proof of the evolutionary importance of smell, **1–2 PERCENT OF OUR GENES AFFECT OLFACTION,** approximately the same percentage involved in the immune system.

Implicit memories are perceptual, emotional, sensory, and often are encoded and retrieved unconsciously. Explicit memories are factual, episodic, temporal, and require conscious coding and retrieval. **A GOOD WINE, WELL PERCEIVED AND DESCRIBED,** lives on in both forms of memory.

Axel and Buck isolated **10,000 DIFFERENT SMELLS.**

Scientists and other experts agree that smell accounts for up to 90 percent of what many perceive as **TASTE AND MOUTHFEEL.**

THE NOSE KNOWS: Exposure to certain easily recognizable smells while forming memories will link the memory to the smell. So (as Wendy implicitly understood as a young girl) eating tangerines while studying for a test, for example, makes it easier to remember the information by recalling the smell of tangerines while taking the test.

DIFFERENT SMELLS OF WINE come from the grape, the winemaking, and the aging.

EACH NOSTRIL can detect different smells.

signals of smell reach the limbic system, the component parts of a smell—wet leather, wildflowers, golden apples, and river rocks—have been identified already. The limbic system recombines these components for analysis by scanning its vast data bank for related matches. With analysis complete, the limbic system triggers an appropriate physiological response.

In the case of Puligny-Montrachet wine, the limbic system might recognize it as a pleasant white wine made from Chardonnay grapes. More experienced wine tasters, with a more highly developed memory data bank, connect that wine to other Puligny wines and recognize it as such. Expert tasters might be able to recall the vineyard, maker, and year. The more we taste, test, and study, the better we become at identification and enjoyment.

OLFACTORY PATHWAY FROM BOTTLE TO BRAIN

We can trace the olfactory pathway, of a bottle of Puligny-Montrachet for example, through the following steps:

- Open the bottle in happy anticipation.
- Pour the wine into a proper glass.
- Swirl the glass to release the wine's aromas.
- Inhale the wine's bouquet deeply and repeatedly.

- Chemical components—esters, ethers, aldehydes—swirl upward through the nostrils on currents of air.

- Midway up the nose, millions of olfactory receptor neurons (olfactory epithelia), with their specialized protein receptors, bind the odorants that form the components of the specific wine profile.

OLFACTORY BULB
OLFACTORY NERVES
INNER CHAMBER OF NOSE
OLFACTORY EPITHELIUM
MUCUS

- Interaction of the odor molecules matched with the right receptors causes the receptors to change shape.

- This change gives rise to an electrical signal that goes first to the olfactory bulb and then to the areas of the brain that convert the electrical signal to the identification of a smell or group of smells.

- The brain associates the smell(s) with perception, impressions, emotions, memories, knowledge, and more.

THE BIOLOGY OF SMELL

The septum, made of cartilage, divides the nose into two separate chambers, or nostrils, each with discretely wired epithelium and olfactory bulbs. Each nostril serves a different function and operates at peak capacity at different times. It's rare for both nostrils, even in the healthiest noses, to work at full capacity simultaneously, and people with a deviated septum often report being able to breathe through only one nostril. Lyall Watson, author of *Jacobson's Organ and the Remarkable Nature of Smell*, reports, "A three-hour cycle of alternation between left and right nostrils goes on, night and day. At night, it contributes to sleep movements." Watson hypothesizes that by day, when we are conscious, right and left nostrils direct information to accordant parts of the brain—the right being the side that perceives, intuits, encodes, and stores implicitly; the left being the side that explicitly analyzes, names, records, and retrieves. "Ideally, we need both. . . . But if a situation is strange and requires action based more on prediction than precedent, you would be better off facing it with a clear left nostril."

Scientists are beginning to be able to identify aroma compounds in wine by name, but tasters are likely to stick with existing lingo. **WHO WOULD WANT TO REMEMBER METHOXYPYRAZINE** for "green bell pepper," or linalool and geraniol for "floral"?

THREE AROMATIC GRAPES
Muscat
Gewürztraminer
Torrontés

A **DEVIATED SEPTUM**, which can cause problems with proper breathing and nasal discharge, is an abnormal configuration of the cartilage that divides the two sides of the nasal cavity. While definitive treatment may require surgery, decongestants, antihistamines, nasal cortisone spray, nasal lavage, and even eating jalapeño peppers and wasabi (which are hot enough to flush a stopped-up nose) can prove temporarily helpful.

HOW WE TASTE

Like smell, taste belongs to our chemical sensing system. Special structures called taste buds detect flavor, and we have, on average, between 5,000 and 10,000 of them, mainly on the tongue but some at the back of the throat and on the palate. Taste buds are the only sensory cells replaced regularly throughout a person's lifetime. Total regeneration takes place approximately every ten days. Scientists are examining this phenomenon, hoping to discover ways to replicate the process to induce regeneration in damaged sensory and nerve cells.

Clustered within each taste bud, gustatory cells have small hairs containing receptors. The gustatory receptors, like the olfactory receptors, sense specific types of dissolved chemicals. Everything we eat and drink must be dissolved—usually by saliva—in order for the gustatory receptors to identify the taste. Once dissolved, the gustatory receptors read then translate a food's chemical structure before converting that information to electrical signals. These electrical signals travel, via the facial and glossopharyngeal nerves, through the nose and on to the brain, where they are decoded and identified as a specific taste.

SALIVATION

Saliva is critical not only to the digestion of food and to the maintenance of oral hygiene but also to flavor. Saliva dissolves taste stimuli, allowing their chemistry to reach the gustatory receptor cells.

Remember being told to chew your food slowly so that you would enjoy your meal more? It's true. Taking more time to chew food and savor beverages allows more of their chemical components to dissolve and more aromas to release. This result provides more material for the gustatory and olfactory receptors to analyze, sending more complex data to the brain, which enhances perception. Taste and smell intensify.

TASTING AND CHEWING increase the rate of salivary flow.

While the majority of our taste buds are located in the mouth, we also have thousands of additional nerve endings—especially on the moist epithelial surfaces of the throat, nose, and eyes—that perceive texture, temperature, and assess a variety of factors, recognizing sensations such as the prickle of sulfur, the coolness of mint, and the burn of pepper. Humans can detect an estimated 10,000 smells and smell combinations, but we can detect just four or five basic flavors—bitter, salty, sour, sweet, and savory (umami). Of these, only sweetness, sourness, and occasionally bitterness apply to wine tasting.

There is **NO SALT** in wine.

The overall word for what we perceive in food and drink through a combination of smelling, tasting, and feeling is taste, but smell is so predominant of the three that wine tasting is actually "wine smelling." Some chemists describe wine as "a tasteless liquid that is deeply fragrant." Taste lets us know whether we're eating an apple or a pear, drinking a Puligny-Montrachet or an Australian Chardonnay. If you doubt the importance of smell in determining taste, hold your nose while eating chocolate or cheese, either of which will tend to taste like chalk.

TASTE PLACE

Old flavor maps place concentrated sweet receptors at the tip of the tongue, bitter at the back, and sour at the sides, but taste buds are distributed broadly throughout the mouth. In wine tasting, it's important to let wine aerate once it reaches your mouth so that it will release more aromas and intensify flavor. Do this by rolling the wine over your tongue and allowing it to linger on the tongue. This process also spreads the wine across a wider array of gustatory receptors and gives them more time to analyze its taste. A good wine will reveal first, middle, and lasting impressions, which are determined largely by aroma and mouthfeel.

MOUTHFEEL

Mouthfeel is literally how a wine feels in the mouth. These feelings are characterized by sensations that delight, prick, and/or pain our tongue, lips, and cheeks and that often linger in the mouth after swallowing or spitting. They can range from the piquant tingle of Champagne bubbles to the teeth-tightening astringency of tannin; from the cool expansiveness of menthol/eucalyptus to the heat of a high-alcohol red; and from the cloying sweetness of a low-acid white to the velvet coating of a rich Rhône. The physical feel of wine is also important to mouthfeel and includes: body, thin to full; weight, light to heavy; and texture, austere, silky, unctuous, and chewy. Each contributes to wine's overall balance. More than just impressions, these qualities can trigger a physical response—drying, puckering, and salivation—that can have wines literally dancing on the tongue and clinging to the teeth.

BITTERNESS IN WINE arises from a combination of high alcohol and high tannin.

WHERE DO YOU EXPERIENCE BITTERNESS?
Back of the tongue
Sides of the mouth
In the throat

Much of **WHAT COMMONLY IS DESCRIBED AS TASTE**—80–90 percent or more—is aroma/bouquet, as sensed and articulated by our olfactory receptors, and mouthfee and texture as sensed by surrounding organs.

WINE TEXTURES
LIGHT: skim milk
MEDIUM: whole milk
FULL: heavy cream

Hypergeusia, hypogeusia, and aguesia—**HEIGHTENED TASTE AND PARTIAL AND TOTAL TASTE LOSS**, respectively—are rare and usually reflect a smell loss, which is often confused with a taste loss.

No scientific evidence shows that our olfactory abilities change over the course of a day, although many winemakers and **WINE PROFESSIONALS BELIEVE THEIR SENSES TO BE KEENER AND THEIR PALATES CLEANER IN THE MORNING**. When evaluating wines, I prefer to taste around 11 AM. Others prefer tasting wine with a slight edge of hunger, which seems to enhance their alertness. Get to know your own cycles!

SMELL AND TASTE TOGETHER

Recent research presents additional proof that taste seldom works alone —as wine tasters have known for centuries—and provides the first clear scientific evidence that olfaction is uniquely "dual." We often smell by inhaling through both nose and mouth simultaneously, adding to smell's complexity.

Smells can reach the olfactory receptors by two paths:

Orthonasal stimulation Odor compounds (smells) reach the olfactory bulb via the external nares or nostrils.

Retronasal stimulation Odor compounds reach the olfactory bulb via the internal nares, located inside the mouth (the respiratory tract at the back of the throat). This is why even if you pinch your nose shut, a strong cheese inhaled through the mouth may still smell. Molecules that stimulate the olfactory receptors float around in your mouth, up through your internal nares, and stimulate the neurons in the olfactory bulb.

According to an article in the journal *Neuron*, researchers reported that the smell of chocolate stimulated different brain regions when introduced into the olfactory system through the nose (orthonasally) than it did when introduced through the mouth (retronasally). The study suggests that sensing odor through the nose may help indicate the availability of food while identification through the mouth may signify receipt of food.

OLFACTORY ABILITIES

Experts agree that, except in rare instances of brain disease or damage, we are born with a relatively equal ability to perceive smell, although our ability to identify and articulate those smells varies widely. In general, women have the advantage over men in perceiving and identifying smells throughout their life cycle. It's not known why, but theories hold that, because women bear the enormous responsibility of conceiving and raising children, a keen sense of smell evolved as an aid to everything from choosing a mate to caring for a family.

Dr. Alan Hirsch of the Smell & Taste Treatment and Research Foundation and experts from the Monell Chemical Senses Center have shed additional light on the evolution and devolution of smell over a lifetime by describing the changes that occur at periods in the life cycle.

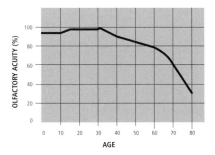

OLFACTORY ACUITY reaches its peak in
young adulthood, around 32 years old.

35 percent of women and 15 percent of men
are **SUPER-TASTERS**.

In utero, the fetus acquires its blood supply through the placenta, via which it may receive odorants that help the baby recognize Mom at birth and which may lead to developing food preferences for what Mom ate or drank. After birth, flavors and smells from food and beverages make their way through mother's milk to the infant. As a result, preferences form toward sweet and away from bitter.

As a child grows, so does his or her ability to recognize and remember different odors, especially those paired with an emotional event. Children usually have a hard time describing smells in words, but they are forming lifelong sensory and emotional impressions. For example, smelling roses in the garden with Mom will have a far different impact on the feeling the scent elicits later in life than if a child first smells roses at a funeral.

The sense of smell reaches its most acute level in both boys and girls at puberty, although girls surge further ahead at the onset of menstruation. This heightened sensitivity to smell will persist throughout their fertile years. Women consistently outscore men in their ability to put names to smells in adulthood, and women give higher ratings on pleasure and intensity of smells and lower ratings on unpleasant aromas. Women's sense of smell is particularly acute at ovulation and during pregnancy.

By age 65, about half the population will experience a decline, on average, of 33 percent in olfactory abilities. A quarter of the population has no ability to smell after 65. A majority of the population will show losses of up to 50 percent in olfactory abilities by age 80.

KINDS OF TASTERS

According to Janet Zimmerman, in her article "Science of the Kitchen: Taste and Texture," approximately one-quarter of the population are "non-tasters," half are "tasters," and one-quarter are "super-tasters." Super-tasters have a significantly higher number of taste buds than tasters, and both groups outnumber non-tasters for taste buds. The averages for the three groups are 96 taste buds per square centimeter for non-tasters, 184 for tasters, and a whopping 425 for super-tasters. Non-tasters are far from picky and seem less conscious of and therefore less engaged with what they eat and drink. Tasters, the largest and least homogeneous group, vary in their personal preferences, tend to enjoy the widest array of food and drink, and relish the act of eating and drinking the most of the three groups. Super-tasters tend to taste everything more intensely.

Sweets are sweeter, bitters are more bitter, and many foods and beverages, including alcohol, taste and feel unpleasantly strong.

ACCOUNTING FOR SMELL AND TASTE

What accounts for ethnic and cultural differences in smell and taste abilities, perceptions, and preferences? According to Monell Chemical Senses Center anthropologist Claudia Damhuis, some odor associations/preferences might be innate, such as an aversion to the odor of rotten food, but the vast majority of them are learned.

THE WAY WE LEARN

The ability to identify and perceive odors, as well as odor preferences, is learned both implicitly and explicitly through a number of variables including environment, culture, custom, context, and a variety of sociocultural factors. Factors that impact cultural differences in odor preferences include:

- Physiological differences, such as the size and presence of glands in different populations

- Differences in hygienic habits

- Acceptability and denial of odors according to cultural norms and etiquette

- Familiarity with specific odors

- The role and function attributed to specific odors

- Cultural differences in food preparations and related olfactory experiences and association

- Precision of language used to express odor perceptions and associations

GENERAL PREFERENCES

Across a great variety of ethnicities, odors can fall into general categories of association: nature, man, civilization, food and drink, and more. A worldwide smell survey conducted by *National Geographic* and Monell found

SUPER-TASTERS CAN BE SUPERSENSITIVE, and they may find wines with tannin and high alcohol too bitter; Cabernet Sauvignon, for example, may not be to their liking. They also may be put off by any sweetness in wine. Non-tasters are the opposite; they might not be bothered by tannin or high alcohol, and sweet wines probably would be perfectly acceptable.

According to Lyall Watson's *Jacobson's Organ and the Remarkable Nature of Smell*, our two square meters of skin come equipped with 3 million sweat glands. People of European and African descent have armpits densely packed with apocrine glands, but PEOPLE OF ASIAN ORIGIN HAVE FAR FEWER, AND SOME HAVE NO ARMPIT GLANDS AT ALL; 90 percent of the population in Japan has no detectable underarm odor. Japanese people who first encountered European traders in the nineteenth century described them as *bata-kusai*—"stinks of butter." Meantime, the French were reveling in their own aromas. Napoléon sent a note to Josephine that read: "I'll be arriving in Paris tomorrow evening. Don't wash."

Mercaptans, described as smelling **UNCOMFORTABLY SKUNKLIKE**, are a natural by-product of fermentation. They can be removed by aeration during the winemaking process.

One culture's special foods and beverages, such as chile peppers, can become highly popular and spread quickly to other groups. Others prove less appealing and tend to stay put. Think of Korea's kimchi; Norway's lutefisk; prairie oysters in the American West; and, in the wine world, Greece's **RETSINA, A WINE FLAVORED BY TREE RESIN.**

English wine writers occasionally use gooseberries to describe a wine's aroma, but **MOST AMERICANS ARE UNFAMILIAR WITH GOOSEBERRIES** and don't know what they smell like.

universal unpleasantness noted across nine regions for fecal odors, human odors, material in decomposition, and mercaptans (sulfur-containing compounds often added to natural gas as a warning agent). Most odors, however, were rated pleasant, including vegetation, lavender, amyl acetate (banana odor), galaxolide (synthetic musk), and eugenol (synthetic clove oil).

CULTURAL DIFFERENCES

Physiology, environment, diet, and language all play roles in cultural preference. The Asian preference for soy rather than dairy products—which carries through even in the smells and tastes of mothers' milk—might account for the Asian cultural aversion to strong cheese. Asian-American communities, families, or individuals may or may not exhibit this aversion, depending on the degree to which they retain these food-and-drink customs or adopt local ones.

Other cultural differences might be environmental, as suggested by a study of the Serer N'Dut of Senegal, who classify their odors in only five categories—scented, milk-fishy, rotten, urinelike, and acidic—or linguistic, as in a cross-cultural French / Vietnamese / American study in which participants' odor categorization didn't correlate with their linguistic categorization.

TOWARD A COMMON LANGUAGE OF SMELL AND TASTE

Smell is a relatively inadequate word for our most primitive and powerful sense. It means both the smells that emanate from us (we are what we eat and drink) as well as the smells we perceive. Over time, wine tasters have done much to create a common language and to savor the intersection where enlivened and articulated senses meet memory, anticipation, association, and personal preferences.

Like colors, aroma falls into basic categories that, when combined, yield the rich symphony that is wine. Ann Noble's *Wine Aroma Wheel* categorizes basic fruit aromas as: citrus, berry, tree, tropical, canned, dried. Other aroma categories include nutty, caramelized, woody, earthy, chemical, pungent, floral, and spicy. See the table on pages 44–45 for a more extensive list of descriptors for wine.

Still, no two people smell or perceive smells alike. It's deeply personal and experiential. Here is our best effort to convey how scent feels and what it means to us:

Wendy says "Puligny-Montrachet" to herself because she loves the word nearly as much as the wine. It serves as a homing signal that brings her to self and center—to a time, place, and wine she loves and to the kind of bonds that endure.

Kevin goes out on his porch with a glass of a favorite, special vintage and looks into the night sky. In every sip are all that he treasures and honors about Windows on the World and a reason to look up at the stars.

We hope and trust that you'll find wine and spirits like this and that you'll share words of them with us. In the meantime, here's to your health, happiness, and savoring wine and life in and with every sense!

in *The Emperor of Scent,* Chandler Burr uses **A PARTICULARLY PUNGENT BURGUNDIAN CHEESE** to illustrate cultural preferences: When they smell Soumaintrain, "Americans think, 'Good God!' The Japanese think, 'I must now commit suicide.' The French think, 'Where's the bread?'"

FOR MORE SOURCES AND RESOURCES on smell and taste, see page 368.

WINE AROMAS AND TASTES

	FRUITY	FLORAL	CARAMELIZED	NUTTY		VEGETAL		SPICY
TROPICAL	Banana	Acacia	Beeswax	Almond	**FRESH HERBS**	Boxwood	**SWEET SPICES**	Cinnamon
	Guava	Chamomile	Brioche	Biscuit		Dill		Clove
	Honeydew	Geranium	Butterscotch	Hazlenut		Eucalyptus		Vanilla
	Lychee	Hawthorn	Caramel	Walnut		Grass		
	Mango	Hibiscus	Chocolate			Mint	**PUNGENT SPICES**	Anise
	Passion fruit	Honeysuckle	Honey			Thyme		Black pepper
	Pineapple	Iris	Malt		**DRIED HERBS**	Black tea		Ginger
CITRUS	Grapefruit	Jasmine	Molasses			Green tea		Licorice
	Lemon	Lavender	Toffee			Hay		Lovage
	Lime	Lilac	White chocolate			Tobacco		Nutmeg
	Orange	Linden			**FRESH VEGETABLES**	Bell pepper		
TREE FRUITS	Apple	Orange blossom				Green pepper		
	Apricot	Peony				Japaleño		
	Elderberry	Potpurri				Sun-dried tomato		
	Green apple	Rose				Tomato		
	Peach	Violet			**COOKED VEGETABLES**	Artichoke		
	Pear	Yarrow				Asparagus		
RED FRUITS	Cherry					Green bean		
	Raspberry					Canned peas		
	Red currant							
	Strawberry							
	Blackberry							
	Black cherry							
	Black currant							
	Plum							
	Date							
	Dried apricot							
	Dried fig							
	Fruitcake							
	Prune							
	Raisin							

MINERAL	WOODY		BIOLOGICAL		DAIRY	CHEMICAL	
Flint	Cedar		ANIMAL	Mousy	Butter	PUNGENT	Nail polish remover (ethyl acetate)
Gravel	Moss			Horsey	Cream		Vinegar (acetic acid)
River rocks	Oak			Wet dog		SULFUR	Burnt match
Slate	Pine			Wet wool			Cooked cabbage
Stone	Resinous		EARTHY	Cheesy			Garlic
	Sandalwood			Forest floor			Natural gas (mercaptans)
	SMOKY	Bacon		Mushroom			Rotten eggs (hydrogen sulfide)
		Coffee		Soy sauce			Rubber
		Leather	LACTIC	Sauerkraut			Skunk
		Tar		Sweaty			Sulfur dioxide
		Toast		Yogurt		PETROLEUM	Diesel
			YEASTY	Baker's yeast			Kerosene
				Bandage			Plastic
				Bread			

Professional wine tasters use hundreds of words to describe the aroma, bouquet, flavor, and taste of wine. Some of them might sound crazy, and the descriptors in this table apply to all wines: young or old, white or red. Many wines will feature only, say, three of these, and some of them are faults, so don't look for them all. Nor do you have to know them all, but they offer a taste of the more common descriptors that you're likely to encounter.

TASTING WINE

You can read all the books (and there are plenty) written on wine to become more knowledgeable on the subject, but the best way to enhance your understanding of wine is to taste as many wines as possible. Reading covers the more academic side of wine, while tasting is more enjoyable and practical. A little of each will do you the most good.

Wine tasting breaks down into five basic steps: color, swirl, smell, taste, and savor. You may wish to follow them with a glass of wine in hand.

COLOR

The best way to determine a wine's color is against a white background—a napkin or tablecloth—holding the glass at an angle in front of it. The range of colors depends of course on whether you're tasting a white or red wine. Here are the colors for both, beginning with the youngest wine and moving to an older wine:

As white wines age, they gain color. Red wines, on the other hand, lose color as they age.

If you can see through a red wine, it's generally ready to drink.

WHITE WINE			RED WINE
PALE YELLOW-GREEN			PURPLE
STRAW YELLOW			RUBY
YELLOW-GOLD			RED
GOLD			
OLD GOLD			BRICK RED
YELLOW-BROWN			RED-BROWN
MADERIZED			
BROWN			BROWN

Color tells you a lot about the wine. Let's consider three reasons that a white wine may have more color:

1. It's older.
2. Different grape varieties give different color. (For example, Chardonnay usually gives a deeper color than Sauvignon Blanc.)
3. The wine aged in wood.

In my classes, it's not unusual to hear that some people believe that a wine is pale yellow-green, while others say it's gold. Everyone begins with the same wine, but color perceptions vary. There are no right or wrong answers because perception is subjective. So you can imagine what happens when we actually taste the wine!

SWIRL

Swirl to allow oxygen to get into the wine. Swirling releases the esters, ethers, and aldehydes that combine with oxygen to yield a wine's bouquet. In other words, swirling aerates the wine and releases more of the aroma. Put your hands over the glass of wine when you swirl to create a more powerful bouquet and aroma.

SMELL

This is the most important part of wine tasting. You can perceive just five flavors—sweet, sour, bitter, salty, savory—but the average person can identify more than 2,000 different scents, and wine has more than 200 of its own. Now that you've swirled the wine and released the bouquet, smell the wine at least three times. You may find that the third smell will give you more information than the first smell did. What does the wine smell like? What type of nose does it have? Again, smell is the most important step in the tasting process, and most people simply don't spend enough time on it.

Pinpointing the nose of the wine helps you identify certain characteristics. I prefer not to use subjective words, so I may say that a wine smells like a white Burgundy. But this description doesn't satisfy most people. They want to know more. What do steak and onions smell like? The answer: "Like steak and onions." See what I mean?

The best way to learn your own preferences for styles of wine is to "memorize" the smell of the individual grape varieties. For white, try

Aroma is the smell of the grapes. **BOUQUET IS THE TOTAL SMELL OF THE WINE.** "Nose" is a word that wine tasters use to describe the bouquet and aroma of the wine.

One of my favorite bouquets comes from older wines, usually of 20 years or more. I call it the **"DEAD LEAF" SMELL** when in the fall the air is full of fallen leaves.

to memorize the three major grape varieties: Chardonnay, Sauvignon Blanc, and Riesling. Keep smelling them, and smelling them, and smelling them until you can identify the differences, one from another. For the reds, it's a little more difficult, but you still can take three major grape varieties: Pinot Noir, Merlot, and Cabernet Sauvignon. Try to memorize those smells without using flowery words, and you'll understand what I mean.

If you remain unconvinced, I have a list of 500 different words commonly used to describe wine. Here's a small excerpt:

acetic	character	legs	seductive
aftertaste	corky	light	short
aroma	developed	maderized	stalky
astringent	earthy	mature	sulfury
austere	finish	metallic	tart
baked-burnt	flat	nose	thin
balanced	fresh	nutty	tired
bitter	grapey	off	vanilla
body	green	oxidized	woody
bouquet	hard	pétillant	yeasty
bright	hot	rich	young

Again, see pages 44–45 for a more extensive list of descriptors.

You're more likely to recognize some of the defects of a wine through your sense of smell. Here's a list of some of the negative smells in wine:

SMELL	CAUSE
VINEGAR	TOO MUCH ACETIC ACID
SHERRY	OXIDATION
DANK, WET, MOLDY, CELLAR SMELL	DEFECTIVE CORK (REFERRED TO AS "CORKED WINE")
SULFUR (BURNT MATCHES)	TOO MUCH SULFUR DIOXIDE

Oxygen can be the best friend of a wine, but it also can be its worst enemy. A little oxygen helps release the smell of the wine (as with swirling),

One of the most difficult challenges in life is to **MATCH A SMELL OR A TASTE** with a word that describes it.

WineSpeak by Bernard Klem includes **36,975 WINE-TASTING DESCRIPTIONS.** Who knew?

but prolonged exposure can be harmful, especially to older wines. Authentic Sherry, from Spain, is made through controlled oxidation.

Each person has a different threshold for sulfur dioxide, and, although most people don't have an adverse reaction, it can prove problematic for individuals with asthma. To protect those sensitive to sulfites, federal law in America requires wineries to label their wines with the warning that the wine contains sulfites. Every wine contains a certain amount of sulfites. They're a natural by-product of fermentation.

TASTE

For many people, tasting wine means taking a sip and swallowing immediately. That's not tasting. You taste with your taste buds, and you have them all over your mouth—on both sides of the tongue, underneath, on the tip, and extending to the back of your throat. If you gulp the wine, you bypass all of those important receptors. When you taste wine, leave it in your mouth for three to five seconds before swallowing. The wine warms up, sending signals about the aroma and bouquet up through the nasal passage then on to the olfactory bulb, and then to the limbic system of the brain. Remember, 90 percent of taste is smell.

WHAT TO THINK ABOUT WHEN TASTING WINE

Be aware of the most important sensations of taste and your own personal thresholds of those tastes. Also, pay attention to where they occur on your tongue and in your mouth. As mentioned earlier, you can perceive just five flavors: sweet, sour, bitter, salty, and savory—but there's no salt in wine, so we're down to four. High alcohol and high tannin usually create bitterness in wine. Sweetness occurs only in wines with residual sugar. Sour (sometimes called "tart") indicates the acidity in wine.

Sweetness The highest threshold is on the tip of the tongue. If there's any sweetness in a wine whatsoever, you'll get it right away.

Acidity Found at the sides of the tongue, the cheek area, and the back of the throat. White wines and some lighter-style red wines usually contain a higher degree of acidity.

Bitterness Tasted on the back of the tongue.

You are born with **10,000 TASTE BUDS.** As you age, the number decreases.

Tasting wine is confirming what the **COLOR AND SMELL** are telling you.

Like my wine bright, rich, mature, developed, **SEDUCTIVE, AND WITH NICE LEGS!**

Aroma is the smell of the grapes. **BOUQUET IS THE TOTAL SMELL OF THE WINE.** "Nose" is a word that wine tasters use to describe the bouquet and aroma of the wine.

Tannin The sensation of tannin begins in the middle of the tongue. Tannin frequently exists in red wines or white wines aged in wood. When the wines are too young, tannin dries the palate to excess. If the wine has a lot of tannin, it can coat your whole mouth, blocking the fruit. Remember, tannin is not a taste: it's a tactile sensation.

Fruit and varietal characteristics These aren't tastes but smells. You'll find the weight or "body" of the fruit in the middle of your tongue.

Aftertaste The overall taste and balance of the components of the wine that lingers in your mouth. How long does the balance last? A long, pleasing aftertaste usually indicates a high-quality wine. The taste of many of the great wines lasts anywhere from one to three minutes, with all their components in harmony.

SAVOR

After you've had a chance to taste the wine, savor it for a few moments. Think about what you just experienced, and ask yourself the following questions to help focus your impressions.

- Was the wine light, medium, or full-bodied?
- For a red wine: Is the tannin in the wine too strong or astringent?
- For a white wine: How was the acidity? Very little, just right, or too much?
- What's the strongest component (residual sugar, fruit, acid, tannin)?
- How long did the balance of the components last (10 seconds, 60 seconds, etc.)?
- Is the wine ready to drink, or does it need more time to age?
- What kind of food would you enjoy with the wine?
- To your taste, is the wine worth the price?
- Most importantly: Do you like it? Is it your style?

Tasting wine is like visiting an art gallery. You wander from room to room, looking at the paintings. Your first impression tells whether you like something. Once you decide you like a piece of art, you want to know more: Who was the artist? What's the history behind the work? How was it made?

BITTER: Think endive or arugula.

TANNIN: Think gritty.

TYPES OF TASTINGS	
HORIZONTAL	Tasting wines from the same vintage
VERTICAL	Comparing wines from different vintages
BLIND	The taster does not have any information about the wines.
SEMI-BLIND	The taster knows only the style of wine (grape) or where it originated.

"The key to great wine is balance, and it is the sum of the different parts that make a wine not only delicious but complete and fascinating as well as worthy of aging."
—FIONA MORRISON, M.W.

"The hardest thing to attain . . . is the appreciation of difference without insisting on superiority."
—GEORGE SAINTSBURY,
Notes on a Cellar-Book

WHAT MAKES A GREAT WINE GREAT?
Varietal character
Balance of components
Complexity
Sense of place
Emotional response

—— **FURTHER READING** ——

Making Sense of Wine by Alan Young

Pocket Guide to Wine Tasting by Michael Broadbent

Vintage Timecharts by Jancis Robinson

Don't forget to **TOAST YOUR FAMILY AND FRIENDS** with the clinking of the glasses. This tradition started in ancient times when the Greeks, afraid of being poisoned by their enemies, shared a little of their wine with one another. If someone had added something to the wine, it would be a short evening for everyone! The clinking of the glasses also is said to drive away the "bad spirits" that might exist and cause the next-day hangover!

So it is with wine. Once oenophiles (wine aficionados) discover a wine that they like, they want to learn everything about it: the grapes; exactly where the vines were planted; the winemaker; the blend, if any; and the history behind the wine.

HOW TO KNOW WHETHER A WINE IS GOOD

The definition of a good wine is one that you enjoy. I cannot emphasize this enough. Trust your own palate, and don't let others dictate your taste to you!

WHEN IS A WINE READY TO DRINK?

This is one of the most frequently asked questions. The answer is very simple: when all components of the wine are in balance to your taste.

THE 60-SECOND WINE EXPERT

I use this 60-second Wine Expert tasting method in my classes for students to record their impressions. The minute divides into four sections: 0 to 15 seconds, 15 to 30 seconds, 30 to 45 seconds, and the final 45 to 60 seconds. Try this with your next glass of wine.

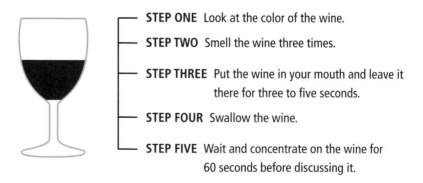

STEP ONE Look at the color of the wine.

STEP TWO Smell the wine three times.

STEP THREE Put the wine in your mouth and leave it there for three to five seconds.

STEP FOUR Swallow the wine.

STEP FIVE Wait and concentrate on the wine for 60 seconds before discussing it.

The first taste of wine will shock your taste buds. This comes from the alcohol content, acidity, and sometimes the tannin. The higher the alcohol or acidity, the more of a shock. For the first wine in any tasting, take a sip and swirl it around in your mouth, but don't evaluate it. Wait another 30 seconds, try it again, and then begin the 60-second wine expert tasting.

0 to 15 seconds If there's any residual sugar / sweetness in the wine, you'll experience it now. If there's no sweetness in the wine, the acidity is usually at its strongest in the first 15 seconds. Focus on the fruit level of the wine and its balance with the acidity or sweetness.

15 to 30 seconds After the sweetness or acidity, evaluate just the fruit sensation. After all, that's ultimately what you want! By 30 seconds, you want a balance of all the components. By this time, you can identify the weight of the wine. Is it light, medium, or full-bodied? Think about what kind of food to pair with this wine (pages 333–334).

30 to 45 seconds Start formulating your opinion of the wine. Not all wines need 60 seconds of thought. Lighter-style wines, such as Rieslings, usually show their best at this point. The fruit, acid, and sweetness of a great German Riesling should be in perfect harmony from this point on. For quality red and white wines, acidity should now balance with the fruit of the wine.

45 to 60 seconds Very often wine writers use the term "length" to des-cribe how long the balance of components continues in the mouth. Concentrate on the length of the wine in these last 15 seconds. In big, full-bodied red wines from Bordeaux and the Rhône Valley, Cabernets from California, Barolos and Barbarescos from Italy, and even some full-bodied Chardonnays, concentrate on the level of tannin in the wine. Just as the acidity and fruit balance are major concerns in the first 30 seconds, you want tannin and fruit balance in the last 30 seconds. If the fruit, tannin, and acid all balance at 60 seconds, then the wine is ready to drink. If the tannin overpowers the fruit at the 60-second mark, consider whether to drink the wine now or put it away for more aging.

It's extremely important, if you want to learn the true taste of the wine, that you take at least one minute to concentrate on all of its components. But 60 seconds is the *minimum* time needed to make a decision about a wine. Many great wines continue to show balance well past 120 seconds. The best wine I ever tasted lasted more than three minutes—that's three minutes of perfect balance of all components!

I make my decision about whether I like the style of a wine within **45 TO 60 SECONDS.**

"Wine is the best of all beverages . . . because it is purer than water, safer than milk, plainer than soft drinks, gentler than spirits, nimbler than beer, and ever so much more pleasant to the educated senses of sight, smell, and taste than any of the drinkable liquids known to us."

—ANDRE L. SIMON, author and founder of the Wine & Food Society

AMERICAN WINE AND THE RED WINES OF CALIFORNIA

AMERICAN WINEMAKING ✶ UNDERSTANDING CALIFORNIA
WINES ✶ THE MAJOR RED GRAPES OF CALIFORNIA:
CABERNET SAUVIGNON, PINOT NOIR, ZINFANDEL, MERLOT,
AND SYRAH ✶ THE RED-GRAPE BOOM

On discovering North America, **LEIF ERIKSSON NAMED IT VINELAND**. More species of native grapes exist in North America than on any other continent.

Huguenots established colonies in Jacksonville, Florida, in 1562 and produced wine using the wild Scuppernong grape. Evidence points to a flourishing wine industry in 1609 at the site of the early Jamestown settlements. In 2004 an **OLD WINE CELLAR WAS DISCOVERED IN JAMESTOWN** with an empty bottle dating back to the seventeenth century.

AMERICAN WINEMAKING

WINE DRINKING HAS jumped by more than a third in the USA over the last 20 years, according to Gallup, with about 30 percent of Americans drinking at least one glass of wine a week. Americans prefer domestic wines: More than three-quarters of all wines consumed by Americans are produced here. Meanwhile, the number of American wineries has tripled in the last two decades—to more than 7,000—and, for the first time in American history, all 50 states produce wine.

Because American wines so dominate the US market, it makes sense to take a detailed look at winemaking here. We often think of the wine industry as "young" in America, but its roots go back some 400 years.

THE EARLY DAYS

Shortly after arriving in America, the Pilgrims and early pioneers, accustomed to drinking wine with meals, delighted in finding grapevines growing wild. These thrifty, self-reliant colonists thought they had found in this species (primarily *Vitis labrusca)* a means of producing their own wine, thereby ending their dependency on costly wine from Europe. They cultivated the local grapevines, harvested the grapes, and made their first American wine. The new vintage possessed an entirely different—and disappointing—flavor when compared to wine made from European grapes. They ordered cuttings of the *Vitis vinifera* vine from Europe, which for centuries had produced the finest wines in the world. Soon ships arrived bearing the tender cuttings, and the colonists, having paid scarce, hard-earned money for these new vines, planted and tended them with great care. They were eager to taste their first wine made from European grapes grown in American soil.

Despite their efforts, few of the European vines thrived. Many died, and those that survived produced few grapes. That meager yield resulted in very poor-quality wine. Early settlers blamed the cold climate, but today we know that their European vines lacked immunity to the New World's plant diseases and pests. For the next 200 years every attempt at establishing varieties of *vinifera*—either intact or through crossbreeding with native vines—failed. Left with no other choice, growers throughout the Northeast and Midwest returned to planting *Vitis labrusca*, North America's vine, and a small wine industry managed to survive.

European wine remained the preferred, though high-priced, choice. The failures of these early attempts to establish a wine industry in the USA, along with the high cost of imported wines, resulted in decreasing demand for wine. Gradually American tastes changed, and wine served at mealtimes marked only special occasions. Beer and whiskey had conquered wine's traditional place in American homes.

The major varieties of wine produced in America come from these species:

American *Vitis labrusca*, such as Catawba, Concord, and Delaware; and *Vitis rotundifolia*, commonly called Scuppernong

European *Vitis vinifera*, such as Cabernet Sauvignon, Chardonnay, Merlot, Pinot Noir, Riesling, Sauvignon Blanc, Syrah, and Zinfandel.

Hybrids A cross between *vinifera* and a native American species, such as Baco Noir, Chancellor, Seyval Blanc, or Vidal Blanc.

WINE IN THE WEST

Wine production in the West began with the Spanish. As Spanish settlers pushed northward from Mexico, the Catholic Church followed, and a great era of mission-building began. Early missions amounted to more than just churches, though; they contained entire communities conceived as self-sufficient fortifications protecting Spanish colonial interests throughout the Southwest and along the Pacific Coast. Besides growing their own food

Early German immigrants imported Riesling grapes and called their finished wine **HOCK**; the French called their wine **BURGUNDY** or **BORDEAUX**; and the Italians borrowed the name **CHIANTI** for theirs.

VITIS LABRUSCA, the "slip-skinned" grape, is native to both the Northeast and the Midwest and produces a unique tatse. Producers use it to make grape juice—the bottled kind you'll find on supermarket shelves. Wine produced from *labrusca* grapes tastes, well, more "grapey" (also described as "foxy") than European wines.

EARLY MISSIONARIES established wineries in the southern parts of California. The first commercial winery was established in what is today Los Angeles.

The grape variety the missionaries used to make their sacramental wine was called **THE MISSION GRAPE.** Unfortunately, it didn't have the potential to produce a great wine.

First Lady Mary Todd Lincoln served American wines in the White House in 1861.

When **ROBERT LOUIS STEVENSON** honeymooned in Napa Valley in 1880, he described the efforts of local winemakers to match soil and climate with the best possible varieties. "One corner of land after another . . . this is a failure, that is better, this is best. So bit by bit, they grope about for their Clos de Vougeot and Lafite . . . and **THE WINE IS BOTTLED POETRY.**"

Welch's grape juice has been around since the late 1800s. It originally was produced by staunch prohibitionists and labeled "**DR. WELCH'S UNFERMENTED WINE.**" In 1892, they renamed it "Welch's Grape Juice" and successfully launched it at the Columbian Exposition in Chicago in 1893.

and making their own clothing, those early settlers also made their own wine, produced primarily for use in the Church. The demand for wine led Father Junípero Serra to bring *Vitis vinifera* vines—brought to Mexico by the Spaniards—from Mexico to California in 1769. These vines took root, thriving in California's moderate climate. The first true California wine industry had begun, albeit on a small scale. Two events occurred in the mid-1800s that resulted in an explosive growth of quality wine production. The 1849 California Gold Rush brought immigrants from Europe and the East Coast along with their winemaking traditions. They cultivated the vines and soon were producing good-quality commercial wine.

The second critical event occurred in 1861, when Governor Downey of California, understanding the importance of viticulture to the state's growing economy, commissioned Agoston Haraszthy to select and import classic *Vitis vinifera* cuttings—such as Cabernet Sauvignon, Chardonnay, Riesling, and Zinfandel—from Europe. Haraszthy traveled to Europe, returning with more than 100,000 carefully selected vines. Not only did these grape varieties thrive in California's climate, but they also produced good-quality wine! Serious California winemaking began in earnest.

In 1863, while California wines were flourishing, European vineyards were facing trouble. Phylloxera—an aphid pest native to the East Coast of America and very destructive to grape crops—began attacking European vineyards. This infestation, which arrived in Europe on cuttings from native American vines exported for experimental purposes, proved devastating. Over the next two decades, the phylloxera blight destroyed thousands of acres of European vines, severely diminishing European wine production just as demand was growing rapidly.

California became virtually the only area in the world producing wine made from European grapes. Demand for its wines skyrocketed. This situation helped develop, almost overnight, two huge markets for California wine. The first market clamored for good, inexpensive, yet drinkable wine produced on a mass scale. The second market sought higher-quality wines. California growers responded to both demands, and by 1876 California was producing more than 2.3 million gallons of wine per year, some of remarkable quality. California had become, for the moment, the new center of global winemaking.

Unfortunately, in that same year, phylloxera arrived in California and began attacking those vineyards. Once there, it spread as rapidly as it had in Europe. With thousands of vines dying, the California wine industry faced financial ruin. To this day, the phylloxera blight remains one of the most destructive crop epidemics of all time.

Luckily, other states had continued producing wine made from *labrusca* vines, and American wine production didn't grind to a complete halt. Meanwhile, after years of research, European winemakers finally found a defense against the pernicious phylloxera aphid. They successfully grafted *Vitis vinifera* vines onto the rootstock of *labrusca* vines, immune to the phylloxera, rescuing their wine industry.

Americans followed suit, and the California wine industry not only recovered but began producing better-quality wines than ever before. By the late 1800s, California wines were winning medals in international competitions, gaining the respect and admiration of the world. It took only 300 years!

PROHIBITION

In 1920, the Eighteenth Amendment to the Constitution created yet another setback for the American wine industry. The National Prohibition Act, also known as the Volstead Act, prohibited the manufacture, sale, transportation, importation, exportation, delivery, or possession of intoxicating liquors for beverage purposes. Prohibition, which continued for 13 years, nearly destroyed what had become a thriving national industry.

But one of the loopholes in the Volstead Act allowed for the manufacture and sale of sacramental wine, medicinal wines for sale by pharmacists with a doctor's prescription, and medicinal wine tonics (fortified wines) sold without prescription. Perhaps more importantly, Prohibition allowed anyone to produce up to 200 gallons of fruit juice or cider a year. The fruit juice, sometimes concentrated, proved ideal for making wine. People bought grape concentrate from California and shipped it to the East Coast. The top of the containers warned:

> CAUTION: DO NOT ADD SUGAR OR YEAST
> OR ELSE FERMENTATION WILL TAKE PLACE!

Some of this yield found its way to bootleggers throughout the country who did just that—but not for long. The government banned the sale of grape juice, preventing illegal wine production. Growers stopped planting, and the American wine industry came to a halt.

Forty different **AMERICAN WINERIES WON MEDALS AT THE 1900 PARIS EXPOSITION**, including those from California, New Jersey, New York, Ohio, and Virginia.

IN 1920, CALIFORNIA HAD MORE THAN 700 WINERIES. By the end of Prohibition, it had just 160.

"PROHIBITION IS BETTER THAN NO LIQUOR AT ALL"

"Once, during Prohibition, I was forced to live for days on nothing but food and water."

—W. C. FIELDS

Fortified wine, or medicinal wine tonic—containing about 20 percent alcohol, which makes it more like a distilled spirit than regular wine—was still available and became America's number-one wine. American wine soon became popular more for its effect than its taste. The word "wino" came into use during the Depression from the name given to those unfortunate souls who turned to fortified wine to forget their troubles.

Prohibition ended in 1933, but its impact reverberated for decades. By its end, Americans had lost interest in quality wine. During Prohibition, farmers around the country had plowed under thousands of acres of valuable grapes. Wineries nationwide shut down, and the winemaking industry dwindled to a handful of survivors, mostly in California and New York. Many growers on the East Coast returned to producing grape juice—the ideal use for the American *labrusca* grape. From 1933 to 1968, grape growers and winemakers had little more than personal incentive to produce any wine of quality. Jug wines, named for the containers in which they were bottled, were inexpensive, nondescript, and mass produced. A few wineries, notably in California, were producing some good wines, but the majority of American wines produced during this period were ordinary.

Although Prohibition proved devastating to the majority of American wine producers, some endured by making sacramental wines. Beringer, Beaulieu, and the Christian Brothers survived this dry time in that way. These wineries didn't have to interrupt production during Prohibition, so they had a jump on those that had to start all over.

In repealing Prohibition, the federal government empowered the states to legislate the sale and transportation of alcohol. Some states handed control to counties and occasionally even municipalities—a tradition that continues today, varying from state to state and often from county to county.

THE RENAISSANCE OF AMERICAN WINE

It's hard to say exactly when the American wine renaissance began, but let's start in 1968, when, for the first time since Prohibition, table wines—those with an alcohol content between 7 and 14 percent—outsold fortified wines, which have an alcohol content between 17 and 22 percent. American wines were improving, but consumers still believed that the best wines came from Europe, especially France.

In the mid-sixties and early seventies, a small group of dedicated California winemakers began concentrating on making high-quality wine to equal Europe's best. Their early wines demonstrated potential and attracted the attention of astute wine writers and wine enthusiasts around the country.

As they continued to improve their product, these winemakers realized that they had to find a way to differentiate their quality wines from California's mass-produced wines—which had generic names: Burgundy, Chablis, or Chianti—and to ally their wines, at least in the minds of wine buyers and consumers, with European wines. Their solution was brilliant: They labeled their best wines by grape variety.

Varietal designation defines the wine by the name of the predominant grape used to produce it: Cabernet Sauvignon, Chardonnay, Pinot Noir, etc. The savvy consumer learned that a wine labeled "Chardonnay" had the general characteristics of any wine made from that grape. Wine buying became easier for both buyers and sellers. Varietal labeling quickly spread throughout the industry and became so successful that, in the 1980s, varietal designation became an American industry standard, forcing the federal government to revise its labeling regulations.

Today, varietal labeling is the norm for the highest-quality American wines. Many other countries have adopted the practice, which has helped bring worldwide attention to California wine. California still produces 90 percent of American wine, but its success has inspired winemakers in other areas of the country to refocus on producing high-quality wines—as we'll see.

—— FURTHER READING ——

American Names for American Wines
  by Frank Schoonmaker

Last Call: The Rise and Fall of Prohibition
  by Daniel Okrent

THE BEST-KNOWN WINERIES OF CALIFORNIA IN THE 1960s AND 1970s:

Almaden	Korbel
Beaulieu	Louis Martini
Beringer	Mirassou
Buena Vista	Parducci
Charles Krug	Paul Masson
Concannon	Sebastiani
Hanzell	Simi
Inglenook	Wente

In the early 1970s, **CHENIN BLANC** was the best-selling white wine and **ZINFANDEL** the best-selling red.

THREE MAJOR GRAPES CONSUMED BY AMERICANS ARE:

1. Chardonnay
2. Cabernet Sauvignon
3. Merlot

TOP AMERICAN MARKETS FOR WINE:

1. New York
2. Los Angeles
3. Chicago
4. Boston
5. San Francisco

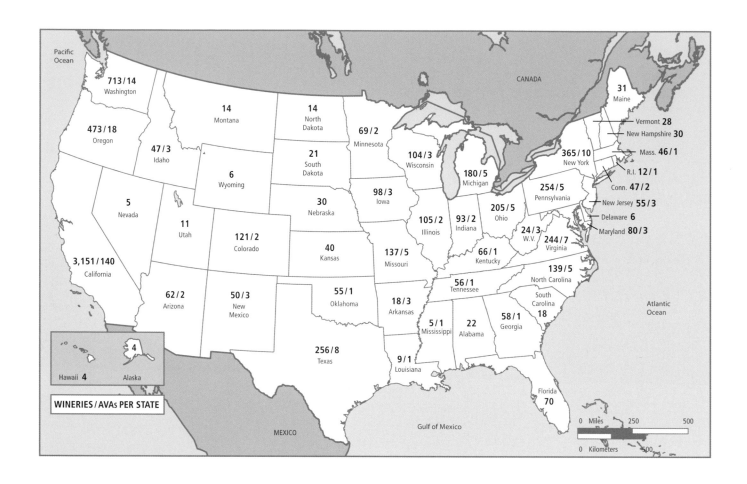

WINERIES / AVAs PER STATE

State	Wineries/AVAs
Washington	713/14
Oregon	473/18
Idaho	47/3
Montana	14
North Dakota	14
Minnesota	69/2
Wyoming	6
South Dakota	21
Nevada	5
Utah	11
Colorado	121/2
Nebraska	30
Iowa	98/3
Wisconsin	104/3
Michigan	180/5
New York	365/10
Maine	31
Vermont	28
New Hampshire	30
Mass.	46/1
R.I.	12/1
Conn.	47/2
New Jersey	55/3
Delaware	6
Maryland	80/3
Pennsylvania	254/5
Ohio	205/5
Indiana	93/2
Illinois	105/2
W.V.	24/3
Virginia	244/7
Kentucky	66/1
Missouri	137/5
Kansas	40
Oklahoma	55/1
Arkansas	18/3
Tennessee	56/1
North Carolina	139/5
South Carolina	18
Georgia	58/1
Alabama	22
Mississippi	5/1
California	3,151/140
Arizona	62/2
New Mexico	50/3
Texas	256/8
Louisiana	9/1
Florida	70
Hawaii	4
Alaska	4

Top five states in **WINE PRODUCTION, 2017:**

1. California
2. Washington
3. New York
4. Oregon
5. Texas

America has **MORE THAN 240 VITICULTURAL AREAS,** 140 of which lie in California.

(WineInstitute.org)

QUALITY AMERICAN WINES

To buy American wines intelligently means knowing about each state as well as the regions within the state. Some states—or even regions within a state—specialize in white wine, others in red; some regions specialize in wine made from a specific grape variety. Therefore, it's helpful to know the American Viticultural Areas (AVAs), the defined grape-growing areas within each state or region.

An AVA is a specific grape-growing area recognized by and registered with the federal government. Styled after the European regional system, AVA designation began in the 1980s. In France, Bordeaux and Burgundy are strictly enforced regional appellations (marked "Appellation d'Origine Contrôlée," or AOC); in Italy, Tuscany and Piedmont are recognized as zones (marked "Denominazione di Origine Controllata," or DOC). So is Napa Valley a defined viticultural area in California. Columbia Valley is an AVA in Washington; both Oregon's Willamette Valley and New York's Finger Lakes district have similar designations.

Winemakers are discovering, as their European counterparts did years ago, which grapes grow best in which particular soils and climatic conditions. The AVA matters for buying wine and will continue to do so as individual AVAs become known for certain grape varieties or wine styles. If an AVA appears on the label, at least 85 percent of the grapes must come from that region.

Let's look at Napa Valley, the best-known AVA in America, renowned for its Cabernet Sauvignon. Within Napa exists a smaller, inner district called Carneros, which has a cooler climate. Chardonnay and Pinot Noir need a cooler growing season to mature properly, so that AVA especially suits these grape varieties. New York's Finger Lakes region is noted for its Riesling, and if you've seen the movie *Sideways*, you know that Santa Barbara is a great place for Pinot Noir.

Not necessarily a guarantee of quality, an AVA designation identifies a specific area well known and established for its wine. It's a geographic point of reference for winemakers and consumers about provenance. The more knowledge you have about a wine's origin by region and grape, the easier it is to buy even unknown brands with confidence. As you learn more about the characteristics of major grapes and styles of wine and which you prefer, you'll be able to identify the AVAs that produce wines you're most likely to enjoy.

The most recent worldwide trend is to ignore all existing standards by giving the highest-quality wines a proprietary name, which helps high-end wineries differentiate their best wines from other wines from the same AVA, from similar varietals, and even from their own other offerings. In America, many of these proprietary wines fall under the category of Meritage (page 83). Examples of American proprietary wines include Dominus, Opus One, and Rubicon.

Because of federal laws governing standards and labels, select wineries increasingly are using proprietary names. Federal law mandates, for example, that, if a label lists a grape, at least 75 percent of the grapes used to make the wine must come from that variety. That's why in stores you see more wines labeled "white blend" or "red blend."

SOME OF THE BEST KNOWN CALIFORNIA AVAS:

Alexander Valley	Los Carneros
Anderson Valley	Napa Valley
Chalk Hill	Paso Robles
Dry Creek Valley	Russian River Valley
Edna Valley	Santa Cruz Mountain
Fiddletown	Sonoma Valley
Howell Mountain	Stag's Leap
Livermore Valley	

In 2017, America had **MORE THAN 7,751 BONDED WINERIES**, up from fewer than 500 in 1970. Of them, more than 90 percent are small and family owned.

2017 WINE IMPORTS TO THE USA

1. Italy
2. Australia
3. France
4. Chile
5. Argentina
6. Spain
7. New Zealand
8. Germany

Wineries in America are opening at the rate of **300 PER YEAR**.

——— FURTHER READING ———

American Vintage by Paul Lukacs

American Wine by Jancis Robinson and Linda Murphy

The Oxford Companion to the Wines of North America by Bruce Cass and Jancis Robinson

Imagine a talented, innovative winemaker in the Columbia Valley of Washington. He or she wants to produce an outstanding, full-bodied Bordeaux-style wine consisting of 60 percent Cabernet Sauvignon blended with several other grapes. Our ambitious winemaker has invested considerable time and labor to produce a really great wine, suitable for aging, that will be ready to drink in five years—and even better in ten.

But how to distinguish this wine, how to attract buyers willing to pay a premium price for an unknown wine? It can't be labeled "Cabernet Sauvignon" because fewer than 75 percent of the grapes used are of that type. For this reason, many producers of fine wine use proprietary names. It's indicative of the healthy state of the American wine industry as well. More and more winemakers are turning out better and better wines, and the very best is yet to come!

THE FUTURE OF AMERICAN WINES

Americans are drinking American wine! More than 75 percent of wines consumed in the USA come from this country—and not just from the top four states: California, Washington, New York, and Oregon. When I began studying wine in 1970, two-thirds of the states had no wineries at all. Now all 50 states are producing wine.

Plenty of books are available on French, Italian, Spanish wines, etc., but comparatively few cover American wines. In the last 20 years, the remarkable rise in the quality of wine production has prompted an increase in wine consumption in America. These two trends keep reinforcing each other, so we can continue to expect great things in American winemaking for many years to come.

American wine also has an enormous "fun factor." Studying and tasting the wines from around this country are exciting! They offer a lesson in geography, history, agriculture, and the passion of American grape growers and winemakers. Wineries here have become major tourist attractions. Wine trails have sprung up all across the country in combination with other historical landmarks. Wine definitely has gone mainstream in America. Our time has arrived. Thanks to the conviction and determination of American producers and the demands of American consumers, I can say proudly that many of the best wines in the world are produced in the United States of America.

UNDERSTANDING CALIFORNIA WINES

No wine-growing area in the world has come so far so quickly as California. Americans historically have had little interest in wine, but from the moment we first became "wine conscious," winemakers in California rose to the challenge. Forty years ago we were asking if California wines measured up to European wines. Now California wines are available worldwide: Exports have increased dramatically in recent years to countries such as Japan, Germany, and Britain. California produces an average of 85 percent of total American wine. If the state were a nation, it would be the fourth leading wine producer in the world!

AN INTRODUCTION TO CALIFORNIA WINES

The map on this page will help familiarize you with the winemaking regions. It's easier to remember them if you divide them into four groups:

THE MAIN VITICULTURAL AREAS

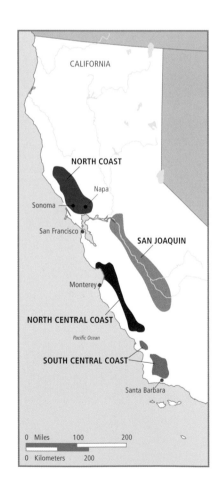

REGION	COUNTIES	BEST WINES
NORTH COAST	NAPA SONOMA MENDOCINO LAKE	CABERNET SAUVIGNON CHARDONNAY MERLOT SAUVIGNON BLANC ZINFANDEL
SAN JOAQUIN VALLEY		INEXPENSIVE JUG WINES
NORTH CENTRAL COAST	MONTEREY SANTA CLARA LIVERMORE	CHARDONNAY GRENACHE MARSANNE ROUSSANE SYRAH VIOGNIER
SOUTH CENTRAL COAST	SAN LUIS OBISPO SANTA BARBARA	CHARDONNAY PINOT NOIR SAUVIGNON BLANC SYRAH

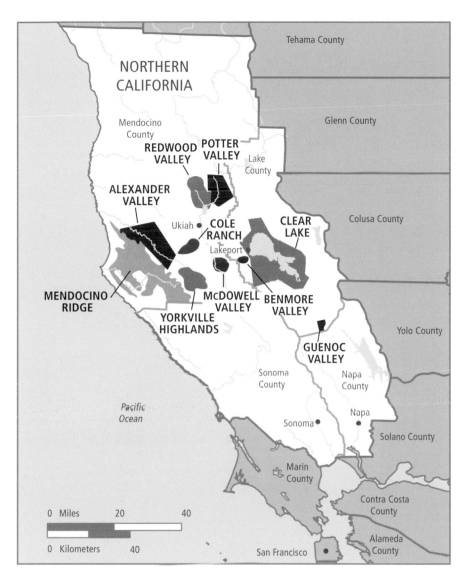

NORTHERN CALIFORNIA

Tehama County

Mendocino County

Glenn County

REDWOOD VALLEY

POTTER VALLEY

Lake County

ALEXANDER VALLEY

Ukiah

COLE RANCH

CLEAR LAKE

Colusa County

Lakeport

MENDOCINO RIDGE

McDOWELL VALLEY

BENMORE VALLEY

YORKVILLE HIGHLANDS

Yolo County

GUENOC VALLEY

Sonoma County

Napa County

Pacific Ocean

Napa

Sonoma

Solano County

Marin County

Contra Costa County

Alameda County

San Francisco

0 Miles 20 40

0 Kilometers 40

CALIFORNIA, PAST AND PRESENT
1970: 240 wineries
2018: 3,151 wineries

California wines dominate American wine consumption, equaling **83 PERCENT OF ALL SALES** in the USA.

California has more than **600,000 ACRES OF WINE VINEYARDS**.

DUTTON Goldfield
CHARDONNAY
DUTTON RANCH
RUSSIAN RIVER VALLEY
2006

If an **INDIVIDUAL VINEYARD** appears on the label, 95 percent of the grapes must come from the named vineyard, which must lie within an approved AVA.

More than 60,000 wine labels are registered in California.

Some **3,000,000 PEOPLE** visit Napa every year.

Although you may be most familiar with Napa and Sonoma, fewer than 10 percent of all California wine comes from these two regions combined. Even so, Napa alone accounts for more than 30 percent of dollar sales of California wines. San Joaquin Valley accounts for 58 percent of the wine grapes planted, much of it for jug wine. Maybe that doesn't seem too exciting—that the production of jug wine dominates California winemaking history—but Americans aren't atypical in this preference. In France, AOC wines account for only 45 percent of all French wines; the rest are everyday table wines.

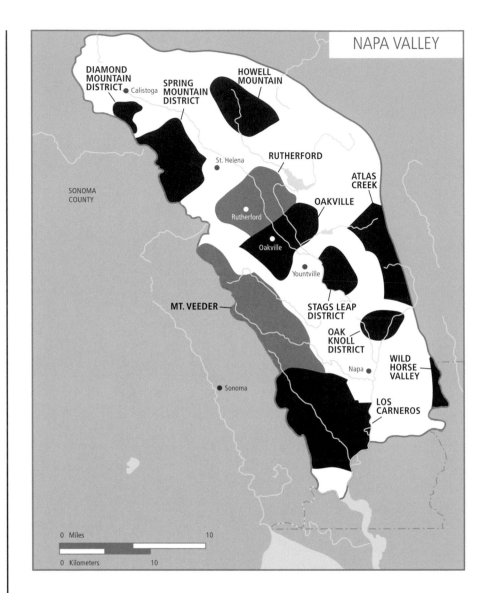

NAPA VALLEY, PAST AND PRESENT

1838: First wine grapes planted in Napa

1858: First winery in Napa Valley

1970: 27 wineries

2018: 400+ wineries

ACRES OF WINE GRAPES planted in Napa: 45,000

TOP GRAPES PLANTED IN NAPA

1. Cabernet Sauvignon (20,759 acres)

2. Chardonnay (7,300 acres)

3. Merlot (5,000 acres)

EARLY EUROPEAN WINEMAKERS:

FRANCE

Paul Masson: 1852

Étienne Thée and Charles LeFranc
   (Almaden): 1852

Pierre Mirassou: 1854

Georges de Latour (Beaulieu): 1900

GERMANY

Beringer Brothers: 1876

Carl Wente: 1883

ITALY

Giuseppe and Pietro Simi: 1876

John Foppiano: 1895

Samuele Sebastiani: 1904

Louis Martini: 1922

Adolph Parducci: 1932

FINLAND

Gustave Niebaum (Inglenook): 1879

IRELAND

James Concannon: 1883

FROM JUG WINES TO GRAPE VARIETIES

Jug wine refers to simple, uncomplicated, everyday drinking wine. These wines sometimes feature a generic style name, such as Chablis or Burgundy. Inexpensive and well made, they originally were bottled in jugs, rather than conventional bottles, hence the name. They are very popular and account for the largest volume of California wine sold in America. The best jug wines in the world come from California. They maintain both consistency and quality from year to year.

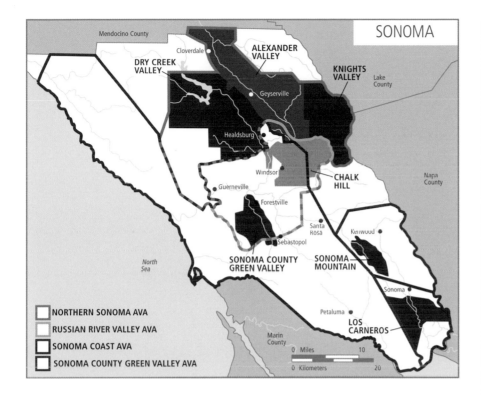

SONOMA

Mendocino County

Cloverdale

DRY CREEK
VALLEY

ALEXANDER
VALLEY

KNIGHTS
VALLEY

Lake
County

Geyserville

Healdsburg

Windsor

CHALK
HILL

Napa
County

Guerneville

Forestville

Santa
Rosa

Kenwood

Sebastopol

North
Sea

SONOMA COUNTY
GREEN VALLEY

SONOMA
MOUNTAIN

Sonoma

Petaluma

LOS
CARNEROS

Marin
County

0 Miles   10

0 Kilometers   20

☐ NORTHERN SONOMA AVA

☐ RUSSIAN RIVER VALLEY AVA

☐ SONOMA COAST AVA

☐ SONOMA COUNTY GREEN VALLEY AVA

Acres of wine grapes **PLANTED IN SONOMA:** more than 60,000

TOP GRAPES PLANTED IN SONOMA
1. Chardonnay (16,500 acres)
2. Pinot Noir (13,700 acres)
3. Cabernet Sauvignon (13,000 acres)

As of 2016, Sonoma had **MORE THAN 450 WINERIES.**

Ernest and Julio Gallo, who began their winery in 1933, are the major producers of jug wines in California. Many people credit the Gallo brothers with converting American drinking habits from spirits to wine.

As early as the 1940s, Frank Schoonmaker—an importer, writer, and one of the first American wine experts—convinced some California winery owners to market their best wines using varietal labels.

Robert Mondavi may be one of the best examples of a winemaker who concentrated solely on varietal wine production. In 1966, he left his family's Charles Krug Winery and started the Robert Mondavi Winery. His role was important to the evolution of varietal labeling of California wines. He was among the first major winemakers to make the total switch that led to higher-quality winemaking. Robert Mondavi was also a great promoter for the California wine industry. "He was able to prove to the public what the people within the industry already knew—that California could produce world-class wines," said California vintner Eric Wente.

Almaden, Gallo, and Paul Masson still produce **JUG WINES**.

E & J Gallo Winery owns **MORE THAN 23,000 ACRES** in California. Gallo produces 75 million cases of wine annually and is the largest winery in the world.

Early California winemakers sent their children to **STUDY ENOLOGY** at Geisenheim in Germany or Bordeaux in France. Today, many European winemakers send their children to the University of California at Davis and to Fresno State University.

WORLD-CLASS IN FORTY YEARS

Many reasons account for California's winemaking success, including:

Location Napa and Sonoma counties, two of the major quality-wine regions, both lie less than a two-hour drive from San Francisco. That proximity encourages Bay Area locals and tourists to visit the wineries in the two counties, most of which offer tastings and sell their wines in their own shops.

Weather Abundant sunshine, warm daytime temperatures, cool evenings, and a long growing season all add up to good conditions for growing many grape varieties. California can experience sudden changes in weather, but a fickle climate doesn't pose a major worry.

The University of California at Davis and Fresno State University Both schools have trained many young California winemakers, and their curricula concentrate on the scientific study of wine, viticulture, and, most important, technology. Their research—focused on soil, hybridization, strains of yeast, temperature-controlled fermentation, and other viticultural techniques—has revolutionized the wine industry worldwide.

Money and Marketing Strategy Marketing may not make the wine, but it certainly helps sell it. As more and more winemakers concentrated on making the best wine they could, American consumers responded with appreciation. They were willing to buy and pay more as quality improved. In order to keep up with consumer expectations, winemakers needed more research, development, and working capital. The wine industry turned to investors, both corporate and individual.

Since 1967, when the now defunct National Distillers bought Almaden, multinational corporations have recognized the profit potential of large-scale winemaking and have entered the wine business aggressively. They've brought huge financial resources and expertise in advertising and promotion that have helped advance American wines domestically and internationally. Other early corporate participants included Pillsbury and Coca-Cola.

On the other side of the investor scale stand the individual investor / growers drawn to the business by their love of wine and their desire to live the winemaking lifestyle. These individuals focus more on producing quality wines.

By the 1990s, both corporate and individual investors had helped California fine-tune its wine industry, which today produces not only delicious and reliable wines in great quantity but also truly outstanding wines, many with investment potential.

EARLY PIONEERS

Some of the pioneers of the back-to-the-land movement include:

"FARMER"	ORIGINAL PROFESSION	WINERY
JAMES BARRETT	ATTORNEY	CHATEAU MONTELENA
TOM BURGESS	AIR FORCE PILOT	BURGESS
BROOKS FIRESTONE	TAKE A GUESS!	FIRESTONE
JESS JACKSON	ATTORNEY	KENDALL-JACKSON
TOM JORDAN	GEOLOGIST	JORDAN
DAVID STARE	CIVIL ENGINEER	DRY CREEK
ROBERT TRAVERS	INVESTMENT BANKER	MAYACAMAS
WARREN WINIARSKI	COLLEGE PROFESSOR	STAG'S LEAP

Clonal selection, wind machines, drip irrigation, biodynamic vineyards, and mechanical harvesting are some **NEW TECHNIQUES** in vineyard management.

The majority of California wines retail from **$9 TO $20.**

In 1970 the average price per acre in Napa was $2,000–$4,000. Today, **ONE PRIME ACRE IN NAPA VALLEY COSTS ABOUT $400,000** unplanted, and it takes an additional $100,000 per acre to plant. This per-acre investment sees no return for three to five years. Add to this the cost of building the winery, buying the equipment, and hiring the winemaker

HOLLYWOOD AND VINE

Many movie actors, directors, and producers have invested in vineyards and wineries throughout California, including Francis Ford Coppola, Candace Cameron and Valeri Bure, Emilio Estevez, Fergie, and John Legend..

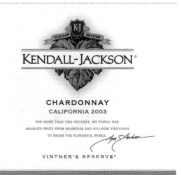

KENDALL-JACKSON

CHARDONNAY
CALIFORNIA 2003

FOR MORE THAN TWO DECADES, MY FAMILY HAS SOURCED FRUIT FROM MOUNTAIN AND HILLSIDE VINEYARDS TO BRING YOU FLAVORFUL WINES.

VINTNER'S RESERVE

OVERHEARD AT A RESTAURANT in Yountville, Napa Valley: "How do you make a small fortune in the wine business?" "Start with a large fortune and buy a winery."

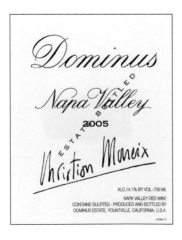

CALIFORNIA VS. EUROPEAN WINEMAKING

European winemaking has established traditions that have remained essentially unchanged for centuries. These practices involve the ways grapes are grown and harvested and in some cases include wine-making and aging procedures.

California maintains few traditions, and winemakers can take full advantage of modern technology. Furthermore, they have the freedom to experiment and create new products. European wine-control laws prohibit some of the experimenting that California winemakers undertake, such as combining different grape varieties to make new styles of wine. Californians thus have greater opportunity to try many new ideas.

Another way in which California winemaking differs is that many California wineries carry a line of wines. Many of the larger houses produce more than 20 different labels. In Bordeaux, most châteaux produce only one or two wines.

Nor can you ignore the fundamentals of wine-growing: California's rainfall, weather patterns, and soil differ from those of Europe. The greater abundance of sunshine in California can result in wines with greater alcohol content, ranging on average from 13.5 percent to 14.5 percent, compared to 12 percent to 13 percent in Europe. This higher alcohol content changes the balance and taste of the wines.

That said, many well-known and highly respected European winemakers have invested in California vineyards to make their own wine. European, Canadian, and Japanese companies own more than 45 California wineries. For example:

- Baron Philippe de Rothschild, then owner of Château Mouton-Rothschild in Bordeaux, and Robert Mondavi, joined forces to produce a wine called Opus One, one of the most influential joint ventures.

- The Moueix family, owners of Château Pétrus in Bordeaux, have vineyards in California. Their wine is a Bordeaux-style blend called Dominus.

- Moët & Chandon owns Domaine Chandon in Napa Valley.

- Roederer grows grapes in Mendocino County and produces Roederer Estate.

- Mumm produces a sparkling wine called Mumm Cuvée Napa.

- Taittinger has its own sparkling wine called Domaine Carneros.

- Spanish sparkling-wine house Codorníu owns a California winery called Artesa.

- Freixenet owns land in Sonoma County and produces a California wine called Gloria Ferrer.

- The Torres family of Spain owns a winery called Marimar Torres Estate in Sonoma County.

- Until recently, Frenchman Robert Skalli (maker of the Fortant de France wines) owned more than 6,000 acres in Napa Valley and the St. Supery winery.

- Tuscan wine producer Piero Antinori owns Antica winery in Napa and partnered with Stag's Leap Wine Cellars in Napa and Chateau Ste. Michelle in Washington on Col Solare.

CALIFORNIA WINE STYLES

"Style" refers to the characteristics of the grapes and wine. It's the signature of the individual winemaker, an artist who tries different techniques to explore the fullest potential of the grapes.

Most winemakers will tell you that 95 percent of winemaking lies in the quality of the grapes. The other 5 percent comes from the winemaker's personal touch. Here are just a few of the hundreds of decisions a winemaker must make when developing his or her style of wine:

- When should the grapes be harvested?

- What varieties of grapes should be blended and in what proportion?

- Should the juice be fermented in stainless steel tanks or oak barrels? How long should it ferment? At what temperature?

- Should the wine age at all? If so, how long? In oak? What kind of oak— American, French?

- How long should the wine age in the bottle before being sold?

The list goes on. Because winemaking has so many variables, producers can create many styles of wine from the same grape variety—so you can choose the style that best suits your taste. With the relative freedom of winemaking in America, the style of California wines continues to be diversity.

But that diversity can cause confusion. The renaissance of the California wine industry began only about 40 years ago. Within that short period, some 2,100 new wineries have been established in California. Today, more than

California wine has **NO CLASSIFICATION LEVELS** that resemble the European system.

"You are never going to stylize the California wines the same way that European wines have been stylized because we have more freedom to experiment. I value my freedom to make the style of wine I want more than the security of the AOC laws. Laws discourage experimentation."

—Louis Martini

STAINLESS STEEL tanks are temperature controlled, allowing winemakers to control the temperature at which the wine ferments. For example, a winemaker could ferment wines at a low temperature to retain fruitiness and delicacy, while preventing browning and oxidation.

Ambassador Zellerbach, who created Hanzell Winery, was one of the first California winemakers to use **SMALL FRENCH OAK AGING BARRELS** because he wanted to recreate a Burgundian style.

FAMOUS VINEYARDS OF CALIFORNIA

Bacigalupi	Hyde
Bancroft Ranch	Martha's Vineyard
Beckstoffer	McCrea
Bien Nacido	Monte Rosso
Durell	Robert Young
Dutton Ranch	S.L.V.
Gravelly Meadow	To-Kalon
Hudson	

Kistler

Sonoma Mountain

Les Noisetiers

№ 15805   2008

In the 2017 vintage, Kistler Vineyards produced **CHARDONNAYS FROM TEN SPECIFIC VINEYARDS!**

3,000 wineries operate here, most of them making more than one wine. The variety of styles reflects the price differences. Cabernet Sauvignons range from Two Buck Chuck to Harlan Estate at more than $500 a bottle—so how do you choose? The constant changes in the wine industry keep California winemaking in a state of flux.

You can't necessarily equate quality with price, though. Some excellent varietal wines produced in California fall well within the budget of the average consumer. On the other hand, some varieties—primarily Chardonnay and Cabernet Sauvignon—may be quite expensive.

As in any market, supply and demand mainly determine price. However, new wineries have start-up costs, which sometimes affect the price of the wine. Older, established wineries, which long ago amortized their investments, can keep prices low when the supply/demand ratio calls for it. Remember, when buying California wine, price doesn't always reflect quality.

PHYLLOXERA REDUX

In the 1980s, phylloxera destroyed a good part of the vineyards of California, costing more than $1 billion in new plantings. But it also proved that good can come from bad.

What's the good news? This time, vineyard owners didn't have to wait to discover a solution. They already knew what to do to replace the dead vines—replant with a different rootstock resistant to phylloxera. The short-term effects were terribly expensive, but the long-term effect was better-quality wine. Why?

In the early days of California grape-growing, little thought went into where a specific grape would grow best. Many Chardonnays were planted in climates that were too warm, and Cabernet Sauvignons in climates too cold. With the onset of phylloxera, vineyard owners had a chance to rectify those errors. When replanting, they matched the climate and soil with the best grape variety. Grape growers also had the opportunity to plant different grape clones. But the biggest change happened to the planting density of the vines themselves. Traditional spacing used by most wineries fell somewhere between 400 and 500 vines per acre. Today, with the new replanting, it's not uncommon to have more than 1,000 vines per acre, and many vineyards have planted more than 2,000 per acre.

The bottom line: If you like California wines now, you'll love them more with time. The quality is already better and the costs are lower—making it a win-win situation for everyone.

RED OR WHITE?

The infographic below represents overall wine consumption in America over the last 40-plus years. In 1970, people drank much more red wine than white. From the mid-1970s into the mid-1990s, tastes shifted to white wine. Since then, the pendulum has swung back to red.

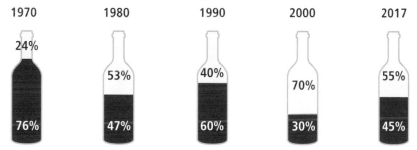

1970	1980	1990	2000	2017
24%	53%	40%	70%	55%
76%	47%	60%	30%	45%

The 1980s obsession with health and fitness urged many people to switch from eating meat and potatoes regularly to fish and vegetables, and that lighter diet called more for white wine than red. "Chardonnay" became the new buzzword, replacing the call for just a glass of white wine. Bars that never stocked wine—nothing decent, anyway—started carrying a fine assortment by the glass, and Chardonnay outsold them all. Today, Cabernet Sauvignon, Merlot, and Pinot Noir have become the new buzzwords.

Over the last 20 years, sales of red wine in America grew by **MORE THAN 125 PERCENT**

The so-called French Paradox and the power of the media also played a key role in the shift. More on that below.

Perhaps the most important reason that red-wine consumption has increased in America is that California is producing better quality red wine than ever before. Remember the phylloxera epidemic that hit the state in the 1980s? Vineyard owners replanted their vines, which allowed for increased red-grape production. Growers then implemented the knowledge they had gained over the years about climate, microclimate, soil, trellising, and other viticultural practices.

Bottom line: California reds are some of the greatest in the world, with more and better yet to come.

THE FRENCH PARADOX

In the early 1990s, the *60 Minutes* news show twice aired a report on a phenomenon known as the French Paradox: The French have a lower rate of heart disease than Americans despite a diet higher in fat. Red wine stood out as one item that the American diet lacks when compared to the French diet, so researchers went looking for a link between the consumption of red wine and a decreased rate of heart disease. In the year following the news of this report, Americans increased their purchases of red wines by 39 percent!

THE MAJOR RED GRAPES OF CALIFORNIA

More than 30 different wine grape varieties grow in California, but these 5 are the most important: Cabernet Sauvignon, Pinot Noir, Zinfandel, Merlot, and Syrah.

CABERNET SAUVIGNON

The most successful red grape in California yields some of the greatest red wines in the world. Remember, Cabernet Sauvignon is the predominant variety in the finest red Bordeaux wines, such as Château Lafite-Rothschild

Besides tannin, **RED WINE CONTAINS RESVERATROL**, which in medical studies has been associated with anticancer properties.

Alcohol, **WHEN CONSUMED IN MODERATION**, will increase HDL (good cholesterol) and decrease LDL (bad cholesterol).

Wine is **FAT-FREE** and contains no cholesterol.

NAPA IS RED-WINE COUNTRY, with 33,784 acres in red grapes versus 10,614 in whites. Leading the red grapes are Cabernet Sauvignon, with 19,894 acres, and Merlot, with 5,734 acres.

More than 1,000 different **CABERNET SAUVIGNONS** from California are available to the consumer.

and Château Latour. Almost all California Cabernets are dry, and, depending on producer and vintage, they range in style from light and ready to drink to extremely full-bodied and long-lived.

My favorite California Cabernet Sauvignons include:

Adobe Road Winery	Diamond Creek	Ovid
Altamura	Duckhorn	Pahlmeyer
Araujo	Dunn Howell Mountain	Paul Hobbs
Arrowood	Eisele	Peter Michael
Beaulieu Private Reserve	Frank Family	Pine Ridge
Beringer Private Reserve	Gallo of Sonoma Estate	Plumpjack
Bevan	Groth Reserve	Pride Mountain
Bond	Hall	Ravena
Bryant Family	Harlan Estate	Ridge Monte Bello
Cakebread	Heitz	Robert Mondavi
Carter	Hess Collection	Sbragia Family
Caymus	Hewitt	Vineyards
Chappellet	Hundred Acre	Schrader
Chateau Montelena	Inglenook Rubicon	Screaming Eagle
Chateau St. Jean,	Jordan	Shafer Hillside Select
Cinq Cépages	Joseph Phelps	Silver Oak
Chimney Rock	Kongsgaard	Snowden
Clos du Val	La Jota	Spottswoode
Colgin	Larkmead	Stag's Leap Cask
Continuum	Laurel Glen	Staglin
Corra	Lewis	Tor
Dalla Valle	Mondavi Reserve	Trefethen
Darioush	Opus One	Whitehall Lane

– BEST VINTAGES OF NAPA VALLEY CABERNET SAUVIGNON –

1994* 1995* 1996* 1997* 1999* 2001** 2002** 2005*
2006** 2007** 2008** 2009** 2010** 2012** 2013**
2014** 2015** 2016

* EXCEPTIONAL VINTAGE   ** EXTRAORDINARY VINTAGE

– BEST RECENT VINTAGES OF SONOMA CABERNET SAUVIGNON–

2007   2010   2012*   2013   2014*   2015   2016*

* EXCEPTIONAL VINTAGE

NAPA VALLEY CABERNET SAUVIGNON		
YEAR	BRIX LEVEL	ABV
1976	22.9	13.6%
2016	25.69	15.4%
(Decanter Magazine)		

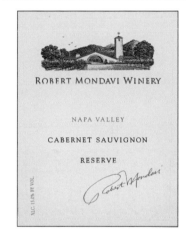

"Reserve" on an American wine label has **NO LEGAL MEANING,** but some wineries, such as Beaulieu Vineyards and Robert Mondavi Winery, use it to designate special wines. BV's Reserve comes from a particular vineyard, and Mondavi's Reserve comes from a special blend of grapes. Other vague terms include "cask" wines, "special selections," and "proprietor's reserve."

MOST CABERNET SAUVIGNONS ARE BLENDED with other grapes, primarily Merlot. To name the grape variety on the label, the winemaker must use at least 75 percent Cabernet Sauvignon.

GREAT OLDER VINTAGES:

1985, 1986, 1987, 1990, and 1991

PINOT NOIR

Sometimes known as the "headache" grape, Pinot Noir is temperamental, expensive, and difficult to grow and make into wine. This great grape of the Burgundy region of France is also one of the principal grapes in Champagne. Many years of experimentation have taken place in California to find the right location to plant Pinot Noir and to perfect fermentation techniques, elevating some of the wines to the level of greatness. Pinot Noir is usually less tannic than Cabernet Sauvignon and matures more quickly, generally within two to five years. Because of the extra growing expenses, the best California Pinot Noirs usually cost more than other varieties.

The three top counties for Pinot Noir are:

Sonoma	Monterey	Santa Barbara
(11,000 acres)	(6,204 acres)	(3,401 acres)

My favorite California Pinot Noirs include:

Acacia	Foxen	Papapietro-Perry
Arista	Gary Farrell	Patz & Hall
Artesa	Goldeneye	Paul Hobbs
Aubert	Hahn	Paul Lato
Au Bon Climat	J. Rochioli	Peter Michael
Belle Clos	Jonata	Pisoni
Bien Nacido Estate	Kistler	Robert Sinskey
Brewer-Clifton	Kosta Browne	Ram's Gate
Byron	Littorai	ROAR
Calera	Lucia	Rochioli
CIRQ	MacMurray	Saintsbury
Dehlinger	Marcassin	Sanford
Domaine de la Côte	Melville	Sea Smoke
Donum	Merry Edwards	Siduri
Etude	Mount Eden	Talley
Flowers	Morgan	Williams Selyem

- BEST RECENT VINTAGES OF CALIFORNIA PINOT NOIR -

SONOMA: 2007* 2009** 2010** 2012* 2013** 2014* 2015** 2016

CARNEROS: 2008* 2009* 2012* 2013* 2014 2015* 2016

SANTA BARBARA: 2009* 2010** 2012* 2013* 2014* 2015 2016

MONTEREY: 2008* 2009** 2010* 2011* 2012* 2013* 2014** 2015 2016

* EXCEPTIONAL VINTAGE   ** EXTRAORDINARY VINTAGE

Carneros, Monterey, Sonoma, and Santa Barbara are great places to grow Pinot Noir because of their cooler climate. **SONOMA HAS THE MOST ACRES OF AND WINERIES FOR PINOT NOIR** in California.

SOUTHERN CALIFORNIA— especially the Santa Barbara area—has become one of the prime locations for Pinot Noir production, with plantings up by more than 200 percent in the past decade.

"Pinot is James Joyce, while Cabernet is Dickens perhaps. Both sell well, but one is easier to understand."

—Decanter magazine

"It's a hard grape to know, as you know. Right? It's, uh, it's thin-skinned, temperamental, ripens early. It's, you know, it's not a survivor like Cabernet, which can just grow anywhere and, uh, thrive even when it's neglected."

—Miles from Sideways

RIDGE 2006
CALIFORNIA
GEYSERVILLE

GRAPES: 70% ZINFANDEL, 18% CARIGNANE,
10% PETITE SIRAH, 2% MATARO
SONOMA COUNTY   14.6% ALCOHOL BY VOLUME
PRODUCED & BOTTLED BY RIDGE VINEYARDS, INC.
18100 MONTE BELLO ROAD, BOX 1810, CUPERTINO, CA 95015

WHITE ZINFANDEL outsells red 6:1 in America.

ZINFANDEL

This historic grape of California went into generic or jug wines in the early years of California winemaking. Over the past 30 years, however, it has developed into one of the best red varietal grapes. The only problem with choosing a Zinfandel wine is that winemakers produce so many different styles. They can taste light and fruity or big, rich, ripe, high-alcohol, spicy, smoky, concentrated, intensely flavored, and with substantial tannin. To say nothing of white Zinfandel!

My favorite Zinfandels include:

Bedrock	Martinelli	Roshambo
Carlisle	Mazzocco	Sbragia
Cline	Merry Edwards	Seghesio
Dehlinger	Rafanelli	Signorello
Dry Creek Winery	Ravenswood	St. Francis
Hartford Family	Ridge	Turley
J. Rochioli	Rosenblum	

– BEST VINTAGES OF NORTH COAST ZINFANDEL –

2003* 2006* 2007* 2008** 2009** 2010*
2012* 2013* 2014** 2015** 2016

* EXCEPTIONAL VINTAGE   ** EXTRAORDINARY VINTAGE

MERLOT

Because Merlot's tannins feel softer and its texture more supple, California winemakers used it for many years only in blends with Cabernet Sauvignon, but Merlot has achieved its own identity as a superpremium variety. It produces a soft, round wine that generally doesn't need the same aging as a Cabernet Sauvignon. Its early maturation and compatibility with food also make it a top seller at restaurants.

My favorite North Coast Merlots include:

Beringer	Lewis Cellars	Plumpjack
Carter	Luna	Pride
Chimney Rock	Markham	The Prisoner
COHO	Matanzas Creek	Provenance
Duckhorn	Newton	Shafer
Franciscan	Palamo	St. Francis
Havens	Pahlmeyer	Whitehall Lane
Hourglass	Pine Ridge	

— BEST VINTAGES OF NORTH COAST MERLOT —

2002* 2004* 2005* 2007* 2009* 2012** 2013**
2014** 2015** 2016

* EXCEPTIONAL VINTAGE ** EXTRAORDINARY VINTAGE

All of California had just **TWO ACRES OF MERLOT** in 1960. Today it has more than 40,000.

SAN LUIS OBISPO and Sonoma counties have the most acreage of Syrah grapes in California.

SYRAH

One of the major grapes of France's Rhône Valley, Syrah makes for some of the best and most long-lived wines in the world. Called Shiraz when it hails from Australia, this spicy, robust wine has seen phenomenal sales in America, where it thrives in California's sunny, warm weather.

My favorite Syrahs include:

Alban	Epoch	Pruett
Bien Nacido Estate	Fess Parker	Qupe
Bonny Doon	Foxen	Sandhi
Cakebread	Justin	Sanguis
Carlisle	Lagier Meredith	Saxum
Clos du Bois	Lewis	Sine Qua Non
Copain	Neyers	Tablas Creek
Dehlinger	Ojai	Tensley
Dumol	Pax	Viader
Edmunds St. John	Peay	Wild Horse
Enfield	Phelps	Zaca Mesa

– BEST VINTAGES OF CALIFORNIA SYRAH –

SOUTH CENTRAL COAST: 2006* 2007* 2008** 2009** 2010** 2012 2013** 2014** 2015 2016

NORTH COAST: 2004** 2006** 2007** 2008* 2009** 2010* 2011* 2012** 2013** 2014** 2015 2016

* EXCEPTIONAL VINTAGE   ** EXTRAORDINARY VINTAGE

THE RED-GRAPE BOOM

The table below tracks the number of acres of California's major red grapes and how those numbers have increased. Note the rapid expansion of the California wine industry!

CALIFORNIA RED-WINE GRAPES

GRAPE	1970	1980	1990	2017
CABERNET SAUVIGNON	3,200	21,800	24,100	90,782
PINOT NOIR	2,100	9,200	8,600	44,578
ZINFANDEL	19,200	27,700	28,000	44,446
MERLOT	100	2,600	4,000	41,131
SYRAH	0	0	400	17,161

MERITAGE WINES

Meritage (rhymes with heritage) is the name for red or white wines made in America from a blend of the classic Bordeaux grapes. Winemakers felt stifled by the legally required 75 percent minimum of a grape that had to go into a bottle for it to bear the name of that variety, so they created this new category because they knew they could make a better wine with a blend of, say, 60 percent of the major grape and 40 percent secondary grapes. Blending gives Meritage producers the same freedom that Bordeaux winemakers have in making their wines.

For red wine, the varieties include:

Cabernet Sauvignon   **Merlot**   **Cabernet Franc**   **Petit Verdot**   **Malbec**

For white wine, the varieties include:

Sauvignon Blanc   **Sémillon**

STYLES OF CALIFORNIA RED WINE

When you buy a Cabernet Sauvignon, Pinot Noir, Zinfandel, Merlot, Syrah, or Meritage wine from California, there's really no good way to know the

In 2017, California had 308,733 acres of red grapes and 183,698 of white grapes.

EXAMPLES OF MERITAGE WINES

Cain Five

Dominus (Christian Moueix)

Insignia (Phelps Vineyards)

Magnificat (Franciscan)

Opus One (Mondavi / Rothschild)

Trefethen Halo

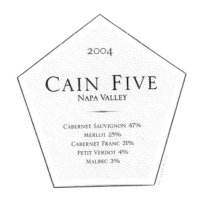

AMID GRAND HOOPLA, Robert Mondavi and Baron Philippe de Rothschild debuted Opus One at Windows on the World, halfway between Bordeaux and Napa. It's a Bordeaux-style blend made from grapes grown in the Napa Valley. It originally was produced at the Robert Mondavi Winery in Napa Valley but now is produced across Highway 29 in its own spectacular winery.

style of the wine just by looking at the label. Unless you know a particular vineyard well, you're stuck with trial-and-error tastings. Just knowing that the same grape can make drastically different styles puts you ahead in the game, though.

California has more than 3,100 wineries, and more than half of them produce red wines, so it's virtually impossible to keep up with the ever-changing styles they produce. Thankfully, more wineries are improving their labeling practices by adding important information, such as whether a wine should be aged, when it's ready to drink, and food pairing suggestions. To avoid unpleasant surprises, find the right retailer who understands both the wine world and your specific tastes.

AGING CALIFORNIA RED WINES

California wines generally taste more accessible when younger than a Bordeaux of the same vintage. That's one reason that California wines sell so well, especially in restaurants.

That said, red wines from California do age well, especially those from the best wineries producing Cabernet Sauvignon and Zinfandel. Some Cabernet Sauvignons from the 1930s, 1940s, and 1950s still drink well for the most part, and some of them taste outstanding, proving the wine's longevity. Zinfandels and Cabernet Sauvignons from the best wineries in great vintages need a minimum of five years of aging before you drink them, and they'll improve over the following ten. That's at least fifteen years of great enjoyment!

FORTY YEARS LATER IN CALIFORNIA

Specific grape varieties now have associations with particular AVAs and even individual vineyards. Go to Napa Valley for Cabernet Sauvignon and Merlot; Anderson Valley, Carneros, Monterey, Santa Barbara, and Sonoma for Pinot Noir; and the South Central Coast, particularly San Luis Obispo, for Syrah.

California winemaking innovation has settled down, but winemakers haven't given up experimentation altogether. Continuing the trend toward diversity, many new grape varieties are coming from California these days. Expect to see more wines made from Barbera, Grenache, Mourvèdre, and especially Syrah.

Alcohol levels also have changed over the past 40 years, especially in the red wines. Most wines around the world have increased in alcohol content but not to the extent that they have in California. Many winemakers are producing wines with more than 15 percent alcohol! That high level can change the balance of a wine if the alcohol replaces elegance and overpowers the varietal character.

5 BEST VALUE RED WINES OF CALIFORNIA UNDER $30

Beaulieu Rutherford Cabernet Sauvignon • Bonny Doon "Le Cigare Volant" • Frog's Leap Merlot • Louis M. Martini Sonoma Cabernet Sauvignon • Ridge Sonoma Zinfandel

See pages 352–355 for a complete list.

WINE COLLECTORS STARTED A FRENZY by buying Cabernet Sauvignon from small California wineries at extraordinary prices. These "cult" wineries produce very little wine—but with hefty price tags.

Araujo	Harlan Estate
Abreau	Scarecrow
Bond	Schrader
Bryant Family	Screaming Eagle
Colgin Cellars	Sine Qua Non
Dalla Valle	Sloan

For the **FIFTIETH ANNIVERSARY OF BEAULIEU'S PRIVATE RESERVE** wine, we tasted every vintage from 1936 to 1986 with winemaker André Tchelistcheff over two days. Everyone was awed by how well many of these vintages aged.

NAPA VALLEY, PAST AND PRESENT
1970: $2,000–$4,000 per acre
2018: $400,000 per acre

Recently, some of the **GREAT WINERIES IN CALIFORNIA WERE SOLD,** including: Mayacamas, Clos Pegase, Qupe, and Araujo.

For the **FIFTIETH ANNIVERSARY OF BEAULIEU'S PRIVATE RESERVE** wine, we tasted every vintage from 1936 to 1986 with winemaker André Tchelistcheff over two days. Everyone was awed by how well many of these vintages aged.

GUIDED TASTING

Pour the first six wines at the same time so you clearly can see the difference in color among the Pinot Noirs, Zinfandels, and Merlots. After you taste these first six wines, choose the grape variety that best suits your personality. That's your eureka moment!

American Pinot Noir Two Pinot Noirs from the same vintage:
1. Carneros Pinot Noir
2. Oregon Pinot Noir

California Zinfandel Two Zinfandels from the same vintage:
3. Sonoma Zinfandel
4. Napa Zinfandel

American Merlot Two Merlots from the same vintage:
5. Washington State Merlot
6. Napa Merlot

California Cabernet Sauvignon One wine tasted alone:
7. Napa Valley Cabernet Sauvignon (medium style and medium price)

California Cabernet Sauvignons Three wines compared (blind tasting): 8, 9, 10. Three different vintages, three different price ranges, or three different California wine regions

Aged Cabernet Sauvignon One wine (more than 8 years old) tasted alone: 11. Napa Valley Cabernet Sauvignon

FOOD PAIRINGS

"With **Cabernet Sauvignon**, lamb, or wild game such as grouse and caribou. With **Pinot Noir**, pork loin, milder game such as domestic pheasant, and coq au vin."   *—Margrit Biever and Robert Mondavi*

"Roast lamb is wonderful with the flavor and complexity of **Cabernet Sauvignon**. The wine also pairs nicely with sliced breast of duck, and grilled squab with wild mushrooms. For a cheese course with mature Cabernet, milder cheeses such as young goat cheeses, St. André and Taleggio, are best so the subtle flavors of the wine can be enjoyed."   *—Tom Jordan*

"With a young **Merlot,** we recommend lamb shanks with crispy polenta or grilled duck with wild rice in Port sauce. One of our favorites is barbecued leg of lamb with a mild, spicy, fruit-based sauce. With older Merlots at the end of the meal, we like to serve Cambazzola cheese and warm walnuts."   *—Margaret and Dan Duckhorn*

"With **Cabernet Sauvignon**, prime cut of well-aged grilled beef; also— believe it or not—with chocolate and chocolate-chip cookies. With **Pinot Noir**, roasted quail stuffed with peeled kiwi fruit in a Madeira sauce. Also with pork tenderloin in a fruity sauce."   *—Janet Trefethen*

"With **Zinfandel**, a well-made risotto of Petaluma duck. With aged **Cabernet Sauvignon**, Moroccan lamb with figs."   *—Paul Draper of Ridge Vineyards*

"With **Cabernet Sauvignon**, lamb or veal with a light sauce."   *—Warren Winiarski of Stag's Leap Wine Cellars*

"**Pinot Noir** is so versatile, but I like it best with fowl of all sorts—chicken, turkey, duck, pheasant, and quail, preferably roasted or mesquite-grilled. It's also great with fish such as salmon, tuna, and snapper."
—*Josh Jensen of Calera Wine Co.*

"With **Cabernet Sauvignon**, Sonoma County spring lamb or lamb chops prepared in a rosemary herb sauce." —*Richard Arrowood*

"My favorite food combination with **Zinfandel** is marinated, butterflied leg of lamb. Have the butcher butterfly the leg, then place it in a plastic bag. Pour in half a bottle of Dry Creek Zinfandel, a cup of olive oil, six mashed garlic cloves, salt and pepper to taste. Marinate for several hours or overnight in the refrigerator. Barbecue until medium rare. While the lamb is cooking, take the marinade, reduce it, and whisk in several pats of butter for thickness. Yummy!" —*David Stare of Dry Creek Vineyard*

"With **Cabernet Sauvignon**, a good rib eye, barbecued with a teriyaki-soy-ginger-sesame marinade; venison or even roast beef prepared with olive oil and tapenade with rosemary, or even lamb. But when it comes to a good Cabernet Sauvignon: nothing at all—just a good book."
—*Bo Barrett of Chateau Montelena Winery*

"With **Cabernet Sauvignon**, try a rich risotto topped with wild mushrooms."
—*Patrick Campbell of Laurel Glen Vineyard*

"**Cakebread Cellars Napa Valley Cabernet Sauvignon** with salmon in a crispy potato crust or an herb-crusted Napa Valley rack of lamb, with mashed potatoes and a red-wine sauce." —*Jack Cakebread*

"I like my **Cabernet Sauvignon** with rack of lamb, beef, or rare duck."
—*Ed Sbragia of Sbragia Family Vineyards*

"With **St. Francis Merlot** Sonoma County, Dungeness crab cakes, rack of lamb, pork roast, or tortellini. With St. Francis Merlot Reserve, hearty minestrone or lentil soup, venison, or filet mignon, or even a Caesar salad."
—*Tom Mackey of St. Francis*

TEST YOUR KNOWLEDGE of the red wines of California by trying the quiz on page 375.

———— FURTHER READING ————

Making Sense of California Wine by Matt Kramer

The New California Wine by Jon Bonné

Wine Atlas of California by James Halliday

The Wine Atlas of California and the Pacific Northwest by Bob Thompson

Wine Spectator's California Wine by James Laube

Wines of California, Deluxe Edition by Mike DeSimone and Jeff Jenssen

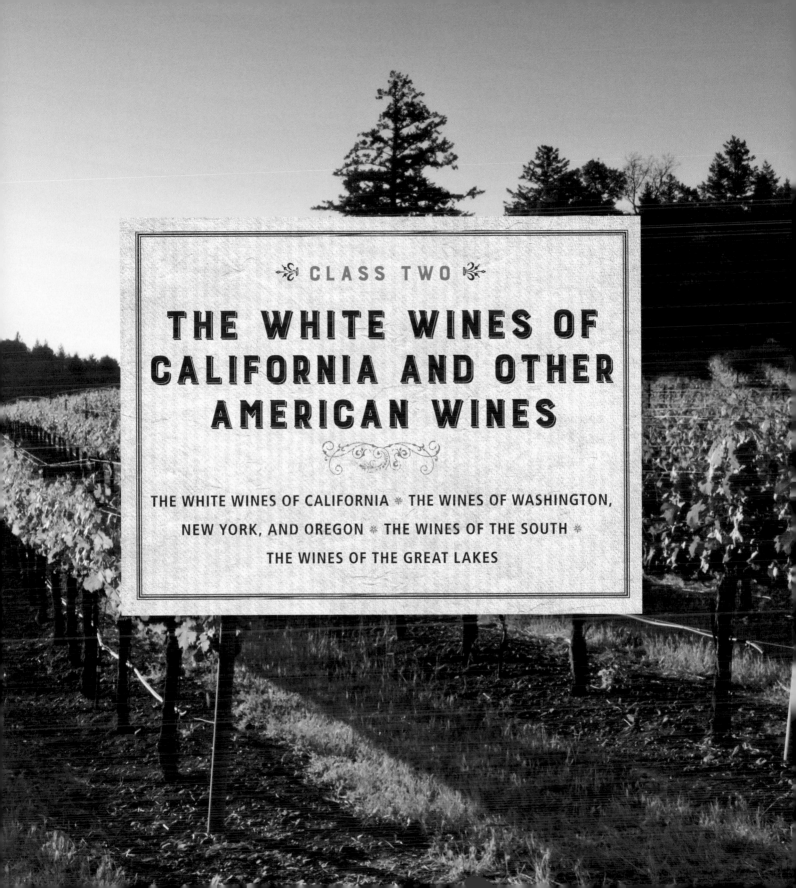

THE WHITE WINES OF CALIFORNIA AND OTHER AMERICAN WINES

THE WHITE WINES OF CALIFORNIA ✳ THE WINES OF WASHINGTON, NEW YORK, AND OREGON ✳ THE WINES OF THE SOUTH ✳ THE WINES OF THE GREAT LAKES

The **THREE LEADING** premium white grapes planted in California in 2016:

1. Chardonnay: 94,532 acres
2. Pinot Gris: 16,728 acres
3. Sauvignon Blanc: 14,752 acres

A THIRD OF ALL GRAPES grown in Sonoma are Chardonnay.

MONTEREY COUNTY HAS THE MOST Chardonnay in California with 16,904 acres.

THE WHITE WINES OF CALIFORNIA

CHARDONNAY

The most important white-wine grape grown in California is Chardonnay. The major regions for California Chardonnay are:

Carneros   Napa   Santa Barbara   Sonoma

This green-skinned grape (*Vitis vinifera*) often ranks as the finest white-grape variety in the world. It's responsible for all the great French white Burgundies, such as Meursault, Chablis, and Puligny-Montrachet. In California, as the most successful white grape, it has yielded wines of tremendous character and magnificent flavor. In the vineyard, yields are fairly low, and the grapes command high prices. The wines often age in small oak barrels, increasing their complexity. Chardonnay is always dry and benefits from aging more than any other American white wine. Superior examples can keep and develop well in the bottle for five years or longer.

The best wineries age these wines in wood, sometimes for more than a year. French oak barrels have doubled in price over the last five years, averaging $1,000 per barrel. Add to this the cost of the grapes and the length of time before the wine is sold, and you can see why the best California Chardonnays cost more than $25.

NOT ALL CALIFORNIA CHARDONNAYS ARE CREATED EQUAL

Put it this way: Grocery stores sell many brands of ice cream. The brands use similar ingredients, but there's only one Ben & Jerry's. The same holds true for wine. Among the many points to consider: Where did the grapes grow? Was the wine barrel-fermented? Did it undergo malolactic fermentation? Is the wine aged in wood or stainless steel? If wood, what type of oak? How long does it remain in the barrel?

MY FAVORITE CALIFORNIA CHARDONNAYS INCLUDE

Acacia	Hanzell	Ramey
Arrowood	Kistler	Ridge
Au Bon Climat	Kongsgaard	Robert Mondavi
Aubert	Landmark	Rombauer
Beringer	Lewis	Rudd Winery
Brewer-Clifton	Littorai	Saintsbury
Cakebread	Marcassin	Sbragia Family
Chalk Hill	Martinelli	Shafer
Chateau Montelena	Merryvale	Silverado
Chateau St. Jean	Mount Eden	Sonoma-Loeb
Diatom	Pahlmeyer Ridge	Talbott
Dutton Goldfield	Paul Hobbs	Testarossa
Ferrari-Carano	Peter Michael	Three Sticks
Flowers	Phelps	Tor
Grgich Hills		

– BEST RECENT VINTAGES OF CALIFORNIA CHARDONNAY –

CARNEROS: 2007** 2009* 2012* 2013* 2014* 2015* 2016

NAPA: 2007* 2008* 2009** 2010** 2012** 2013** 2014** 2016

SONOMA: 2004** 2005** 2009** 2010** 2012** 2013** 2014** 2015* 2016

SANTA BARBARA: 2009* 2012 2013* 2014* 2015* 2016

* EXCEPTIONAL VINTAGE ** EXTRAORDINARY VINTAGE

California has more **CHARDONNAY** planted than any country **IN THE WORLD**!

Some **800 DIFFERENT CALIFORNIA CHARDONNAYS** are available to the consumer.

CHARDONNAY IS THE MOST POPULAR VARIETY sold in America.

In 2012, 2013, and 2014 California had the **LARGEST GRAPE CROPS IN HISTORY**—more than 4 million tons—and great quality.

Robert Mondavi realized that no one was buying Sauvignon Blanc, so he changed its name to **FUMÉ BLANC.** Strictly a marketing maneuver—it was still the same wine. Result: sales took off. Mondavi decided not to trademark the name, allowing anyone to use it (and many producers do).

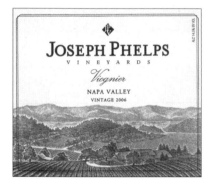

CALIFORNIA TRENDS THROUGH THE DECADES

1960s and 1970s: **JUG WINES** (Chablis, Burgundy)

1980s: **VARIETAL WINES** (Chardonnay, Cabernet Sauvignon)

1990s: **VARIETAL LOCATION** (Napa Cabernet Sauvignon, Santa Barbara Pinot Noir)

2000s: **SPECIFIC VINEYARDS** for specific varieties

Today: **CONSISTENTLY GREAT WINES** from all regions

OTHER MAJOR CALIFORNIA WHITE-WINE GRAPES

Sauvignon Blanc Sometimes labeled "Fumé Blanc," this is one of the grapes used in making the dry white wines of the Graves region of Bordeaux and the white wines of Sancerre and Pouilly-Fumé in the Loire Valley of France as well as New Zealand. California Sauvignon Blanc makes one of the best dry white wines in the world. Winemakers sometimes age it in small oak barrels and occasionally blend it with the Sémillon grape.

Chenin Blanc In California, this grape—one of the most widely planted in the Loire Valley—yields a very attractive, soft, light-bodied wine. It's usually made very dry or semisweet. It's a perfect apéritif wine, simple and fruity.

Viognier One of the major white grapes from France's Rhône Valley, Viognier thrives in warmer and sunny climates, so it's a perfect grape for the weather conditions in certain areas of California. It has a distinct fragrant bouquet. Not as full-bodied as most Chardonnays, nor as light as most Sauvignon Blancs, it's an excellent food wine.

MY FAVORITE CALIFORNIA SAUVIGNON BLANCS INCLUDE

Brander	Grey Stack	Merry Edwards
Caymus	Honig	Orin Swift
Chalk Hill	Joseph Phelps	Quintessa
Chateau St. Jean	Kenwood	Robert Mondavi
Dry Creek	Kunde	Silverado
Ferrari-Carano	Mason	Simi
Girard	Matanzas Creek	Vogelzang

CALIFORNIA WINE TRENDS

The 1960s saw expansion and development. The 1970s brought growth, especially in the number of wineries established in California and the corporations and individuals that invested in them. The 1980s and 1990s fostered experimentation in grape-growing as well as in winemaking and marketing techniques.

Over the past 20 or so years, winemakers finally had a chance to step back and fine-tune their wines. Today, they're producing wines with tremendous structure, finesse, and elegance that many lacked in the early years of the California winemaking renaissance. They also are making wines that can give pleasure when young and great wines that I hope I will be around to share with my grandchildren. The benchmark for quality has increased to such a level that the best wineries have improved, but more important to the consumer is that even the wines under $20 are better than ever before.

Another trend has pushed wineries toward specializing in particular grape varieties. Forty years ago, I would have talked about which wineries in California were best overall. Today, I'm more likely to talk about which AVA, winery, or individual vineyard makes the best Chardonnay or which winery makes the best Sauvignon Blanc.

Chardonnay remains the major white-grape variety by far in California. Sauvignon Blancs / Fumé Blancs have improved greatly, and they're easier to consume young. They still don't have the cachet of a Chardonnay, but they pair better with most foods. Other white-grape varieties, such as Riesling and Chenin Blanc, aren't meeting with the same success, and they're harder to sell. Still, to keep it interesting, some winemakers are planting more European varieties, including Viognier and Pinot Gris.

—— FURTHER READING ——

The Far Side of Eden and Napa by James Conaway

Making Sense of California Wine by Matt Kramer

The New California Wine by Jon Bonné

Wine Atlas of California by James Halliday

The Wine Atlas of California and the Pacific Northwest by Bob Thompson

Wine Spectator's California Wine by James Laube

Wines of California, Deluxe Edition by Mike DeSimone and Jeff Jenssen

2018	
CALIFORNIA	NEW YORK
602,000 acres	37,000 acres
3,151 wineries	365 wineries
WASHINGTON	OREGON
50,000 acres	30,400 acres
713 wineries	473 wineries

THE PACIFIC NORTHWEST WINE-GROWING REGION includes Washington, Oregon, Idaho, and British Columbia.

WASHINGTON'S WINE PRODUCTION

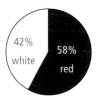

42% white

58% red

WASHINGTON, PAST AND PRESENT
1970: 10 wineries (9 acres)
2018: 713 wineries (50,000 acres)

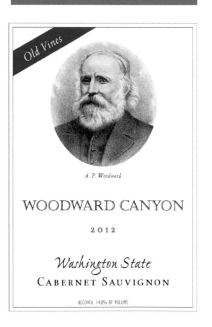

Old Vines

A. P. Woodward

WOODWARD CANYON

2012

Washington State
CABERNET SAUVIGNON

ALCOHOL 14.8% BY VOLUME

THE WINES OF WASHINGTON

Washington's wine industry has matured considerably in the last 40 years, and the state has some of the best wine regions of the world. It has taken people a while to understand and appreciate these wines for many reasons, not least of which is weather. Ask the average wine drinker about winemaking in this region of America, and one of the most common responses you'll get is, "How do you make great wine in a rainy climate like Seattle's?"

The Cascade Mountains—which include two active volcanoes, Mount Rainier and Mount St. Helens—split Washington State into two regions: east and west. On the eastern side of this mountain range, geologic cataclysms—dramatic lava flows from 15 million years ago and monstrous floods during the last ice age—created soil conditions ideal for growing superior grapes and making high-quality wine. An enormous difference exists between Washington's west coast maritime climate and its eastern continental climate: 60 inches of annual rainfall along the Pacific versus just 8 in eastern Washington, where wine grapes thrive in its arid, hot summers. The eastern wine-growing region also has an ideal irrigation system

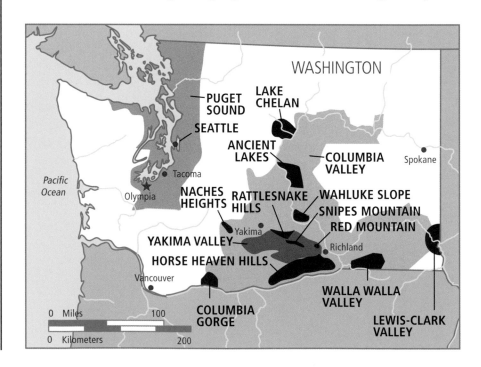

In 2016, Washington gained **ANOTHER AVA**, Lewis-Clark Valley, bringing the total to 14.

Chateau Ste. Michelle is the **WORLD'S LARGEST RIESLING PRODUCER** and formed a winemaking partnership with the famous German wine producer Dr. Loosen to produce a Riesling wine called Eroica.

QUARTERBACKS WITH WINERIES IN WASHINGTON: Drew Bledsoe (New England Patriots), Dan Marino (Miami Dolphins), Damon Huard (Kansas City Chiefs)

In 2016, Washington had its **LARGEST HARVEST.**

―――――― FURTHER READING ――――――
Washington Wines & Wineries
   by Paul Gregutt
The Wine Project by Ron Irvine

partly deriving from the Columbia River, which helps produce perfectly ripe grapes. The Columbia Valley receives more than 300 days of sunshine a year.

Unlike California, Washington's winemaking history is all about the present and future. Only 10 wineries were operating here in 1970; today there are more than 700. It was wheat to grapes, orchards to vineyards, and Rieslings to reds (think Cabernet Sauvignon, Merlot, and Syrah). From 1970 until recently, Washington produced mostly white wines: Riesling and Chardonnay. Now producers here make more red wine. Still, Washington remains the number-one American producer of Riesling, and its Chardonnays, with their balance, great fruit, and lively acidity, are some of the best in the country.

The major red grapes are:

Cabernet Sauvignon	Merlot	Syrah
(10,293 acres)	(8,235 acres)	(3,103 acres)

The major white grapes grown in Washington are:

Chardonnay	Riesling
(7,654 acres)	(6,320 acres)

MY FAVORITE WASHINGTON PRODUCERS INCLUDE

Andrew Will	Doyenne	Owen Roe
Betz Family	Fidelitas	Pepper Bridge
Canoe Ridge	Gramercy Cellars	Quilceda Creek
Cayuse	Hogue Cellars	Reynvaan
Charles Smith	Januik	Seven Hills
Chateau Ste. Michelle	L'Ecole No. 41	Sparkman Cellars
Columbia Crest	Leonetti Cellar	Spring Valley
Columbia Winery	Long Shadows	Woodward Canyon
DiStefano	McCrea Cellars	

– BEST RECENT VINTAGES OF WASHINGTON WINES –
2005* 2006* 2007* 2008** 2009* 2010*
2012** 2013* 2014** 2015** 2016
* EXCEPTIONAL VINTAGE   ** EXTRAORDINARY VINTAGE

THE WINES OF NEW YORK

New York is the third largest wine-producing state in America, with ten AVAs. The three main wine regions in New York are:

Finger Lakes   with the largest wine production east of California
Hudson Valley   concentrating on premium farm wineries
Long Island   New York's red-wine region

Of the 9,400 acres of vines in the Finger Lakes, only 2,100 acres are planted with *vinifera* grapes. The rest are *labrusca* and hybrids. New York's Hudson Valley is one of America's oldest wine-growing regions. Huguenots planted grapevines here in the 1600s. Benmarl in Marlboro, New York, is America's oldest continuously operated vineyard. The Hudson Valley boasts the oldest active winery in America: Brotherhood, which recorded its first vintage in 1839. Alex and Louisa Hargrave started the first winery on Long Island in 1973. In 2015 *Wine Enthusiast* magazine chose New York as the wine region of the year, beating out Champagne, Chianti, Sonoma, and Washington.

The three main categories of grapes grown here are:

Native American	European	French-American
Vitis labrusca	*Vitis vinifera*	hybrids

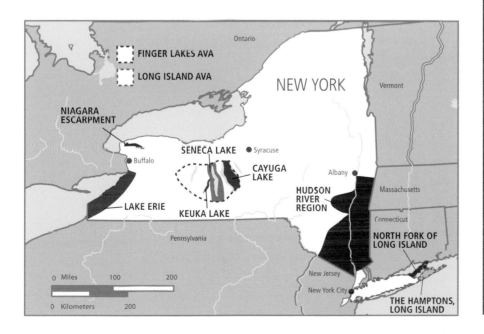

NEW YORK HAS 365 WINERIES, up from fewer than 10 in 1970.

From 2001 to 2017, **MORE THAN 200 WINERIES** have opened in New York.

In the **THREE MAJOR REGIONS,** the Finger Lakes region has 130 wineries, the Hudson Valley has 43, and Long Island has 77.

Long Island has more than 200 days of sunshine and a longer growing season, making it perfect for **MERLOT, CABERNET FRANC, AND BORDEAUX-STYLE WINES.**

Finger Lakes wineries **PRODUCE 85 PERCENT** of New York's wine.

NATIVE AMERICAN VARIETIES

Vitis labrusca vines remain popular among grape growers in New York because they are hardy and can withstand cold winters. Among the most familiar grapes of the *Vitis labrusca* family are Catawba, Concord, and Delaware. Until the last decade, these grapes accounted for most New York wines. Words such as "foxy," "grapey," "Welch's," and "Manischewitz" often describe these wines—a sure sign of *Vitis labrusca*.

EUROPEAN VARIETIES

About 50 years ago, some New York wineries began to experiment with the traditional European (*Vitis vinifera*) grapes. Dr. Konstantin Frank, a Russian viticulturist skilled in cold-climate grape growing, came to America and catalyzed efforts to grow *Vitis vinifera* in New York. This was unheard of—and laughed at—back then. Other winemakers predicted that he'd fail, that it was impossible to grow *vinifera* in New York's cold and capricious climate.

"What do you mean?" Frank replied. "I'm from Russia—it's even colder there."

Most people remained skeptical, but Charles Fournier of Gold Seal Vineyards gave Frank a chance to prove his theory. Sure enough, Frank succeeded with *vinifera* and has produced some world-class wines, especially his Riesling and Chardonnay. So have many other New York wineries, thanks to the vision and courage of Frank and Fournier.

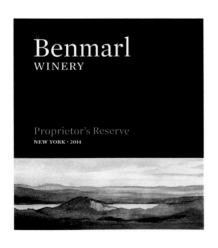

FRENCH-AMERICAN VARIETIES

Some New York and East Coast winemakers have planted French-American hybrid varieties, which combine European taste characteristics with American vine hardiness to withstand the cold winters in the Northeast. French viticulturists originally developed these varieties in the nineteenth century. Seyval Blanc and Vidal are the most prominent white-wine varieties; Baco Noir and Chancellor are the most common reds.

The most significant developments in New York wine are taking place on Long Island and in the Finger Lakes region. Both have experienced tremendous growth of new vineyards. Since 1973, grape-growing acreage on Long Island has increased from 100 acres to more than 4,000, with more expansion expected in the future.

The wines of the Finger Lakes region continue to improve as the winemakers work with grapes that thrive in the cooler climate, including European varieties such as Riesling, Chardonnay, and Pinot Noir.

The predominant use of *Vitis vinifera* varieties allows Long Island wineries to compete more effectively in the world market, and Long Island's longer growing season offers greater potential for red grapes.

The Millbrook and Whitecliff wineries in the Hudson Valley have shown that this region can produce world-class wines—not only white, but red too, from grapes such as Pinot Noir and Cabernet Franc.

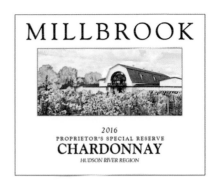

WINERIES TO LOOK FOR IN NEW YORK

THE FINGER LAKES

Anthony Road	Fox Run	Ravines
Atwater Estate	Glenora	Red Newt Cellars
Château Lafayette	Heart & Hands	Red Tail Ridge
Landing	Hermann J. Wiemer	Sheldrake Point
Damiani	Heron Hill	Standing Stone
Dr. Konstantin Frank	Keuka Lake Vineyards	Wagner
Forge Cellars	Lamoreaux Reneau	

THE HUDSON VALLEY

Benmarl	Clinton Vineyards	Whitecliff
Brotherhood	Millbrook	

LONG ISLAND

Bedell	Martha Clara	Pellegrini
Channing Daughters	McGregor	Pindar
Damiani	Osprey's Dominion	Raphael
Grapes of Roth	Palmer	Shinn Estate
Lenz	Paumanok	Wölffer
Macari	Peconic Bay	

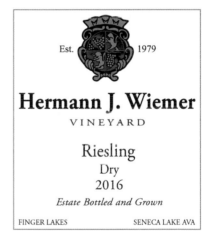

> **– BEST RECENT VINTAGES OF NEW YORK WINES –**
> 2012* 2013 2014* 2015 2016
> ** EXCEPTIONAL VINTAGE*

More than 70 percent of Oregon wineries are located in the **WILLAMETTE VALLEY.**

The Columbia Valley and Walla Walla Valley AVAs encompass parts of Oregon as well as Washington.

Both the **WILLAMETTE VALLEY AND BURGUNDY, FRANCE,** lie at 45 degrees North latitude.

Willamette Valley is pronounced Wil-AM-it, **DAMN IT!**

More than half of Oregon's vineyards are planted with Pinot Noir.

OREGON STATE LAW requires that a wine labeled "Pinot Noir" must contain 100 percent Pinot Noir.

THE WINES OF OREGON

Although growers planted grapes and vintners made wine as early as 1847, Oregon's modern viticultural era began roughly 40 years ago with a handful of intrepid wine pioneers, including David Lett (Eyrie winery) Dick Erath (Erath winery), and Dick Ponzi (Ponzi winery). This new breed of grape growers and winemakers believed that cool-climate varietals such as Pinot Noir, Chardonnay, and Pinot Gris not only would grow in Oregon but would produce world-class wines—and they have! What separated Oregon winemaking from its neighbors in California and Washington was the importation of French clones from Burgundy and Alsace.

The major grapes grown in Oregon are:

Pinot Noir	Pinot Gris	Chardonnay
(17,744 acres)	(3,705 acres)	(1,482 acres)

Most Oregon wineries are small, family-owned, artisanal producers. Their proximity to the city of Portland and Oregon's beautiful coastline make this a must-visit wine region.

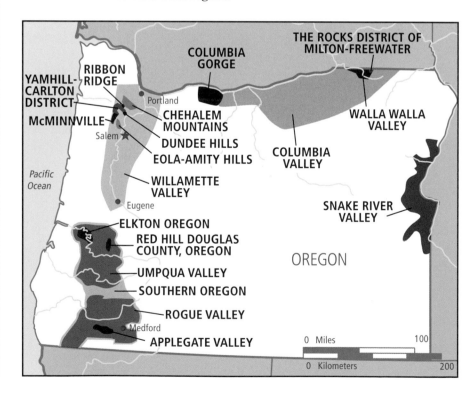

The **KING ESTATE** in Oregon is the largest producer of Pinot Gris in America.

MY FAVORITE OREGON PRODUCERS INCLUDE

A to Z	Chehalem	Lingua Franca
Adelsheim	Cristom	Nicolas & Jay
Alexana	Domaine Drouhin	Penner-Ash
Archery Summit	Domaine Serene	Ponzi
Argyle	Eminent Domaine	Résonance
Artisanal	Elk Cove	Rex Hill
Beaux Frères	Erath	Shea
Benton Lane	Evening Land	Sokol Blosser
Bergström	Eyrie	Soter
Bethel Heights	Ken Wright	St. Innocent
Brick House	King Estate	Tualatin

- BEST RECENT VINTAGES OF OREGON WINES -

2005* 2006* 2008** 2009* 2010**
2012** 2014** 2015** 2016**

* EXCEPTIONAL VINTAGE   ** EXTRAORDINARY VINTAGE

—— **FURTHER READING** ——

The Northwest Wine Guide by Andy Perdue

Wines of the Pacific Northwest by Lisa Shara Hall

WINES OF THE SOUTH

TEXAS

Missionaries planted the first vineyard in Texas in 1662. Texas's oldest winery, Val Verde, has been in operation since 1883. You might not think the climate would make for good wine, but the wineries of Texas are committed to growing primarily Cabernet Sauvignon and Chardonnay. Recent plantings of Malbec and Viognier point to an interesting future. The state has eight AVAs. The largest, Texas Hill Country, has more than 600 acres and 70 wineries.

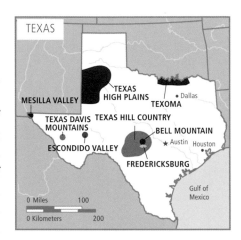

VIRGINIA

Records from Jamestown show that colonists planted vineyards and made wine in the Virginia colony in 1609. Before he became the third American president, Thomas Jefferson served as minister to France and imported some of that country's great wines, planting his own vineyard in Virginia. It proved as challenging back then as it is today. George Washington was unsuccessful with his vineyard. Even in 1979, Virginia only had six wineries.

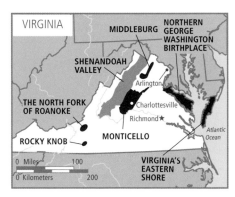

The number-one grape is Chardonnay, but Viognier has become an increasingly popular white grape. Norton, a native grape, has a strong following, and beautiful red blends also have succeeded. Northern Virginia has seen

the most growth in the last seven to ten years and has produced tremendous wines. Virginia is one of the fastest-growing wine regions in the country.

NORTH CAROLINA

Explorer Giovanni de Verrazano receives credit for discovering the Scuppernong grape in the Cape Fear River Valley in 1524. Sir Walter Raleigh explored the Carolinas in the late 1500s and wrote that the land overflowed with grapes. This was the first grape cultivated in America and is to this day the official fruit of North Carolina.

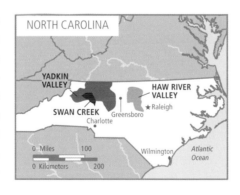

Medoc vineyard in Brinkleyville was the state's first commercial winery, established in 1835, and once led the country in wine production. Since 2001, the number of wineries has more than quadrupled with a new focus on *vinifera* grapes. Most of the grapes are planted in the northwestern and Piedmont regions of the state. The most important grape-growing area is the Yadkin Valley, North Carolina's first AVA, recognized in 2003. It includes more than 35 wineries and 400 acres devoted to vineyards.

NORTH CAROLINA RANKS TENTH in the USA with 139 wineries and 1,800 acres of vines.

Duplin Winery in Rose Hill is the largest and oldest winery in North Carolina and the world's largest producer of **SCUPPERNONG WINE**.

WELL-KNOWN NORTH CAROLINA WINERIES

Biltmore Winery

Childress Vineyards

RagApple Lassie Vineyards

RayLen Vineyards

Shelton Vineyards

Westbend Vineyards

Colorado ranks twelfth with 121 wineries.

WELL-KNOWN MISSOURI WINERIES

Augusta Winery

Blumenhof Winery

Chaumette Vineyards & Winery

Les Bourgeois Winery and Vineyards

Montelle Winery

Mount Pleasant Winery

St. James Winery

Stone Hill Winery

The NORTON GRAPE VARIETY is sometimes called Cynthiana.

The Heck family, CREATORS OF KORBEL, began their winemaking careers in Missouri.

MISSOURI

Growers first planted wine grapes in Missouri in the early 1800s. At one time, Missouri ranked second in production, just behind New York (before California started making wine). The oldest winery is Stone Hill, established in 1847. Many German immigrants settled in Hermann, Missouri, in 1837 because of its resemblance to the Rhine Valley in Germany, planting vineyards on both sides of the Missouri River. Hermann held its first Weinfest in the fall of 1848, a tradition that continues in today's Octoberfest celebrations. Augusta became the first federally recognized AVA in 1980.

Today, Missouri grows a combination of *Vitis labrusca* (Concord) as well as French hybrids (Vignoles), but its most important grape is Norton, which produces a pleasant dry-style red wine. Norton originated in Virginia, but today it's Missouri's official grape.

THE WINES OF THE GREAT LAKES

PENNSYLVANIA

William Penn planted the first vineyard in Pennsylvania in 1683, and Pennsylvania is the site of America's first commercial vineyard—the Pennsylvania Vine Company, established in 1793. Pennsylvania is a "control state," meaning that the state purchases all the wines and sells them through their stores. Pennsylvania is one of the largest single buyers of wines in America. It's also the fifth largest wine-grape producer in the nation.

Like New York, Pennsylvania produces wines from Native American grapes such as Concord and Niagara; *vinifera* grapes such as Cabernet Sauvignon and Chardonnay; and also hybrids such as Seyval Blanc and Chambourcin. Most of Pennsylvania's wineries lie in the warmer, southeastern portion of the state, such as York, Bucks, Chester, and Lancaster counties.

PENNSYLVANIA RANKS SIXTH in the USA with 254 wineries and more than 14,000 acres of vines.

WELL-KNOWN PENNSYLVANIA WINERIES

Allegro Vineyards

Arrowhead Wine Cellars

Blue Mountain

Chaddsford Winery

J. Maki

Manatawny Creek

Pinnacle Ridge Winery

VaLa Vineyards

OHIO

The first vineyards were planted here in 1823, and by 1842 there were 1,200 acres under vine. The oldest and largest winery in Ohio is Meier's, established in 1856. In the 1860s, Ohio was the largest producer of wine in the country. Most of the vineyards were planted with Native American grapes, and Ohio became famous for its sparkling Catawba. Unfortunately the

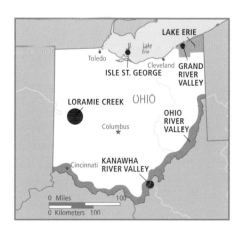

OHIO RANKS EIGHTH in the USA with 205 wineries and 1,500 acres of vines.

At the turn of the twentieth century, dozens of wineries operated on the islands of Lake Erie and produced thousands of gallons of wine. It became known as the **LAKE ERIE GRAPE BELT.**

MICHIGAN RANKS NINTH in the USA with 180 wineries and 13,700 acres of vines.

majority of the vines died from disease, and Prohibition severely curtailed the wine industry.

More than 30 different grapes are planted in Ohio, a blend of *Vitis labrusca*, hybrids such as Seyval Blanc and Chambourcin, and more recently *Vitis vinifera* such as Riesling and Cabernet Franc. Through the efforts of the Ohio State Viticultural and Enology programs, the quality of the wines has improved dramatically.

MICHIGAN

Of the 14,200 acres of grapes in Michigan, only about 3,000 are used for producing wine. But the Riesling grape thrives in the cool climate, and plantings have increased substantially over the last ten years.

The maritime climate greatly influences Michigan winemaking. The Leelanau Peninsula, home to more than 50 percent of Michigan's wineries, benefits from the Lake Effect in many ways. The snow insulates the vines during winter, slowing bud break in spring and preventing damaging frost, which makes the growing season last much longer. The Michigan Grape Council is testing other areas in the state to find the best

grape-growing land and to increase production, which will mean more quality wines from Michigan.

ILLINOIS

In 1778, French settlers in La Ville de Maillet (now Peoria) brought the winemaking expertise of their homeland to Illinois. The village featured a winepress and an underground wine vault. In the 1850s, farmers started planting the Concord grape. Emile Baxter and Sons opened a winery in Nauvoo in 1857, along the banks of the Mississippi River. Baxter's Vineyards remains Illinois's oldest operating winery, run by a fifth generation of Baxters. More recently, the Illinois wine industry has exploded, growing from just 12 wineries in 1997 to more than 100 today. Acreage devoted to grape production also has grown at a tremendous rate, and today Illinois consistently ranks among the top wine-producing states.

5 BEST VALUE WHITE WINES OF AMERICA UNDER $30

Chateau St. Jean Chardonnay • Columbia Crest Sémillon-Chardonnay • Dr. Konstantin Frank Riesling • Frog's Leap Sauvignon Blanc • King Estate Pinot Gris

See pages 352–355 for a complete list.

Château Grand Traverse first produced **ICE WINE** in 1983.

ILLINOIS RANKS THIRTEENTH in the USA with 105 wineries and more than 1,100 acres of vines.

WELL-KNOWN ILLINOIS WINERIES

Alto Vineyards

Baxter's Vineyards

Fox Valley Winery

Galena Cellars

Hickory Ridge Vineyard

Lynfred Winery

Mary Michelle Winery & Vineyard

Owl Creek Vineyard

Spirit Knob Winery and Winery

Vahling Vineyards

TEST YOUR KNOWLEDGE of American wines by trying the quiz on page 377.

GUIDED TASTING

Start with an unoaked, low-alcohol Riesling, which will leave the palate refreshingly light. Then move on to food-friendly Sauvignon Blancs, and work your way through some great Chardonnays.

American Riesling One Riesling tasted alone:
　　1. Finger Lakes, New York, Riesling

American Sauvignon Blanc Two Sauvignon Blancs compared:
　　2. Sonoma County Sauvignon Blanc
　　3. Napa Valley Sauvignon Blanc

American Chardonnay One Chardonnay tasted alone:
　　4. Unoaked California Chardonnay

Two Chardonnays compared (blind tastings):
　　5. Blind Tasting 1:
　　Unoaked California Chardonnay versus heavily oaked California
　　　　Chardonnay
　　　　OR Sonoma Valley Chardonnay versus Napa Valley Chardonnay
　　6. Blind Tasting 2:
　　White Burgundy versus Napa or Sonoma Valley Chardonnay
　　　　OR New York Chardonnay versus California Chardonnay
　　　　OR Australian Chardonnay versus California Chardonnay
In both blind tastings, select wines of the same quality, vintages within a year of each other, and in the same price range.

Four Chardonnays from four different AVAs:
　　7. Sonoma County Chardonnay
　　8. Santa Barbara Chardonnay
　　9. Monterey Chardonnay
　　10. Carneros Chardonnay

Aged Chardonnay (more than five years old) tasted alone:
　　11. Aged Napa Valley Chardonnay

GRGICH HILLS

Napa Valley
CHARDONNAY
2002

PRODUCED AND BOTTLED BY
GRGICH HILLS CELLAR, RUTHERFORD, CA

FOOD PAIRINGS

"With **Chardonnay**: oysters, lobster, a more complex fish with beurre blanc, pheasant salad with truffles. With **Sauvignon Blanc:** traditional white meat or fish course, sautéed or grilled fish (as long as it isn't an oily fish)."
—Margrit Biever and Robert Mondavi

"With **Chardonnay**: fresh boiled Dungeness crab cooked in Zatarain's crab boil, a New Orleans–style boil. Serve this with melted butter and a large loaf of sourdough French bread. With **Sauvignon Blanc**, "I like fresh salmon cooked in almost any manner. Personally, I like to take a whole fresh salmon or salmon steaks and cook them over the barbecue in an aluminum foil pocket. Place the salmon, onion slices, lemon slices, copious quantities of fresh dill, salt, and pepper on aluminum foil and make a pocket. Cook over the barbecue until barely done. Place the salmon in the oven to keep it warm while you take the juices from the aluminum pocket, reduce the juices, strain, and whisk in some plain yogurt. Enjoy!"
—David Stare, Dry Creek

"With **Chardonnay**: ceviche, shellfish, salmon with a light hollandaise sauce."
—Warren Winiarski, Stag's Leap Wine Cellars

"With **Chardonnay**: barbecued whole salmon in a sorrel sauce. With White Riesling: sautéed bay scallops with julienne vegetables."
—Janet Trefethen

"With **Chardonnay**: Sonoma Coast Dungeness crab right from the crab pot, with fennel butter as a dipping sauce."
—Richard Arrowood

"With **Chardonnay**: salmon, trout, or abalone, barbecued with olive oil and lemon leaf and slices."
—Bo Barrett, Chateau Montelena Winery

"With my Cakebread Cellars Napa Valley **Chardonnay**: bruschetta with wild mushrooms, leek-and-mushroom-stuffed chicken breast, and halibut with caramelized endive and chanterelles."
—Jack Cakebread

"With **Chardonnay**: lobster or salmon with lots of butter."
—Ed Sbragia, Sbragia Family Vineyards

CLASS THREE

FRENCH WINE AND THE RED WINES OF BORDEAUX

UNDERSTANDING FRENCH WINE ✳ THE RED WINES OF BORDEAUX ✳

MÉDOC ✳ GRAVES ✳ POMEROL ✳ ST-ÉMILION ✳

BORDEAUX VINTAGES ✳ CHOOSING A RED BORDEAUX

In 2016, France was the **NUMBER-TWO PRODUCER** of wines in the world.

UNDERSTANDING FRENCH WINE

BEFORE WE BEGIN this class, you should know a few important points about all French wines. First look at the map of France again to familiarize yourself with the main wine-producing areas. As we progress, you'll understand why geography is so important.

This table offers a quick rundown of which areas produce which styles of wine:

WINE REGIONS	STYLES	MAJOR GRAPES
ALSACE	MOSTLY WHITE	RIESLING, GEWÜRZTRAMINER
BORDEAUX	RED AND WHITE	SAUVIGNON BLANC, SÉMILLON, MERLOT, CABERNET SAUVIGNON, CABERNET FRANC
BURGUNDY	RED AND WHITE	PINOT NOIR, GAMAY, CHARDONNAY
CHAMPAGNE	SPARKLING WINE	PINOT NOIR, CHARDONNAY, PINOT MEUNIER
CÔTES DU RHÔNE	MOSTLY RED	SYRAH, GRENACHE, MOURVÈDRE
LANGUEDOC-ROUSSILLON	RED AND WHITE	CARIGNAN, GRENACHE, SYRAH, CINSAULT, MOURVÈDRE
LOIRE VALLEY	MOSTLY WHITE	SAUVIGNON BLANC, CHENIN BLANC, CABERNET FRANC
PROVENCE	RED, WHITE, AND ROSÉ	GRENACHE, SYRAH, MOURVÈDRE, CINSAULT, CLAIRETTE BLANCHE

Five major regions of Languedoc-Rousssillon:

1. Corbières-Boutenac
2. Faugères
3. La Clape
4. Minervois-La Livinière
5. St-Chinian

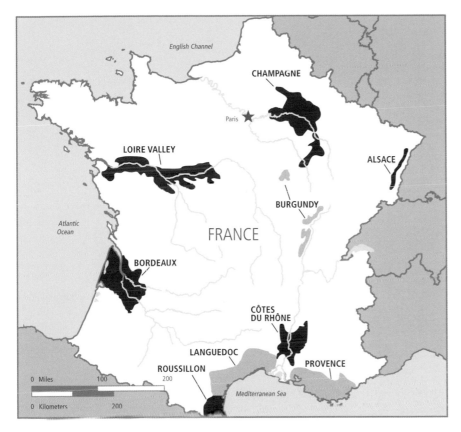

If you're interested in wine, you're bound to encounter French wine at one time or another. Why? Because of the thousands of years of history and winemaking tradition, because of the great diversity and variety of wines from the many different regions, and because French wines have the reputation for ranking among the best in the world. The reason for this goes back to quality control.

Appellation d'Origine Contrôlée These strict government laws regulate French winemaking. If you don't want to say "Appellation d'Origine Contrôlée" all the time, you simply can say "AOC."

Vins de pays This category is growing in importance. A 1979 French legal decision liberalized the rules for this category, permitting the use of non-traditional grapes in certain regions and even allowing winemakersrs to label wines with the varietal rather than the regional name. For exporters to the American market, where consumers are becoming accustomed to

Why would Georges Duboeuf, Louis Latour, and many other famous winemakers start wineries in Languedoc and Roussillon? **THE LAND IS MUCH LESS EXPENSIVE** compared to regions such as Burgundy or Bordeaux, so the winemakers can produce moderately priced wines and still get a good return on their investment.

IN PROVENCE, look for the producers Domaine Ott, Domaine Tempier, Château Routas, and Château d'Esclans (Whispering Angel).

AMERICANS LOVE FRENCH WINE.
The USA is the number-one export market especially for wine from Champagne, Loire, Burgundy, Rhône, and Bordeaux.

The regions **MOST ACTIVE IN THE PRODUCTION OF *VIN DE PAYS*** varietal wines are Languedoc and Roussillon in southwest France. Once called the "wine lake" because of the vast quantities of anonymous wine made there, Languedoc has more than 700,000 acres of vineyards and produces more than 200 million cases a year, about a third of the total French output.

ABOUT 45 PERCENT of all French wines are worthy of the AOC designation.

There are nearly **500 AOC FRENCH WINES**.

1 HECTOLITER = 26.42 gallons
1 HECTARE = 2.471 acres

FAMOUS NON-AOC FRENCH WINES available in America include: Moreau, Boucheron, and René Junot.

buying wines by grape variety—Cabernet Sauvignon or Chardonnay, for example—this change makes their wines much easier to sell.

Vins de table These ordinary table wines represent almost 35 percent of all wines produced in France. Most French wine is meant to be consumed as a simple beverage. Many of the *vins de table* appear under proprietary names and are the French equivalent of California jug wines. Don't be surprised if you go into a grocery store in France to buy wine and find it in a plastic container with no label! You can see the color through the plastic—red, white, or rosé—but the only marking on the container is the alcohol content, ranging from 9 to 14 percent. Choose your wine depending on how sharp you need to feel for the rest of the day!

When you buy wines, keep the distinctions between *vins de pays* and *vins de table* in mind because there's a difference between them not only in quality but also in price.

BORDEAUX GRAPE ACREAGE

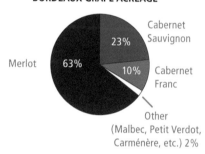

Cabernet Sauvignon 23%

Merlot 63%

Cabernet Franc 10%

Other (Malbec, Petit Verdot, Carménère, etc.) 2%

Until 1970 Bordeaux regularly produced **MORE WHITE WINE THAN RED.**

BORDEAUX WINE PRODUCTION

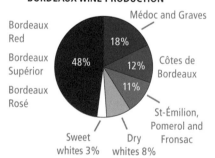

Bordeaux Red
Bordeaux Supérior
Bordeaux Rosé
48%

Médoc and Graves 18%

Côtes de Bordeaux 12%

St-Émilion, Pomerol and Fronsac 11%

Sweet whites 3%   Dry whites 8%

FRANCE HAS the most acres of Merlot in the world, followed by Italy and then California.

THE RED WINES OF BORDEAUX

THIS PROVINCE OF France teems with excitement and history, and its wines speak for themselves. You'll find this region much easier to understand than Burgundy because fewer landholders own bigger plots of land, and, as the wine-loving author Samuel Johnson once said, "He who aspires to be a serious wine drinker must drink claret"—the old word for the dry red table wine known as Bordeaux.

Some 57 wine regions in Bordeaux produce high-quality wines that can carry the Bordeaux name on the label according to AOC rules. Of those, four stand out for red wine:

Médoc	Graves / Pessac-Léognan	Pomerol	St-Émilion
40,676 acres	12,849 acres	1,986 acres	23,062 acres
(only red)	(red and dry white)	(only red)	(only red)

The Médoc has seven important communes, or subsidiary appellations, that you should know:

Haut Médoc	Margaux	Pauillac	St-Julien
Listrac	Moulis	St-Estèphe	

The three major grapes are:

Merlot	Cabernet Franc	Cabernet Sauvignon

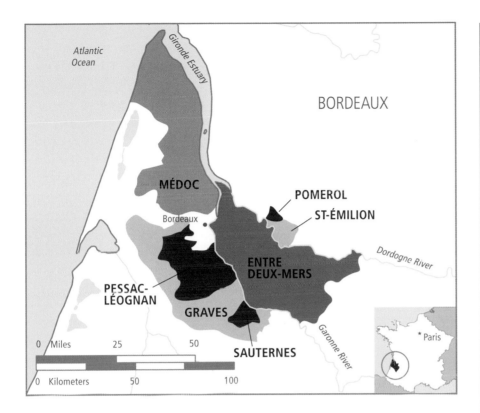

In dollar value, America is **THE SECOND-LARGEST IMPORTER** of Bordeaux wines.

Two other grapes that sometimes go into Bordeaux wines are **PETIT VERDOT AND MALBEC.**

27 PERCENT of France's AOC wines come from the Bordeaux region.

WINES PRICED BETWEEN $8 AND $25 account for 80 percent of all Bordeaux wines.

PROPRIETARY WINES YOU MAY KNOW:

Baron Philippe	Michel Lynch
Lacour Pavillon	Mouton-Cadet
Lauretan	

MAJOR SHIPPERS OF REGIONAL WINES FROM BORDEAUX INCLUDE:

Baron Philippe de Rothschild

Barton & Guestier (B & G)

Borie-Manoux

Cordier

Dourthe Kressmann

Dulong

Eschenauer

Ets J-P Moueix

Sichel

Yvon Mau

Unlike Burgundy, where winemakers must use 100 percent Pinot Noir to make most red wines (and 100 percent Gamay for Beaujolais), the red wines of Bordeaux almost always come from a blend of grapes. As a rule of thumb, the regions and villages to the west, or left, of the Garonne, use primarily the Cabernet Sauvignon grape, and those to the right, or east, of the Dordogne use mostly Merlot.

The three different quality levels of Bordeaux wine are:

Bordeaux This lowest AOC level consists of nice, inexpensive, consistent "drinking" wines. Sometimes these proprietary wines go by a kind of brand name, such as Mouton-Cadet, rather than by the sub-region or vineyard. Cost: $.

Region Only grapes and wines made in the specified 60 areas can go by their regional names: Pauillac and St-Émilion, for example. These are more expensive than those labeled simply "Bordeaux." Cost: $$.

PROPRIETARY BORDEAUX
Appellation Bordeaux Contrôlée

REGIONAL
Appellation Pauillac Contrôlée

CHÂTEAU
Appellation Pauillac Contrôlée
with château name

Region + Château Château wines come from individual vineyards, and Bordeaux has more than 7,000 of them. As far back as 1855, Bordeaux officially classified the quality levels of some of its châteaux. Hundreds have received official recognition for their quality. In the Médoc, for example, the 61 highest-level châteaux are called Grands Crus Classés. The Médoc level below that, Cru Bourgeois, has 246 châteaux. Other areas have their own classification systems. Cost: $$–$$$$.

MAJOR RED BORDEAUX CLASSIFICATIONS

REGION	CLASSIFICATION	YEAR ESTABLISHED	CLASSIFIED CHÂTEAUX
GRAVES	GRANDS CRUS CLASSÉS	1959	12
MÉDOC	GRANDS CRUS CLASSÉS	1855	61
MÉDOC	CRUS BOURGEOIS	1920 (REVISED 1932, 1978, 2003, 2010)	246
POMEROL	NO OFFICIAL CLASSIFICATION		
ST-ÉMILION	PREMIERS GRANDS CRUS CLASSÉS	1955 (REVISED 1996, 2006, 2012)	18
ST-ÉMILION	GRANDS CRUS CLASSÉS	1955 (REVISED 1996, 2006, 2012)	85

CHÂTEAUX

When most people think of châteaux, they picture grandiose homes filled with valuable art and antiques, surrounded by rolling vineyards—but most châteaux aren't like that at all. A château could be a mansion on a large estate, yes, but it also could be a modest home with a two-car garage. The best quality and therefore the most expensive wines of Bordeaux come from châteaux, and some of the best known Grands Crus Classés command the highest wine prices in the world! No one wants to memorize the names of thousands of châteaux, though, so let's take a closer look at the most important classification in Bordeaux.

MÉDOC

GRAND CRU CLASSÉ

TYPICAL MÉDOC BLEND

10–20% Cabernet Franc ——

25–40% Merlot ——

60–80% Cabernet Sauvignon ——

For the International Exposition of 1855, Emperor Napoleon III asked wine brokers to select the best wines to represent France. The brokers agreed to create the classification with the proviso that it never become official. They ranked the top Médoc wines according to price, which at the time directly correlated with quality. According to this system, the top four (now five) vineyards, or *crus*, produced "first-growth" wines; the next fourteen best made second-growth; and so on until the fifth-growth producers, thereby creating what became—*voilà!*—the Official Classification of 1855, on the next page.

According to French law, a château is a house attached to a vineyard having a specific number of acres as well as winemaking and storage facilities on the property. A château wine must meet these criteria. **THE TERMS *DOMAINE*, *CLOS*, AND *CRU* ARE USED ALSO.**

If you see a château on the label, French law dictates that **THE CHÂTEAU REALLY EXISTS** and belongs to that winemaker.

Grands Crus Classés represent LESS THAN 5 PERCENT of Bordeaux wines.

> *"For a given vintage there is quite a consistent ratio between the prices of the different classes, which is of considerable help to the trade. So a fifth growth would always sell at about half the price of a second. The thirds and fourths would get prices halfway between the seconds and the fifths. The first growths are getting about 25 percent over the second growths."*
>
> —Ch. Cocks, *Bordeaux et Ses Vins*, 1868

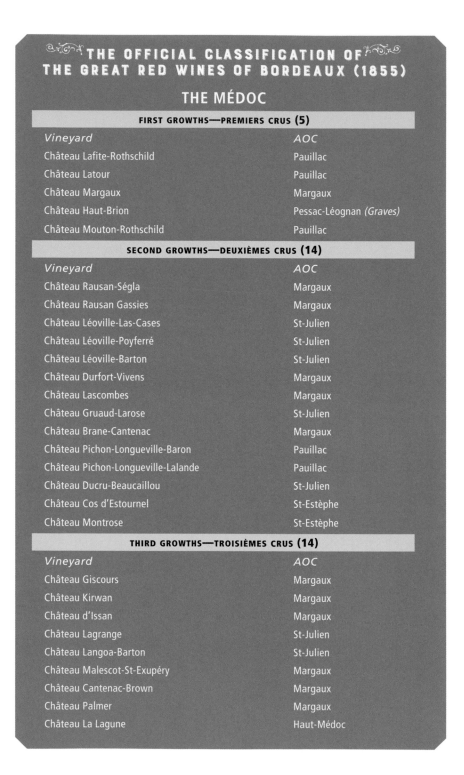

THE OFFICIAL CLASSIFICATION OF THE GREAT RED WINES OF BORDEAUX (1855)

THE MÉDOC

FIRST GROWTHS—PREMIERS CRUS (5)

Vineyard	AOC
Château Lafite-Rothschild	Pauillac
Château Latour	Pauillac
Château Margaux	Margaux
Château Haut-Brion	Pessac-Léognan *(Graves)*
Château Mouton-Rothschild	Pauillac

SECOND GROWTHS—DEUXIÈMES CRUS (14)

Vineyard	AOC
Château Rausan-Ségla	Margaux
Château Rausan Gassies	Margaux
Château Léoville-Las-Cases	St-Julien
Château Léoville-Poyferré	St-Julien
Château Léoville-Barton	St-Julien
Château Durfort-Vivens	Margaux
Château Lascombes	Margaux
Château Gruaud-Larose	St-Julien
Château Brane-Cantenac	Margaux
Château Pichon-Longueville-Baron	Pauillac
Château Pichon-Longueville-Lalande	Pauillac
Château Ducru-Beaucaillou	St-Julien
Château Cos d'Estournel	St-Estèphe
Château Montrose	St-Estèphe

THIRD GROWTHS—TROISIÈMES CRUS (14)

Vineyard	AOC
Château Giscours	Margaux
Château Kirwan	Margaux
Château d'Issan	Margaux
Château Lagrange	St-Julien
Château Langoa-Barton	St-Julien
Château Malescot-St-Exupéry	Margaux
Château Cantenac-Brown	Margaux
Château Palmer	Margaux
Château La Lagune	Haut-Médoc

Château Desmirail	Margaux
Château Calon-Ségur	St-Estèphe
Château Ferrière	Margaux
Château d'Alesme (formerly Marquis d'Alesme)	Margaux
Château Boyd-Cantenac	Margaux

FOURTH GROWTHS—QUATRIÈMES CRUS (10)

Vineyard	AOC
Château St-Pierre	St-Julien
Château Branaire-Ducru	St-Julien
Château Talbot	St-Julien
Château Duhart-Milon-Rothschild	Pauillac
Château Pouget	Margaux
Château La Tour-Carnet	Haut-Médoc
Château Lafon-Rochet	St-Estèphe
Château Beychevelle	St-Julien
Château Prieuré-Lichine	Margaux
Château Marquis de Terme	Margaux

FIFTH GROWTHS—CINQUIÈMES CRUS (18)

Vineyard	AOC
Château Pontet-Canet	Pauillac
Château Batailley	Pauillac
Château Grand-Puy-Lacoste	Pauillac
Château Grand-Puy-Ducasse	Pauillac
Château Haut-Batailley	Pauillac
Château Lynch-Bages	Pauillac
Château Lynch-Moussas	Pauillac
Château Dauzac	Haut-Médoc
Château d'Armailhac (called Château Mouton-Baron-Philippe from 1956 to 1988)	Pauillac
Château du Tertre	Margaux
Château Haut-Bages-Libéral	Pauillac
Château Pédesclaux	Pauillac
Château Belgrave	Haut-Médoc
Château Camensac	Haut-Médoc
Château Cos Labory	St-Estèphe
Château Clerc-Milon-Rothschild	Pauillac
Château Croizet Bages	Pauillac
Château Cantemerle	Haut-Médoc

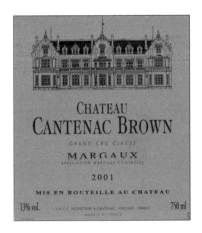

UNDERSTANDING THE 1855 CLASSIFICATION

As you can see, the 1855 classification can look a little cumbersome, so I've separated the classification into growths, communes, and the number of vineyards in each. My table shows which communes have the most first growths—all the way down to fifth growths. It also shows which commune corners the market on all growths. A quick glance offers some instant facts to guide you when you buying a Médoc Bordeaux: Pauillac has the most first-growths and the most fifth-growths. Margaux sweeps the third growths and the overall châteaux count, and only Margaux has a château in each category. St-Julien has no first- or fifth-growths, but its strengths lie in second- and fourth-growths.

BOX SCORE OF THE 1855 CLASSIFICATION

COMMUNE	1ST	2ND	3RD	4TH	5TH	TOTAL
MARGAUX	1	5	10	3	2	21
PAUILLAC	3	2	0	1	12	18
ST-JULIEN	0	5	2	4	0	11
ST-ESTÈPHE	0	2	1	1	1	5
HAUT-MÉDOC	0	0	1	1	3	5
GRAVES	1	0	0	0	0	1
CHÂTEAUX	5	14	14	10	18	61

THE HISTORY OF THE 1855 CLASSIFICATION

Much has changed over the last century and a half. Some vineyards have doubled or tripled production by buying neighboring land; the châteaux have seen many changes of ownership; and, like all businesses, the wine industry in Bordeaux has seen good times and bad. The 1855 classification has remained stable, but both it and its relative meaning have changed slightly over the years. Here are three examples.

In 1920, Baron Philippe de Rothschild assumed control of the family vineyard, but he refused to accept that in 1855 the brokers had ranked the château a second-growth (two years after his great-grandfather, an

Englishman, bought it). Baron Philippe felt it should have been classified a first-growth from the beginning, and he fought for years to change the designation. When that change finally came in 1973, the château's motto changed from

> *Premier ne puis, second ne daigne, Mouton suis.*
> First, I cannot be. Second, I do not deign to be. Mouton I am.

to

> *Premier je suis, Second je fus, Mouton ne change.*
> First, I am. Second, I used to be. Mouton doesn't change.

In the early 1970s, Château Margaux and all Bordeaux wines were having a difficult time, even at the highest level. The family who owned Château Margaux then was struggling financially and didn't put enough time or money into running the vineyard, so the quality of the wine fell from its traditional excellence. Then, in 1977, the Franco-Greek Mentzelopoulos family bought the château for $16 million, and since then the quality of the wine has risen even beyond its first-growth standards.

The cru bourgeois Château Larose-Trintaudon is **THE LARGEST VINEYARD IN THE MÉDOC** area, making nearly 100,000 cases of wine per year.

Château Gloria, which lies in the commune of St-Julien, didn't exist in 1855. Starting in the 1940s, Henri Martin, the mayor of St-Julien, bought parcels of second-growth vineyards. As a result, the château he founded now produces top-quality wine not included in the 1855 classification.

Also keep in mind that the techniques that winemakers use today differ from those used in 1855 and make for better wine. Some of the châteaux in the 1855 classification deserve a lesser ranking, and others deserve a better one, but, even after more than 150 years, the classification still offers a valid and useful guide to quality and price.

CRU BOURGEOIS

The Crus Bourgeois are châteaux originally classified in 1920. Rather than remaining fixed like the Official Classification, the Crus Bourgeois designation varies over time. In 1932, it featured 444 properties, but in 1962 it listed only 94. The latest classification of Crus Bourgeois of the Médoc and Haut-Médoc took place in 2010 and has 246 châteaux. Because of the high quality of the 2000, 2003, 2005, 2009, 2010, and 2015 vintages, you'll find some of today's best values in the Cru Bourgeois classification.

Look for these producers:

Château Chasse-Spleen	Château Les Ormes-Sorbet
Château Coufran	Château Marbuzet
Château d'Angludet	Château Meyney
Château de Lamarque	Château Monbrison
Château de Pez	Château Patache d'Aux
Château Fourcas-Hosten	Château Phélan-Ségur
Château Greysac	Château Pibran
Château Haut-Marbuzet	Château Pontensac
Château Labégorce-Zédé	Château Poujeaux
Château La Cardonne	Château Siran
Château Larose-Trintaudon	Château Sociando-Mallet
Château Les Ormes-de-Pez	Château Vieux Robin

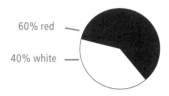

60% red

40% white

In 1987, the northern Graves region established the **PESSAC-LÉOGNAN** (for both reds and whites) communal appellation.

Guests at an exclusive hotel in the vineyards of Château Smith-Haut-Lafitte can enjoy **TREATMENTS FEATURING GRAPEVINE EXTRACT,** crushed grape seeds, and grapeseed oil.

MERLOT IS THE MAJOR GRAPE used to produce wine in the Pomerol region. Very little Cabernet Sauvignon goes into these wines.

Château Pétrus makes as much wine in one year as Gallo makes in **SIX MINUTES.**

GRAVES

The most famous château here, which we saw in the 1855 classification, is Château Haut-Brion. Other good red Graves wines classified in 1959 as Grands Crus Classés include:

Château Bouscaut
Château Carbonnieux
Château de Fieuzal
Château Haut-Bailly
Château La Mission-Haut-Brion
Château La Tour-Martillac

Château Malartic-Lagravière
Château Olivier
Château Pape-Clément
Château Smith-Haut-Lafitte
Domaine de Chevalier

POMEROL

The smallest of the top red-wine regions in Bordeaux, Pomerol produces only 15 percent as much wine as St-Émilion, so Pomerol wines are relatively scarce and, if you do find them, expensive. The red wines of Pomerol tend to be softer, fruitier, and ready to drink sooner than Médoc wines. No official classification exists, but here are some of the finest Pomerols on the market:

Château Beauregard
Château Bourgneuf
Château Clinet
Château Gazin
Château La Conseillante
Château La Fleur-Pétrus
Château La Pointe
Château Lafleur
Château Latour-à-Pomerol

Château L'Église Clinet
Château L'Évangile
Château Le Pin
Château Nénin
Château Petit-Village
Château Pétrus
Château Plince
Château Trotanoy
Vieux Château-Certan

ST-ÉMILION

One of the most beautiful villages in France, St-Émilion produces about two-thirds as much wine as the Médoc. A century after the Médoc classification came the St-Émilion classification, which features 18 first growths comparable to the Médoc's Grand Cru Classé wines.

PREMIERS GRANDS CRUS CLASSÉS A (HIGHEST LEVEL)

Château Angélus	Château Chevâl Blanc
Château Ausone	Château Pavie

PREMIERS GRANDS CRUS CLASSÉS B

Château Beau-Séjour-Bécot	Château La Gaffelière
Château Beauséjour- Duffau-Lagarrosse	Château La Mondotte
	Château Larcis Ducasse
Château Belair-Monange	Château Pavie Macquin
Château Canon	Château Troplong Mondot
Château Canon-La-Gaffelière	Château Trottevieille
Château Clos Fourtet	Château Valandraud
Château Figeac	

Below that level, here are the important Grands Crus Classés and other St-Émilion wines generally available in America:

Château Bellevue	Château Haut-Corbin
Château Dassault	Château La Tour-Figeac
Château de Ferrand	Château Monbousquet
Château Faugères	Château Pavie Decesse
Château Fonplégade	Château Soutard
Château Fonroque	Château Tertre Daugax
Château Fombrauge	Château Yon Figeac
Château Franc Mayne	Clos des Jacobins
Château Grand-Corbin	

GRAPE VARIETIES OF ST-ÉMILION

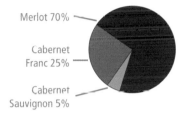

Merlot 70%

Cabernet Franc 25%

Cabernet Sauvignon 5%

OTHER RED BORDEAUX REGIONS

Côtes de Blaye

Côtes de Bourg

Fronsac

In Bordeaux, the earliest harvest since 1893 took place in 2003. **THAT VINTAGE SUFFERED** summer heat waves, fierce storms, and hail, reducing production to the lowest level since 1991.

Many experts consider the decade of 2000–2010 **THE BEST IN THE HISTORY OF BORDEAUX.**

Drink your lighter vintages, such as 2011 and 2012, while you **WAIT PATIENTLY** for your great vintages such as 2009, 2010, and 2015 to mature.

Bordeaux produces **60–70 MILLION CASES** (720–840 million bottles) of wine for each vintage.

"Great vintages take time to mature. Lesser wines mature faster than the greater ones. . . . Patience is needed for great vintages, hence the usefulness and enjoyment of lesser vintages. . . . Often vintages which have a poorer rating—if young—will give a greater enjoyment than a better-rated vintage—if young."

—Alexis Lichine

BORDEAUX VINTAGES

Now that you know the greatest red-wine regions of Bordeaux, here are some of their best vintages.

– LEFT BANK OF THE GARONNE RIVER –
MÉDOC, ST-JULIEN, MARGAUX, PAUILLAC, ST-ESTÈPHE, GRAVES

GREAT OLDER VINTAGES	GREAT VINTAGES	GOOD VINTAGES
1982	1990	1994
1985	1995	1997
1986	1996	1998
1989	2000	1999
	2003	2001
	2005	2002
	2009	2004
	2010	2006
	2015	2007
	2016	2008
		2011
		2012
		2014
		2017

– RIGHT BANK OF THE DORDOGNE RIVER –
ST-ÉMILION, POMEROL

GREAT OLDER VINTAGES	GREAT VINTAGES	GOOD VINTAGES
1982	1990	1995
1989	1998	1996
	2000	1997
	2001	1999
	2005	2002
	2009	2003
	2010	2004
	2015	2006
	2016	2007
		2008
		2011
		2012
		2014
		2017

CHOOSING A RED BORDEAUX

Remember, Bordeaux wines are blends. Do you want a Merlot-style Bordeaux, such as St-Émilion or Pomerol, or a Cabernet style, such as Médoc or Graves? Keep in mind that Merlot is more accessible and easier to drink when young.

Next, do you want to drink the wine now or age it? A great château Bordeaux in a great vintage needs a minimum of ten years to age. Down a level, a Cru Bourgeois or a second label of a great château in a great vintage needs at least five years. Drink a regional wine within two or three years of the vintage, and a wine labeled simply "Appellation Bordeaux Contrôlée" as soon as it hits store shelves.

Then select the right vintage for what you want. If you're looking for a wine to age, you need a great vintage. If you want a wine ready to drink now and from a greater château, choose a lesser vintage. If you want a wine ready to drink now and a great vintage, look for a lesser château.

As we've seen, not all Bordeaux wines are very expensive. They all have different price ranges, so don't let cost expectations prevent you from finding and enjoying a good value. Some red Bordeaux do cost much more than others, however. These factors separate a $30 bottle from a $300 bottle:

- Where the grapes grew
- Age of the vines (usually the older the vine, the better the wine)
- Yield of the vine (lower yield = higher quality)
- Winemaking technique (how long aged in wood, etc.)
- Vintage

The best way to get the best value for your money is to use the pyramid method. Let's say you like Château Lafite-Rothschild—top of the pyramid in the margin—but you can't afford it. What to do? Look for the region, which is Pauillac. Now you have a choice: Go back to the 1855 classification and look for a fifth-growth wine from Pauillac that represents the region at a lower price. Still too pricey? Drop another level on the pyramid and go for a Cru Bourgeois from Pauillac, or buy a regional wine labeled "Pauillac."

I've never memorized the 7,000 châteaux. If at a wine store I find a château I don't know, I look at the region. If it comes from Pauillac and from a good vintage and it costs $25 to $30, I buy it—because chances are good that the wine will be good, and everything in wine is about hedging your bets.

"The French drink their Bordeaux wines too young, afraid that the Socialist government will take them away. The English drink their Bordeaux wines very old because they like to take their friends down to their wine cellars with the cobwebs and dust to show off their old bottles. The Americans drink their Bordeaux wines exactly when they are ready to be drunk because they don't know any better."

—author unknown

Some ORGANIC / BIODYNAMIC ESTATES in Bordeaux:

Château Climens (Sauternes)
Château Durfort-Vivens (Margaux)
Château Fonplégade (St-Émilion)
Château Fonroque (St-Émilion)
Château Palmer (Margaux)
Château Pontet Canet (Pauillac)
Château La Tour-Figeac (St-Émilion)

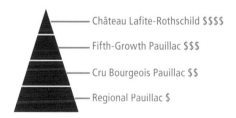

— Château Lafite-Rothschild $$$$
— Fifth-Growth Pauillac $$$
— Cru Bourgeois Pauillac $$
— Regional Pauillac $

The first growths Château Margaux, Château Latour, Château Lafite-Rothschild, and Château Mouton-Rothschild use less than 40 percent of the crop for their wines. **THE REST GOES INTO THEIR SECOND LABELS.**

In 2011, **ROBERT PARKER CONDUCTED A BORDEAUX TASTING** at WineFuture in Hong Kong, choosing "estates that produce wines of first-growth quality . . . and because they are undervalued and very smart acquisitions." He selected the following châteaux: Château Angelus, Château Brane-Cantenac, Château Clos Fourtet, Château Cos d'Estournel, Château Haut Bailly, Château La Conseillante, Château La Fleur Pétrus, Château Le Gay, Château Léoville Las Cases, Château Léoville Poyferré, Château Lynch Bages, Château Malescot St. Exupéry, Château Palmer, Château Pape Clément, Château Pichon Baron, Château Pichon Lalande, Château Pontet-Canet, Château Rauzan Ségla, Château Smith Haut Lafitte, and Château Trotanoy.

Another good way to avoid sky-high Bordeaux prices is to take the time to look for second-label wines. These wines come from the youngest parts of a vineyard, making them lighter in style, quicker to mature, and less expensive than first-label wines.

CHÂTEAU	EXAMPLES OF SECOND-LABELS
CHÂTEAU HAUT-BRION	LE CLARENCE DE HAUT-BRION
CHÂTEAU LAFITE-ROTHSCHILD	CARRUADES DE LAFITE
CHÂTEAU LATOUR	LES FORTS DE LATOUR
CHÂTEAU LÉOVILLE-BARTON	LA RÉSERVE LÉOVILLE-BARTON
CHÂTEAU LÉOVILLE-LAS-CASES	LE PETIT LION
CHÂTEAU LYNCH-BAGES	ECHO DE LYNCH-BAGES
CHÂTEAU MARGAUX	PAVILLON ROUGE DU CHÂTEAU MARGAUX
CHÂTEAU MOUTON-ROTHSCHILD	LE PETIT MOUTON
CHÂTEAU PALMER	ALTER EGO
CHÂTEAU PICHON LALANDE	RÉSERVE DE LA COMTESSE
CHÂTEAU PICHON-LONGUEVILLE	LES TOURELLES DE LONGUEVILLE
DOMAINE DE CHEVALIER	L'ESPIRIT DE CHEVALIER

FORTY YEARS LATER IN BORDEAUX

The most dramatic change in the entire wine world in the last four decades has been the worldwide demand for the best châteaux of Bordeaux. In 1985, the most important market for Bordeaux was the UK. In the 1980s and 1990s, interest in Bordeaux shifted to the Americans and Japanese. Today, Asia has become the new and growing market, particularly Hong Kong, South Korea, and China. All of which means increasingly higher prices for the best Bordeaux. In a way, it's the end of an era. As a young man, my first "eureka" wine moment came when I discovered that a 20-year-old Bordeaux cost less than $25—a lot of money for a college student but worth it. Few people today, young or otherwise, can afford the $3,000 price tag for one bottle of Château Pétrus 2005, which probably won't be ready to drink for another decade! The great châteaux have become wines of prestige reserved to the wealthy.

That said, we common folk still can find some excellent values from the other 7,000 châteaux. Since 1990, quality has filtered down to the entire region, which is making the best wines in Bordeaux history, especially in the Médoc, St-Émilion, Graves, Côtes de Bourg, and Côtes de Blaye.

---

5 BEST VALUE RED WINES OF BORDEAUX UNDER $30

Château Cantemerle • Château Greysac • Château La Cardonne • Château Larose-Trintaudon • Confidences de Prieure Lichine

See pages 358–359 for a complete list.

GUIDED TASTING

Bordeaux wines have a reputation of being expensive and requiring long aging, which isn't entirely true: 80 percent of all Bordeaux wines retail at between $8 and $25, and you can drink most of those either when you buy them or within two years of purchase. The two important points to consider as you taste these wines are the various hierarchies—quality classifications, growths, and labels—and the effects of the aging process.

Bordeaux Four wines tasted together:
1. Appellation Bordeaux Controlée
2. Appellation Region Controlée
3. Château: Cru Bourgeois
4. Château: Grand Cru Classé

When the **FOUR SEASONS RESTAURANT IN NEW YORK** opened in 1959, they served 1918 Château Lafite-Rothschild for $18, or a 1934 Château Latour for $16. They also offered a 1945 Château Cos d'Estournel for $9.50.

NIXON'S FAVORITE WINE WAS CHÂTEAU MARGAUX. He always had a bottle of his favorite vintage waiting at his table from the cellar of the famous "21" Club in New York.

LUXURY WINERIES

Bernard Arnault, CEO of LVMH and the richest man in France, owns Château d'Yquem, Château Cheval Blanc, and Krug Champagne. Brothers Alain and Gerard Wertheimer, who own Chanel, also own Château Canon and Château Rauzan-Ségla. Francois Pinault, CEO of Kering (Balenciaga, Yves St. Laurent, Gucci, Alexander McQueen), owns Château Latour. He's also Salma Hayek's husband. Lucky guy!

MIS EN BOUTEILLE AU CHATEAU
CHATEAU LES ORMES DE PEZ
SAINT-ESTÈPHE
1995
13.0%Vol   750ml
APPELLATION SAINT-ESTÈPHE CONTRÔLÉE
A. CAZES, PROPRIETAIRE A SAINT ESTEPHE (FRANCE)
PRODUCE OF FRANCE

Second Labels Two wines from the same producer, tasted together:
  5. Second-label Château wine
  6. First-label Château wine

The Bordeaux Growth Hierarchy Three wines tasted together, each wine from the same vintage:
  7. Château: Cru Bourgeois
  8. Château: Third, Fourth, or Fifth Growth
  9. Château: Second Growth

The Aging Process One wine tasted alone:
  10. Aged Bordeaux (at least ten years old)

FOOD PAIRINGS

"With **Château La Louvière Rouge**: roast leg of lamb or grilled duck breast."
  —*Denise Lurton-Moulle of Château La Louvière, Château Bonnet*

"For **Bordeaux red**, simple and classic is best! Red meat, such as beef and particularly lamb, as we love it in Pauillac. If you can grill the meat on vine cuttings, you are in heaven."
—*Jean-Michel Cazes of Château Lynch-Bages and Château Les Ormes-de-Pez*

"Sunday lunches at Le Pin include lots of local oysters with chilled white Bordeaux followed by thick entrecôte steaks on the barbecue with shallots and a selection of the family's **Pomerols, Margaux, or Côtes de France red Bordeaux.**   —*Jacques and Fiona Thienpont of Château Le Pin*

"With **red Bordeaux**: duck breast with wild mushrooms or guinea hen with grapes."   —*Antony Perrin of Château Carbonnieux*

"With red Bordeaux, especially **Pomerol** wine, lamb is a must."
          —*Christian Moueix*

TEST YOUR KNOWLEDGE of the red wines of Bordeaux by trying the quiz on page 379.

——— **FURTHER READING** ———

Bordeaux by Oz Clarke

Bordeaux by Robert M. Parker Jr.

The Bordeaux Atlas and Encyclopedia of Chateaux by Hubrecht Duijker and Michael Broadbent

Bordeaux Legends by Jane Anson

The Complete Bordeaux by Stephen Brook

The Finest Wines of Bordeaux by James Lawther

Grands Vins by Clive Coates

CLASS FOUR

THE RED WINES OF BURGUNDY AND THE RHÔNE VALLEY

UNDERSTANDING THE RED WINES OF BURGUNDY ✳ BEAUJOLAIS ✳
CÔTE CHÂLONNAISE ✳ CÔTE D'OR ✳ THE RHÔNE VALLEY ✳ ROSÉ

UNDERSTANDING THE RED WINES OF BURGUNDY

BURGUNDY REPRESENTS ONE of the most difficult subjects in the study of wines. People may say, "There's *so much* to know," and "It looks so hard." If you're having trouble understanding these wines, don't feel like you're alone. After the French Revolution in 1789, all the vineyards were sold off in small parcels. Then the Napoleonic Code instituted equal inheritance among heirs, which fragmented vineyards further. Burgundy has many villages and vineyards, and, yes, they're all important. You must memorize more than 1,000 names and more than 110 appellations to become a Burgundy wine expert. I'm going to help you decode the mysteries—regions, names, labels—but to understand, enjoy, and speak about Burgundy wines intelligently, you really need to know only 15 to 25 names.

The main red wine–producing regions are:

Beaujolais   Côte Châlonnaise   Côte d'Or { Côte de Nuits / Côte de Beaune

The two major grape varieties are:

Pinot Noir   Gamay

Under AOC laws, all red Burgundies must come from the Pinot Noir grape, except Beaujolais, which comes from the Gamay grape.

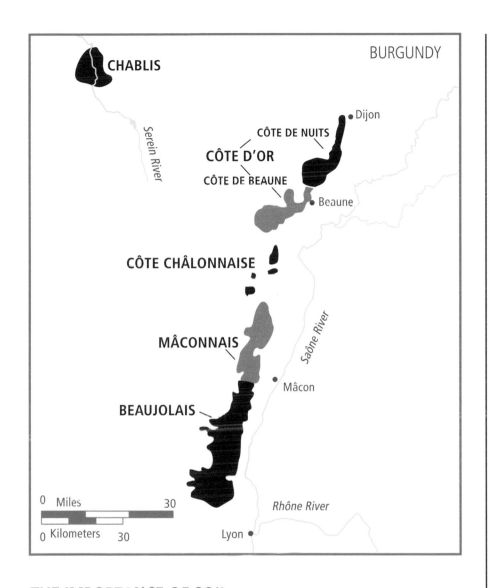

CHABLIS

Serein River

CÔTE DE NUITS

CÔTE D'OR

CÔTE DE BEAUNE

• Dijon

• Beaune

CÔTE CHÂLONNAISE

MÂCONNAIS

Saône River

BEAUJOLAIS

• Mâcon

| 0 | Miles | 30 |

| 0 | Kilometers | 30 |

Rhône River

Lyon •

Burgundy's reputation for winemaking dates as far back as 51 B.C.

THE MAGNIFICENT AND DIFFICULT PINOT NOIR

Pinot Noir's fame originates in Burgundy. It's difficult to make this thin-skinned grape into a great wine. It's susceptible to many diseases, and too much sunlight (heat) during the growing season kills the chances of a balanced wine. But if a grower proves both passionate and patient, a great Pinot Noir offers less tannin, less extraction of color, and less body. The best Pinot Noirs from Burgundy don't flex dense muscle but rather display an elegant finesse.

THE IMPORTANCE OF SOIL

Any producer of quality Burgundy will say that soil represents the most important element in making those wines. Terroir—soil composition, the slope of the land, and climatic conditions—determines whether a wine ranks as a Village, Premier Cru, or Grand Cru. On a trip I took to Burgundy, it rained for five straight days. On the sixth day, workers gathered at the bottom of the vineyard slopes with pails and shovels, collecting the soil that had run down the hillside to return it to the vineyard. That's how important soil is to Burgundy wines.

BEAUJOLAIS

Made from 100 percent Gamay grapes, Beaujolais typically tastes light and fruity, is meant to be consumed young, and can be chilled. Most bottles cost between $8 and $20, although price varies with quality. Beaujolais reigns as the best-selling Burgundy in America probably because there's so much of it, it's so easy to drink, and it's affordable.

All grapes in the Beaujolais region are picked by hand, and Beaujolais has three different quality levels:

Beaujolais This basic Beaujolais accounts for the majority produced. Cost: $.

Beaujolais-Villages This classification comes from certain villages, and 35 of them produce consistently better wines. Most Beaujolais-Villages contain a blend of wines from these villages, and the label usually doesn't feature a particular village name. Cost: $$.

Cru Named for the village that produces this highest quality of Beaujolais. Cost $$$$.

There are ten crus (villages):

Brouilly	Fleurie	Moulin-à-Vent
Chénas	Juliénas	Régnié
Chiroubles	Morgon	St-Amour
Côte de Brouilly		

Also look for these shippers / producers:

Bouchard	Duboeuf	Jadot
Drouhin		

How long you keep a Beaujolais depends on the quality level and the vintage. Beaujolais and Beaujolais-Villages will last between one and three years. Crus can last longer because they have more fruit and tannin. Some Beaujolais Crus maintain their excellence after more than ten years. But these prove the exception rather than the rule.

Beaujolais Nouveau releases on **THE THIRD THURSDAY IN NOVEMBER** amid great hoopla. Restaurants and retailers all vie to offer the new Beaujolais to their customers first.

BEAUJOLAIS NOUVEAU

Beaujolais Nouveau tastes even lighter and fruitier than your basic Beaujolais. This "new" Beaujolais undergoes fermentation and bottling and appears on retailer shelves in a matter of weeks, giving the winemaker a virtually instant return. Like a movie trailer, it also offers an indication of the quality of the vintage and style that the winemaker will produce for the regular Beaujolais the following spring. Drink Beaujolais Nouveau young, within six months of bottling. If you're holding a bottle significantly older than that . . . well, now's the time to give it to your "friends."

As a young wine student, I visited the Beaujolais region. In one village, I ordered a glass of Beaujolais, and the waiter brought me a chilled glass of wine. Every book I'd read always said to serve red wines at room temperature, but when it comes to Beaujolais Nouveau, Beaujolais, and Beaujolais-Villages, **CHILL THEM SLIGHTLY TO BRING OUT THE FRUIT AND ACIDITY.** Try a chilled Beaujolais in the summer, and you'll see what I mean. Beaujolais Crus have more fruit and tannin, though, and taste better at room temperature.

"Beaujolais is one of the very few red wines that can be drunk as a white. Beaujolais is my daily drink. And sometimes I blend one-half water to the wine. It is the most refreshing drink in the world."

—Didier Mommessin

— BEST RECENT VINTAGES OF BEAUJOLAIS —
2009** 2012* 2014* 2015** 2016 2017*
* EXCEPTIONAL VINTAGE ** EXTRAORDINARY VINTAGE

FOOD PAIRINGS

Beaujolais goes well with light, simple meals and cheeses that don't over-power. Try to match Beaujolais with veal, fish, or fowl, and take note of what some of the experts say:

"A lot of dishes can be eaten with **Beaujolais**. What you choose depends on the appellation and vintage. With charcuteries and pâtés, you can serve a young **Beaujolais or Beaujolais-Villages**. With grilled meat, more generous and fleshy wines, such as **Juliénas** and **Morgon crus,** can be served. With meats cooked in a sauce—for example, coq au vin—I would suggest a **Moulin-à-Vent cru** from a good vintage."
— *Georges Duboeuf*

"**Beaujolais** with simple meals, light cheeses, grilled meat—everything except sweets."
— *André Gagey of Louis Jadot*

CÔTE CHÂLONNAISE

These classic Pinot Noir wines offer tremendous value, and you should know three villages from this area:

| Mercurey | Givry | Rully |
| 95% red | 90% red | 50% red |

Of these, Mercurey (sounds like "ray") is most important, producing wines of high quality. Because they're not well known in America, Mercurey wines often make for a very good value. Look for these shippers/producers when buying Côte Châlonnaise wines:

If you see the word "monopole" on a Burgundy label, it comes from **JUST ONE WINERY.**

MERCUREY	GIVRY	RULLY
CHÂTEAU DE CHAMIREY	CHOFFLET-VALDENAIRE	ANTONIN RODET
DOMAINE DE SUREMAIN	DOMAINE JABLOT	
FAIVELEY	DOMAINE THENARD	
MICHEL JUILLOT	LOUIS LATOUR	

CÔTE D'OR

This is the beating heart of Burgundy. The Côte d'Or—pronounced "coat door"—means "gold coast." One theory holds that the region takes its name from autumnal foliage . . . as well as the income it brings to winemakers. Because the area is very small, its best wines rank among the priciest in the world. If you want a $9.99 bottle, look elsewhere!

The Côte d'Or consists of two regions:

Côte de Beaune — 70% red

Côte de Nuits — 95% red

The highest-quality red Burgundy wines come from the Côte de Nuits.

As with the white wines of the same region, these reds also have quality levels: regional, Village, Premier Cru, and Grand Cru. Scant Grand Cru wine is produced, but it has the highest quality and is extremely expensive. Regional wine, on the other hand, is more readily available, but very few rate as outstanding.

Quantity

—Regional (Bourgogne) —

— Bourgogne Côte d'Or —

———Village———

—Premier Cru vineyards —

—Grand Cru vineyards —

Quality

To understand the wines of the Côte d'Or, familiarize yourself with the most important villages, some of the Premier Cru vineyards, and of course the Grand Cru vineyards.

Bourgogne
Appellation Contrôlée

LEROY

GENERIC WINES ARE LABELED SIMPLY "BURGUNDY" OR "BOURGOGNE." A higher level of generic wines will say "Côte de Beaune Villages" or "Côte de Nuits Villages,"containing a blend of different Village wines.

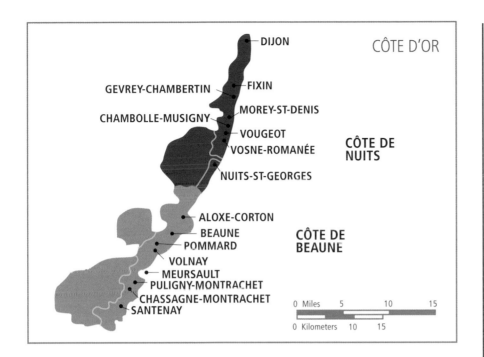

CÔTE D'OR

Map showing regions from Dijon south through the Côte de Nuits (DIJON, FIXIN, GEVREY-CHAMBERTIN, MOREY-ST-DENIS, CHAMBOLLE-MUSIGNY, VOUGEOT, VOSNE-ROMANÉE, NUITS-ST-GEORGES) and the Côte de Beaune (ALOXE-CORTON, BEAUNE, POMMARD, VOLNAY, MEURSAULT, PULIGNY-MONTRACHET, CHASSAGNE-MONTRACHET, SANTENAY).

Burgundy has more than 500 Premier Cru vineyards.

CÔTE DE BEAUNE

MOST IMPORTANT VILLAGES	MY FAVORITE PREMIER CRU VINEYARDS	GRAND CRU VINEYARDS
ALOXE-CORTON	CHAILLOTS FOURNIÈRES	CORTON CORTON BRESSANDES CORTON CLOS DU ROI CORTON MARÉCHAUDE CORTON RENARDES
BEAUNE	BRESSANDES CLOS DES MOUCHES FÈVES GRÈVES MARCONNETS	
POMMARD	ÉPENOTS RUGIENS	
VOLNAY	CAILLERETS CLOS DES CHÊNES SANTENOTS TAILLEPIEDS	

The Cote d'Or has **32 GRAND CRU VINEYARDS:** 24 red, 8 white, 24 from the Côte de Nuits, 8 from the Côte de Beaune.

By far the most-produced red Grand Cru is **CORTON,** representing about 25 percent of all Grand Cru red wines.

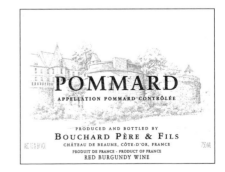

POMMARD
APPELLATION POMMARD CONTRÔLÉE

PRODUCED AND BOTTLED BY
BOUCHARD PÈRE & FILS
CHÂTEAU DE BEAUNE, CÔTE-D'OR, FRANCE
PRODUIT DE FRANCE · PRODUCT OF FRANCE
RED BURGUNDY WINE

In the 1800s, some villages in Burgundy added the name of their most famous **VINEYARD TO THE NAME OF THE VILLAGE.** Gevrey became Gevrey-Chambertin, and Puligny became Puligny-Montrachet. Can you name the others?

CHAMBERTIN CLOS DE BÈZE was Napoléon's favorite wine, of which he reportedly said: "Nothing makes the future look so rosy as to contemplate it through a glass of Chambertin." Perhaps he ran out at Waterloo!

Tucked between the Grands Crus La Tâche and La Romanée-Conti in Vosne-Romanée, La Grande-Rue ascended from being a Premier Cru **TO THE GRAND CRU LEVEL IN 1992.**

Clos de Vougeot is Burgundy's largest Grand Cru vineyard, at 125 acres and with more than 80 owners. Each owner makes his or her own winemaking decisions, such as when to pick the grapes, fermentation style, and how long to age the wine in oak. **ALL CLOS DE VOUGEOT IS NOT CREATED EQUAL.**

CÔTE DE NUITS

If you haven't been paying close attention to geography, start now. The majority of Grand Cru vineyards lie in this area.

MOST IMPORTANT VILLAGES	MY FAVORITE PREMIER CRU VINEYARDS	GRAND CRU VINEYARDS
CHAMBOLLE-MUSIGNY	CHARMES LES AMOUREUSES	BONNES MARES (PARTIAL) MUSIGNY
FLAGEY-ÉCHÉZEAUX		ÉCHÉZEAUX GRANDS-ÉCHÉZEAUX
GEVREY-CHAMBERTIN	AUX COMBOTTES CLOS ST-JACQUES LES CAZETIERS	CHAMBERTIN CHAMBERTIN CLOS DE BÈZE CHAPELLE-CHAMBERTIN CHARMES-CHAMBERTIN GRIOTTE-CHAMBERTIN LATRICIÈRES-CHAMBERTIN MAZIS-CHAMBERTIN MAZOYÈRES-CHAMBERTIN RUCHOTTES-CHAMBERTIN
MOREY-ST-DENIS	CLOS DES ORMES LES GENEVRIÈRES RUCHOTS	BONNES MARES (PARTIAL) CLOS DE LA ROCHE CLOS DE TART CLOS DES LAMBRAYS CLOS ST-DENIS
NUITS-ST-GEORGES	LES ST-GEORGES PORETS VAUCRAINS	
VOSNE-ROMANÉE	BEAUX-MONTS	LA GRANDE-RUE LA ROMANÉE LA ROMANÉE-CONTI LA ROMANÉE-ST-VIVANT LA TÂCHE MALCONSORTS RICHEBOURG
VOUGEOT		CLOS DE VOUGEOT

THE IMPORTANCE OF GEOGRAPHY

Geography helps make you a smart buyer. If you know the key villages and vineyards, you're more likely to make a better purchase. You don't have to memorize all the villages and vineyards, though. A label often contains all the information you need. Take a look at this one, and follow along:

Where is the wine from? France

What type of wine is it? Burgundy

Which region is it from? Côte d'Or

Which area? Côte de Nuits

Which village? Chambolle-Musigny

Anything else? Yes, the wine comes from Musigny, one of the 32 Grand Cru vineyards.

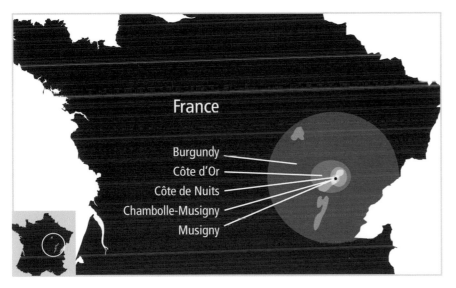

The more you zoom in, the better the quality of the wine, and the more it likely will cost. Why? Supply and demand. The growers and shippers of the Côte d'Or have a problem that all businesspeople envy: not enough supply to meet the demand. This has been the case for years and will continue because Burgundy is a small region that produces a limited amount of wine. (Bordeaux, by comparison, produces three times as much wine as Burgundy.)

VILLAGE ONLY = VILLAGE WINE $

VILLAGE + VINEYARD = PREMIER CRU $$

VINEYARD ONLY = GRAND CRU $$$$

In a restaurant, you order a Village wine—Gevrey-Chambertin, for example—and by mistake the waiter brings you a Grand Cru Le Chambertin. **WHAT WOULD YOU DO?**

Beginning with the 1990 vintage, all Grand Cru Burgundies must include the words **"GRAND CRU" ON THE LABEL.**

BURGUNDY WINE HARVEST IN CASES	
REGIONAL APPELLATIONS	2,136,674
BEAUJOLAIS	11,503,617
CHABLIS	755,188
CÔTE CHÂLONNAISE	357,539
CÔTE D'OR: CÔTE DE NUITS	511,594
CÔTE D'OR: CÔTE DE BEAUNE	1,391,168
MÂCONNAIS	2,136,674
OTHER APPELLATIONS	339,710
TOTAL HARVEST	**19,132,164**

(average number of cases over a five-year period for red and white)

In the 1960s, Burgundy wines were fermented and vatted for up to three weeks. Today's Burgundy wines usually are **FERMENTED AND VATTED FOR 6 TO 12 DAYS.**

BURGUNDY, PAST AND PRESENT
1970s: 15 percent domaine-bottled
2016: 60 percent domaine-bottled

KNOW YOUR VINTAGES and—because of the delicacy of the Pinot Noir grape—buy from a merchant who handles Burgundy wines with care.

FORTY YEARS LATER IN BURGUNDY

The red wines of Burgundy still stand as the benchmark for Pinot Noir throughout the world. Over the last 40 years, the great wines of Burgundy have improved—and of course become more expensive! The good wines have become more consistent and increased in quality. Both the shippers (*négociants*) and the estate-bottled producers are making the best wines that Burgundy has ever known. Better clonal selection, vineyard management, and a new generation of winemakers will continue this greatness for decades.

Look for these shippers / producers:

Bouchard Père et Fils	Jaffelin	Joseph Drouhin
Chanson	Louis Jadot	

Some fine estate-bottled wines are available in limited quantities in America. Look for the following:

Armand Rousseau	Henri Lamarche	Mongeard-Mugneret
Clerget	Jayer	Parent
Comte de Voguë	Jean Grivot	Pierre Damoy
Daniel Rion	Leroy	Pierre Gelin
Denis Mortet	Louis Trapet	Potel
Dujac	Lucien Le Moine	Pousse d'Or
Faiveley	Maison Champy	Prince de Mérode
Georges Roumier	Marquis d'Angerville	Romanée-Conti
Groffier	Méo Camuzet	Tollot-Beaut
Henri Gouges	Michel Gros	Vincent Girardin

> — BEST RECENT VINTAGES OF CÔTE D'OR —
> 1999* 2002** 2003* 2005** 2009** 2010** 2012**
> 2013* 2014** 2015** 2016* 2017**
>
> * EXCEPTIONAL VINTAGE   ** EXTRAORDINARY VINTAGE

> 5 BEST VALUE RED WINES OF BURGUNDY UNDER $30
>
> "Caves Jean Ernest Descombes" • Château de Mercey Mercurey Rouge •
> Louis Jadot Château des Jacques Moulin-à-Vent • Domaine Bouchard Pinot Noir •
> Joseph Drouhin Côte de Nuits-Village • Georges Duboeuf Morgon

See pages 358–359 for a complete list.

VALUE BURGUNDIES: Chorey-les-Beaune from Tollot-Beaut, Alex Gambal, Arnoux, and Champy

Burgundy, 2016: **WORST FROSTS** in more than 30 years.

Many wine writers and Burgundy lovers describe the taste of Pinot Noir as **SEDUCTIVE AND SMOOTH.**

FOOD PAIRINGS

"White wine is never a good accompaniment to red meat, but a light red **Burgundy** can match a fish course (not shellfish). Otherwise, for light red Burgundies, white meat—not too many spices; partridge, pheasant, and rabbit. For heavier-style wines, lamb and steak are good choices."

—*Robert Drouhin*

—— FURTHER READING ——

Burgundy by Anthony Hanson

Burgundy by Robert M. Parker Jr.

The Great Domaines of Burgundy by Remington Norman

Making Sense of Burgundy by Matt Kramer

The Original Grand Crus of Burgundy by Charles Curtis

The Wines of Burgundy by Clive Coates

"With red **Beaujolais** wines, such as Moulin-à-Vent Château des Jacques, for example, a piece of pork like an andouillette from Fleury is beautiful. A **Gamay**, more fruity and fleshy than Pinot Noir, goes perfectly with this typical meal from our terroir. My favorite food combination with a red **Burgundy** wine is poulet de bresse demi d'oeil. The very thin flesh of this truffle-filled chicken and the elegance and delicacy from the great **Pinot Noir**, which comes from the best terroir, go together beautifully."

—*Pierre Henry Gagey of Louis Jadot*

"With **Château Corton Grancey**, filet of duck in a red-wine sauce. Otherwise, **Pinot Noir** is good with roast chicken, venison, and beef. Mature wines are a perfect combination for our local cheeses, Chambertin and Citeaux."

—*Louis Latour*

THE RHÔNE VALLEY

The winemaking regions of the Rhône Valley fall into two distinct areas: northern and southern. The most famous reds from the northern region include:

Crozes-Hermitage	Côte Rôtie	Hermitage
(3,059 acres)	(580 acres)	(345 acres)

Also look for St-Joseph and Cornas.

The most famous reds from the southern region are:

Châteauneuf-du-Pape	Gigondas
(7,907 acres)	(3,036 acres)

The two major grape varieties in the Rhône Valley are:

Grenache	Syrah

From the North, Côte Rôtie, Crozes-Hermitage, and Hermitage come primarily from the Syrah grape. These are the region's biggest and fullest wines. From the South, Châteauneuf-du-Pape can contain a blend of as many as 13 different grape varieties, but the best producers use a higher percentage of Grenache and Syrah in the blend.

When I worked as a sommelier, diners often asked me to recommend a big, robust red Burgundy to complement a rack of lamb or filet mignon. To their surprise, I didn't recommend a Burgundy at all. The best bet is a red Rhône. Typically bigger and fuller than Burgundies, Rhône wine usually has a higher alcohol content, and the reason goes back to geography. The Rhône Valley lies in southeastern France, south of Burgundy, where the climate runs sunny and hot. The sun gives the grapes more sugar, which boosts the alcohol level. The rocks in the soil also retain the intense summer heat, both day and night. By law, Rhône Valley winemakers must create wines containing a specified amount of alcohol. For example, AOC regulations require

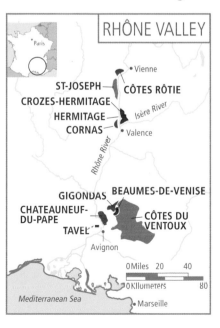

RHÔNE VALLEY

Some of the oldest vineyards in France lie in the Rhône Valley. Hermitage, for example, has been in existence for **MORE THAN 2,000 YEARS.**

THE CRUS OF THE RHÔNE VALLEY

North	South
Château-Grillet (white)	Beaumes de Venise (red, natural sweet)
Condrieu (white)	Cairanne (red)
Cornas (red)	Châteauneuf-du-Pape (red, white)
Côte-Rôtie (red)	
Crozes-Hermitage (red, white)	Gigondas (red, rosé)
Hermitage (red, white)	Lirac (red, rosé, white)
St-Joseph (red, white)	Rasteau (red, natural sweet)
St-Peray	Tavel (rosé)
	Vacqueyras (red, rosé, white)
	Vinsobres (red)

LEADING ACREAGE OF GRENACHE / GARNACHA

France: 237,000 acres

Spain: 205,000 acres

Italy: 55,000 acres

America: 10,000 acres

Australia: 9,900 acres

LEADING ACREAGE OF SYRAH/SHIRAZ

France: (169,000 acres)

Australia: (105,000 acres)

WINES MADE IN THE RHÔNE VALLEY

Red 93%

White 7%

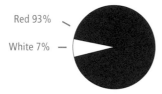

Côtes du Rhône wine can come from grapes grown in either or both of the two Rhône regions, but **MORE THAN 90 PERCENT OF ALL CÔTES DU RHÔNE** wines come from the southern region.

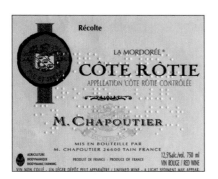

REGION	HOURS OF SUNSHINE PER YEAR
Burgundy	2,000
Bordeaux	2,050
Châteauneuf-du-Pape	2,750

a 10.5 percent minimum for Côtes du Rhône and 12.5 percent for Châteauneuf-du-Pape. A simple Côtes du Rhône parallels a Beaujolais, except the Côtes du Rhône has more body and alcohol. (A Beaujolais must contain a minimum of just 9 percent alcohol.)

The two most famous white wines of the Rhône Valley, Condrieu and Château Grillet, are made from the Viognier grape. There's a white Châteauneuf-du-Pape as well as a white Hermitage, but only a few thousand cases are produced each year.

Unlike Bordeaux and Burgundy, Rhône Valley wines have no official classification system, but the different quality levels are:

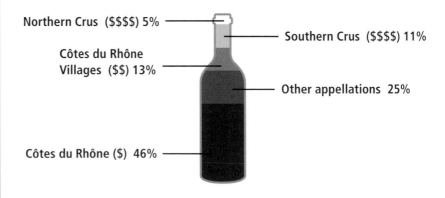

Northern Crus ($$$$) 5%

Southern Crus ($$$$) 11%

Côtes du Rhône Villages ($$) 13%

Other appellations 25%

Côtes du Rhône ($) 46%

CHÂTEAUNEUF-DU-PAPE

Châteauneuf-du-Pape means "the pope's new castle," so named for the Avignon palace in which Pope Clement V resided in the fourteenth century, heralding the nearly 70-year Avignon Papacy. Winemakers can use 13 different grapes for Châteauneuf-du-Pape. Those who use more of the best grapes—like a chef cooking only with the finest, organic ingredients, for example—produce the best-tasting and the most expensive wines. A $25 bottle of Châteauneuf-du-Pape may contain only 20 percent of top-quality grapes (Grenache, Mourvèdre, Syrah, and Cinsault). A $75 bottle may contain 90 percent of those top-quality grapes.

CHOOSING A RED RHÔNE WINE

First decide whether you prefer a light Côtes du Rhône or a bigger, more flavorful one, such as an Hermitage. Then consider the vintage and the producer. Two of the oldest and best-known firms are M. Chapoutier and Paul Jaboulet Aîné.

Here are some of the best producers:

NORTHERN RHÔNE

Delas Frères	Jean-Louis Chave	Paul Jaboulet Aîné
E. Guigal	Jean-Luc-Colombo	René Rostaing
Ferraton Père et Fils	Marc Sorel	Stéphane Ogier
Francois Villard	M. Chapoutier	Yves Cuilleron
Jamet		

SOUTHERN RHÔNE, CHÂTEAUNEUF-DU-PAPE

Beaucastel	Domaine du Pégaü	Domaine St-Préfert
Bosquet des Papes	Domaine de la Vielle	Domaine Vacheron-
Château La Nerthe	Julienne	Pouizin
Château Rayas	Domaine du Vieux	Le Vieux Donjon
Clos des Papes	Télégraphe	Mont Redon
Domaine de la Janasse	Domaine Giraud	Roger Sabon & Fils
Domaine du Banneret		

SOUTHERN RHÔNE, GIGONDAS

Château de St-Cosme	Notre Dame des	Pierre-Henri Morel
Domaine La	Paillières	Tardieu-Laurent
Bouissièrel	Olivier Ravoire	

The medieval **PAPAL COAT OF ARMS** appears on some Châteauneuf-du-Pape bottles. Only owners of vineyards can use this coat of arms on their labels.

THE 13 GRAPES ALLOWED IN CHÂTEAUNEUF-DU-PAPE

Grenache	Muscardin
Syrah	Vaccarèse
Mourvèdre	Picardin
Cinsault	Clairette
Picpoul	Roussanne
Terret	Bourboulenc
Counoise	

The first 4 grapes represent 92 percent of the grapes used, with Grenache by far the most.

CÔTES DU VENTOUX IS A GOOD VALUE.
One of the most widely available wines to look for in this category is La Vieille Ferme.

An exception to the aging rule, Hermitage is the best and **THE LONGEST-LIVED OF RHÔNE WINES**. In a great vintage, Hermitage wines can last for more than 50 years.

OLDER GREAT VINTAGES
NORTH: 1983, 1985, 1988, 1989, 1990, 1991
SOUTH: 1985, 1988, 1989, 1990

RHÔNE VALLEY VINTAGES CAN BE TRICKY: a good year in the North may be a bad year in the South, and vice versa.

Rhône Valley wines prove that not all great wines need age. Here's when to drink them:

Tavel Within two years

Côtes du Rhône Within three years

Crozes-Hermitage Within five years

Châteauneuf-du-Pape After five years, but higher quality Châteauneuf-du-Pape tastes better after ten

Hermitage Within seven to eight years, but a great vintage tastes best after fifteen

FORTY YEARS LATER IN THE RHÔNE VALLEY

Four decades ago, the red wines of Burgundy and Bordeaux overshadowed Rhône Valley wines. Today all three are equals, except the best quality value wines come from the Rhône. The region also has benefited from great weather over the last decade, especially in the south. All of which makes for superb wines at a reasonable cost.

— **BEST VINTAGES OF RED RHÔNE VALLEY WINES** —
NORTH: 1999* 2003* 2005* 2006* 2007* 2009** 2010**
2011* 2012* 2013* 2014 2015** 2016

SOUTH: 1998* 2000* 2001* 2003* 2004* 2005** 2006*
2007** 2009* 2010** 2011* 2012* 2015** 2015 2016

* EXCEPTIONAL VINTAGE ** EXTRAORDINARY VINTAGE

5 BEST VALUE RED WINES OF THE RHÔNE VALLEY UNDER $30

Château Cabrières Côte du Rhône • Château de Trignon Gigondas • Guigal Côtes du Rhône • Michel Poniard Crozes-Hermitage • Perrin & Fils Côtes du Rhône

See pages 358–359 for a complete list.

GUIDED TASTING

In order of importance, the three points to know about red Burgundy wines are the producer, vintage, and quality ranking. Take note of these details after tasting each wine in this flight. Whether it's a simple, medium-bodied Côtes du Rhône; a spicy Crozes-Hermitage; or a voluptuous, high-alcohol Châteauneuf-du-Pape, these are some of the greatest wines in the world and still offer some of the best values.

Beaujolais Two Beaujolais wines compared:
1. Beaujolais Villages
2. Beaujolais Cru

Côte Châlonnaise One wine tasted alone:
3. A wine from Côte Châlonnaise

Côte d'Or Two Côte de Beaune wines compared:
4. Village wine
5. Premier Cru

Two Côte de Nuits wines compared:
6. Village wine
7. Premier Cru

Côtes du Rhône Three Côtes du Rhône wines compared:
8. Côtes du Rhône
9. Crozes-Hermitage
10. Châteauneuf-du-Pape

AMERICAN IMPORTS of Rhône wines have risen more than 200 percent in the last five years

If you **PREFER SWEET WINES**, try Beaumes-de-Venise, made from the Muscat grape.

FOOD PAIRINGS

"Red Rhône wines achieve their perfection from ten years and beyond and are best when combined with game and other meats with a strong flavor. A good dinner could be wild mushroom soup and truffles with a white Beaucastel, and stew of wild hare à la royale [with foie gras and truffles] served with a red **Château de Beaucastel**."

> —*Jean Pierre and François Perrin of Château de Beaucastel*

"My granddad drinks a bottle of Côtes du Rhône a day, and he's in his eighties. It's good for youth. It goes with everything except old fish! Hermitage is good with wild boar and mushrooms. A Crozes Hermitage complements venison or roast rabbit in a cream sauce, but you have to be very careful with the sauce and the weight of the wine. Beef ribs and rice go well with a **Côtes du Rhône**, as does a game bird like roast quail. **Tavel**, slightly chilled, is refreshing with a summer salad. **Muscat de Beaumes-de-Venise** is a beautiful match with foie gras."

> —*Frédéric Jaboulet*

With a **Côtes du Rhône**, Michel Chapoutier recommends poultry, light meats, and cheese. **Côte Rôtie** goes well with white meats and small game. **Châteauneuf-du-Pape** complements the ripest of cheese, the richest venison, and the most lavish civet of wild boar. An **Hermitage** is suitable with beef, game, and any full-flavored cheese.

TEST YOUR KNOWLEDGE of the red wines of Burgundy and the Rhône Valley by trying the quiz on page 381.

——— **FURTHER READING** ———
The Wines of the Rhône Valley by Robert M. Parker Jr.

ROSÉ

This style was probably the first type of red wine. In the early days of wine-making (as in B.C.), most red wines were made to be consumed immediately, and most vintners didn't age them. Thus, most wines made from red grapes looked more pink than the deep, dark red wines we have today.

My earliest memories of rosé are rosados from Portugal. The two most famous were Mateus and Lancers. They appealed to us poor college students because they were inexpensive, easy to drink (some sweetness and slightly sparkling), and the empty bottles made good candleholders for dorm rooms! When I started working in a restaurant, the rosé on the wine list came from a region in the Rhône Valley called Tavel. It tasted totally dry and quite different from the Portuguese rosados. Then, in the 1970s, a California winery took the market by storm with White Zinfandel, which created a new category: "blush" wine.

In my 40-year career in wine, rosé was always an afterthought. Stores and restaurants usually stocked one or two. The most popular was rosé Champagne, and sales of both still and sparkling rosé were seasonal. Until recently, they were considered cheap, sweet wines. Not anymore! Rosé has become one of the leading categories of wine sales in America. Today, some rosés, especially from France, are very expensive ($100+) and are on allocation!

WHAT IS ROSÉ?

By leaving the skins to soak with the juice (maceration), winemakers extract both color and tannin from red grapes. A rosé is a red wine with less color. If it has less color, then it also has lower tannins than red wine, making it easier to drink with more fruit accessible up front—less maceration, low tannins, more fruit. Any grape that vintners use to make red wine can make rosé. In Provence, the primary grapes are Carignan, Cinsault, Grenache, Syrah, Mourvèdre, and Cabernet Sauvignon. In Tavel, it's Grenache.

The original name for Sutter Home's White Zinfandel was "Oeil de Perdrix," which means **EYE OF THE PARTRIDGE.**

Two methods of making **ROSÉ CHAMPAGNE**: 1) add red wine to the blend; 2) leave the red grape skins in contact with the must for a short period of time.

Retail sales of rosé in the USA increased by **MORE THAN 50 PERCENT** in 2017!

Rosé makes **A GREAT APERITIF** and goes well with light, textured foods.

WHO MAKES THE BEST ROSÉ?

COUNTRY	REGION	SUBREGION
1. FRANCE	PROVENCE	BANDOL
	RHÔNE VALLEY	TAVEL, GIGONDAS, LIRAC,
	LOIRE	ANJOU
	CHAMPAGNE	
	LANGUEDOC-ROUSSILLON	
	JURA	
2. ITALY	ABRUZZO	
(ROSATO)	FRIULI	
	TRENTINO	
	SICILY	
	CALABRIA	
	APULIA	
	VALLE D'AOSTA	
3. SPAIN	NAVARRA	
(ROSADO)	ALICANTE	
	JUMILLA	
4. AMERICA	CALIFORNIA	
	LONG ISLAND	
5. GERMANY	BADEN	
(ROSEWEIN)	WURTTEMBERG	

CORSICA has a long history of making rosé with French, Italian, and Spanish grapes such as Carignan, Vermentino, and Garnacha. Look for Clos Canarelli and Domaine Abbatucci.

National **ROSÉ DAY** in America is June 10.

TAVEL

This rosé stands apart from most others because of its unusual dryness. It comes primarily from the Grenache grape, although nine grape varieties can go into the blend. At heart, Tavel is just like a red wine, with all the same components but less color. How does that happen? It's all about the vatting process.

With short-vatted wines, the grape skins ferment with the must for a short time, only long enough to impart that rosé color. With long-vatted wines—such as Châteauneuf-du-Pape or Hermitage—the skins ferment longer with the must, giving a rich, ruby color to the wine.

GARRIGUE, a Mediterranean herb, is one of the distinct aromas of Provençal rosé.

——— **FURTHER READING** ———
Rosé Wine by Jennifer Simonetti-Bryan

PROVENCE

This is France's oldest wine-producing region, dating back more than 2,600 years. It has a classic Mediterranean climate, with mild winters and warm summers. Provence contains eight AOC regions. The largest is Côtes de Provence and the most famous is Bandol. The primary grape of Bandol is Mourvèdre, and rosé accounts for 90 percent of all Provençal wines.

My favorite Provence producers include:

Château d'Esclans	Clos Sainte Magdeleine	Domaine Tempier
Château de Pibarnon	Domaine de Trevallon	La Bastide Blanche
Château Font du Broc	Domaine Hauvette	Terrebrune
Château Simone	Domaine Ott	

OTHER ROSÉS

My favorite Tavel producers include:

Château d'Aqueria	Château de Trinquevedel

My favorite Loire producers include:

Claude Riffault Sancerre	Rosé Lucien-Crochet Sancerre Rosé
Domaine Vacheron Sancerre Rosé	

My favorite American rosés include:

Hartford Court Rosé of Pinot Noir (California)	Soter North Valley Highland Rosé (Oregon)
Provenance (California)	Wolffer Estate (Long Island)

SHADES OF ROSÉ

Provence pink ← → ← Other regions →

Cinsault, Grenache, Syrah

Cabernet Sauvignon, Merlot, Montepulciano d'Abruzzo, Pinot Noir, Sangiovese, Tempranillo, Zinfandel

The longer the juice remains in contact with the grape skins, the darker it becomes.

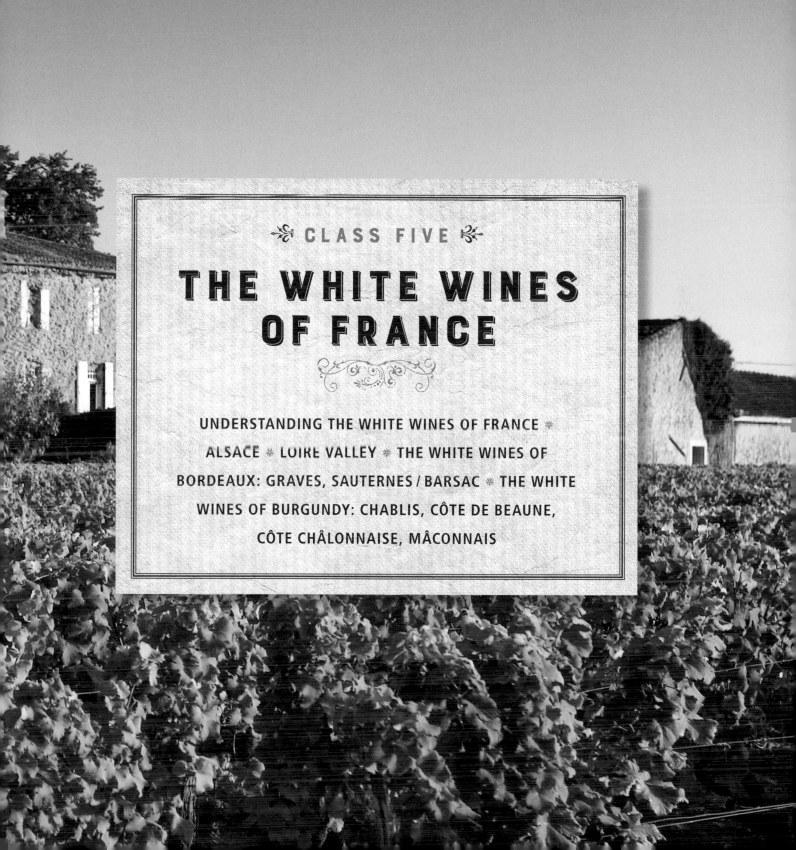

THE WHITE WINES OF FRANCE

UNDERSTANDING THE WHITE WINES OF FRANCE *
ALSACE * LOIRE VALLEY * THE WHITE WINES OF
BORDEAUX: GRAVES, SAUTERNES / BARSAC * THE WHITE
WINES OF BURGUNDY: CHABLIS, CÔTE DE BEAUNE,
CÔTE CHÂLONNAISE, MÂCONNAIS

UNDERSTANDING THE WHITE WINES OF FRANCE

The major white wine–producing Regions of France are:

Alsace   **Loire Valley**   **Bordeaux**   **Burgundy**

CHAMPAGNE is another major white-wine producer, but that's for another class.

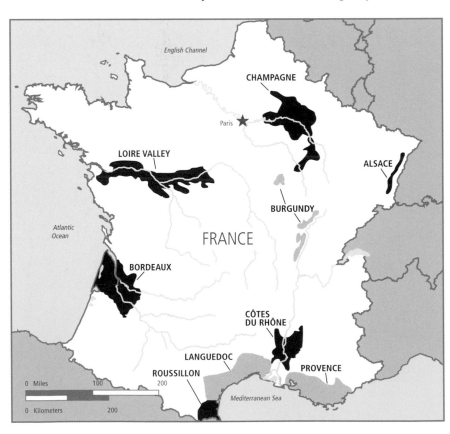

Let's start with Alsace and the Loire Valley because these two regions specialize in white wines. As you can see from the map, Alsace, the Loire Valley, and Chablis (a white wine–producing region of Burgundy) all lie in the northern half of France. These areas produce predominantly white wines because of the shorter growing season and cooler climate best suited for growing white grapes.

ALSACE

People often confuse the wines from Alsace with those from Germany. But the confusion can be justified because, from 1871 to 1919, Alsace belonged to Germany and both wines are sold in tall bottles with tapering necks. To confuse matters further, Alsace and Germany grow the same grape varieties. But when you think of Riesling, what are your associations? You'll probably answer "Germany" and "sweetness." That's a typical response, and that's because German winemakers add a small amount of naturally sweet unfermented grape juice back into the wine to create the distinctive German Riesling. The winemaker from Alsace ferments every bit of the sugar in the grapes, which is why 90 percent of all Alsace wines are totally dry.

Another fundamental difference between wine from Alsace and wine from Germany is the alcohol content. Wine from Alsace has 11 to 12 percent alcohol, while most German wine has a mere 8 to 9 percent.

The four white grapes grown in Alsace you should know are:

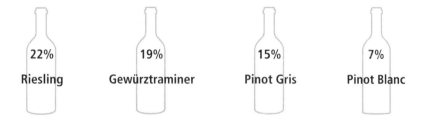

| 22% | 19% | 15% | 7% |
| Riesling | Gewürztraminer | Pinot Gris | Pinot Blanc |

ALSACE HAS LITTLE RAINFALL, especially during the grape harvest. The town of Colmar—the Alsace wine center—is the second driest in France. That's why they say a "one-shirt harvest" will be a good vintage.

38,500 ACRES OF GRAPES are planted in Alsace, but the average plot of land for each grower is only 5 acres.

Pinot Gris is the same grape as Pinot Grigio.

THE THREE AOCS OF ALSACE

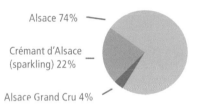

Alsace 74%

Crémant d'Alsace (sparkling) 22%

Alsace Grand Cru 4%

All wines produced in **ALSACE ARE AOC-DESIGNATED** and represent nearly 20 percent of all AOC white wines in France.

TWO GREAT SWEET (LATE HARVEST) WINES from Alsace are Vendange Tardive (like German Auslese) and Sélection de Grains Nobles (like German Beerenauslese).

AS THIS LABEL INDICATES, Hugel & Fils began producing wine in 1639.

TYPES OF WINE PRODUCED IN ALSACE

Virtually all Alsace wines are dry, and 90 percent of the wines produced are white. Riesling is the major grape planted here, and it's responsible for the highest-quality wines of the region. Alsace is also known for its Gewürztraminer, which stands in a class by itself. Most people either love it or hate it because Gewürztraminer has a very distinctive style. *Gewürz* is the German word for "spice," which aptly describes the wine. Pinot Blanc and Pinot Gris are becoming increasingly popular among the growers of Alsace as well.

QUALITY LEVELS OF ALSACE WINES

The shipper's reputation determines the quality of Alsace wines rather than any labeling on the bottle. That said, the vast majority of any given Alsace wine is the shipper's varietal. A very small percentage is labeled with a specific vineyard's name, especially for an Alsace Grand Cru. Some wines are labeled "Réserve" or "Réserve Personelle," terms not legally defined.

CHOOSING AN ALSACE WINE

Consider two important factors in choosing a wine from Alsace: the grape variety and the reputation and style of the shipper. Some of the most reliable shippers include:

Domaine Dopff au Moulin	Domaine Trimbach
Domaine Hugel & Fils	Domaine Weinbach
Domaine Léon Beyer	Domaine Zind-Humbrecht
Domaine Marcel Deiss	

The majority of grape growers (approximately 4,600) in Alsace don't grow enough grapes to make it economically feasible to produce and market their own wine. Instead, they sell their grapes to a shipper who produces, bottles, and markets the wine under its own name. The art of making high-quality Alsace wine lies in the selection of grapes that each shipper makes.

Alsace is known also for its **FRUIT BRANDIES**, or *eaux-de-vie*:

  FRAISE: strawberries

  FRAMBOISE: raspberries

  KIRSCH: cherries

  MIRABELLE: yellow plums

  POIRE: pears

SHOULD ALSACE WINES BE AGED?

In general, most Alsace wines are made to be consumed young—from one to five years after bottling. In Alsace, as in any fine-wine area, a small percentage of great wines may be aged for ten years or more.

FOR THE TOURIST: Visit the beautiful wine village of Riquewihr, which has buildings that date from the fifteenth and sixteenth centuries.

FORTY YEARS LATER IN ALSACE

I'm enjoying the same producers, such as Trimbach and Hugel, as I did decades ago. A dry, crisp, acidic Riesling is still one of my favorite wines to have at the beginning of a meal, especially with a fish appetizer. Pinot Blanc is a perfect summer picnic wine or for wine by the glass at a restaurant, and the famous Gewürztraminer is one of the most unique and flavorful wines in the world.

The best part about Alsace wines is that they are still very affordable, of good quality, and available throughout America.

Alsace produces 9 percent of its red wines from the Pinot Noir grape. These generally are **CONSUMED IN THE REGION** and rarely are exported.

– BEST RECENT VINTAGES OF ALSACE –

2005** 2007** 2008** 2009** 2010**
2011** 2012** 2013* 2014* 2015** 2016

* EXCEPTIONAL VINTAGE   ** EXTRAORDINARY VINTAGE

—— **FURTHER READING** ——

Alsace and Its Wine Gardens by S. F. Hallgarten

Alsace Wines and Spirits by Pamela Vandyke Price

FOOD PAIRINGS

"Alsace wines are not suited only to classic Alsace and other French dishes. For instance, I adore **Riesling** with raw fish specialties such as Japanese sushi and sashimi, while our **Gewürztraminer** is delicious with smoked salmon and brilliant with Chinese, Thai, and Indonesian food.

"**Pinot Blanc** is round, soft, not aggressive . . . an all-purpose wine . . . that can be used as an apéritif, with all kinds of pâté and charcuterie, and also with hamburgers. Perfect for brunch—not too sweet or flowery."

—*Étienne Hugel*

"**Riesling** with fish—blue trout with a light sauce. **Gewürztraminer** as an apéritif; with foie gras or any pâté at meal's end; or with Muenster cheese or a stronger cheese such as Roquefort." —*Hubert Trimbach*

LOIRE VALLEY

Starting at the city of Nantes, a bit upriver from the Atlantic Ocean, the Loire Valley stretches inland for six hundred miles along the Loire River.

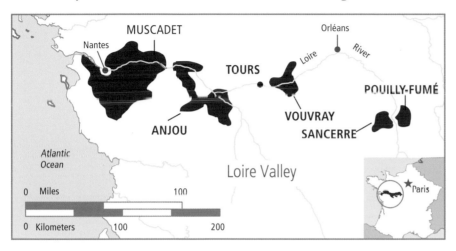

Loire Valley

You should be familiar with two white-grape varieties here:

Sauvignon Blanc   Chenin Blanc

In the Loire Valley, more than 50 percent of the AOC wines produced are white, and 96 percent of those are dry. Rather than choosing by grape variety and shipper, as you would in Alsace, choose Loire Valley wines by style and vintage. These are the main styles:

Muscadet A light, dry wine, made from 100 percent Melon de Bourgogne grapes. If you see the phrase "sur lie" on a Muscadet wine label, it means that the wine aged on its lees (sediment) for at least one winter.

Pouilly-Fumé A dry wine that has the most body and concentration of all the Loire Valley wines. It's made with 100 percent Sauvignon Blanc. The distinct nose of Pouilly-Fumé comes from a combination of the Sauvignon Blanc grape and the soil of the Loire Valley.

Sancerre Striking a balance between full-bodied Pouilly-Fumé and light-bodied Muscadet, it's made with 100 percent Sauvignon Blanc.

Vouvray This "chameleon" can be dry, semisweet, or sweet and is made from 100 percent Chenin Blanc.

The Loire Valley is the **LARGEST WHITE-WINE REGION** in France and second largest in sparkling-wine production.

Most Pouilly-Fumé and Sancerre wines are **NOT AGED IN WOOD**.

MY FAVORITE PRODUCERS

MUSCADET: Choblet, Métaireau, Marquis de Goulaine, Sauvion

POUILLY-FUMÉ: Château de Tracy, Colin, Dagueneau, Guyot, Jean-Paul Balland, Jolivet, Ladoucette, Michel Redde

SANCERRE: Archambault, Château de Sancerre, Domaine Fournier, Henri Bourgeois, Jean Vacheron, Jolivet, Lucien Crochet, Roblin, Sauvion

SAVENNIERES: Château d'Epiré, Damien Laureau, Domaine du Closel, Nicolas Joly

VOUVRAY: Domaine d'Orfeuilles, Huët

Other Sauvignon Blanc wines from the Loire to **TRY: MENETOU-SALON AND QUINCY**. For Chenin Blanc, try **SAVENNIÈRES**.

POUILLY-FUMÉ

Many people ask whether Pouilly-Fumé is smoked because they automatically associate the word *fumé* with smoke. Two of the many theories about the origin of the word come from the white morning mist that blankets the area. As the sun burns off the mist, it looks like smoke rising. Others say it's the "smokelike" bloom on Sauvignon Blanc grapes.

WHEN ARE THE WINES READY TO DRINK?

Generally, Loire Valley wines are meant to be consumed young. The exception is a sweet Vouvray, which can be aged for a longer time. Here are more specific guidelines:

Muscadet	Sancerre	Pouilly-Fumé
one to two years	two to three years	three to five years

POUILLY-FUMÉ VS. POUILLY-FUISSÉ

Students often ask whether these similarly named wines are related. Pouilly-Fumé is made from 100 percent Sauvignon Blanc and comes from the Loire Valley. Pouilly-Fuissé is made from 100 percent Chardonnay and comes from the Mâconnais region of Burgundy (page 189).

FORTY YEARS LATER IN THE LOIRE VALLEY

I am still enamored of the quality and diversity of the white wines of the Loire Valley. Forty years ago, the most important Loire Valley wine was Pouilly-Fumé. Today Sancerre is the most popular Loire wine in America. Both wines come from the same grape variety, 100 percent Sauvignon Blanc, both are medium-bodied with great acidity and fruit balance, and both are perfect food wines. Muscadet continues to be a great value, and Vouvray is still the best example of the quality that the Chenin Blanc grape can achieve. The wines have maintained their style and character, representing great value for the consumer.

FOR RED WINES look to Bourgueil, Chinon, and Saumur, all made from the Cabernet Franc grape.

Like rosé? Try a Sancerre rosé made from Pinot Noir. The Loire Valley also produces the **WORLD-FAMOUS ANJOU ROSÉ.**

– BEST RECENT VINTAGES OF THE LOIRE VALLEY –
2005* 2009* 2010* 2015* 2016**
*EXCEPTIONAL VINTAGE ** EXTRAORDINARY VINTAGE*

FOOD PAIRINGS

"All you have to do is look at the map to see where **Muscadet** is made: by the sea where the main fare is shellfish, clams, and oysters.

"With Pouilly-Fumé, smoked salmon; turbot with hollandaise; white meat chicken; veal with cream sauce.

"Shellfish, simple food of the sea because **Sancerre** is drier than Pouilly-Fumé."
                                                                    —*Baron Patrick de Ladoucette*

"A nice semidry Vouvray with fruit and cheese. **Muscadet** is good with a huge variety of excellent and fresh 'everyday' foods, including all the seafood from the Atlantic Ocean, the fish from the river—pike, for instance—game, poultry, and cheese (mainly goat cheese). Of course, there is a must in the region of Nantes: freshwater fish with the world-famous butter sauce, the beurre blanc, invented at the turn of the century by Clémence, who happened to be the chef at Goulaine."
                                                                    —*Robert, Marquis de Goulaine*

The Loire Valley is famous not only for its wines but also as a **SUMMER RETREAT FOR ROYALTY**. Elegant and sometimes enormous châteaux embellish the countryside.

THE WHITE WINES OF BORDEAUX

BORDEAUX DOESN'T MEAN JUST RED WINE

That's a misconception. Two of the five major areas of Bordeaux—Graves and Sauternes—are known for their excellent white wines. Sauternes is world-famous for its sweet white wine. The major white-grape varieties used in both areas are:

Sauvignon Blanc   **Sémillon**

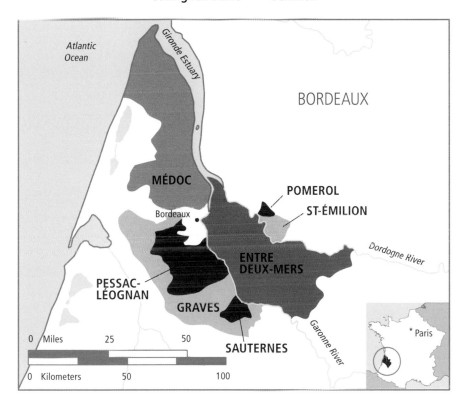

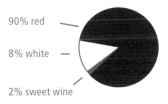

BORDEAUX PRODUCTION

90% red

8% white

2% sweet wine

GRAND CRU CLASSÉ DE GRAVES

Château Olivier

PESSAC-LÉOGNAN
APPELLATION PESSAC-LÉOGNAN CONTROLÉE

GROUPEMENT FONCIER AGRICOLE DU CHATEAU OLIVIER
J.-J. DE BETHMANN - PROPRIÉTAIRE
LÉOGNAN - 33850 - GIRONDE - FRANCE

MIS EN BOUTEILLE AU CHATEAU

12,5% vol   PRODUCE OF FRANCE   75 cl

GRAVES

Graves means "gravel"—the type of soil found in the region. White Graves wines are classified by two levels of quality:

Graves   **Pessac-Léognan**

The most basic Graves is called simply Graves. Wines labeled "Graves" come from the southern portion of the region surrounding Sauternes.

When the original edition of the *Complete Wine Course* came out in 1985, the appellation "Pessac-Léognan" had not yet been established. Since 1987, this **"NEW" APPELLATION IS YOUR GUARANTEE** of the finest dry white wines in Bordeaux.

CLASSIFIED WHITE CHÂTEAU WINES make up only 3 percent of the total production of white Graves.

THE STYLE OF CLASSIFIED white château wines varies according to the ratio of Sauvignon Blanc and Sémillon used. Château Olivier, for example, consists of 65 percent Sémillon, and Château Carbonnieux of 65 percent Sauvignon Blanc.

The best wines are produced in Pessac-Léognan, which lies mostly north of Graves, near the city of Bordeaux. The best wines are known by the name of a particular château, a special vineyard that produces the best-quality grapes. The grapes grown for these wines enjoy better soil and better growing conditions overall. The classified château wines and the regional wines of Graves are always dry.

CHOOSING A GRAVES WINE

Buy a classified château wine. The classified châteaux are:

Château Bouscaut*	Château La Tour-Martillac
Château Carbonnieux*	Château Laville-Haut-Brion
Château Couhins-Lurton	Château Malartic-Lagravière
Domaine de Chevalier	Château Olivier*
Château Haut-Brion	Château Smith-Haut-Lafitte
Château La Louvière*	

* The largest producers and the easiest to find

FORTY YEARS LATER IN WHITE BORDEAUX

The dry white wines of Bordeaux never were considered equal to the great red châteaux and sweet whites of Sauternes. That has changed over the last 40 years. Winemakers have spent millions of dollars on state-of-the-art equipment, and new vineyard management has created great white-wine production, especially in the Pessac-Léognan.

Few other regions in the world blend Sauvignon Blanc and Sémillon and age them in oak. Winemakers here have been very careful to integrate the fruit and oak together to maintain the freshness and crispness of the wine. Recent vintages have been outstanding.

– BEST RECENT VINTAGES OF WHITE GRAVES –
2000* 2005* 2007* 2009* 2010* 2014* 2015* 2016
* EXCEPTIONAL VINTAGE

FOOD PAIRINGS

"Oysters, lobster, Rouget du Bassin d'Arcachon with a **Châteaux Olivìer**."
—*Jean-Jacques de Bethmann*

"With **Château La Louvière Blanc**: grilled sea bass with a beurre blanc, shad roe, or goat cheese soufflé. With **Château Bonnet Blanc**: oysters on the half-shell, fresh crab salad, mussels, and clams."
—*Denise Lurton-Moullé*

"With a young **Château Carbonnieux Blanc**: chilled lobster consommé, or shellfish, such as oysters, scallops, or grilled shrimp. With an older **Carbonnieux**: a traditional sauced fish course or a goat cheese."
—*Anthony Perrin*

SAUTERNES/BARSAC

Sauternes is always sweet, meaning that not all the grape sugar has turned into alcohol during fermentation. Dry Sauternes doesn't exist. The Barsac district, adjacent to Sauternes, has the option of using Barsac or Sauternes as its appellation. The main grape varieties in Sauternes are:

Sémillon   **Sauvignon Blanc**

The two different quality levels in style are

Regional ($)   Classified château ($$$–$$$$)

Sauternes is still producing one of the best sweet wines in the world. With the extraordinary vintages of 2009, 2011, 2014, and 2015 you'll be able to find excellent regional Sauternes if you buy from the best shippers. These wines represent a good value for your money, considering the labor involved in production, but they won't have the same intensity of flavor as that of a classified château.

Sauternes is **EXPENSIVE TO PRODUCE** because several pickings must take place before the crop is entirely harvested. The harvest can last into November.

BORDEAUX HAS MORE SÉMILLON grapes planted than Sauvignon Blanc.

WHEN BUYING REGIONAL SAUTERNES look for these reputable shippers: Baron Philippe de Rothschild and B&G.

SAUTERNES CLASSIFICATIONS

FIRST GREAT GROWTH—GRAND PREMIER CRU

CHÂTEAU D'YQUEM*

FIRST GROWTH—PREMIERS CRUS

CHÂTEAU CLIMENS* (BARSAC)	CHÂTEAU LAFAURIE-PEYRAGUEY*
CHÂTEAU CLOS HAUT-PEYRAGUEY*	CHÂTEAU RABAUD-PROMIS
CHÂTEAU COUTET* (BARSAC)	CHÂTEAU RIEUSSEC*
CHÂTEAU DE RAYNE-VIGNEAU*	CHÂTEAU SIGALAS-RABAUD*
*CHÂTEAU GUIRAUD	CHÂTEAU SUDUIRAUT*
CHÂTEAU LA TOUR BLANCHE*	

SECOND GROWTHS—DEUXIÈMES CRUS

CHÂTEAU BROUSTET (BARSAC)	CHÂTEAU FILHOT*
CHÂTEAU CAILLOU (BARSAC)	CHÂTEAU LAMOTHE
CHÂTEAU D'ARCHE	CHÂTEAU LAMOTHE-GUIGNARD
CHÂTEAU DE MALLE*	CHÂTEAU MYRAT (BARSAC)
CHÂTEAU DOISY-DAËNE (BARSAC)	CHÂTEAU NAIRAC* (BARSAC)
CHÂTEAU DOISY-DUBROCA (BARSAC)	CHÂTEAU ROMER DU HAYOT*
CHÂTEAU DOISY-VÉDRINES* (BARSAC)	CHÂTEAU SUAU (BARSAC)

These châteaux are the most readily available in America.

GRAVES VS. SAUTERNES

If the same grapes make dry Graves and sweet Sauternes, why the difference in styles? The best Sauternes comes primarily from the Sémillon grape. Second, to make Sauternes, the winemaker leaves the grapes on the vine longer until a mold called *Botrytis cinerea* ("noble rot") forms. When that happens, the water within them evaporates, and they shrivel. Sugar concentrates as the grapes "raisinate." Then, during the winemaking process, not all the sugar is allowed to ferment into alcohol: hence, the high residual sugar.

In 2011, **ONE BOTTLE OF CHÂTEAU D'YQUEM 1811 SOLD FOR $117,000,** the most money ever paid for a white wine.

Château d'Yquem makes a dry white wine simply called Y. By law, **DRY WINE MADE IN SAUTERNES CANNOT BE CALLED APPELLATION SAUTERNES.** It can be called only Appellation Bordeaux. Chateau d'Yquem didn't produce a wine in 2012 due to poor weather conditions.

CHÂTEAU RIEUSSEC IS OWNED by the same family as Château Lafite-Rothschild.

– BEST VINTAGES OF SAUTERNES –

1986* 1988* 1989* 1990* 1995 1996 1997* 1998
2000 2001* 2002 2003* 2005** 2006* 2007* 2008*
2009** 2010* 2011** 2013* 2014** 2015** 2016

EXCEPTIONAL VINTAGE **EXTRAORDINARY VINTAGE*

JUST DESSERTS

My students always ask, "What do you serve with **Sauternes**?" Here's a lesson I learned when I first encountered the wines of Sauternes.

Many years ago, I was invited to one of the châteaux of the region for dinner. My group was offered appetizers of foie gras, and, to my surprise, Sauternes was served with it. All the books I had ever read said to serve drier wines first and sweeter wines later, but I thought it best not to question my host's selection.

When we sat down for the first dinner course (fish), once again we were served a Sauternes. This continued through the main course—rack of lamb—when *another* Sauternes was served.

I thought for sure our host would serve a great old red Bordeaux with the cheese course, but I was wrong again. With the Roquefort cheese came a very old Sauternes.

With dessert on its way, of course I expected another Sauternes and waited with anticipation for the final choice. You can imagine my surprise when a dry red Bordeaux—Château Lafite-Rothschild—accompanied dessert!

Our host's point was that Sauternes doesn't have to be served only with dessert. All the Sauternes went well with the courses because all the sauces complemented the wine and food. In fact, the only wine that didn't go well with dinner was the Château Lafite-Rothschild with dessert, but we drank it anyway!

Hopefully this anecdote will inspire you to serve Sauternes with everything. I prefer to enjoy Sauternes by itself; I'm not a believer in the "dessert wine" category. This dessert wine is dessert in itself.

OTHER SWEET-WINE PRODUCERS in Bordeaux: Ste-Croix-du-Mont and Loupiac.

NOT CLASSIFIED BUT OF OUTSTANDING QUALITY: Château Fargues, Château Gilette, and Château Raymond Lafon.

THE WHITE WINES OF BURGUNDY

One of the finest wine-producing areas in the world, Burgundy is one of the major regions that holds an AOC designation in France. However, people often are confused about what a Burgundy really is because the name has been borrowed so freely.

Burgundy is *not* a synonym for red wine, even though the color known as burgundy obviously comes from the red wine. Adding to the confusion (especially in the past) is that many red wines around the world were labeled simply "Burgundy" even though they were ordinary table wines. Some wineries, especially in America, continue to label their wines as Burgundy, but these wines bear no resemblance to authentic French Burgundy wines.

The main regions within Burgundy are:

Chablis   Côte d'Or { Côte de Nuits
                             Côte de Beaune

Côte Châlonnaise   Mâconnais   Beaujolais

Before we explore Burgundy, region by region, it's important to know the types of wine produced there. Take a look at the infographic below, which breaks down the types of wine and tells you the percentages of white and reds.

68 percent of all Burgundy is white, and 32 percent is red.

> **THE APÉRITIF KIR** is a mixture of white wine and crème de cassis liqueur made from black currants. It was the favorite drink of the mayor of Dijon, Canon Kir, who added the sweet cassis to balance the high acidity of the local white wine made from the Aligoté grape.

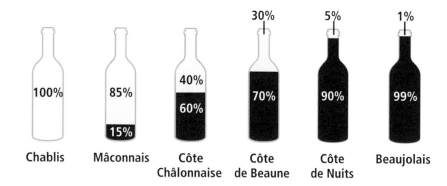

Chablis	Mâconnais	Côte Châlonnaise	Côte de Beaune	Côte de Nuits	Beaujolais
100%	85% / 15%	40% / 60%	30% / 70%	5% / 90%	1% / 99%

Burgundy is so famous for its red wines that people may forget that some of the finest, most renowned and expensive white wines of France come from here. The three areas in Burgundy that produce world-famous white wines that we'll examine are:

Chablis   Côte de Beaune   Mâconnais

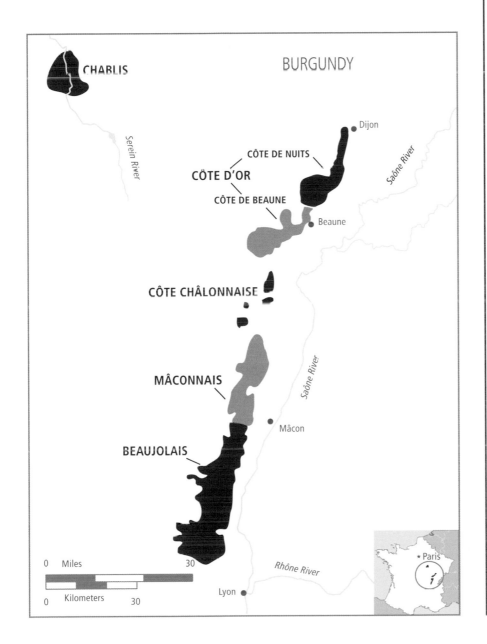

Although **CHABLIS BELONGS TO THE BURGUNDY REGION,** it is a three-hour drive south from there to the Mâconnais area.

The largest city in Burgundy is known not for its wines but for **ANOTHER WORLD-FAMOUS PRODUCT.** The city is Dijon, and the product is mustard.

FOR THE TOURIST: Some of the best hotels lie in the city of Beaune. My favorites include Hôtel Le Cep, Hostellerie Le Cèdre, and Hôtel de la Poste.

CÔTE D'OR PRODUCTION

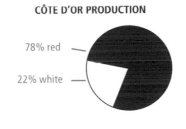

78% red

22% white

BURGUNDY

37.5% 44 Villages

53% 23 Regional Appellations

10% 645 Premier Cru Vineyards

1.5% 32 Grand Cru Vineyards

\For great value try a **REGIONAL BURGUNDY WINE,** such as Bourgogne Blanc.

The average yield for a Village wine in Burgundy is **360 GALLONS PER ACRE.** For the Grand Cru wines, it's 290 gallons per acre, a notably higher concentration, which produces a more flavorful wine.

MOST PREMIER CRU WINES give you the name of the vineyard on the label, but others are called simply Premier Cru, a blend of different cru vineyards.

BURGUNDY AND NEW OAK

25% Village wine

40–70% Premier Cru

80–100% Grand Cru

You need to know only one white-grape variety: Chardonnay. All the great white Burgundies come from 100 percent Chardonnay. Although Chardonnay grapes make all the best white Burgundy wines, the three areas produce many different styles. Much of this difference has to do with where the grapes grow and the winemaking procedures. For example, the northern climate of Chablis produces wines with more acidity than those in the southern region of Mâconnais.

As for vinification, after workers harvest the grapes in the Chablis and Mâconnais areas, most of the grapes ferment and age in stainless steel tanks. In the Côte de Beaune, a good percentage of the wines ferment in small oak barrels and also age in oak barrels. The wood adds complexity, depth, body, taste, and longevity to the wines.

All white Burgundies have one trait in comon: They are dry.

BURGUNDY CLASSIFICATIONS

The type of soil and the angle and direction of the slope primarily determine quality, divided into the following levels:

Regional Appellations $

Village wine Bears the name of a specific village. $$

Premier Cru From a specific vineyard with special characteristics, within one of the named villages. Usually a Premier Cru wine will list on the label the village first and the vineyard second. $$$

Grand Cru From a specific vineyard that possesses the best soil and slope in the area and meets or exceeds all other requirements. In most areas of Burgundy, the village doesn't appear on the label—only the Grand Cru vineyard name. $$$$+

THE USE OF WOOD

Each wine region in the world has its own way of producing wines. Wine always fermented and aged in wood—until the introduction of cement tanks, glass-lined tanks, and, most recently, stainless steel tanks. Despite these technological improvements, many winemakers prefer the more traditional methods. For example, some of the wines from Louis Jadot ferment in wood as follows:

- One-third of the wine ferments in new wood.
- One-third ferments in year-old wood.
- One-third ferments in older wood.

Jadot's philosophy holds that the better the vintage, the newer the wood: Younger wood imparts more flavor and tannin, which might overpower wines of lesser vintage. Thus they generally reserve younger woods for aging the better vintages.

CHABLIS

Chablis lies in the northernmost area in Burgundy, and it produces only white wine. All French Chablis comes from of 100 percent Chardonnay grapes. The name "Chablis" suffers from the same misinterpretation and overuse as the name "Burgundy." Because the French didn't take the necessary legal precautions to protect the use of the name, "Chablis" now randomly applies to many ordinary bulk wines from other countries. As a result, Chablis has developed associations with some very undistinguished wines, but this isn't the case with French Chablis. The French take their Chablis very seriously. These are classifications and quality levels for Chablis:

Petit Chablis The most ordinary Chablis; rarely seen in America.

Chablis This wine comes from grapes grown anywhere in the Chablis district, also known as a Village wine.

Chablis Premier Cru Good-quality Chablis that comes from specific high-quality vineyards.

Chablis Grand Cru The highest classification of Chablis and the most expensive because of its limited production. Only seven vineyards in Chablis can be called Grand Cru.

Of these quality levels, the best value is a Chablis Premier Cru.

Chablis has more than 250 GRAPE GROWERS, but only a handful age their wine in wood.

CHABLIS VILLAGE $

CHABLIS PREMIER CRU $$

CHABLIS GRAND CRU $$$$

ONLY 247 ACRES of grapes are planted in Chablis Grand Cru vineyards.

DOMAINE LAROCHE USES SCREW CAPS
on all their wines, including the Grand Crus.

If you're interested in only the best Chablis, here are the most important Premier Cru vineyards and the seven Grands Crus:

SOME OF THE TOP PREMIER CRU VINEYARDS OF CHABLIS	
CÔTE DE VAULORENT	MONTMAINS
FOURCHAUME	MONTS DE MILIEU
LECHET	VAILLON
MONTÉE DE TONNERRE	

THE SEVEN GRAND CRU VINEYARDS OF CHABLIS	
BLANCHOTS	PREUSES
BOUGROS	VALMUR
GRENOUILLES	VAUDÉSIR
LES CLOS	

CHOOSING A CHABLIS

The two major aspects to look for in Chablis are the shipper and the vintage. The most important shippers of Chablis to America include:

A. Regnard & Fils	Domaine Chantemerle	Albert Pic & Fils
La Chablisienne	Domaine Laroche	Louis Jadot
François Raveneau	Domaine Moreau-	Guy Robin
René Dauvissat	Naudet	Robert Vocoret
Jean Dauvissat	Drouhin Vaudon	William Fèvre
Joseph Drouhin		

WHEN TO DRINK CHABLIS

Chablis	Premier Cru	Grand Cru
within two years	two to four years	three to eight years

– BEST RECENT VINTAGES OF CHABLIS –
2006* 2007* 2008* 2009* 2010** 2011* 2012** 2013*
2014** 2015* 2016
EXCEPTIONAL VINTAGE

The **WINTER TEMPERATURES** in some parts of Chablis can match those of Norway. Frost hit Chablis in 2016 and resulted in little production or quality.

CÔTE DE BEAUNE

This is one of the two major areas of the Côte d'Or. The wines produced here are some of the finest examples of dry white Chardonnay produced in the world and serve as a benchmark for winemakers everywhere.

The three most important white wine–producing villages of the Côte de Beaune are:

Meursault   Puligny-Montrachet   Chassagne-Montrachet

All three produce their white wine from the same grape—100 percent Chardonnay. These are my favorite white wine–producing villages and vineyards in the Côte de Beaune.

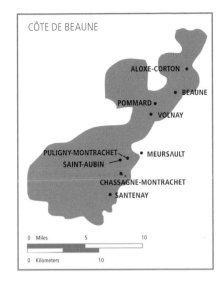

CÔTE DE BEAUNE

MOST IMPORTANT VILLAGES	MY FAVORITE PREMIER CRU VINEYARDS	GRAND CRU VINEYARDS
ALOXE-CORTON		CORTON-CHARLEMAGNE CHARLEMAGNE
BEAUNE	CLOS DES MOUCHES	
CHASSAGNE-MONTRACHET	LES RUCHOTTES MORGEOT	BÂTARD-MONTRACHET* CRIOTS-BÂTARD-MONTRACHET MONTRACHET*
MEURSAULT	BLAGNY LA GOUTTE D'OR LES CHARMES LES GENEVRIÈRES LES PERRIÈRES PORUZOTS	
PULIGNY-MONTRACHET	CLAVOILLONS LES CAILLERETS LES CHAMPS GAIN LES COMBETTES LES FOLATIÈRES LES PUCELLES LES REFERTS	BÂTARD-MONTRACHET* BIENVENUE-BÂTARD MONTRACHET CHEVALIER-MONTRACHET MONTRACHET*

* The vineyards of Montrachet and Bâtard-Montrachet overlap between the villages of Puligny-Montrachet and Chassagne-Montrachet.

The **LARGEST GRAND CRU,** in terms of production, is Corton-Charlemagne, which represents more than 50 percent of all white Grand Cru wines.

In 1879, the villages of Puligny and Chassagne added the name of the most well known Grand Cru vineyard, Montrachet, to their own names.

THE CÔTE DE NUIT is primarily a red wine–producing region, but the villages of Vougeot and Musigny make some exceptional white wines.

FROM ST. AUBIN, try the great Chardonnays of Pierre-Yves Colin-Morey, Philippe Colin, Alain Chavy, and Maroslavac-Leger.

QUALITY LEVELS OF BURGUNDY

NAME OF VILLAGE $

Puligny-Montrachet
APPELLATION CONTROLÉE

Louis Latour
MIS EN BOUTEILLE PAR LOUIS LATOUR
NÉGOCIANT A BEAUNE (COTE-D'OR)

NAME OF VILLAGE + PREMIER CRU VINEYARD $$

Puligny-Montrachet
LES REFERTS
APPELLATION CONTROLÉE

Louis Latour
MIS EN BOUTEILLE PAR LOUIS LATOUR
NÉGOCIANT A BEAUNE (COTE-D'OR), FRANCE

NAME OF GRAND CRU VINEYARD $$$

Montrachet
APPELLATION CONTROLÉE

MIS EN BOUTEILLE PAR
LOUIS LATOUR, NÉGOCIANT A BEAUNE (CÔTE-D'OR), FRANCE

WHAT MAKES EACH BURGUNDY WINE DIFFERENT?

In Burgundy, one of the most important factors in making a good wine is soil. The quality of the soil is the main reason that there are three levels and price points among a Village, a Premier Cru, and a Grand Cru wine. "The difference among the Village wine, Puligny-Montrachet, and the Grand Cru Montrachet is not in the type of wood used in aging or how long the wine is aged in wood. The primary difference is in the location of the vineyards, i.e. the soil and the slope of the land," says Robert Drouhin of Maison Joseph Drouhin.

Another major factor that differentiates each wine is the vinification procedure, the "recipe" the winemaker uses. It's the same as if you were to compare chefs at three different restaurants: They may start out with the same ingredients, but what they do with those ingredients matters.

– BEST RECENT VINTAGES OF CÔTE DE BEAUNE WHITE –

2002* 2005* 2006* 2007* 2008* 2009* 2010*
2012* 2013* 2014** 2015** 2016
*EXCEPTIONAL VINTAGE **EXTRAORDINARY VINTAGE*

CÔTE CHÂLONNAISE

This is is the least known of the major wine districts of Burgundy. Although the Châlonnaise produces red wines such as Givry and Mercurey (see Class Four, "The Red Wines of Burgundy and the Rhône Valley"), it also produces some very good white wines that not many people know, which means value for you—specifically the wines of Montagny and Rully. These wines are of the highest quality produced in the area, similar to the white wines of the Côte d'Or but less costly.

Look for the wines of Antonin Rodet, Faiveley, Louis Latour, Moillard, Olivier Leflaive, Jacques Dury, Chartron & Trébuchet, Marc Morey, and Vincent Girardin.

MÂCONNAIS

The southernmost white wine–producing area in Burgundy, the Mâconnais, has a climate warmer than that of the Côte d'Or and Chablis. Mâcon wines are, in general, pleasant, light, uncomplicated, reliable, and a great value. From basic to best, here are the different quality levels of Mâconnais wines:

The Mâconnais region has a **VILLAGE NAMED CHARDONNAY**, where the grape's name reportedly originated.

1. Mâcon Blanc
2. Mâcon Supérieur
3. Mâcon-Villages
4. St-Véran
5. Pouilly-Vinzelles
6. Pouilly-Fuissé

Of all Mâcon wines, Pouilly-Fuissé is unquestionably one of the most popular. It ranks among the highest-quality Mâconnais wines, fashionable to drink in the USA long before most Americans discovered the splendors of wine. As wine consumption increased here, Pouilly-Fuissé and other famous areas such as Pommard, Nuits-St-Georges, and Chablis became synonymous with the best wines of France and frequently appeared on restaurants' wine lists.

Mâcon-Villages is the best value. Why pay more for Pouilly-Fuissé—sometimes three times as much—when a simple Mâcon will do just as nicely?

My favorite Mâconnais producers include

Château de Fuissé	J. J. Vincent & Fils	Louis Jadot
Château des Rontets	Joseph Drouhin	Nicolas Potel
J-A Ferret	Les Héritiers du Comte Lafon	

Since **MÂCON WINES USUALLY DON'T AGE IN OAK,** they are ready to drink as soon as they are released.

IF YOU'RE TAKING A CLIENT OUT on a limited expense account, Mâcon is a safe wine to order. If the sky's the limit, go for the Meursault!

– BEST RECENT VINTAGES OF MÂCON WHITE –
2009** 2010** 2011 2012** 2013 2014* 2015* 2016
*EXCEPTIONAL VINTAGE **EXTRAORDINARY VINTAGE*

ESTATE-BOTTLED WINE is made, produced, and bottled by the owner of the vineyard.

DOMAINE LEFLAIVE'S WINES ARE NAMED FOR CHARACTERS AND PLACES IN A LOCAL MEDIEVAL TALE. The chevalier of Puligny-Montrachet, missing his son who was fighting in the Crusades, amused himself in the ravinelike vineyards (Les Combettes) with a local maiden (Pucelle), only to welcome the arrival of another son (Bâtard-Montrachet) nine months later.

BURGUNDY REVIEW

Now that you're familiar with the different white wines of Burgundy, how to choose the right one? First look for the vintage. With Burgundy, it's especially important to buy a good year. After that, your choice becomes a matter of taste and cost. If price is no object, aren't you lucky?

Also, after some trial and error, you may find that you prefer the wines of one shipper over another. Here are some of the shippers to look for when buying white Burgundy:

Bouchard Père & Fils	Labouré-Roi	Prosper Maufoux
Chanson	Louis Jadot	Ropiteau Frères
Domaine Faiveley	Louis Latour	
Joseph Drouhin	Olivier Leflaive Frères	

Although 80 percent of Burgundy wines sell through shippers, some fine estate-bottled wines are available in limited quantities in America. The better ones include:

WINE	VILLAGE
Château Fuissé	Pouilly-Fuissé
Domaine Bachelet-Ramonet	Chassagne-Montrachet
Domaine Boillot	Meursault
Domaine Bonneau du Martray	Corton-Charlemagne
Domaine Coche-Dury	Meursault, Puligny-Montrachet
Domaine des Comtes Lafon	Meursault
Domaine Étienne Sauzet	Puligny-Montrachet
Domaine Leflaive	Meursault, Puligny-Montrachet
Domaine Lucien le Moine	Corton-Charlemagne
Domaine Matrot	Meursault
Domaine Philippe Colin	Chassagne-Montrachet
Domaine Vincent Girardin	Chassagne-Montrachet
Jean Chartron	Chevalier-Montrachet
Ramonet	Montrachet
Tollot-Beaut	Corton-Charlemagne

---

5 BEST VALUE WHITE WINES OF FRANCE UNDER $30

Pascal Jolivet Sancerre • Trimbach Riesling • William Fèvre Chablis •
Château Larrivet-Haut-Brion • Louis Jadot Mâcon

See pages 359–360 for a complete list.

FORTY YEARS LATER IN WHITE BURGUNDY

If you're looking for pure unoaked Chardonnay at its best, the crisp flavorful Chablis region of France will satisfy your tastes. Over the last 40 years, these wines have only improved. Through enhanced frost protection, the region has increased its vineyard acreage from 4,000 to 12,000 acres since the late 1950s without losing its quality. Great news for the consumer.

The white wines of the Mâconnais and Châlonnaise represent some of the great value wines made from 100 percent Chardonnay, yet most usually cost less than $20 a bottle. Wines labeled "Bourgogne Blanc" are fantastic values.

One of the big changes, especially in Mâcon, is the inclusion of the grape variety on the label. With increased competition from new-world Chardonnay producers, the French government finally has accepted that Americans and other countries buy wines by grape variety.

The great white wines of the Côte d'Or have achieved greatness in the last 40 years. For me, these are the best white wines in the world! The new generation of winemakers has studied around the world, leading to more control in the vineyards and in the cellars, plantings of new clones, and picking lower yields. Chaptalization, the once prevalent addition of sugar to the fermenting juice to increase the alcohol content, rarely happens today, which means the wines have a better natural balance.

GUIDED TASTING

Start with a lighter-styled Riesling from Alsace, and end with a sweet Sauternes from Bordeaux. Pay attention to the balance of fruit and acid, and note that some high-acid wines taste better with food, especially shellfish.

Riesling One Riesling, tasted alone:
   1. Alsace Riesling

Melon de Bourgogne and Sauvignon Blanc Two wines from the Loire Valley, compared:
   2. Muscadet
   3. Pouilly-Fumé

Sauvignon Blanc and Sémillon One Bordeaux, tasted alone:
   4. Château from Graves or Pessac-Léognan

Chardonnay Four wines from Burgundy, compared:
    5. Unoaked Mâcon-Villages
    6. Oaked Chablis Premier Cru
    7. Village wine, such as Meursault
    8. Premier Cru, such as Puligny-Montrachet Les Combettes

Gewürztraminer One Alsace wine, tasted alone:
    9. Gewürztraminer

Sémillon One Sauternes, tasted alone:
    10. Bordeaux, Château from Sauternes

FOOD PARINGS

When you choose a white Burgundy, you have a gamut of wonderful food possibilities. Mâconnais wines are suitable for picnics as well as for formal dinners—you might select one of the fuller-bodied Côte de Beaune wines or an all-purpose Chablis.

"Drink young **Chablis** or **St-Véran** with shellfish. Fine **Côte d'Or** wines match well with any fish or light white meat, such as veal or sweetbreads."

Robert Drouhin

"A basic **Village Chablis** is good as an apéritif and with hors d'oeuvre and salads. A great **Premier Cru** or **Grand Cru Chablis** needs something more special, such as lobster. It's an especially beautiful match if the wine has been aged a few years."

—*Christian Moreau*

"My favorite food combination with white **Burgundy** wine is, without doubt, homard grillé Breton [blue lobster.] Only harmonious, powerful, and delicate wines are able to go with the subtle, thin flesh and very fine taste of the Breton lobster. **Chablis** is a great match for oysters, snails, and shellfish, but a **Grand Cru Chablis** should be had with trout. With Village wines of the **Côte de Beaune**, which should be had at the beginning of the meal, try a light fish or quenelles [light dumplings]. **Premier Cru** and **Grand Cru** wines can stand up to heavier fish and shellfish such as lobster—but with a wine such as **Corton-Charlemagne**, smoked Scottish salmon is a tasty choice."

—*Pierre Henry Gagey*

"**Chablis** with oysters and fish. With **Corton-Charlemagne**, filet of sole in a light Florentine sauce. Otherwise, the **Chardonnays** of Burgundy complement roast chicken, seafood, and light-flavored goat cheese particularly well."

—*Louis Latour*

TEST YOUR KNOWLEDGE of the white wines of France by trying the quiz on page 383.

—————— **FURTHER READING** ——————

Burgundy by Anthony Hanson

Burgundy by Robert M. Parker Jr.

Making Sense of Burgundy by Matt Kramer

Côte D'Or: A Celebration of the Great Wines of Burgundy by Clive Coates

The Wines of Burgundy by Clive Coates

CLASS SIX

THE WINES OF SPAIN

UNDERSTANDING THE WINES OF SPAIN ❋ RIOJA ❋ RIBERA DEL
DUERO ❋ PENEDÈS ❋ PRIORAT ❋ THE WHITE WINES OF SPAIN

UNDERSTANDING THE WINES OF SPAIN

AALTO

2005   RIBERA DEL DUERO
DENOMINACIÓN DE ORIGEN

Former winemaker at Vega Sicilia, Mariano Garcia and his business partner, Javier Zaccagnini, founded Aalto in 1999 and make just two wines: Aalto and Aalto PS. **ADD BOTH TO YOUR WINE CELLAR.**

SPAIN HAS THOUSANDS of years of grape growing and winemaking history and ranks as the world's third largest producer of wine, after France and Italy, but Spain also has more acres of grapevines than any other country on earth—nearly 3 million!

Since joining the European Union in 1986, Spain has benefited from an infusion of capital into its vineyards and wineries. Modern technology, including stainless steel fermenters and new trellis systems, has helped create outstanding wines from all of its wine regions. To offset the dry climate and frequent droughts, especially in the center and south of the country, irrigating grapevines became legal in 1996, which has increased both the quality and volume of Spain's wine production.

Spain established its Denominación de Origen (DO) laws in 1970 and revised them in 1982. Similar to the AOC laws of France and Italy's DOC, Spain's DO laws control a region's boundaries, grape varieties, winemaking practices, yield per acre, and most importantly the aging of the wine before it can be released. Today Spain has 69 DO regions, including 2 higher-level Denominación de Origen Calificada (DOC) regions, Rioja and Priorat.

Here are the most important regions along with the most important grapes grown there:

REGION	VARIETY
RIOJA	TEMPRANILLO
RIBERA DEL DUERO	TEMPRANILLO (TINTO FINO)
PENEDÈS	MACABEO, CABERNET SAUVIGNON, CARIÑENA, GARNACHA
PRIORAT	GARNACHA, CARIÑENA
RUEDA	VERDEJO
RÍAS BAIXAS	ALBARIÑO
JEREZ (SHERRY)	PALOMINO

OTHER WINE-PRODUCING AREAS OF SPAIN INCLUDE

Bierzo

Castilla-La Mancha

Jumilla

Navarra

Toro

IN TORO, look for Numanthia, Bodegas Ordoñez, Dominio de Valdepusa, and Marqués de Griñón. In Jumillo, look for Bodegas El Nido. In Bierzo, look for Godelia.

GRENACHE **IS THE FRENCH NAME** of Garnacha, a Spanish grape brought to France during the Avignon Papacy.

FINCA means "estate" or "farm."

Vinos de Pagos means that the wine comes from **A SINGLE ESTATE.**

The word *joven* occasionally appears on a wine label, indicating that the wine is unoaked or slightly oaked and should be **DRUNK "YOUNG."**

More than 600 grape varieties grow here, but you'll most likely find these in a wine store or restaurant:

NATIVE VARIETIES		INTERNATIONAL VARIETIES	
WHITE	**RED**	**WHITE**	**RED**
ALBARIÑO VERDEJO MACABEO (VIURA)	TEMPRANILLO (TINTO FINO) GARNACHA MONASTRELL CARIÑENA	CHARDONNAY SAUVIGNON BLANC	CABERNET SAUVIGNON MERLOT SYRAH

RIOJA

CRIANZA

Rioja lies fewer than 200 miles to the southwest of Bordeaux, which has influenced Rioja winemaking since the 1800s. During the 1870s, the phylloxera blight, traveling from north to south, arrived in Bordeaux and nearly destroyed the wine industry there. Many Bordeaux landowners and winemakers relocated to Rioja, still blight-free, for the similar climate and growing conditions. As they established their own vineyards and wineries, they affected how Spaniards made Rioja, an influence still apparent today.

Despite a surge in diverse and interesting wines from elsewhere in Spain, Rioja still reigns as the country's principal red wine region, offering both quality and quantity to match the world's best. Today the region has more than 150,000 acres of grapevines, 41 percent of those planted during the last ten years. Rioja continues to innovate within its traditional style and offers a tremendous range of quality at price points appealing to beginners and collectors alike. The new, emerging style is bigger and more concentrated. Wineries making this style include Allende, Palacios, Remelluri, Remirez de Ganuza, and Remondo.

The primary red grapes used in Rioja wines are

Tempranillo   Garnacha

but the grape variety doesn't always appear on wine labels. There's no official classification system for Rioja, but the three quality levels are:

Crianza Released after two years of aging, at least one in oak. Cost: $.

Reserva Released after three years of aging, at least one in oak. Cost: $$.

Gran Reserva Released after five to seven years of aging, at least two in oak. Cost: $$$.

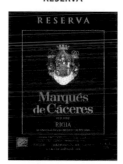

RESERVA

GRAN RESERVA

Bodegas Dinastia Vivanco in Briones, Rioja, is the world's **BEST WINE MUSEUM.** If you go, spend the day—it's that good!

CHOOSING A RIOJA WINE

All you need to know is the quality level you want and the reputation of the Rioja winemaker or shipper. That's it! You also may know a Rioja wine by its proprietary name. Look for these bodegas, or wineries, along with some of their better-known proprietary names.

Baron de Ley	Bodegas Roda
Bodegas Bretón	Bodegas Tobía
Bodegas Dinastía Vivanco	Contino
Bodegas Lan	CVNE (Imperial, Viña Real)
Bodegas Montecillo	El Coto
Bodegas Muga (Muga Reserva, Prado Enea, Torre Muga)	Finca Allende
	Finca Valpiedra
Bodegas Obalo	La Rioja Alta (Viña Alberdi, Viña Ardanza)
Bodegas Remírez de Ganuza	
Bodegas Riojanas (Monte Real, Viña Albina)	López de Heredía
	Marqués de Cáceres

Marqués de Murrieta
Marqués de Riscal
Martínez Bujanda
  (Conde de Valdemar)

Palacios Remondo
Remelluri
Señorio de San Vicente
Ysios

Three of the best American importers of Spanish wine are Steve Metzler (Classical Wines), Jorge Ordoñez (Fine Estates from Spain), and Eric Solomon (European Cellars).

— BEST VINTAGES OF RIOJA —

1994* 1995* 2001** 2004** 2005** 2009* 2010**
2011* 2012* 2014 2015 2016 2017

*EXCEPTIONAL VINTAGE ** EXTRAORDINARY VINTAGE

ESTABLISHED IN 1852, Marqués de Murrieta was the first commercial bodega in Rioja.

Wine Spectator voted Imperial Gran Reserva 2004 the **THE WORLD'S BEST WINE IN 2014.**

Some of the top Rioja winemakers say that the 2001 and 2004 vintages are the **BEST THEY EVER HAVE TASTED.**

In 2012, *Wine Enthusiast* named Ribera del Duero **WINE REGION OF THE YEAR.**

TINTO
PESQUERA
RIBERA DEL DUERO
Denominación de Origen

Aborigen N°1   *Manuel Millares*

VEGA-SICILIA
COSECHA 1982   "UNICO"

The word *cosecha*, which means "harvest" or "vintage," appears on some labels. It also can indicate a wine that has little barrel aging. Producers often use it for their **MODERN-STYLE WINES.**

RIBERA DEL DUERO

When I wrote the first edition of this book, cooperatives made most Ribera del Duero wines—except Spain's most famous winery, Bodegas Vega Sicilia, which has been making wine since the 1860s. But one wine does not a region make. Then, in the 1980s, Pesquera wine received great reviews from wine critics, helping to stimulate quality wine production in the region and setting the stage for astounding growth. Today Ribera del Duero has more than 280 wineries, covering nearly 50,000 acres, and a new generation of quality winemakers is emerging. Aging requirements are the same here as in Rioja (Crianza, Reserva, Gran Reserva).

The major wine grapes used in Ribera del Duero are:

Cabernet Sauvignon	Malbec	Tempranillo
Garnacha	Merlot	

My favorite Ribera del Duero producers include:

Aalto	Bodegas Los Astrales	Hacienda Monasterio
Abadía Retuerta	Bodegas Matarromera	Legaris
Alejandro Fernandez	Bodegas Valderiz	Montecastro
Arzuaga	Bodegas y Viñedas	Pago de los Capellanes
Bodegas Alion	Condado de Haza	Pesquera
Bodegas Emilio Moro	Dominio de Pingus	Vega Sicilia
Bodegas Felix Callejo	García Figuero	Viña Mayo
Bodegas Hermanos Sastre		

— BEST VINTAGES OF RIBERA DEL DUERO —
1996* 2001** 2004** 2005** 2009** 2010**
2011** 2012* 2013 2014 2015** 2016
* EXCEPTIONAL VINTAGE   ** EXTRAORDINARY VINTAGE

PENEDÈS

Just outside Barcelona, the Penedès region produces the famous sparkling wine called Cava, protected—like Champagne in France—under its own DO. We'll learn more about Cava in class 11, but these are the major grapes used in wines from Penedès:

CAVA	RED	WHITE
CHARDONNAY	CABERNET SAUVIGNON	CHARDONNAY
MACABEO	GARNACHA	MACABEO
PARELLADA	MERLOT	PARELLADA
XAREL-LO	TEMPRANILLO	RIESLING GEWÜRZTRAMINER

The best-known Spanish sparkling wines in America are Freixenet and Codorníu, two of the biggest producers of bottle-fermented sparkling wines in the world. (The Ferrer family, which owns Freixenet, also makes Segura Viudas Cava, which you also may have seen in wine stores.) For traditional-method sparkling wines, these are very reasonably priced.

Penedès also has a reputation for high-quality table wine. The most famous wine from the Torres family, a name synonymous with quality, is Gran Coronas Black Label, made with 100 percent Cabernet Sauvignon. It's rare and expensive, but they also produce a full range of fine wines in all price categories.

My favorite Penedès producers include:

Albet i Noya   Marques de Monistrol
Jean Leon   Torres (Mas La Plana)

PRIORAT, PAST AND PRESENT
1995: 16 wineries
2016: 102 wineries

One of Spain's wine mavericks, Alvaro Palacios started at his family's winery in Rioja and has expanded into Priorat and Bierzo, two regions that he helped revitalize. His L'Ermita Priorat is **ONE OF SPAIN'S MOST HIGHLY RATED AND EXPENSIVE WINES.** For better value, try the Finca Dofi. For the best value, Les Terrasses.

Priorat wines must have a minimum of **13.5 PERCENT ALCOHOL.**

PRIORAT

South of Penedès lies Priorat, a region that epitomizes the Spanish wine renaissance. Carthusian monks farmed vineyards here for more than 800 years until the government auctioned their land to local farmers in the early 1800s. In the late 1800s, phylloxera forced most farmers to stop planting grapes, and many began cultivating hazelnuts and almonds instead. By 1910, cooperatives were making most of the wine here, and until about 25 years ago Priorat was known mostly for producing sacramental wine.

In the late 1980s, some of the most well-known Spanish wine producers, including René Barbier and Alvaro Palacios, revived the old Carthusian vineyards. Today Priorat produces some of the best red wine in Spain, as attested by the Spanish government, which awarded Priorat the highest status of DOC in 2003. Priorat vineyards lie at an altitude between 1,000 and 3,000 feet above sea level. Most are too steep to maneuver mechanical equipment, so growers use mules—just like the old days!

These are the grapes that go into red Priorat wines:

NATIVE VARIETIES	INTERNATIONAL VARIETIES
GARNACHA CARIÑENA	CABERNET SAUVIGNON MERLOT SYRAH

Because of extremely low yields and demand, it's hard to find an inexpensive Priorat. The best bottles easily sell for more than $100 each.

My favorite Priorat producers include:

Alvaro Palacios	Clos Martinet	Mas La Mola
Clos Daphne	Clos Mogador	Pasanau
Clos de L'Obac	La Conreria d'Scala Dei	Vall Llach
Clos Erasmus	Mas Igneus	

– BEST VINTAGES OF PRIORAT –

2001** 2004** 2005** 2006* 2007 2009*
2010** 2011 2012* 2013* 2014* 2015* 2016

* EXCEPTIONAL VINTAGE ** EXTRAORDINARY VINTAGE

THE WHITE WINES OF SPAIN

RUEDA

The wines of Rueda, northwest of Madrid, have been well known for centuries, but until the 1970s Ruedas were made with the Palomino grape and fortified in a style similar to Sherry. The new style of Rueda white wine comes from Verdejo, Viura, and occasionally Sauvignon Blanc grapes and tastes dry, fruity, and fresh.

RÍAS BAIXAS

Near Santiago de Compostela in Galicia (north of Portugal), Rías Baixas also began making outstanding white wines in the 1980s. More than 90 percent of Rías Baixas wine comes from the Albariño grape.

5 BEST VALUE RED WINES OF SPAIN UNDER $30

Alvaro Palacios Camins del Priorat • Bodegas Monticello Reserva • El Coto Crianza • Pesquera Tinto Crianza • Marqués de Cáceres Crianza

See page 365 for a complete list.

TEST YOUR KNOWLEDGE of the wines of Spain by trying the quiz on page 385.

—— **FURTHER READING** ——

The New and Classical Wines of Spain by Jeremy Watson

The New Spain by John Radford

The Peñín Guide to Spanish Wine (annual) edited by José Peñín

Rioja and Northwest Spain by Jesus Barquin, Luis Gutierrez, and Victor de la Serna

GUIDED TASTING

In a complex tasting, you always want to drink from lightest to heaviest so the previous wine you've tasted doesn't overpower the next one. To achieve that end, we're going to start with a young Rioja tasted on its own and then, rather than going region by region—in which case, a Rioja Gran Reserva will overwhelm a Ribera del Duero Crianza—we'll proceed instead by classification level, from youngest to oldest. As you go, pay attention to the tastes that wines from the same region have in common.

Rioja One Rioja tasted alone:
   1. Rioja Joven

Crianza Three wines compared:
   2. Rioja Crianza
   3. Ribera del Duero Crianza
   4. Priorat Crianza

Reserva Three wines compared:
   5. Rioja Reserva
   6. Ribera del Duero Reserva
   7. Priorat Reserva

Gran Reserva Three wines compared:
   8. Rioja Gran Reserva
   9. Ribera del Duero Gran Reserva
   10. Priorat Gran Reserva

FOOD PAIRINGS

One of the tenets of good pairings holds that what grows together goes together, so with Spanish wines, regardless of the region or classification, you can't go wrong with typical Spanish foods, such as tortilla española (potato frittata), tapas in general, and in particular jamon iberico and cheeses such as Manchego or cabra (goat).

CLASS SEVEN

THE WINES OF ITALY

UNDERSTANDING THE RED WINES OF ITALY ❋ TUSCANY ❋

PIEDMONT ❋ VENETO ❋ SICILY ❋

OTHER IMPORTANT ITALIAN REGIONS

UNDERSTANDING THE RED WINES OF ITALY

More than **ONE MILLION GROWERS** own the 2 million acres of vineyards in Italy.

MY FAVORITE WINE-PRODUCING
REGIONS IN ITALY INCLUDE

Veneto

Piedmont

Tuscany

ITALY HAS BEEN making wine for more than 3,000 years, and today it ranks as one of the world's largest producers. (France and Italy vie every year for the distinction of largest.) Grapevines grow everywhere here. As one retailer of fine Italian wine once told me, "There is no country. Italy is one vast vineyard from north to south."

From everyday drinking to serious tasting, Italian wines are good for any occasion. The country has 20 wine regions, 96 provinces, and more than 500 different grape varieties. But don't worry. To master the basics, concentrate on the 3 major regions below, along with their major red-grape varieties, and you'll soon have Italy in the palm of your hand.

REGION	TUSCANY	PIEDMONT	VENETO
VARIETY	SANGIOVESE	NEBBIOLO	CORVINA

Like the French AOC, the Denominazione di Origine Controllata (DOC) defines numerous aspects of Italian wine production, but the biggest difference between the two is that Italy's DOC mandates aging requirements. The DOC laws went into effect in 1963 and govern:

- regional boundaries
- allowable grape varieties
- grape percentages
- wine produced per acre
- alcohol content
- aging requirements

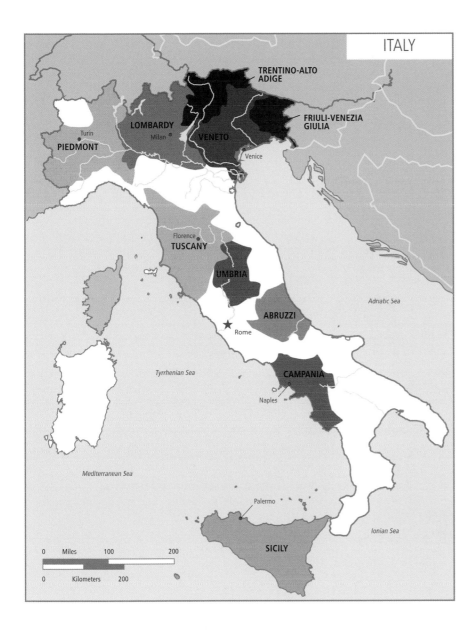

ITALY

DOCG WINES

TUSCANY

Brunello di Montalcino

Carmignano

Chianti

Chianti Classico

Elba Aleatico Passito

Montecucco Sangiovese

Morellino di Scansano

Vernaccia di San Gimignano

Vino Nobile di Montepulciano

PIEDMONT

Acqui or Brachetto d'Acqui

Alta Langa

Barbera d'Asti

Barbera del Monteferrato Superiore

Barbaresco

Barolo

Dolcetta Diano d'Alba

Dolcetto di Dogliani Superiore

Dolcetto di Ovada Superiore

Erbaluce di Caluso

Gattinara

Gavi or Cortese di Gavi

Ghemme

Moscato d'Asti or d'Alba

Roero

Ruche di Castagnole Monferrato

VENETO

Amarone della Valpolicella

Bardolino Superiore

Conegliano Valdobbiadene-Prosecco

Recioto della Valpolicella

Recioto di Gambellara

Recioto di Soave

Soave Superiore

During the 1980s, the Ministry of Agriculture took quality control a step further by adding the higher-ranking DOCG. The G stands for "Garantita" and means that tasting-control boards guarantee the stylistic authenticity of a wine. A third classification, Indicazione Geografica Tipica (IGT) indicates that a wine doesn't meet DOC requirements, but many of these wines drink at a higher level than DOC table wine.

DOCG WINES FROM OTHER REGIONS
Aglianico de Taburno
Aglianico del Vulture Superiore
Albana di Romagna
Castelli di Jesi Verdicchio Riserva
Cerasuolo di Vittoria
Cesanese del Piglio
Colli Asolani Prosecco
Colli Bolognesi Classico Pignoletto
Colli Euganei Fior d'Arancio
Colli Orientali del Friuli Picolit
Conero
Fiano di Avellino
Franciacorta
Frascati Superiore
Greco di Tufo
Lison
Montepulciano d'Abruzzo Colline Teramane
Oltrepo Pavese Metodo Classico
Piave Malanotte
Ramandolo
Sagrantino di Montefalco
Scanzo
Sforzato di Valtellina
Taurasi
Torgiano Riserva Montefalco
Valtellina Superiore
Verdicchio del Castelli di Jesi Classico Riserva
Verdicchio di Matelica Riserva
Vermentino di Gallura
Vernaccia di Serrapetrona

ITALIAN WINE QUALITY LEVELS

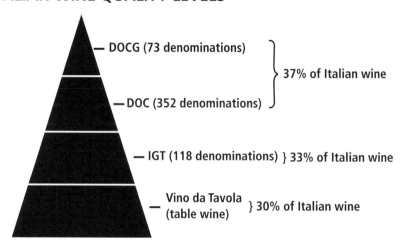

- DOCG (73 denominations)
- DOC (352 denominations) } 37% of Italian wine
- IGT (118 denominations) } 33% of Italian wine
- Vino da Tavola (table wine) } 30% of Italian wine

As a comparison, 30 years ago table wine represented 90 percent of all Italian wine.

ITALIAN WINE NAMES

For Bordeaux, you most often see the name of a château, and you look for the grape variety on California bottles. But in Italy, different winemaking regions have different ways of naming their wines: by grape variety, district or village, or a proprietary name. Note the examples below.

EXAMPLES OF GRAPE VARIETY	EXAMPLES OF DISTRICT OR VILLAGE	EXAMPLES OF PROPRIETARY NAMES
BARBERA	BARBARESCO	ORNELLAIA
NEBBIOLO	BAROLO	SASSICAIA
PINOT GRIGIO	CHIANTI	SUMMUS
SANGIOVESE	MONTALCINO	TIGNANELLO

TUSCANY

Tuscan winemaking has a long history, dating back nearly 3,000 years to the Etruscans, who lived here in pre-Roman times. Chianti is a wine region of Tuscany and also the most well known of all its wines. The name "Chianti" first appears in records from A.D. 700. Brolio, a major producer, has been making it since 1141. More than 30 generations of the family have tended to the vineyards and made the wine.

CHIANTI

Current DOCG rules require winemakers to use at least 80 percent Sangiovese to produce Chianti, but the rules also encourage the use of other grapes by allowing a previously unprecedented 20 percent of nontraditional grapes (Cabernet Sauvignon, Merlot, Syrah, etc.). Over the last quarter century, this shift and better vineyard development and winemaking techniques have improved the quality and reputation of Chianti greatly.

The different levels of Chianti are:

Chianti The basic level. Cost: $.

Chianti Classico From the inner historic district of Chianti. These wines must age for two years. Cost: $$.

Chianti Classico Riserva From a Classico area and aged at least 27 months. Cost: $$$$.

Chianti Classico Gran Selezione The highest level. All grapes for these wines can come only from the winery's own vineyard (estate-bottled) and must age for a minimum of 30 months. Cost: $$$$.

Many producers of Chianti Classico and Classico Riserva use **100 PERCENT SANGIOVESE** to set themselves apart.

CHOOSING A CHIANTI

Chianti varies considerably in style—depending on the blend of grapes—so first find the style that you like best. Then always buy from a shipper or producer with a good, reliable reputation.

Quality Chianti producers include:

Antinori	Castello del Terriccio	Monsanto
Antinori Tenuta Belvedere	Castello di Ama	Montepeloso
	Castello di Bossi	Nozzole
Badia a Coltibuono	Castello di Volpaia	Petra
Belguardo	Fattoria di Magliano	Podere Chiano
Brolio	Fattoria le Pupille	Podere Grattamacco
Brancaia	Fontodi	Querciabella
Capannelle	Frescobaldi	Ricasoli
Castellare di Castellina	Le Macchiole	Ruffino
Castello Banfi	Melini	San Felice
Castello dei Rampolla	Michele Satta	Vignamaggio

OTHER TUSCAN WINES

Tuscany produces many other types of wine, but you should know Brunello di Montalcino, Vino Nobile di Montepulciano, Carmignano, and the Super Tuscans from Bolgheri in Maremma.

BRUNELLO DI MONTALCINO

The stunningly beautiful village of Montalcino sits atop a hill surrounded by 5,000 acres of vineyards. The wines come from 100 percent Brunello grapes (another name for Sangiovese) and rank among the best in the world. This is one of my absolute favorite red wines. Brunello di Montalcino received DOCG status in 1980. Beginning with the 1995 vintage, Brunellos must age in oak for at least two years, instead of the previous three. The result? A fruitier, more accessible wine. In 2008, Brunello winemakers voted to maintain 100 percent Sangiovese for their wines, not blending it with any other varieties. If you buy a good Brunello, it probably needs five to ten years of additional aging before it reaches peak drinkability.

Because of its limited supply, Brunello di Montalcino is sometimes very expensive. For **ONE OF THE BEST VALUES IN TUSCAN RED WINE,** look for Rosso di Montalcino and Rosso di Montepulciano, especially in great years.

	ACRES	WINERIES
Chianti Classico	18,000	964
Brunello de Montalcino	8,645	258
Vino Nobile di Montepulciano	3,025	76

More than 150 producers grow Brunello, and my favorites include:

Altesino	Col d'Orcia	Poggio Antico
Antinori	Collosorbo	Poggio il Castellare
Barbi	Constanti	Poliziano
Biondi-Santi	Fuligni	San Felice
Capanna	Gaja	San Filippo
Caparzo	Il Marroneto	Silvio Nardi
Carpineto	La Fuga	Siro Pacenti
Castelgiocondo	La Poderina	Soldera
Castello Banfi	Lisini	Tenuta di Sesta
Casanova di Neri	Livio Sassetti	Uccelliera
Ciacci Piccolomini d'Aragona	Marchesi de Frescobaldi	Valdicava

In 1975, just 30 **BRUNELLO PRODUCERS MADE** 800,000 bottles. Today 258 producers make more than 9 million bottles!

VINO NOBILE DI MONTEPULCIANO

This "noble wine from Montepulciano" village comes primarily (at least 70 percent) from the Sangiovese varietal known as Prugnolo gentile. Like Montalcino, Montepulciano is a must-visit town for wine-loving tourists. The region has more than 75 wineries and more than 3,000 acres of vines.

My favorite producers include:

Avignonesi	Fassati	Poggio alla Sala
Bindella	Fattoria del Cerro	Poliziano
Boscarelli	Icario	Salcheto
Carpineto	La Braccesca	Valdipiatta
Dei		

CARMIGNANO

This smaller region has been producing great wines since Roman times, but it has become increasingly popular in the last 20 years. DOCG regulations hold that Carmignano must contain at least 50 percent Sangiovese, 10–20 percent Cabernet Sauvignon or Cabernet Franc, plus other indigenous grapes. The wine also must age for at least three years.

For Carmignano, look for:

Artimino	Poggiolo	Villa di Capezzana

THE SUPER TUSCANS

Sometimes called the Wild West because of its landscapes and winemaking, Bolgheri's vineyards cover more than 2,000 acres. Grapes have grown here since the nineteenth century, but Bolgheri has risen to international prominence in the last 30 years. Unlike Brunello and Vino Nobile, Bolgheri wines can be made with red Bordeaux grapes, such as Cabernet Sauvignon, Cabernet Franc, and Merlot. Sometimes it also includes Syrah, Petit Verdot, and of course the traditional Sangiovese.

Decades ago, the DOC didn't allow the use of certain grapes, such as Cabernet Sauvignon, and in the 1970s, as was the case in Bordeaux, the market for Chianti wines was suffering. To skirt DOC regulations and make better wines—as we saw California winemakers do with Meritage wines—Italian vintners created their own style of wine legally qualifying simply as *vino da tavola*, or table wine. Today these wines, governed by the IGT classification, have a world-class reputation and have become known as the Super Tuscans that you've probably seen on wine lists at good Italian restaurants.

Bolgheri wines have three distinct styles. First: most wines are a red Bordeaux blend; second: a blend of Cabernet Franc and Cabernet Sauvignon; third: a blend of Cabernet Sauvignon, Merlot, and Syrah.

My favorite Super Tuscans include:

Brancaia Ilatraia	Le Macchiole	Petra
Ca' Marcanda	Luce	Rocca di Frassinello
Cabreo Il Borgo	Masseto	Sassicaia
Castello del Terriccio	Montepeloso	Solaia
Excelsus	Mazzei Tenuta Belguardo	Summus
Fattoria le Pupille	Olmaia	Tenuta di Biserno
Guado al Tasso	Ornellaia	Tignanello
		Tua Rita

SOUTHERN COASTAL TUSCANY

Some 40 years ago, when I first visited Tuscany, the only wine of merit was Chianti, and it wasn't made very well. (Today, it's a world-class wine.) About 20 years ago, I started hearing more about another part of Tuscany called Maremma. It once consisted largely of marshland. Today it's home to the DOCG wine Morellino di Scansano and the Super Tuscans. Morellino is the local name for Sangiovese, and Scansano is a medieval village in the region. Bolgheri, another small village in the region, is where in the 1940s

Tenuta San Guido produced Sassicaia, the first Super Tuscan wine. These are the major grapes used in the area:

RED	WHITE
CABERNET FRANC	TREBBIANO
CABERNET SAUVIGNON	VERMANTINO
MERLOT	SAUVIGNON BLANC
SANGIOVESE	
SYRAH	

My favorite Bolgheri producers include:

Guado al Tasso   **Ornellaia**   **Tenuta San Guido**
Michele Satta   **Sassicaia**

- BEST RECENT VINTAGES OF CHIANTI CLASSICO -
2006** 2007** 2010** 2011* 2013* 2015** 2016

- BEST RECENT VINTAGES OF BRUNELLO DI MONTALCINO -
2004** 2006** 2007** 2008* 2010** 2011*
2012** 2015** 2016

- BEST RECENT VINTAGES OF BOLGHERI -
2006** 2007** 2008* 2009* 2010** 2011* 2012*
2013* 2015** 2016

* EXCEPTIONAL VINTAGE   ** EXTRAORDINARY VINTAGE

BRICCO: a hillside vineyard.

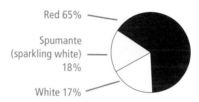

PIEDMONT WINE PRODUCTION

Red 65%

Spumante (sparkling white) 18%

White 17%

PIEDMONT

Some of the biggest and best red wines in the world come from Piedmont. The major grapes that grow there are:

Barbera	Dolcetto	Nebbiolo
(41,000 acres)	(16,000 acres)	(9,000 acres)

Two of the best DOCG Tuscan wines hail from the villages of Barbaresco and Barolo. These "heavyweight" wines come from the Nebbiolo variety and have the fullest style and a high alcohol content. Be careful when you try to match young vintages of these wines with your dinner because they may overpower the food.

	BARBARESCO VS.	BAROLO
GRAPE	NEBBIOLO	NEBBIOLO
MINIMUM ALCOHOL CONTENT	12.5%	12.5%
STYLE	LIGHTER, BUT FINE AND ELEGANT	MORE COMPLEX, MORE BODY
MINIMUM AGING	TWO YEARS, ONE IN WOOD	THREE YEARS, ONE IN WOOD
DEFINITION OF "RISERVA"	AGED FOUR YEARS	AGED FIVE YEARS
PRODUCTION	3 MILLION BOTTLES	10 MILLION BOTTLES

These are the Crus of Barolo:

Barolo	Cannubi	Monforte d'Alba
Briccolina	Castiglione Falletto	Monvigliero
Bricco Rocche	Cerequio	Mosconi
Bricco San Pietro	La Morra	Ravera
Brunate	Le Coste	Serralunga d'Alba
Bussia		

My favorite Piedmont producers include:

A. Conterno	G. Conterno	Paolo Scavino
Antonio Vallana	Gaja	Pio Cesare
B. Giacosa	La Spinetta	Pira
Borgogno	Luciano Sandrone	Produttori del
C. Rinaldi	M. Chiarlo	Barbaresco
Ceretto	Marcarini	Prunotto
Conterno Fantino	Marchesi di Barolo	Renato Ratti
Damilano	Marchesi di Gresy	Roberto Voerzio
Domenico Clerico	Mascarello e Figlio	Schiavenza
Erbaluce di Caluso	Massolino	Vietti
Fontanafredda		

For aging, Giuseppe Colla of Prunotto advises that, for a good vintage, you set aside a Barbaresco for at least four years and a Barolo for six before drinking. In a great vintage, age a Barbaresco for six and a Barolo for eight. Patience is a virtue—especially with wine. Also keep in mind that many Piedmont wines have changed over the last decade. Past wines were more tannic and difficult to appreciate when young, but many today are much easier to drink.

```
–  BEST VINTAGES OF PIEDMONT WINES  –
  1996**  1998*  1999*  2000**  2001**  2004**  2005*  2006**
      2007**  2008**  2009*  2010**  2011**  2012*
           2013*  2014  2015**  2016
           * EXCEPTIONAL VINTAGE  ** EXTRAORDINARY VINTAGE
```

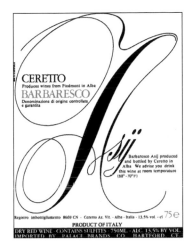

Another great Piedmont wine is called **GATTINARA.** Look for the Antoniolo Reservas.

Three reasons to visit **PIEDMONT IN THE FALL:** the harvest, the food, and the white truffles.

GREAT OLDER VINTAGES of Piedmont: 1982, 1985, 1988, 1989, 1990

AMARONE della Valpolicella: dry
RECIOTO della Valpolicella: sweet

VENETO

This is Italy's largest wine-producing region. Even if you don't recognize the name immediately, you've probably had a Venetian wine at some point, such as a Valpolicella, Bardolino, or Soave. All three are consistent, easy to drink, and don't need aging. They don't match the quality of a Brunello di Montalcino or a Barolo, but they're very good table wines that fit everyone's budget. The best of the three is Valpolicella. Look for Valpolicella Superiore made using the *ripasso* method, which adds the grape skins from Amarone wine back to Valpolicella, giving it more alcohol and flavor. Easy-to-find Veneto producers are:

Allegrini	Folonari	Suavia
Anselmi	Quintarelli	Zenato
Bolla	Santa Sofia	

AMARONE

The word "Amarone" derives from *amaro*, meaning "bitter," and *-one* (OH-nay), meaning "big." It's a type of Valpolicella wine made by allowing the ripest grapes (Corvina, Rondinella, and Molinara) from the top of each bunch to raisinate on straw mats. Amarone winemakers ferment most of the sugar, bringing the alcohol content to 14–16 percent. The minimum alcohol level is 14 percent.

Since 1990, the vineyards in Valpolicella have doubled in size. My favorite producers of Amarone include:

Allegrini	Nicolis	Tommaso Bussola
Bertani	Quintarelli	Romano dal Forno
Cesari	Tedeschi	Zenato
Masi	Tommasi	

– BEST VINTAGES OF AMARONE –
1990** 1993 1995** 1997** 1998** 2000* 2001*
2003* 2004** 2006* 2008** 2009* 2010*
2011* 2012* 2013* 2014 2015* 2016
* EXCEPTIONAL VINTAGE   ** EXTRAORDINARY VINTAGE

SICILY

Long famous for the sweet fortified Marsala wines and the Zibibbo (Muscato) wines from the island of Pantelleria, Sicily didn't have any icon wines until recently. Most of the wine made here went in bulk to France and Northern Italy for blending. Then, in 1983, the government began a program to increase the use of international grapes, such as Chardonnay, Cabernet Sauvignon, and Syrah. That initiative also included new vineyard techniques and winery management—and it worked! By 2000, wineries were focusing on making their best wines with indigenous grapes, especially Nero d'Avola and Nerello Mascalese for the reds and Grillo, Catarratto, and Inzolia for the whites.

Sicily is the largest island in the Mediterranean and the fourth largest wine producing region in Italy, and I've visited it three times over the last 20 years. The first time, there still wasn't enough happening to write about. Ten years ago, I felt the same way. In 2017, I spent a month visiting more than 50 wineries from the west coast to Mt. Etna. Since my first visit, many changes have increased the quality of the wine and given the overall industry a new direction. Today the island has 453 producers, 23 DOC wines, and 1 DOCG wine. The old saw holds true here: What's old is new again—and the best is yet to come.

THE LAND

Sicily is the hottest and driest region of Italy. During my visit in summer 2017, the temperature hit 90–95°F every day, with no rainfall and lots of wind. Overall the island has poor soil, and farmers grow grapes on hills and mountains. One Sicilian winemaker told me that there is Sicily and there is Mt. Etna. The vineyards in Etna sometimes feel like the moon. The volcanic soil is black, and when your foot goes down, lava dust comes up! These are the most important regions and their wines:

Marsala	fortified wine
Faro	red wine only
Siracusa	red (Nero d'Avola), white, and Muscato
Noto	Moscato
Vittoria	Cerasuolo di Vittoria
Mt. Etna	80 percent red, 20 percent white
Menfi	red, white, and rosato

John Woodhouse, an Englishman, came across **MARSALA WINE** in 1773 and brought it to the UK to compete with Sherry and Port.

A winemaker told me that Sicily has five official languages: Italian (Sicilian), Greek, Latin, Arabic, and Hebrew, reflecting the **HISTORY AND DIVERSITY** of the island.

2011: IGT Terre Siciliane established
2013: The Consorzio established, with 98 percent of producers joining
2017: More DOCs

70 percent of Sicily's **RAIN FALLS** in Etna.

Riccardo Cotarello, **THE TRAVELING WINE WIZARD,** is Italy's top wine consultant and has helped tremendously in raising the quality of Sicilian wines over the past decade..

An **ACTIVE VOLCANO**, Mt. Etna last erupted in March 2017.

It takes **200 YEARS** for lava to turn into dirt.

MARC DE GRAZIA, the great importer of Italian wines into America, owns a vineyard on Mt. Etna.

SICILY WINE PRODUCTION

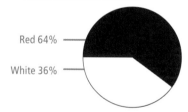

Red 64%

White 36%

GELATO AND CANNOLI were made first in Sicily.

THE GRAPES OF SICILY

Because of the weather conditions, growers here can produce organic grapes easily.

RED

INDIGENOUS VARIETIES	
NERO D'AVOLA	THE REGION'S SIGNATURE GRAPE
NERELLO MASCALESE	THE PRIMARY GRAPE IN RED ETNA WINES
NERELLO CAPPUCCIO	BLENDED WITH NERELLO MASCALESE ON MT. ETNA.
FRAPPATO	A LIGHTER GRAPE
PERRICONE	THIS GRAPE MAKES FULL BODIED, HEAVY WINES.

INTERNATIONAL VARIETIES	
CABERNET SAUVIGNON	
MERLOT	
SYRAH	

WHITE

INDIGENOUS VARIETIES	
GRILLO	VINTNERS ARE MAKING THIS BASE WINE FOR MARSALA INTO SPARKLING WINE AND BLENDING IT WITH INTERNATIONAL GRAPES SUCH AS CHARDONNAY.
CATARRATTO	THE MOST PLANTED WHITE GRAPE (60 PERCENT OF VINEYARDS), KNOWN AS THE BLENDING GRAPE IN MARSALA
INZOLIA	THE ISLAND'S BEST VARIETY FOR DRY WHITE WINE
ZIBIBBO (MUSCATO)	THIS GRAPE MAKES THE SWEET, AROMATIC WINE FROM PANTELLERIA.

INTERNATIONAL WHITE GRAPES	
CHARDONNAY	
SAUVIGNON BLANC	

Made from Nero d'Avola and Frappato grapes, Cerasuolo di Vittoria is Sicily's only DOCG wine. In terms of style, Nerello Mascalese falls somewhere between a Pinot Noir (soft fruit) and a Nebbiolo (high acidity and tannins). Of the international grapes now in Sicily, the reigning winemaker favorite is Syrah, which loves a lot of sun and heat. Some of the best wines I tasted in Sicily came from the Syrah grape. If you like sweet wine, try Moscato from Pantelleria and Malvasia delle Lipari.

The IGT Terre Sicilane classification, established in 2011, covers all wines made in Sicily, and the DOC Sicilia, created in 2017, covers higher quality wines from anywhere on the island.

CHOOSING A SICILIAN WINE

Over the last 15 years, the number of wineries has tripled. Look for these producers

Abbazia Santa Anastasia	Feudo Maccari	Murana
Baglio Curatolo	Feudo Montoni*	Palari*
Baglio di Pianetto	Feudo Principe di Butera	Passopisciaro Contrada*
Barone Villagrande	Firriato	Planeta*
Benanti*	Frank Cornelissen	Regaleali
Cantine Russo	Georghi Tondi	Settesoli
Cusumano*	Gulfi	Spadafora*
Donna Fugata* (Ben Ryé)	Lantieri (Lipari)	Tasca d'Almerita* (Almerita)
Duca di Salaparuta	Marco de Bartoli* (Passito di Pantelleria)	Tenuta delle Terre Nere
Fatascia	Morgante	Tenuta Rapitalia
Feudo Disisa		Terrazze dell'Etna

My favorite producers

My favorite icon wines of Sicily include:

Corvo Duca Enrico	Feudo Maccari Sicilia Mahâris
Cos Nero d'Avola Sicilia Contrada	Marco de Bartoli Marsala Superiore
Cusumano Nero d'Avola Sicilia Sàgana	Passopisciaro Terre Sicillane Contrada
Donnafugata Passito di Pantelleria Ben Ryé	Planeta Chardonnay Sicilia
Duca di Salaparuto	Rosso del Conte
Duca Enrico	Spadafora Sole dei Padre
	Tenuta Delle Terre Nere
	Etna Prephylloxera La Vigne di Don Peppino

A Mt. Etna red wine **MUST CONTAIN** a minimum 80% of Nerello Mascallese.

FEUDO means feudal estate.

Sicily specializes in my top **THREE NECESSITIES** in life: olive oil, bread, and wine.

80% of Mt. Etna is **RED WINE**.

— BEST RECENT VINTAGES OF RED ETNA —

2010*   2011   2012   2013   2014*   2015   2016   2017

EXCEPTIONAL VINTAGE

— BEST RECENT VINTAGES OF SICILY —

2014**   2015   2016   2017

**EXTRAORDINARY VINTAGE*

OTHER IMPORTANT ITALIAN REGIONS

All 20 of Italy's wine regions produce good or great wine, so it's worth taking a quick look at the lesser-known regions, the predominant grapes that grow there, the best wines to try, and some of my favorite producers that make them.

REGION	GRAPE	WINE	PRODUCERS
ABRUZZO	MONTEPULCIANO D'ABRUZZO	MONTEPULCIANO EMIDIO PEPE MASCIARELLI	ELIO MONTI LA VALENTINA
CAMPANIA	AGLIANICO FIANO GRECO SANGIOVESE	GRECO DI TUFO FIANO DI AVELLINO TAURASI	FEUDI DI SAN GREGORIO MASTRO- BERARDINO MOLETTIERA MONTEVETRANO MUSTILLI QUINTODECIMO VILLA MATILDE
FRIULI-VENEZIA GIULIA	PINOT BIANCO PINOT GRIGIO CHARDONNAY SAUVIGNON BLANC		LIVIO FELLUGA MARCO FELLUGA MARIO SCHIOPETTO
LOMBARDY	NEBBIOLO TREBBIANO	FRANCIACORTA (SPARKLING) LUGANA VALTELLINA (GRUMELLO, SASSELLA, INFERNO, VALGELLA)	**SPARKLING PRODUCERS:** BELLAVISTA CA' DEL BOSCO **VALTELLINA PRODUCERS:** CONTI SERTOLI FAY NINO NEGRI RAINOLDI

TRI-VENETO encompasses Trentino, Alto-Adige, and Friuli. Some of the best white wines of Italy come from those regions.

In Friuli-Venezia Giulia and Trentino-Alto Adige, the wines are **IDENTIFIED BY PRODUCER AND GRAPE VARIETY** rather than a specific wine name.

IN BASILICATA, try Terre degli Svevi Aglianico.

ITALY'S WINE PRODUCTION

50% white | 50% red

REGION	GRAPE	WINE	PRODUCERS
TRENTINO-ALTO ADIGE	**WHITE GRAPES:** PINOT BIANCO PINOT GRIGIO CHARDONNAY SAUVIGNON GEWÜRZTRAMINER **RED GRAPES:** CABERNET FRANC CABERNET SAUVIGNON LAGREIN MERLOT		ALOIS LAGEDE CANTINA DI TERLANO COLTERENZIO FERRARI FORADORI H. LUN ROTALIANO TEROLDEGO TIEFENBRUNNER TRAMIN
UMBRIA	TREBBIANO SAGRANTINO SANGIOVESE MERLOT	ORVIETO SAGRANTINO DI MONTEFALCO TORGIANO ROSSO RISERVA	ARNALDO CAPRAI CASTELLO DELLE REGINE LUNGAROTTI PAOLO BEA

THE WHITE WINES OF ITALY

When the first edition of this book was published in 1985, I didn't discuss Italian white wines. At that time, Italian winemakers were putting their best efforts into making red wines. The most popular whites available were Orvieto Soave, Frascati Pinot Grigio, and Verdicchio—still easy to drink, inexpensive, everyday wines. Today, the best Italian regions for white wine are Trentino-Alto Adige and Friuli-Venezia Giulia (Collio). In them, growers have planted more international grapes such as Chardonnay, Riesling, and Sauvignon Blanc. These, along with indigenous grapes such as Cortese, Arneis, Vermentino, Grechetto, Fiano, Garganega, Falanghina, and the famous Zibibbo—used for the sweet wines of

Sicily—make for very good white wines, which vintners throughout Italy are producing.

MY FAVORITE WHITE WINES OF ITALY INCLUDE:

STYLE	PRODUCERS
VERNACCIA DI SAN GIMIGNANO	ANTINORI CERVARO DELLA SALA CHARDONNAY
GAVI	JERMANN "VINTAGE TUNINA"
COLLIO CHARDONNAYS	LA SCOLCA GAVI DEI GAVI BLACK LABEL
VERDICCHIO DEI CASTELLI DI	BRUNO GIACOSA ROERO ARNEIS
JESI CLASSICO SUPERIORE	CANTINA TERLANO TERLANER CLASSICO
	LIVIO FELLUGA SAUVIGNON BLANC

FORTY YEARS LATER IN ITALY

For the Italians, wine used to be an everyday affair, like salt and pepper, to enhance the taste of food. Since then, winemaking has become a business, and Italian winemakers have shifted from making casual-drinking wines to better-made wines that prove much more marketable internationally. They've done so by using modern technology, updated vineyard management, and modern vinification procedures. They also have experimented with non-traditional grape varieties, such as Cabernet Sauvignon and Merlot. Remember, we're not talking about California; Italy has literally *thousands* of years of traditions that are changing. Vintners there have had to unlearn winemaking techniques that go back dozens of generations in order to make better wines for the export market.

The prices of Italian wines have increased tremendously as well over the last 25 years—not good news for consumers. Some of the wines from Italy have become among the most expensive in the world. Many certainly are worth it, but the value to the consumer isn't the same as it was 40 years ago.

5 BEST VALUE ITALIAN WINES UNDER $30

Allegrini Valpolicella Classico • Castello Banfi Toscana Centine • Michele Chiarlo Barbera d'Asti • Morgante Nero d'Avola • Taurino Salice Salentino

See page 361 for a complete list.

PINOT GRIGIO is a white-grape variety found in Alsace, France, where it's called Pinot Gris. It also grows with success in Oregon and California.

The most planted white variety in Piedmont is **MOSCATO** (25,000 acres).

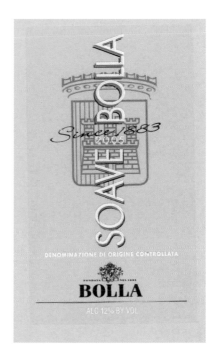

SINGLE-VINEYARD LABELING is one of the *newest trends* in Italy.

In Italy, consumption of bottled water and beer are both increasing, while **WINE CONSUMPTION IS DECREASING**.

GUIDED TASTING

Many people know something about French or American wines but very little about Italian wines, so this tasting is all about discovery and finding new wine styles made from grapes such as Sangiovese or Nebbiolo. For the Piedmont tasting, following the advice of Renato Ratti, you'll start with the lighter-style Barbera, move to the fuller-bodied Barbaresco, and then you will appreciate a Barolo fully as well as the Amarone.

Tuscany Three wines compared:
1. Chianti Classico Riserva
2. Vino Nobile di Montelpulciano
3. Brunello di Montalcino

Piedmont Three wines compared:
4. Barbera or Dolcetto
5. Barbaresco
6. Barolo

Veneto One wine tasted alone:
7. Amarone

When **DRINKING THE RED WINES OF PIEDMONT**, start with the lighter-style Barbera and Dolcetto, move to the fuller-bodied Barbaresco, and then you can appreciate a Barolo fully. As vintner Renato Ratti said, "Barolo is the wine of arrival."

FOOD PAIRINGS

In Italy, wine is made to go with food. No meal is served without it. Take it from these experts.

"**Chianti** with prosciutto, chicken, pasta, and of course pizza. Pair a **Chianti Classico Riserva** with a hearty prime-rib dinner or a steak."
                                        —*Ambrogio Folonari of Ruffino*

"A **Chianti** is good with all meat dishes, but I save the **Brunello** for 'stronger' dishes, such as steak, wild boar, pheasant, and other game, as well as Pecorino Toscano cheese."   —*Ezio Rivella of Castello Banfi*

"**Barbaresco** with meat and veal, and also with mature cheeses that are not too strong, such as Emmenthaler and Fontina. Avoid Parmesan and goat cheese when you have a Barbaresco. If you're having a **Barolo**, my favorite is roast lamb."   —*Angelo Gaja*

"Piedmontese wines show better with food than in a tasting."
                                        Angelo Gaja

"When you're having Italian wines, you must not taste the wine alone. You must have them with food."
                                        —Giuseppe Colla of Prunotto

"I enjoy light-style **Dolcetto** with all first courses and all white meat—chicken and veal especially—but not fish. The wine doesn't stand up well to spicy sauce, but it's great with tomato sauce and pasta."

—Giuseppe Colla of Prunotto

"**Barbera** and **Dolcetto** are good with chicken and lighter foods. However, **Barolo** and **Barbaresco** need to be served with heavier dishes. Better yet, brasato al Barolo—wine-braised meat, such as pheasant, duck, or wild rabbit. For a special dish, try risotto al Barolo (rice cooked with Barolo). When serving wine with dessert, strawberries or peaches with **Dolcetto**."

—Renato Ratti

"With young **Chianti**, roast chicken, squab, or pasta with meat sauce. To complement an older Chianti, a wide pasta with meat braised in Chianti, pheasant or other game, wild boar, or roast beef.

—Lorenza de'Medici of Badia a Coltibuono

"I enjoy **Chianti** with the grilled foods for which Tuscany is famous, especially its bistecca alla Fiorentina, but also poultry and even hamburgers. With **Chianti Classico Riserva**, wild boar and fine aged Parmesan cheese. The wine is a perfect match for roast beef, roast turkey, lamb, or veal."

—Piero Antinori

With a **red Sicilian wine**, lamb, pork, or goat. Try red mullet, swordfish, or tuna with a **white Sicilian**.

TEST YOUR KNOWLEDGE of the wines of Italy by trying the quiz on page 385.

——— **FURTHER READING** ———

Into Italian Wine by Geralyn Brostrom and Jack Brostrom

Italian Wine by Victor Hazan

Italian Wines for Dummies by Mary Ewing Mulligan and Ed McCarthy

The Simon & Schuster Pocket Guide to Italian Wines by Burton Anderson

Vino Italiano by Joseph Bastianich and David Lynch

Wine Atlas of Italy by Burton Anderson

THE WINES OF AUSTRALIA AND NEW ZEALAND

AUSTRALIAN WINE EXPORTS TO AMERICA
1990: 578,000 cases
2017: 20,000,000 cases

THE AUSTRALIAN GRAPE HARVEST

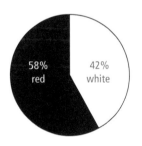

58% red

42% white

Australia has 65 wine regions and, in 2017, almost **2,500 WINERIES**.

THE WINES OF AUSTRALIA

After the British lost the colonies in the American War of Independence (as they call it), they looked to other colonial opportunities, founding Sydney in New South Wales in 1788. The wine industry there began that same year. At first, the country produced mostly fortified wines. Cabernet Sauvignon vine cuttings from Château Haut-Brion in Bordeaux were planted near Melbourne in the 1830s. James Busby brought Syrah cuttings from

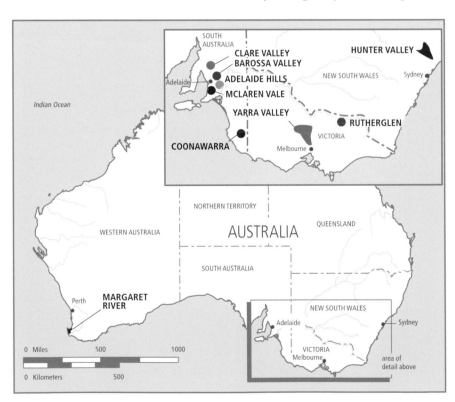

Australia is now the third largest exporter of wine to America, and **YELLOW TAIL** is the top imported wine. Sales rocketed from 200,000 cases in 2001 to nearly 8 million cases in 2016.

Australia has some of the oldest Shiraz (Syrah) grape vines in the world, many of them more than **100 YEARS OLD.**

the Chapoutier vineyards in the Rhône Valley in 1832 and planted them in Hunter Valley. Many of the largest or most prestigious wine companies here—Henschke, Lindemans, Orlando, Penfolds, Seppelt—were founded in the nineteenth century and produce excellent wines today.

Once better known for kangaroos and surfing, Australia ranks as the world's sixth largest wine producer. The shift to quality grape varieties began in the 1970s and has continued with tremendous speed. From 1988 to 2008, exports of Australian wines increased nearly 100 percent, and now exports exceed $3 billion!

The country has 65 wine-growing regions, called Geographical Indications. You don't need to know them all, but you should familiarize yourself with the best regions and their best wines:

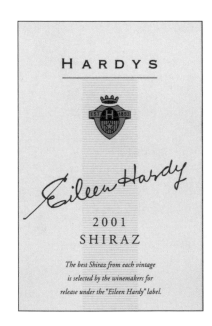

HARDYS

Eileen Hardy

2001
SHIRAZ

*The best Shiraz from each vintage
is selected by the winemakers for
release under the "Eileen Hardy" label.*

TASMANIA is known for sparkling wines,
and **RUTHERGLEN** for fortified wine

REGION	VARIETIES
SOUTH AUSTRALIA	
ADELAIDE HILLS	CHARDONNAY, SAUVIGNON BLANC
BAROSSA VALLEY	SHIRAZ, GRENACHE
CLARE VALLEY	RIESLING
COONAWARRA	CABERNET SAUVIGNON
McLAREN VALE	SHIRAZ, GRENACHE
NEW SOUTH WALES	
HUNTER VALLEY	SÉMILLON
VICTORIA	
YARRA VALLEY	CHARDONNAY, PINOT NOIR
WESTERN AUSTRALIA	
MARGARET RIVER	CABERTNET SAUVIGNON, CHARDONNAY, SAUVIGNON BLANC, SÉMILLON

South Australia produces almost half of the country's wines. It also remains one of the few wine regions in the world never to have succumbed to phylloxera, so many growers here still plant using the vines' own rootstock.

More than 100 different grape varieties grow in Australia, but none of them is indigenous.

The main white grape varieties are:

Chardonnay	Sauvignon Blanc	Sémillon	Riesling
(65,000 acres)	(17,000 acres)	(14,000 acres)	(10,000 acres)

The main red varietials are:

Shiraz / Syrah	Cabernet Sauvignon	Merlot	Pinot Noir
(104,000 acres)	(65,000 acres)	(23,000 acres)	(12,000 acres)

The Australian wine industry's Label Integrity Program (LIP) took effect with the 1990 vintage. It doesn't govern as many aspects of wine production as France's AOC laws, but the LIP does regulate and oversee vintage, varietal, and Geographical Indication regulations.

To conform to the LIP and the Australian Food Standards Code, Australian wine labels must provide a great deal of information. Take a look at the label in the right margin. The producer is Penfolds. For blends that list varieties, labels must show the percentages of each varietal, and the first grape must have the highest percentage. If the label specifies a Geographical Indication—Clare Valley here—at least 85 percent of the

More than 75 percent of Australian wine is bottled with a **SCREW CAP.**

Australia's most coveted **WINE AWARD**, established in 1962, takes its name from wine-bar owner Jimmy Watson and goes to the best one-year-old red wine each year. The first 15 went to wines labeled "Burgundy type" or "Claret type." Only in 1976 did a wine labeled with a grape variety win the trophy.

wine must originate there. If a vintage appears, 95 percent of the wine must come from that vintage.

Since 1994, Australia and most other wine countries have conformed to an EU wine agreement that calls for an end to the use of borrowed generic names, such as Burgundy, Champagne, Port, and Sherry. One of Australia's most famous wines is Penfolds Grange Hermitage, so, to adhere to the agreement, Penfolds dropped "Hermitage," a wine produced in France's Rhône Valley. Even with its "new" name, Penfolds Grange remains one of Australia's greatest wines.

MY FAVORITE AUSTRALIAN PRODUCERS INCLUDE:

Cape Mentelle	Cabernet Sauvignon
Clarendon Hills	Hickinbotham Grenache
Cullen Wines	Diana Madeline
d'Arenberg	The Dead Arm Shiraz
De Bortoli	Noble One
Grant Burge	Meshach Shiraz
Hardy's	Chateau Reynella Cellar No. One Shiraz
Henschke	Cyril Cabernet Sauvignon, Hill of Grace
Hentley Farm	The Beauty
Jamshead	Seville Syrah
Jim Barry	McRae Wood Shiraz
Kaesler	Old Bastard Shiraz
Katnook	Odyssey Cabernet Sauvignon
Leeuwin Estate	Art Series Chardonnay or Cabernet Sauvignon
Mollydooker Shiraz	Velvet Glove
Mount Mary	Quintet
Noon Winery	Reserve Cabernet Sauvignon
Penfolds	Grange, Bin 707 Cabernet Sauvignon
Petaluma	Adelaide Hills Shiraz
Peter Lehmann	Reserve Riesling or Sémillon
Powell & Son	Brennecker Grenache
Shaw & Smith	M3 Vineyard Adelaide Hills Chardonnay
Tahbilk	Eric Stevens Purbrick Shiraz or Cabernet Sauvignon
Torbreck Vintners	Run Rig
Vasse Felix	Margaret River Chardonnay and Sémillon

Voyager	Margaret River Sauvignon Blanc / Sémillon
Wirra Wirra	RSW Shiraz and Angelus Cabernet Sauvignon
Wolf Blass	Black Label Shiraz
Yalumba	The Menzies Coonawarra Cabernet Sauvignon
Yering Station	Shiraz, Viognier

— BEST RECENT VINTAGES OF WINES — FROM BAROSSA, COONAWARRA, AND MCLAREN VALE:

2004** 2005** 2006* 2008* 2009 2010**
2012** 2013* 2014 2015 2016 2017

*EXCEPTIONAL VINTAGE   **EXTRAORDINARY VINTAGE*

5 BEST VALUE WINES OF AUSTRALIA UNDER $30

Jacob's Creek Shiraz Cabernet • Leeuwin Estate Siblings Shiraz •
Lindeman's Chardonnay Bin 65 • Penfolds "Bin 28 Kalimna" Shiraz •
Rosemount Estate Shiraz Cabernet (Diamond Label)

See page 356 for a complete list

VASSE FELIX

Chardonnay

2007 MARGARET RIVER

The vintage in Australia occurs in the **FIRST HALF OF THE YEAR**. Growers harvest grapes from February to May.

2006 had the **LATEST HARVEST** ever. 2013 had the **EARLIEST HARVEST** ever. **MARGARET RIVER WINES** had a great vintage in 2013.

TEST YOUR KNOWLEDGE of the wines of Australia by trying the quiz on page 387.

—— FURTHER READING ——

Australian Wine Companion by James Halliday

THE WINES OF NEW ZEALAND

New Zealand features beautiful coastlines, rolling hills, magnificent mountains, and outstanding weather. It's also the home of bungee jumping, which accurately captures the vitality and exuberance of its wine industry. The country recorded its first vintage in 1836 and by 1985 had approximately 15,000 acres of vines. The majority—mostly Müller Thurgau—produced large volumes of low-end wine, however. Winemakers produced so much wine that they created a huge surplus, and as a result the government offered cash to any grower who agreed to uproot a quarter of his or her vineyard, an event known as the Vine Pull. This massive purge of inferior wine grapes led to a resurgence of interest in high-quality wine and to widespread plantings of Sauvignon Blanc, Pinot Noir, and Chardonnay. This shift marked the New Zealand wine industry's new beginning. Over the last 30 years, the vineyards and wines here have grown by leaps and

95 percent of New Zealand's population lives within **30 MILES** of the ocean.

TOTAL ACRES OF GRAPES

1985	15,000 acres
1986	11,000 acres (Vine Pull)
2017	80,000 acres

NEW ZEALAND, PAST AND PRESENT:

1985: 100 wineries
2016: 692 wineries

NEW ZEALAND'S WINE PRODUCTION

80% white

20% red

More than 90 percent of New Zealand wines are **SEALED WITH SCREW CAPS.**

New Zealand is the number-one producer of **SAUVIGNON BLANC** in the world.

Besides wine, New Zealand is famous for its dairy products and wool. Wineries let **SHEEP GRAZE FREELY THROUGHOUT THE VINEYARDS** during the winter to keep the fields clear of grass and weeds.

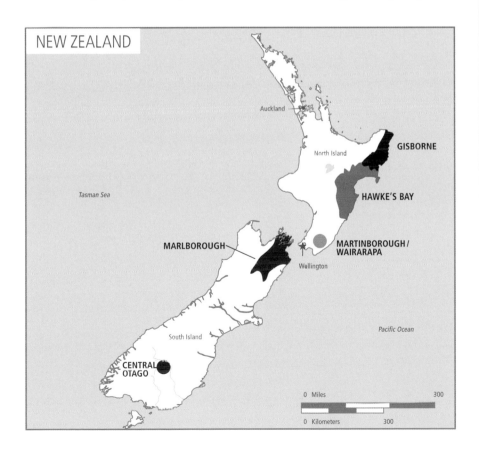

NEW ZEALAND

Auckland
North Island
Tasman Sea
GISBORNE
HAWKE'S BAY
MARLBOROUGH
MARTINBOROUGH / WAIRARAPA
Wellington
South Island
Pacific Ocean
CENTRAL OTAGO

0 Miles 300
0 Kilometers 300

New Zealand had only 1,000 acres of **PINOT NOIR** in 1996. In 2016, more than 11,000 acres were planted.

bounds, and the international wine community recognizes New Zealand's Sauvignon Blanc and Pinot Noir wines as world-class.

The frenzy has calmed somewhat, but the wines still are evolving. With more than 25 different grape varieties at their disposal, winemakers are just beginning to understand the full potential of New Zealand's soil and weather. Think of the vineyard owners and vintners here as the new kids on the block, and you'll have a good sense of the potential that this country has to produce even more world-class wines. The New Zealand public relations theme, "The best is yet to be discovered," pretty much says it all.

The two islands, North and South, that comprise the country have ten wine regions between them. The five most important and their best wines are:

REGION	VARIETIES
NORTH ISLAND	
GISBORNE	CHARDONNAY
HAWKE'S BAY	BORDEAUX BLENDS, CHARDONNAY, SYRAH
MARTINBOROUGH / WAIRARAPA	PINOT NOIR
SOUTH ISLAND	
MARLBOROUGH	SAUVIGNON BLANC, PINOT NOIR
CENTRAL OTAGO	PINOT NOIR

The most southerly grapes harvested in the world come from Central Otago.

The main grape varieties of New Zealand are:

Sauvignon Blanc   Pinot Noir   Chardonnay

Look for Pinot Gris and Syrah in the coming years.

MARLBOROUGH SAUVIGNON BLANC

Sauvignon Blanc accounted for less than 4 percent of New Zealand's total grape crop 30 years ago. Today the Marlborough region contains more than half of the country's vineyards and produces 90 percent of its Sauvignon Blanc. As such, New Zealand touts itself as the Sauvignon Blanc capital of the world, but the terroir here differs significantly from France and California. Wine writers describe the wine as having crisp, mineral, acidic flavors of grapefruit, lime, or other tropical fruit and assertive, herbaceous, pungent, racy, vibrant aromas—sometimes even like cat pee! What's not to like?

My Favorite New Zealand Wineries include:

Amisfield	Esk Valley	Quartz Reef
Astrolabe	Felton Road	Rippon
Ata Rangi	Forrest	Sacred Hill
Babich	Giesen	Saint Clair
Bell Hill	Greywacke	Seresin
Brancott (Montana)	Kim Crawford	Spy Valley
Cloudy Bay	Kumeu River	Te Mata
Craggy Range	Matua Valley	Trinity Hill
Dog Point	Mud House	Two Paddocks
Dry River	Nautilus Palliser	Villa Maria
Escarpment		

70 percent of New Zealand vines are **10 YEARS OLD** or younger.

New Zealand had a **RECORD LEVEL OF PRODUCTION** in 2014.

See page 363 for a complete list

GUIDED TASTING

Australia produces wines from many different grape varieties, so the first part of this tasting introduces you to the country's diversity. In the case of New Zealand, which specializes in Sauvignon Blanc and Pinot Noir above other grapes, the goal is to understand how those wines compare with and differ from wines produced from those same varieties elsewhere in the world. Don't taste the New Zealand wines after the Australia wines or vice versa, however. Taste the two countries separately. A Coonawarra Cabernet Sauvignon will overpower a New Zealand Sauvignon Blanc, and an Oregon Pinot Noir will overpower a Clare Valley Riesling.

Australia Four white wines compared:

1. Clare Valley Riesling
2. Adelaide Hills Sauvignon Blanc
3. Hunter Valley Sémillon
4. Margaret River Chardonnay

Three red wines compared:

5. Yarra Valley Pinot Noir
6. McLaren Vale Shiraz
7. Coonawarra Cabernet Sauvignon

New Zealand Two Sauvignon Blancs compared:

1. Marlborough Sauvignon Blanc
2. Sancerre

Two Pinot Noirs compared:
  3. Cenral Otago Pinot Noir
  4. Oregon Pinot Noir

TEST YOUR KNOWLEDGE of the wines of New Zealand by trying the quiz on page 387.

—— **FURTHER READING** ——
Buyer's Guide to New Zealand Wines by Michael Cooper

FOOD PAIRINGS

To complement the bold acidity and bright, spicy fruit of an Australian **Shiraz**, pair it with Chinese food—particularly a pork dish—or kebabs. New Zealand **Pinot Noir** will sit nicely alongside duck, lamb, or lobster dishes. Both Australian **Chardonnay** and New Zealand **Sauvignon Blanc** will go well with seafood. Have the heavier meats such as crab, lobster, and salmon with the Chardonnay and lighter fare, such as oysters and shrimp, with the Sauvignon Blanc.

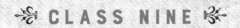

CLASS NINE

THE WINES OF
SOUTH AMERICA

UNDERSTANDING THE WINES OF SOUTH AMERICA *

CHILE * ARGENTINA * OTHER SOUTH AMERICAN WINES

UNDERSTANDING THE WINES OF SOUTH AMERICA

As in most of the Western Hemisphere, winemaking in South America began with the arrival of the Spanish in the sixteenth century. Conquistadors and colonists brought vines with them for sacramental purposes, and those vines spread with the Church. The various nations of South America have been making wine for centuries but, until recently, only for domestic consumption. In the twentieth century, political upheaval interfered with the production of quality wine, but the stability that followed refocused the entire industry. Growers paid closer attention to proper planting and cultivation of international varieties while also developing signature varieties, such as Carménère, Malbec, and Tannat. With the rise of the export market in the last 40 years, vintners here have modified the styles of the wines that they make. The wine industries in this part of the world have grown by leaps and bounds, show no signs of slowing, and offer fantastic value for the international consumer.

On average, Chile stretches just 109 miles wide, but it has more than 2,500 miles of Pacific coastline and many different climates, from desertlike conditions in the north to glaciers in the south.

THE WINES OF CHILE

IN THE MIDDLE of Chile, within 150 miles of Santiago, the capital, lies the perfect Mediterranean-style climate for growing outstanding wine grapes: warm days, cool nights, and ocean winds. The majestic snow-capped

Andes—more than 13,000 feet above sea level on average and the world's longest mountain range—supply all the water necessary for growing grapes through both flood and drip irrigation.

The Spanish first planted grapes here in 1551 and produced the first wine in 1555. In the mid-1800s, vineyard owners imported French grape varieties, such as Cabernet Sauvignon and Merlot, but not until the phylloxera epic ravaged Europe and America starting in the 1870s did Chilean wines develop a meaningful export market. Industry growth ground to a halt in 1938, however, when the government banned the planting of new vineyards, a prohibition that lasted until 1974 and severely damaged the country's wine quality. In 1979, Torres, the Spanish wine family, introduced modern technology, such as stainless steel fermenting vats, sparking Chile's modern wine industry. In the 1990s, Chile stood on the verge of producing world-class wine, primarily reds and specifically Cabernet Sauvignon. In those days, the industry was still a work in progress, but what a difference 20 years can make—and not just in better wines! Chile's new and improving infrastructure has transformed the country into a destination for tourists and investors alike.

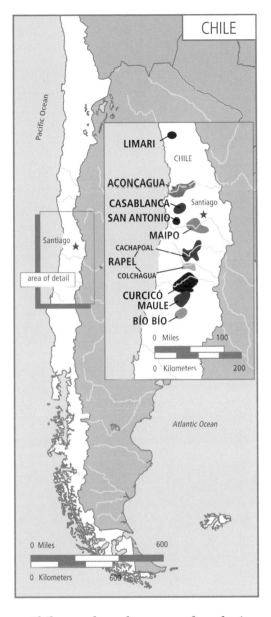

CHILE

Pacific Ocean

LIMARI

CHILE

ACONCAGUA

CASABLANCA

SAN ANTONIO

MAIPO

CACHAPOAL

RAPEL

COLCHAGUA

CURCICÓ

MAULE

BÍO BÍO

Santiago

Santiago

area of detail

0 Miles 100

0 Kilometers 200

Atlantic Ocean

0 Miles 600

0 Kilometers 600

CHILE, PAST AND PRESENT
1995: 12 wineries
2017: more than 100

After a long day of tasting Chilean wines, it's a tradition to end with the national drink— a **PISCO SOUR**: brandy mixed with lemon and / or lime juice, simple syrup, egg white, and a dash of Angostura bitters. The longer the day, the more Pisco you must have!

COUSIÑO-MACUL

CABERNET SAUVIGNON

2016

VALLE DEL MAIPO

14% vol.   75 cl

Chile is the **FOURTH LARGEST EXPORTER** of wine to America.

THE TOP FIVE CHILEAN WINE BRANDS IN THE AMERICA

Concha y Toro

Walnut Crest

San Pedro

Santa Rita

Santa Carolina

(Impact Databank)

FOREIGN INVESTMENT IN CHILE

FOREIGN WINERY	COUNTRY	CHILEAN WINERY
ANTINORI	ITALY	ALBIS
DAN ODFJELL	NORWAY	ODFJELL VINEYARDS
O. FOURNIER	SPAIN	O. FOURNIER
QUINTESSA	USA / CALIFORNIA	VERAMONTE
TORRES WINERY	SPAIN	MIGUEL TORRES WINERY

THE FRENCH CONNECTION

FRENCH INVESTOR	CHILEAN WINERY
BARON PHILIPPE DE ROTHSCHILD	ALMAVIVA
BRUNO PRATS & PAUL PONTALLIER	AQUITANIA
CHÂTEAU LAFITE-ROTHSCHILD	LOS VASCOS
CHÂTEAU LAROSE-TRINTAUDON	CASAS DEL TOQUI
GRAND MARNIER	CASA LAPOSTOLLE
WILLIAM FÈVRE	FÈVRE

Chilean wineries adhere to EU label requirements, so a wine must contain 85 percent of the grape variety, vintage, or domaine of origin (DO) that appears on the label. Today winemakers have a lot of freedom: Old traditions, such as aging wines in French oak barrels; new technologies, including stainless steel fermentors; and better vineyard management, including drip irrigation, have combined to produce better wines. Even though Chile's winemaking industry is still learning, experimenting, and growing, *its red wines are the best values in the world* in the $15 to $25 range!

Identifying the major winemaking regions can prove tricky in a country so narrow. The best way to look at Chile is west-east and north-south. From west to east, three different climatic conditions exist:

Coastal cool climate

Central valley warm climate

Andes Mountains cool or warm climate

From north to south, the most important regions are:

Casablanca Valley   Maipo Valley   Rapel Valley / Colchagua

The major red grapes are:

Cabernet Sauvignon   Carménère   Merlot   Syrah

and new plantings of Malbec, Carignan, Pinot Noir, and Cinsault are adding diversity to the Chilean landscape.

The major white grapes are:

Chardonnay   Sauvignon Blanc

CARMÉNÈRE

Bordeaux heavily influenced Chile's wine industry in its early days, which is why Cabernet Sauvignon ranks as the country's number-one red grape variety. In the 1850s, Chileans planted other Bordeaux grapes, including Merlot and Cabernet Franc. Then, in 1994, DNA analysis revealed that a substantial amount of grapes produced and sold as Merlot were actually another Bordeaux grape, Carménère, a thick-skinned grape that has soft, sweet tannins and low acidity.

The potential marketing disaster quickly became a positive opportunity. Carménère has become one of the top varieties in Chile, which remains the

OTHER REGIONS AND THEIR WINES INCLUDE

Aconcagua: Cabernet Sauvignon

Bío Bío: Pinot Noir

Cachapoal: Cabernet Sauvignon

Cafayate: Malbec, Cabernet Sauvignon, Tannat, Torrontés

Curicó: Cabernet Sauvignon, Sauvignon Blanc

Limari: Cabernet Sauvignon

Maule: Cabernet Sauvignon

Neuquen: Sauvignon Blanc, Merlot, Pinot Noir, Malbec

San Antonio: Chardonnay

Uco Valley: Sémillon, Malbec

CABERNET SAUVIGNON accounts for 32 percent of the total acreage of premium grapes planted in Chile.

THE SEVEN LARGEST WINERIES IN CHILE	
WINERY	DATE FOUNDED
San Pedro	1865
Errazuriz	1870
Santa Carolina	1875
Santa Rita	1880
Concha y Toro	1883
Undurraga	1885
Canepa	1930

More than 40 percent of all winemakers in Chile are **WOMEN**.

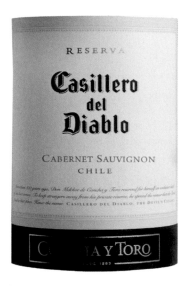

only country in the world to produce it as a single varietal. But even in 1997, Carménère lacked consistency from winery to winery; most bottles tasted green and herbaceous. Over the last ten years, the quality has increased dramatically. To make a great wine from the Carménère varietal:

- It must be planted in claylike, well-drained soil.
- Older vines make for better wine.
- Because it ripens late, it needs good weather.
- At the end of the harvest, growers must remove the vines' leaves and expose the grapes to maximum sunlight.
- It's better blended with Cabernet Sauvignon or Syrah.
- Oak aging is necessary for at least twelve months to integrate the fruit, tannins, and acidity.

You can enjoy this wine young—three to seven years—and the best will cost you $20 or more . . . still a great value!

MY FAVORITE CHILEAN PRODUCERS INCLUDE

Almaviva	Miguel Torres
Anakena (Ona)	Montes (Alpha M, Folly)
Aquitania	Morandé
Arboleda	Neyen
Caliterra (Cenit)	O. Fournier (Centauri)
Carmen (Grande Vidure)	Odfjell
Casa Lapostolle (Cuvée Alexandre, Clos Apalta)	Santa Carolina (Viña Casa blanca)
Casa Silva	Santa Rita (Casa Real)
Chadwick	Seña
Concha y Toro (Don Melchor)	Tamaya
Cono Sur (Ocio)	Tarapaca (Reserva Privada)
Cousiño Macul (Finis Terrae, Antiguas Reservas, Lota)	Undurraga (Altazor)
	Valdivieso (Caballo Loco, Eclat)
De Martino	Los Vascos (Le Dix de Los Vascos)
Echeverria	
Emiliana Orgánico	Veramonte (Primus)
Errazuriz (Don Maximiano)	Viña Koyle
Leyda	Viña San Pedro
Matetic (EQ)	William Fèvre

— BEST RECENT VINTAGES OF CHILE —

CASABLANCA: 2011   2012**   2013*   2014   2015**
2016   2017   2018**

MAIPO: 2005**   2006*   2007**   2008*   2010*   2011*   2012**
2013*   2014   2015**   2016   2017   2018**

COLCHAGUA: 2005*   2007*   2010   2011   2012*
2013*   2014   2015*   2016   2017   2018**

* EXCEPTIONAL VINTAGE   ** EXTRAORDINARY VINTAGE

5 BEST VALUE WINES OF CHILE UNDER $30

Arboleda Carmenère • Casa Lapostolle "Cuvée Alexandre" Merlot • Concha y Toro
Puente Alto Cabernet • Montes Cabernet Sauvignon • Veramonte Sauvignon Blanc

See page 357 for a complete list.

TEST YOUR KNOWLEDGE of the wines of
Chile by trying the quiz on page 387.

——— **FURTHER READING** ———

The Wines of Chile by Peter Richards

THE WINES OF ARGENTINA

The wine tradition here dates back to Spanish colonization. As with many of the great wine producing countries in the Americas, missionaries first planted and cultivated vines. In this case, Jesuits did so in 1544 in Mendoza and to the north in San Juan. Because its wines were well made and inexpensive, Argentina never exported them; they were consumed domestically. But much has changed in the last 20 years, including a tremendous amount of new investment, not just financial but also in terms of world-renowned experts owning their own vineyards and wineries here.

The second largest country in South America, Argentina has great climatic conditions and soil, especially for red wines. Because the country receives 300 days of sunshine and just eight inches of rain annually, the Argentineans have established an elaborate network of canals and dams to irrigate their vineyards.

Argentina has more than 1,000 wineries, more than 600 of them in Mendoza.

From north to south, the most important regions and their best wines are:

REGION	VARIETIES
NORTH	
SALTA	TORRONTÉS RIOJANO, CABERNET SAUVIGNON
CAFAYATE	MALBEC, CABERNET SAUVIGNON, TANNAT, TORRONTÉS RIOJANO
CUYO	
MENDOZA	MALBEC, TEMPRANILLO, CABERNET SAUVIGNON
UCO VALLEY	SÉMILLON, MALBEC
PATAGONIA	
SAN JUAN	BONARDA, SYRAH
RIO NEGRO	PINOT NOIR, TORRONTÉS RIOJANO
NEUQUÉN	SAUVIGNON BLANC, MERLOT, PINOT NOIR, MALBEC

More than 70 percent of the country's 500,000 vineyard acres lie in Mendoza, but, of these seven, keep your eye on Salta.

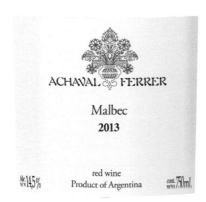

The major red grape varieties are:

Cabernet Sauvignon	Merlot	Tempranillo
Malbec	Syrah	

The major white grape varieties are:

Sauvignon Blanc   Torrontés Riojano

All Argentinean wines contain 100 percent of the grape varietal named on the label.

FOREIGN INVESTMENT IN ARGENTINA

With an average price of $30,000 per acre, it's no wonder that so many influential companies have invested in Argentina in recent years.

FOREIGN WINERY	COUNTRY	ARGENTINEAN WINERY
CHANDON	FRANCE	BODEGAS CHANDON
CONCHA Y TORO	CHILE	TRIVENTO, SAN MARTIN
CORDORNÍU	SPAIN	SÉPTIMA WINERY
HESS	SWITZERLAND	COLOMÉ WINERY
O. FOURNIER	SPAIN	O. FOURNIER
PAUL HOBBS	USA	VIÑA COBOS
PERNOD RICARD	FRANCE	ETCHART WINERY
SOGRAPE VINHOS	PORTUGAL	FINCA FLICHMAN

THE BORDEAUX CONNECTION

BORDEAUX WINERY	REGION	ARGENTINEAN WINERY
CHÂTEAU CHEVAL BLANC	FRANCE	CHEVAL DES ANDES
CHÂTEAU LE BON PASTEUR	POMEROL	CLOS DE LOS SIETE
CHÂTEAU LE GAY	POMEROL	MONTEVIEJO
CHÂTEAU LÉOVILLE POYFERRE	ST-JULIEN	CUVELIER LOS ANDES
CHÂTEAU MALARTIC-LAGRAVIERE	PESSAC-LÉOGNAN	BODEGAS DIAMANDES
CHÂTEAUX CLARKE, DASSAULT, AND LISTRAC	ST-ÉMILION	FLECHAS DE LOS ANDES
LURTON	FRANCE	FRANÇOIS LURTON

In the 1980s and '90s, annual domestic consumption dropped from 20-plus gallons of wine per person per year to just 8. When the value of the peso collapsed in the Argentine Great Depression (1998–2002), exporting

Argentineans consume about half a pound of beef per person per day, and many of the wineries have **EXCEPTIONAL RESTAURANTS,** from Francis Mallman 1884 to Urban at O. Fournier.

Take the family to **PATAGONIA,** where the most dinosaur fossils in the world are located.

Michel Rolland, **THE MOST FAMOUS WINE CONSULTANT IN THE WORLD,** has invested his winemaking expertise into an estate of five wineries called Clos de los Siete, all within eyesight of one another. His partners include top winemakers and viticulturists. *Wine Advocate* wrote of the 2007 vintage that "there may be no finer red wine value in Argentina." The four other wineries involved in the group are Monteviejo, Flechas de los Andes, Cuvelier los Andes, and Diamandes.

became more profitable. With foreign investment and winemaking consultants already in place, Argentina seized the perfect time to enter the world market, using the Malbec grape to establish its national identity. Today Argentina ranks as the largest producer of wines in South America, fifth largest in the world, and sixth largest consumer of wines in the world. With thousands of acres that still can be planted, it's the up-and-coming country to watch for new wines and regions, and the quality-to-price ratio remains one of the world's best. Look for more and better wines over the next 20 years.

MY FAVORITE ARGENTINEAN PRODUCERS

Achaval Ferrer (Finca Mirador)

Alta Vista (Alto)

Bodega Noemìa de Patagonia

Bodega Norton (Perdriel
   Single Vineyard)

Catena Zapata (Adrianna Vineyard)

Cheval des Andes

Clos de los Siete

Cuvelier los Andes (Grand Malbec)

Enrique Foster (Malbec Firmado)

Etchart

Finca Flichman

Finca Sophenia

François Lurton (Chacayes)

Kaiken

Luca (Nico by Luca)

Luigi Bosca (Icono)

Matervini

Mendel (Finca Remota)

O. Fournier (Alfa Crux Malbec)

Proemio

Salentein (Primum Malbec)

Septima

Susana Balbo

Terrazas (Malbec Afincado)

Tikal (Locura)

Trapiche

Val de Flores

Viña Cobos (Marchiori Vineyard)

Weinert

– BEST RECENT VINTAGES OF MENDOZA MALBEC –
2005* 2006** 2007 2009* 2010* 2011* 2012*
2013** 2014 2015 2016* 2017* 2018**
* EXCEPTIONAL VINTAGE ** EXTRAORDINARY VINTAGE

---

5 BEST VALUE WINES OF ARGENTINA UNDER $30

Alamos Chardonnay • Catena Malbec • Clos de los Siete Malbec •
Salentein Malbec • Susana Balboa Cabernet Sauvignon

See page 355 for a complete list

OTHER WINES OF
SOUTH AMERICA

In addition to high-quality Cabernet Sauvignons from Chile and Argentina, South America is diversifying its overall portfolio of grape varieties, including increased plantings of Merlot, Syrah, Tempranillo, and Sauvignon Blanc. Chile specializes in Carménère, as we've seen, and Argentinean winemakers have taken a strong stance with Malbec, another less popular grape that originated in France and features less prominently in Bordeaux blends. Uruguay is laying claim to Tannat, a grape with roots in the foothills of the Pyrenees. Look especially toward Uruguay and the southern regions of Brazil for new developments in South American wines.

GUIDED TASTING

In Argentina, if a wine label displays the name of the grape, the bottle must contain 100 percent of that variety. Chile, on the other hand, conforms to the 85 percent standard set by EU regulations, so Chilean wines often

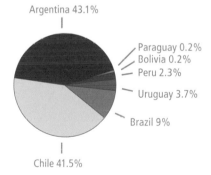

SOUTH AMERICAN WINE PRODUCTION

Argentina 43.1%

Paraguay 0.2%
Bolivia 0.2%
Peru 2.3%

Uruguay 3.7%

Brazil 9%

Chile 41.5%

consist of blends and thus can vary wildly in style, depending on the varieties that the winemakers used. Neither country has an official classification system, so it's harder to show you what to do. You always want to taste from lighter to heavier, though, and in this part of the world the price usually indicates the body or weight of the wine. Below we'll focus on Argentinean Malbec and Chilean Cabernet Sauvignon—the two major red grapes of the continent, so the easiest to find in the export market. It's harder to find other single-variety bottles, such as Merlot and Tannat. If you can find them, taste them alone for a broader perspective of the diversity of the red wines of South America.

Argentinean Malbec Three wines compared:
1. Light ($)
2. Medium ($$)
3. Full ($$$)

Chilean Carménère Two wines compared:
4. Light ($)
5. Full ($$)

Chilean Cabernet Sauvignon Three wines compared:
6. Light ($)
7. Medium ($$)
8. Full ($$$)

FOOD PAIRINGS

For Chilean and Argentinean **Cabernet Sauvignons**, a traditional meat dish, such as steak, grilled beef tenderloin, or grilled lamb. **Carménère** overall has relatively low levels of acidity, so it will pair well with foods that have a smaller fat content. Try it with grilled vegetables, an eggplant stew, or grilled chicken. **Malbec** has softer tannins than Cabernet Sauvignon, so you can enjoy it with a leaner cut of meat, such as skirt or flank steak. It also goes great with pizza, empanadas, or a simple pasta with a tomato and meat sauce. The strong tannins of **Tannat** make it a good match for rich lamb dishes and particularly strong cheeses.

TEST YOUR KNOWLEDGE of the wines of Argentina by trying the quiz on page 387.

——— **FURTHER READING** ———

Wines of Argentina by Michel Rolland and Enrique Chrabolowsky

THE WINES OF GERMANY

UNDERSTANDING GERMAN WINE ❋
GERMAN WINE STYLES ❋ PRÄDIKATSWEIN LEVELS ❋
HOW TO BUY GERMAN WINE

In Germany, 100,000 grape growers cultivate nearly 255,000 acres of vines, meaning **THE AVERAGE HOLDING PER GROWER IS 2.5 ACRES.**

WHO'S VINEYARD IS IT?
PIESPORTER GOLDTRÖPFCHEN:
350 owners
WEHLENER SONNENUHR:
250 owners
BRAUNEBERGER JUFFE:
180 owners

On a globe, put your finger on Germany, and then spin it westward into North America. You're pointing to **NEWFOUNDLAND, CANADA.**

One mechanical harvester can do the **WORK OF 60 PEOPLE.**

UNDERSTANDING GERMAN WINE

Today Germany—a minor player on the world wine stage—features more than 1,400 wine villages and 2,600-plus vineyards. No problem, right? But if you had to study German wines before 1971, you would have had 30,000 different names to remember! A large assortment of people used to own very small parcels of land, which is why there were so many names. Then, in an effort to reduce confusion, the West German government passed a law in 1971, mandating that a vineyard consist of at least twelve and a half acres of land. That legislation cut the list of vineyard names considerably, but it increased the number of owners.

Germany produces only 2 or 3 percent of the world's wines. (The national beverage is beer, remember.) What wines it does produce depend largely on the weather. Why? Germany is the northernmost country in Europe in which vines can grow, and 80 percent of the quality vineyards lie on hilly slopes—which means forget about mechanical harvesting!

The following graphic will give you a better idea of the hilly conditions that farmers face in order to grow grapes that produce the highest-quality wines in Germany.

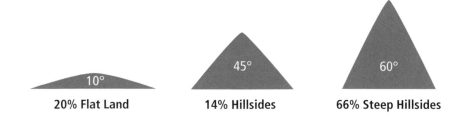

| 10° | 45° | 60° |
| **20% Flat Land** | **14% Hillsides** | **66% Steep Hillsides** |

North Sea

Hamburg

GERMANY

Berlin

SAALE-UNSTRUT

SAXONY

Rhein River

AHR

Bonn

MITTELRHEIN

MOSEL

RHEINGAU

HESSISCHE BERGSTRASSE

Frankfurt

NAHE

Mosel River

RHEINHESSEN

FRANCONIA

PFALZ

BADEN WÜRTTEMBERG

Munich

0 Miles 100 200

0 Kilometers 200

GERMAN WINE PRODUCTION

35% red

65% white

85%

If a wine label gives the grape variety—Riesling, for example—85 percent of the wine must be made from the Riesling grape.

If a German wine shows a vintage on the label, 85 percent of the grapes used must be from that year. Top German wine producers use 100 percent of the grape variety and the vintage on the label.

Germany has been growing the **RIESLING GRAPE SINCE 1435.**

Some 75 years ago, most German wines tasted dry and very acidic. Even in finer restaurants, servers offered **A SPOONFUL OF SUGAR** with a German wine to **balance the acidity**.

Germany has more than **56,000 ACRES OF RIESLING.** North America comes next with 21,000 acres. Australia has 10,800, and Alsace, France, has 8,600 acres.

THE WINEMAKING REGIONS OF GERMANY

Germany has 13 official winemaking regions, but just four of them produce the best German wines. They are:

Rheinhessen	Rheingau	Mosel	Pfalz
		(Mosel-Saar-Ruwer until 2007)	(Rheinpfalz until 1992)

Rhein wines generally have more body than Mosels, which usually have higher acidity and lower alcohol levels than Rheins. Mosels show more autumn fruits such as apples, pears, and quince, while Rhein wines show more summer fruits such as apricots, peaches, and nectarines.

Look for these important villages in each of the four chief regions:

Rheinhessen Oppenheim, Nackenheim, Nierstein

Rheingau Eltville, Erbach, Rüdesheim, Rauenthal, Hochheim, Johannisberg

Mosel Erden, Piesport, Bernkastel, Graach, Ürzig, Brauneberg, Wehlen

Pfalz Deidesheim, Forst, Wachenheim, Ruppertsberg, Dürkheimer

GERMAN GRAPE VARIETIES

Riesling This is the most widely planted and the best grape variety produced in Germany. If you don't see "Riesling" on the label, the wine probably has little if any Riesling grape. Remember, if the label gives the grape variety, the wine must contain at least 85 percent of that grape, according to German law. Of the grapes planted in Germany, 23 percent are Riesling.

Müller Thurgau A cross between Riesling and Chasselas, it accounts for 12.5 percent of Germany's wines.

Silvaner This grape variety accounts for just 5 percent of Germany's wines.

GERMAN WINE STYLES

Simply put, German wine balances sweetness with acidity and low alcohol. Remember the equation:

Sugar + Yeast = Alcohol + Carbon Dioxide

The sugar ultimately comes from the sun. If your vines are growing on a southerly slope and you have a good year, you'll get a lot of sun and therefore the right amount of sugar to produce a good wine. Many times, however, German winemakers aren't so fortunate, and they don't get enough sun to ripen the grapes properly. The result: higher acidity and lower alcohol. To compensate, some winemakers add sugar to the must before fermentation to increase the amount of alcohol. This process, called chaptalization, is verboten for higher-quality German wines.

The three basic styles of German wine are:

Trocken	Halbtrocken	Fruity
Dry	Medium-dry	Semidry to very sweet

But those designations don't take into account the ripeness levels of the wine, which matters!

SÜSSRESERVE

A common misconception about German wine holds that, after fermentation, the remaining residual sugar gives the wine its sweetness naturally. On the contrary, some wines are fermented dry. Many German winemakers withhold a certain percentage of unfermented grape juice from the same vineyards, variety, and sweetness level. This Süssreserve contains natural sugar, which winemakers add back to the wine after fermentation. The finest estates don't use the Süssreserve method but do rely on stopping the fermentation to achieve their style.

RIPENESS LEVELS

As a result of the 1971 legislation, German wine falls into two main categories:

Deutscher Wein The lowest designation given to a wine grown in Germany, it never carries the vineyard name and rarely leaves the country.

Qualitätswein Literally, quality wine, which also falls into two types:
1. *Qualitätswein bestimmter Anbaugebiete* QbA indicates a quality wine from one of the 13 specified regions.
2. *Prädikatswein* This is a quality wine with distinction—the good stuff, in other words. Vintners may not be chaptalize these wines.

Given good weather, the longer the grapes remain on the vine, **THE SWEETER THEY BECOME**—but the winemaker takes a risk when doing this because bad weather could ruin the crop.

TERPENES, organic compounds found in German Riesling, sometimes give aromas of kerosene or gasoline.

TYPICAL VINTAGE YEAR IN GERMANY

Prädikatswein 45%

Deutscher Wein 6%

QbA 49%

Schloss Johannisberger
2007er Riesling Spätlese
PRÄDIKATSWEIN

THE STORY OF SPÄTLESE

The story goes that, at the **VINEYARDS OF SCHLOSS JOHANNISBERG,** the monks couldn't pick the grapes until the abbot of Fulda gave his permission. During the harvest of 1775, the abbot was away attending a synod. That year the grapes were ripening early, and some had started to rot on the vine. The concerned monks dispatched a rider to ask the abbot's permission to pick the grapes. By the time the rider returned with the official assent, the monks despaired but went ahead with the harvest anyway. To their amazement, the wine was one of the best they had ever tasted. That was the beginning of Spätlese-style wines.

In **1921,** the first Trockenbeerenauslese was made in the Mosel region.

PRÄDIKATSWEIN LEVELS

In increasing order of quality, price, and ripeness at harvest, here are the six Prädikatswein levels:

Kabinett Light, semidry wines made from normally ripened grapes.

Spätlese "Late-picking," meaning that this medium-style wine comes from grapes picked after the normal harvest. The extra days of sun give the wine more body and a more intense taste.

Auslese "Out-picked," meaning that the grapes come from particularly ripe bunches, which yield a medium-to-fuller style of wine. If you've ever grown fruit, you've probably done the same by picking the especially ripe ones, leaving the others on the vine.

Beerenauslese "Berry picking," which signifies that growers have selected individual grapes. These luscious grapes go into the rich dessert wines for which Germany is renowned. Beerenauslese is made usually only two or three times a decade.

Trockenbeerenauslese A step above the Beerenauslese, and don't let the big words scare you. These grapes are dried (trocken), so they're more like raisins. These raisinated grapes produce the richest, sweetest, and most expensive honeylike wine.

Eiswein A very rare, sweet, concentrated wine made from grapes left on the vine and pressed while frozen. According to law, this wine must come from grapes at least ripe enough to make a Beerenauslese.

EDELFÄULE

Botrytis cinerea, called *Edelfäule* in German, is a mold that attacks grapes, as we saw in the section on Sauternes (page 179). It's also instrumental in the production of Beerenausleses and Trockenbeerenausleses. Noble rot occurs late in the growing season when nights are cool and heavy with dew, mornings are foggy, and days are warm. When noble rot attacks the grapes, they shrivel, and their water content evaporates, leaving concentrated sugar. Grapes affected by this mold may not look very appealing, but don't let looks deceive you: The proof is in the wine!

CHOOSING A GERMAN WINE

Make sure it comes from one of the four major regions. Next, see if the wine comes from the Riesling grape. Riesling shows the best-tasting characteristics and denotes a quality wine. Also note the vintage. It's especially important with German wines to know whether the wine comes from a good year. The final and most important consideration is to buy from a reputable grower or producer.

So what's the difference between a $100 Beerenauslese and a $200 Beerenauslese—besides a hundred bucks? The major difference is the grapes. The $100 bottle probably comes from Müller-Thurgau grapes or Silvaner, while the $200 bottle no doubt comes from Riesling. The wine region also partially determines quality. Traditionally, the best Beerenausleses and Trockenbeerenausleses come from the Rhein area or the Mosel.

Quality is higher in wine when:
- The grapes come from great vineyards.
- The grapes grew in a great climate or come from a great vintage.
- The wine is produced from low yields.
- Great winemakers produce the wine

Today, most German wines, including Beerenauslese and Trockenbeerenauslese, are bottled in spring and early summer. Many no longer receive additional cask or tank maturation because **BARREL AGING DESTROYS THE FRUIT**.

MY FAVORITE GERMAN PRODUCERS

MOSEL

C. von Schubert	Friedrich-Wilhelm-	Meulenhof
Dr. H. Thanisch	Gymnasium	Rheinhold Haart
Dr. Loosen	Fritz Haag	S. A. Prum
Dr. Pauly-Bergweiler	J. J. Prüm	Schloss Leiser
Egon Müller	Joh. Jos. Christoffel Erben	Selbach-Oster
	Kesselstatt	St. Urbans-Hof

RHEINHESSEN

Keller	Strub

RHEINGAU

Georg Breuer	Peter Jacob Kühn	Schloss Johannisberg
Josef Leitz	Robert Weil	Schloss Vollrads
Kessler		

PFALZ

Basserman-Jordan	Dr. Bürklin Wolf	Lingenfelder
Darting	Dr. Deinhard	Muller-Catoir

HOW TO BUY A GERMAN WINE

Read the label carefully. German wine labels give you plenty of information. For example, take a look at the label at the right.

Joh. Jos. Christoffel Erben is the producer.

Mosel is the region (one of the main four).

2001 is the year in which the grapes were harvested.

Ürzig is the town and **Würzgarten** is the vineyard from which the grapes originate. (Just as a person from New York is a New Yorker, the Germans add the suffix "-er" to Ürzig to make Ürziger.)

Riesling is the grape variety, which means this wine contains at least 85 percent Riesling.

Auslese is the ripeness level, in this case from bunches of overripe grapes.

Qualitätswein mit Prädikat is the quality level of the wine.

A.P. Nr. 2 602 041 008 02 is the official testing number, which shows that a panel of tasters tasted that wine and that it passed the government's strict quality standards.

Gutsabfüllung means "estate-bottled."

OTHER WORDS ON GERMAN WINE LABELS

Erste Lage Select vineyards outside Mosel and Rheingau.

Erstes Gewächs Used only in Rheingau for the best vineyards making the best dry wines.

Grosse Lage Germany's best vineyards, the highest level for non dry wines.

Grosses Gewächs "Great Growth," used in every region except Rheingau for the best vineyards making the best dry wines.

All Qualitätswein and Prädikatswein must **PASS A TEST BY AN OFFICIAL LABORATORY** and tasting panel to be given an official number, prior to the wine's release.

A.P. Nr. 2 602 041 008 02

2 = The government referral office or testing station

602 = Location code of bottler

041 = Bottler ID number

008 = Bottle lot

02 = The year the wine was tasted by the board

VDP: A classification with higher standards than German wine laws.

PAST GREAT VINTAGES of Beerenauslese and Trockenbeerenauslese: 1985, 1988, 1989, 1990, 1996.

RIESLING ALWAYS USED TO RIPEN in October and was picked until mid-November. Since 2000, Riesling is ready to harvest in September.

The **2010 VINTAGE** in Germany was one of the smallest harvests in 30 years.

The 2014 vintage in Germany had the **HIGHEST MEDIAN TEMPERATURE** in the last 100 years.

In 2015 Germany had **A STELLAR HARVEST.**

RECENT TRENDS

Germany is producing higher-quality wines than ever before, and international interest in these wines has increased. Lighter-style Trockens (dry), Halbtrockens (medium-dry), Kabinetts, and even Spätleses can serve easily as apéritifs or accompany light or grilled food—spicy or Pacific Rim cuisines in particular. If you haven't had a German wine ever or in a long time, vintages such as 2010, 2011, and 2015 show the greatness of German white wines. Plus, with more modern designs, those old hard-to-read Gothic script labels have become more user-friendly.

Pinot Noir, called Spätburgunder here, grows on about 30,000 acres. German winemakers have always made red wine, albeit in fairly small amounts until recently. Increasing temperatures from climate change mean that vintners in the southern regions of Baden and Würtemberg are making more of it than in years past.

– BEST RECENT VINTAGES OF GERMAN WHITE WINES –

2001** 2002* 2003* 2004* 2005** 2006* 2007**
2008* 2009** 2010** 2011** 2012 2013 2015** 2016 2017**

*EXCEPTIONAL VINTAGE ** EXTRAORDINARY VINTAGE*

5 BEST VALUE WHITE WINES OF GERMANY UNDER $30

Dr. Loosen Riesling • J. J. Prüm Wehlener Sonnenuhr Spätlese • Josef Lietz Rüdesheimer Klosterlay Riesling Kabinett • Selbach-Oster Zeltinger Sonnenuhr Riesling Kabinett • Strub Niersteiner Olberg Kabinett or Spätlese

See page 360 for a complete list.

GUIDED TASTING

People don't know or understand German white wines as well as French or Californian wines and often dismiss them for being light-bodied and having higher levels of residual sugar. Don't make that mistake. Learn the main regions, villages, vineyards, classifications, and a little German pronunciation, and you'll find it easy to understand and enjoy the charm and elegance of these great German white wines.

Quality German Wine One wine tasted alone:
1. Any Qualitätswein from Germany

Kabinett Two Kabinetts compared:
2. Mosel Riesling Kabinett
3. Rheinhessen Riesling Kabinett

Spätlese Two Spätleses compared:
4. Mosel Riesling Spätlese
5. Pfalz Riesling Spätlese

Auslese Two Ausleses compared:
6. Mosel Riesling Auslese
7. Rheingau Riesling Auslese

FOOD PAIRINGS

With **Riesling Spätlese Halbtrocken**: "We have a tradition of cooking freshwater fish that come from a number of small creeks in the Palatinate Forest, so my personal choice would be trout, either herbed with thyme, basil, parsley, and onion and cooked in wine; or smoked with a bit of horse-radish. We find it to be a very versatile wine, a very good match with a whole range of white meat. Pork is traditional in the Palatinate region, as are chicken and goose dishes."

— Rainer Lingenfelder of Weingut Lingenfelder Estate, Pfalz

"There's a wide variety of food that goes very well with—and this is the key—a fruity, only moderately sweet, well-balanced **Riesling Spätlese**. Start with mild curries and sesame- or ginger-flavored, not-too-spicy dishes. Or try either gravlax or smoked salmon. You can even have Riesling Spätlese with a green salad in a balsamic vinaigrette, preferably with a touch of raspberry, as long as the dressing is not too vinegary. Many people avoid pairing wine with a salad, but it works beautifully.

"For haute cuisine, fresh duck or goose liver lightly sautéed in its own juice, or veal sweetbreads in a rich sauce. Also salads with fresh greens, fresh fruit, and fresh seafood marinated in lime or lemon juice or balsamic vinegar.

"With an old, ripe **Spätlese**: roast venison, dishes with cream sauces, and any white-meat dish stuffed with or accompanied by fruit. It is also delicious with fresh fruit itself or as an apéritif."

With **Riesling Spätlese Halbtrocken**: "This is a food-friendly wine, but the first thing that comes to mind is fresh seafood and fresh fish. Also wonderful with salads with a mild vinaigrette, and with a course that's often difficult to match: cream soups. If we don't know exactly what to drink with a particular food, Spätlese Halbtrocken is usually the safe bet.

"It may be too obvious to say foie gras with **Eiswein**, but it is a classic."

—Johannes Selbach of Selbach-Oster, Mosel

SELBACH-OSTER HAS PARTNERED with veteran California winemaker Paul Hobbs and planted a Riesling vineyard in the Finger Lakes region of New York.

TEST YOUR KNOWLEDGE of the white wines of Germany by trying the quiz on page 389.

——— **FURTHER READING** ———

The Gault-Millau Guide to German Wines by Armin Diel and Joel Payne

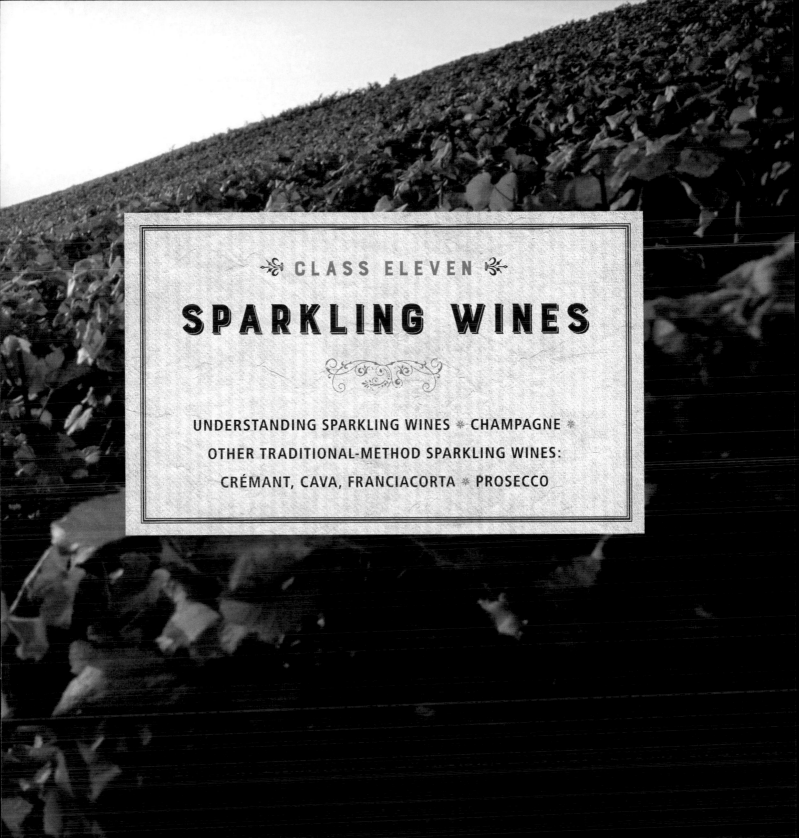

~❦~ CLASS ELEVEN ~❦~

SPARKLING WINES

UNDERSTANDING SPARKLING WINES * CHAMPAGNE *

OTHER TRADITIONAL-METHOD SPARKLING WINES:

CRÉMANT, CAVA, FRANCIACORTA * PROSECCO

The balance of the fruit and acidity, together with the bubbles, makes **GOOD CHAMPAGNE**.

UNDERSTANDING SPARKLING WINE

AMERICANS ARE HAVING a great time drinking lots of sparkling wine. With more than half of the market, California dominates sales. Champagne sales are holding their own. Prosecco is booming, and so is Franciacorta. Cava from Spain and Crémants from France round out the list. Champagne is the most famous of the bunch, so let's start there.

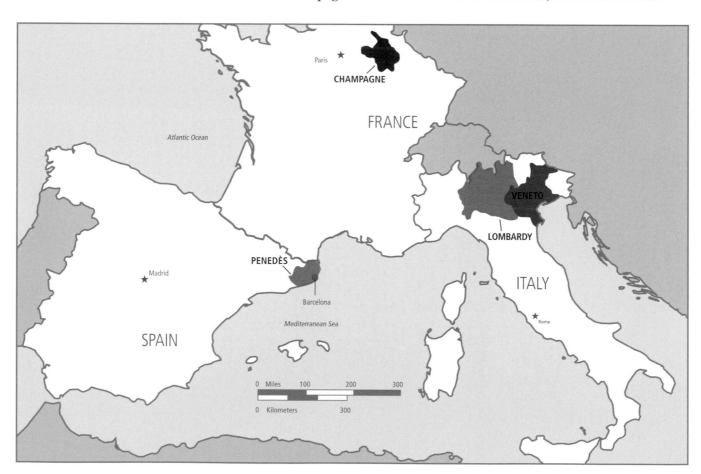

CHAMPAGNE

Champagne is a sparkling wine that everyone drinks on New Year's Eve, birthdays, and other anniversaries, but it's so much more than that. It's France's northernmost winemaking region, an hour and a half northeast of Paris. That location matters because, in cooler, more northerly climates, including that of the Champagne region, grapes have a higher acidity than in most other regions. That's one reason that Champagne has its distinct taste. Acidity in Champagne not only imparts freshness to the wines, but it also increases their longevity.

The region consists of four main areas:

Marne Valley   Côte des Blancs   Reims Mountain   Aube

which together have 43,680 acres of vineyards. More than 20,000 growers sell to around 250 *négociants*, or shippers. Winemakers can use three grapes to produce Champagne:

Chardonnay 27%

Pinot Meunier 35%

Pinot Noir 38 %

In France, only sparkling wines from the Champagne region may be called Champagne. Some American producers use the name on their sparkling wine labels, but don't be fooled—or compare them with proper Champagnes.

The three major types of Champagne are:

Nonvintage/multiple vintage A blend of two or more harvests, 60 to 80 percent from current harvest and 20 to 40 percent from previous vintages. more than 80 percent of the Champagnes produced are not vintage dated. This means they contain blends of several years' wines. nonvintage Champagne is more typical of the house style than vintage Champagne.

Until around 1850, all Champagne tasted **SWEET**.

Champagne houses market about two-thirds of Champagne's wines, but they own **LESS THAN 10 PERCENT OF THE VINEYARDS**.

Vintage From a single vintage. vintage champagne must contain 100 percent of that vintage year's harvest.

"Prestige" cuvée From a single vintage with longer aging requirements.

Unlike most of the rest of the wine industry, each individual house decides whether to declare a vintage year, so not every year is a vintage. (See the end of this section for the best vintages.) Prestige Champagnes usually meet the following requirements to receive that designation:

- Best grapes from the highest-rated villages
- Made from only the first pressing of the grapes
- More bottle aging than nonvintage Champagnes
- From vintage years only
- Small quantities

MÉTHODE CHAMPENOISE

Champagne is made by a process called *méthode champenoise*. Outside Champagne, that method is called *méthode traditionnelle, método tradicional*, classic method, etc. The EU doesn't allow the designation of *méthode champenoise* for sparkling wines from outside the Champagne region. This is the ten-step process:

Harvest This usually takes place in late September or early October.

In 2011, Champagne had its **EARLIEST HARVEST** since 1822.

Pressing AOC regulations allow only two pressings of the grapes. Prestige cuvée Champagnes usually come exclusively from the first pressing. The *taille*, or second pressing, often is blended with the cuvée to make vintage and nonvintage Champagnes.

First fermentation In this step, the must becomes wine. Remember the formula:

Sugar + Yeast = Alcohol + Carbon Dioxide

Most Champagnes ferment first in stainless steel tanks. The first fermentation takes two to three weeks and, because the carbon dioxide dissipates, produces still wines.

Blending This is the most important step in Champagne production. Each of the still wines comes from a single grape variety from a single village. Here the winemaker has many decisions to make, the three most important being:

1. Which of the three grapes to blend and in what proportions?
2. From which vineyards?
3. Which years or vintages to blend? Should the blend come from the wines of only the current harvest, or should several vintages be blended together?

Liqueur de tirage After blending, the winemaker adds this mixture of sugar and yeast, which begins the second fermentation. Then the wine goes into the bottle with a temporary cap.

Second fermentation In this fermentation, the carbon dioxide remains in the bottle, creating the bubbles. The second fermentation also creates natural sediment.

Aging The amount of time that the wine ages on its lees largely determines its quality. Nonvintage champagnes must age for at least 15 months after bottling. Vintage Champagnes must age for at least three years after bottling.

Riddling The wine bottles now go into A-frame racks, necks down. The *remueur*, or riddler, goes through the racks, bottle by bottle, slightly turning

DOM PÉRIGNON ages for six to eight years before releasing to market.

"It's not a Burgundy; it's not a Bordeaux; it's a white wine; it's a sparkling wine that should be kept no longer than two to three years. It should be consumed young."
—Claude Taittinger

"R.D." on a Champagne wine label means that the wine was **RECENTLY DISGORGED**.

each and gradually tipping it farther downward. After six to eight weeks, the bottle stands almost completely upside down, the sediment resting in the neck of the bottle. (Barbe-Nicole Ponsardin, widow—*veuve* in French—of François Clicquot, invented this process in 1816.)

Disgorging The top of the bottle goes into a supercooled brine solution to freeze it. A *dégorgeur* removes the temporary bottle cap, and, propelled by the carbon dioxide, out flies the frozen sediment.

Dosage Pronounced doh-SAZH, this mixture of wine and sugar goes into the bottle after disgorging. At this point, the winemaker determines whether he or she wants a sweeter or a drier Champagne. These are the sweetness levels of Champagnes:

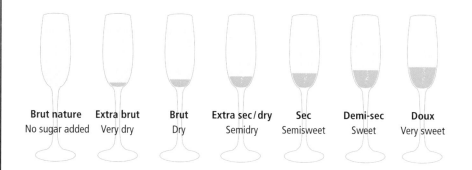

Brut nature	Extra brut	Brut	Extra sec/dry	Sec	Demi-sec	Doux
No sugar added	Very dry	Dry	Semidry	Semisweet	Sweet	Very sweet

Recorking A real cork replaces the temporary bottle cap. After that, a protective wire cage, called a *muselet*, goes around the neck of the bottle and holds a metal cap atop the cork.

As you can see, this method is laborious, intensive, and expensive, which is why Champagne frequently costs more than other quality wines, sparkling or otherwise. Because the contents are pressurized, the bottles also must be thicker and stronger than ordinary wine bottles, another additional cost.

DIFFERENT STYLES OF CHAMPAGNE

The general rule: The more white grapes in the blend, the lighter the style; the more red grapes, the fuller the style. Blanc de blanc Champagne comes from 100 percent Chardonnay grapes. Blanc de noir comes from 100 percent Pinot Noir. Some producers ferment their wines in wood. Bollinger ferments some of its portfolio this way, and Krug ferments all of its wines in this manner, which gives their Champagne fuller body and bouquet than if fermented in stainless steel.

CHOOSING A CHAMPAGNE

First, determine the style you prefer, light-bodied to full, and the sweetness level, from brut nature to doux. Then buy your Champagne from a reliable shipper/producer. Champagne has more than 4,000 producers, and each takes pride in its house style and strives for a consistent blend, year after year. It's not a hard and fast rule, but the styles of these nationally distributed houses generally conform to the categories below. Also keep in mind that supply and demand largely dictate the prices of prestige cuvée Champagnes.

LIGHT, DELICATE	LIGHT TO MEDIUM	MEDIUM	MEDIUM TO FULL	FULL, RICH
A. CHARBAUT ET FILS JACQUESSON LANSON	BILLECART-SALMON BRUNO PAILLARD DEUTZ G. H. MUMM LAURENT-PERRIER NICOLAS FEUILLATTE PERRIER-JOUËT POMMERY RUINART PÈRE & FILS TAITTINGER	CHARLES HEIDSIECK MOËT & CHANDON PIPER-HEIDSIECK POL ROGER SALON	DRAPPIER HENRIOT LOUIS ROEDERER	A. GRATIEN BOLLINGER KRUG VEUVE CLICQUOT

To evaluate a Champagne, look at the bubbles, an integral part of the wine that creates texture and mouthfeel. The better wines have smaller bubbles and more of them. In a good Champagne, the bubbles last longer.

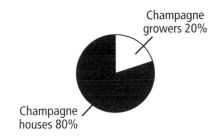

Champagne growers 20%

Champagne houses 80%

Some of my favorite Champagne **GROWER-PRODUCERS** include: Béreche, Jacques Selosse, Egly-Ouriet, Larmandier-Bernier, Marc Hebrart, Marie-Courtin, Pierre Peters, Tarlant, Vilmart & CIE, and C. Boucharn.

How many bubbles does a bottle of Champagne have? According to scientist Bill Lembeck, **49 MILLION!**

AGING CHAMPAGNE

As a rule, Champagne is ready to drink as soon as you buy it, but in some cases you can age it. Drink nonvintage Champagnes within two to three years and vintage and prestige cuvée Champagnes within 10 to 15 years. If you're still saving that bottle of Dom Pérignon from 15 years ago, don't wait any longer. Open it!

– BEST VINTAGES OF CHAMPAGNE–

1995** 1996** 1998 1999 2000 2002** 2004** 2005
2006** 2008* 2009* 2012** 2013*

* EXCEPTIONAL VINTAGE ** EXTRAORDINARY VINTAGE

OTHER TRADITIONAL-METHOD SPARKLING WINES

CRÉMANT

Champagne comes from a defined area in northeast France, and the word can appear on a bottle only if the wine comes from this region. Eight other regions of France—notably Alsace, Bordeaux, Burgundy, Jura, and the Loire Valley—produce sparkling wines also made with the *méthode champenoise*. They contain roughly half the carbonation of Champagne, but these wines also follow strict regulations, such as permitted grape varieties, yield per acre, and minimum aging. AOC laws recognized Crémants (meaning creamy, describing the mouthfeel of their lower carbon dioxide levels) starting in the 1970s and 1980s.

CRÉMANT D'ALSACE

The most French Crémant comes from Alsace, representing 22 percent of the region's wine production. Winemakers here primarily use Pinot Gris, Pinot Blanc, Pinot Noir, and Riesling. My favorite Crémant d'Alsace producers include:

Lucien Albrecht **Gustave Lorentz** **Pierre Sparr**

FROST in the spring and vine rot and mildew during the growing season in 2016 meant that year wasn't a great vintage for Champagne.

The **"PÉT-NAT"** style stands for "pétillant naturel" (natural sparkling). Winemakers bottle the wine before it finishes its first fermentation, so it contains less carbon dioxide. It cannot come from the Champagne region because by law Champagne can be made only with the *méthode champenoise*.

LUXEMBOURG also has a Crémant that adheres to AOC / EU regulations.

CRÉMANT DE BOURGOGNE

Vintners can use any grape grown in Burgundy to make this wine. About 7 percent of Burgundy production is Crémant. My favorite Crémant de Bourgogne producers include:

Bailly-Lapierre	Boisset	Louis Bouillot
Simonnet-Febvre		

Look for Eminent or Grand Eminent Crémants from Burgundy, the highest level of quality.

CRÉMANT DU JURA

Made mostly with Chardonnay and Pinot Noir, this is a very important wine in the Jura, representing more than 20 percent of the region's wine production. My favorite Crémant d'Alsace producers include:

Domaine de Savagny	Domaine Rolet	Tissot

CRÉMANT DE LOIRE

Vintners can use many grapes for this wine, but the best examples come from Chenin Blanc. My favorite Crémant d'Alsace producers include:

Bouvet-Ladubay	Gratien & Meyer	Langlois-Château de Loire

CAVA

In northeastern Spain, the Penedès region of Catalonia—30 miles southwest of Barcelona—has been making sparkling wines using the traditional method for more than 160 years. The major grapes used are Chardonnay, Macabeo, Parellada, and Xarel-lo, and the name of this wine, made official in 1970, refers to the caves where winemakers stored the wines for fermentation and aging. You probably have heard of two top producers, Freixenet and Codorníu. The Ferrer family, which owns Freixenet, also makes Segura Viudas. Cava offers great value for sparkling wines made with the traditional method. My favorite Cava producers include:

Codorníu	Raventos	Segura Viudas
Freixenet	Recaredo Mata	
Juve y Camps	Casanovas	

FRANCIACORTA

Like Champagne and Cava, this sparkling wine from Lombardy, Italy, is made using the traditional method. The permitted grape varieties are Chardonnay, Pinot Nero (Pinot Noir), and Pinot Bianco. Nonvintage bottles must age for a minimum of 18 months, and vintage wines for a minimum of 30 months. Look for these easy-to-find and high-quality producers:

Bellavista	Berlucchi	Ferghettina
Ca' del Bosco		

As with Champagne, Franciacorta has **SWEETNESS LEVELS** from Brut to Demi-Sec.

PROSECCO

All of my students know at least three Italian wines: Chianti, Pinot Grigio, and now, in the last ten years, Prosecco. It's been around a long time, though. It dates back to the fourteenth century. I first mentioned Prosecco in the 25th anniversary edition of this book, a decade ago, as a sidebar about this sparkling wine from the Veneto region that was becoming popular. In 2018, it was the fastest growing Italian wine in America!

It's easy to see why: The name is easy to pronounce; it doesn't contain as much carbonation as Champagne; and it has a fruit-forward taste, low alcohol, and budget-friendly prices (most under $20). The reason? Winemakers use the Charmat-Martinotti method, in which the second fermentation takes place in huge stainless-steel or glass tanks. The major grape is Glera, an Italian variety, and the wine can be made only in the Veneto and a small part of the Friuli-Venezia Giulia region. Prosecco also defines sweetness levels differently. Brut is the driest, next is extra dry, and the sweetest is called dry. Go figure!

Prosecco is made to be consumed young, so don't age it—but do try it in a cocktail. The most famous is the Bellini, created in the 1930s at the famous Harry's Bar in Venice, frequented by Ernest Hemingway and Orson Wells. They no doubt enjoyed the two parts Prosecco to one part fresh white peach puree. Enjoy!

Look for these easy-to-find Prosecco producers:

Bellissima	Lunetta	Nino Franco
La Marca	Mionetto	Zonin

PROSECCO WAS ORIGINALLY THE NAME OF THE GRAPE and, in 2008, became the name of the region. The best Prosecco is designated DOCG. The style is medium weight, aromatic, and fresh. It has high acidity, elegance, balance, and low alcohol (11.5–12%).

"Prosecco in Venice is like beer in Milwaukee." —Lettie Teague, *The Wall Street Journal*

Because of the difficult weather conditions for the 2017 vintage, expect Prosecco prices to increase by 10 to 15 percent.

PROSECCO SALES in America increased 35 percent last year.

"My dear girl, there are some things that just aren't done, such as drinking Dom Perignon '53 above the temperature of 38° Fahrenheit. That's just as bad as listening to the Beatles without earmuffs!"

—Sean Connery as James Bond, in *Goldfinger* (1964)

ROGER MOORE preferred Dom Perignon 1962, and **PIERCE BROSNAN** drank Bollinger 1961.

New Champagne bottles are lighter by 7 percent and **MORE ENVIRONMENTALLY FRIENDLY.** Two big changes: The bottles are slimmer, and the punt at the bottom is deeper and wider.

OPENING A BOTTLE OF SPARKLING WINE

Sabering a bottle makes for a fun—if hazardous—party trick best left to the experts, but everyone should know how to open a bottle of Champagne properly because even doing it manually can prove dangerous. The pressure inside is around 6 atmospheres, or nearly 90 pounds per square inch. That's three times the pressure in a car tire! At all steps below, point the bottle away from yourself, others, or anything fragile.

1. Chill the bottle well.
2. Remove the foil from the top of the bottle.
3. Place your hand on top of the cork and keep it there until you're done. This may seem awkward during some of the subsequent steps, but you'll understand the importance of this step if you've ever seen or had a cork blast off unexpectedly in the middle of the process.
4. Untwist the wire tab to release the cage. You can either remove the cage—carefully—or leave it on top of the cork.
5. Gently place a cloth napkin over the cork. (If the cork suddenly pops, the napkin will absorb the force.)
6. Grasp the napkin-wrapped cork with your dominant hand and the body of the bottle with the other. Twist the bottle in one direction and the cork in the other, easing it out slowly and gently, until it releases. Don't launch it with a loud pop and a lot of wasted foam.

Popping the cork may sound and look fun, but that allows carbon dioxide to escape, and that's what gives Champagne its signature sparkle. If you open a bottle of Champagne properly, as above, it can sit for hours with very little loss of carbonation.

GLASSWARE

No matter which Champagne you decide to drink, you should serve it in the proper glass. One story holds that the modern coupe—a footed glass with a shallow cup widening toward the rim—derives from the shape of the breast of Helen of Troy. The Ancient Greeks did drink wine from a breast-shaped cup (a *mastos*), but most surviving examples have handles and no stem or foot. Another story, centuries later, holds that the coupe was molded from the left breast of Marie Antoinette, queen of France— also unlikely. Either way, the larger surface area of a coupe means that Champagne loses its bubbles more quickly, so today it's served in a flute or tulip glass, which also helps concentrate the aromas of the wine in the glass.

CHAMPAGNE VS. SPARKLING WINE

Champagne is made using the *méthode champenoise*; it comes from the Champagne region of France; and in my opinion it's the world's best sparkling wine because that region has the ideal combination of elements necessary for producing excellent sparkling wine. The area has fine chalk soil; the grapes used for sparkling wine grow best here; and the climate of the location is perfect for this style.

Many different regions all over the world produce sparkling wines, but quality varies widely. Spain produces excellent Cava, made using the método tradicional. Germany has Sekt, and Italy has Spumante, which means "sparkling," and from Veneto the increasingly popular Prosecco. In America, California and New York are the main producers. California yields many fine examples, including Domaine Carneros, Domaine Chandon, Iron Horse, J, Korbel, Mumm Cuvée Napa, Piper-Sonoma, Roederer Estate, Scharffenberger, and Schramsberg. Many of the larger California wineries also market their own sparkling wines. New York is known for Paumanok, Sparkling Point, and Dr. Konstantin Frank. Oregon produces Soter and Argyle. From New Mexico, try Gruet.

Most sparkling wines not made using the classic method are made with secondary fermentation taking place in steel tanks, called the Charmat-Martinotti method, as with Prosecco. Some of the tanks used in this method can produce 100,000 bottles of sparkling wine in one batch!

The Moët-Hennessy Group, responsible for the production of Dom Pérignon in France also, owns Domaine Chandon. **THE SAME WINEMAKER** flies to California to help make the Domaine Chandon blend.

America is the **TOP IMPORTER** of Champagne.

40 percent of all sparkling wines consumed in America are imported, and about 20 percent of the sparkling wines made here use **THE CLASSIC METHOD.**

THE TOP FIVE CHAMPAGNES SOLD IN THE WORLD IN 2017

1. Moët & Chandon
2. Veuve Clicquot
3. Nicolas Feuillatte
4. G. H. Mumm
5. Laurent Perrier

GUIDED TASTING

There's no better way to celebrate your newfound knowledge of wine. Taste a couple of sparkling wines of Europe, then try two American sparkling wines, before raising two glasses of Champagne. Cheers.

European Sparkling Wine Two sparkling wines, compared:
  1. Prosecco
  2. Cava Brut

California Sparkling Wines Two sparkling wines, compared:
  3. Sparkling wine from Anderson Valley
  4. Sparkling wine from Napa Valley

Champagne Two Champagnes, compared:
  5. Nonvintage Champagne
  6. Vintage Champagne

FOOD PAIRINGS

Champagne is one of the most versatile wines that you can drink with a number of foods, from apéritif to dessert. Try these expert-recommended combinations.

"Never with sweets. A **Comtes de Champagne Blanc de Blancs** with seafood, caviar, or pâté of pheasant. Also never with cheese because the bubbles do not go well."
                                             —*Claude Taittinger*

"With **brut nonvintage**: a light hors d'oeuvre, such as mousse of pike. With **vintage Champagne**: pheasant, lobster or other seafood. With a **rosé Champagne** a strawberry dessert."
                                             —*Christian Pol Roger*

COMMON CHAMPAGNE AROMAS	
apple	yeast (bread dough)
toast	hazelnuts
citrus	walnuts

Serve **BRUT AND EXTRA DRY** as apéritifs or throughout the meal. **SERVE SEC AND DEMI-SEC** with desserts and wedding cake.

TEST YOUR KNOWLEDGE of sparkling wines by trying the quiz on page 391.

——— FURTHER READING ———
Champagne by Peter Liem

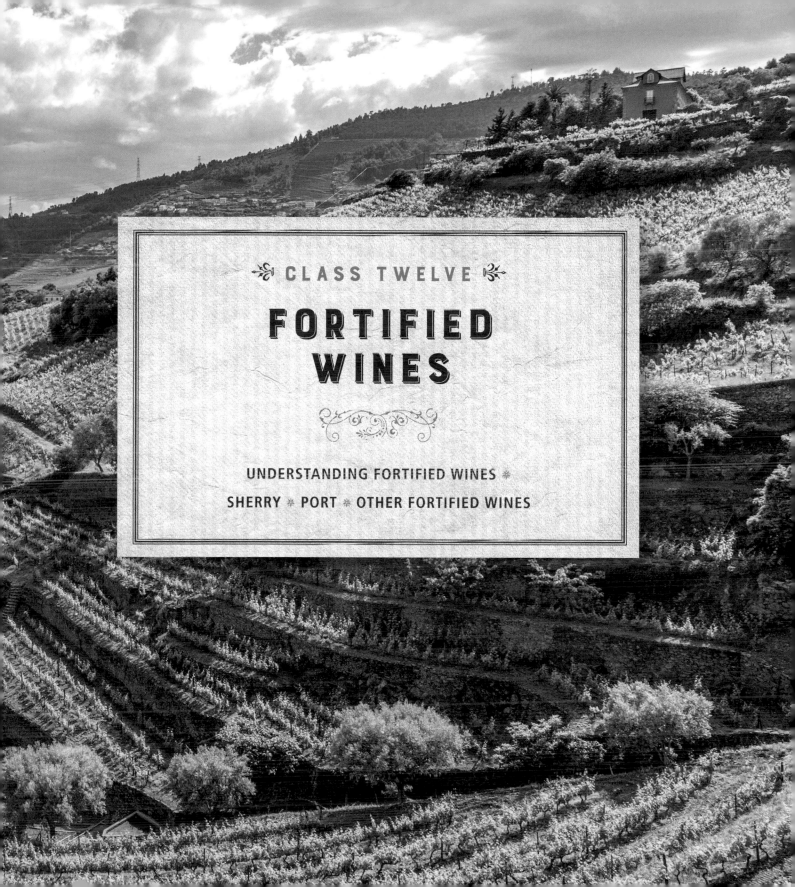

FORTIFIED WINES

UNDERSTANDING FORTIFIED WINES *
SHERRY * PORT * OTHER FORTIFIED WINES

Sherry accounts for **LESS THAN 3 PERCENT OF SPANISH WINE** production.

CHRISTOPHER COLUMBUS'S SHIPS were built in Puerto de Santa María, and the arrangements with Queen Isabella of Castile for his journey of discovery took place there as well.

PALOMINO accounts for 90 percent of the planted vineyards in Jerez.

UNDERSTANDING FORTIFIED WINES

Fortified wines are made in a two-stage process. Vintners first make the base wine and then add a neutral brandy (distilled wine) to raise the alcohol content. That addition happens at different stages, resulting in differing levels of sweetness. Different fortified wines also use different colors of grapes. Sherry comes from white grapes, while Port uses a blend of different red grapes.

SHERRY

The world's two greatest fortified wines are Sherry and Port. They have much in common, but the end result is two very different styles. What separates Port from Sherry is when the winemaker adds the brandy. For Port, it's added during fermentation. The extra alcohol kills the yeast and halts fermentation, which is why Port tastes so sweet. For Sherry, the brandy is added after fermentation. Port usually has 20 percent alcohol. Sherry, by comparison, usually has around 18 percent. Let's start with Sherry, produced in sunny southwestern Spain.

The area within these three towns makes up the Sherry triangle:

Jerez de la Frontera   **Puerto de Santa María**   **Sanlúcar de Barrameda**

The English pronunciation of Xeres, the old spelling of the first town's name, gives us the name of the wine in English.

The two main grape varieties used to make Sherry are:

Palomino   **Pedro Ximénez**

The different types of Sherry are:

Manzanilla	Fino	Amontillado	Oloroso	Cream
dry	dry	dry to medium-dry	dry to medium-dry	sweet

In the Sherry world, PX stands for the Pedro Ximénez grape. Cream Sherry is a blend of PX and Oloroso.

CONTROLLED OXIDATION

Normally vintners carefully guard against letting air into wine during the winemaking process, but that's exactly what transforms wine into Sherry. To do so, winemakers place the wine in barrels, about two-thirds full, and place the bung, or stopper, loosely in the barrel so as to admit air. They store the barrels in a bodega, in this case an aboveground storage structure. During the process, some wine evaporates—at least 3 percent a year (called the Angels' Share). Now you know why the people of Jerez are so happy all the time. They're breathing in Sherry!

THE SOLERA METHOD

The next step in making Sherry is called fractional blending, achieved through the Solera method. In this process, aging and maturation take place by means of the continuous blending of several vintages. At the bottling stage, wine is drawn from the barrels—never more than a third of the barrel's content—to make room for the new vintage. This blending maintains the house style by using the "mother" wine as a base and refreshing it with younger wines.

Some Soleras can contain a blend of **10 TO 20 DIFFERENT HARVESTS.**

CHOOSING A SHERRY

Your best guide is the producer, who buys the grapes and does the blending. Ten producers account for 60 percent of the export market, and the top producers include:

Croft	Hidalgo	Sandeman
Emilio Lustau	Osborne	Savory and James
González Byass	Pedro Domecq	Williams & Humbert
Harveys		

In today's Sherry, the wine ages only in
AMERICAN OAK.

STORAGE

After opening, Sherry lasts longer than a regular table wine because of its higher alcohol content, which acts as a preservative. But once opened, it will begin to lose its freshness. To drink Sherry at its best, finish the bottle within two weeks of opening and refrigerate the opened bottle. Treat Manzanilla and Fino Sherry as white wines, and drink them within a day or two.

GUIDED TASTING

Remember that Sherries, because they're fortified, have a higher alcohol content than regular wine. Pour accordingly and limit the tasting to one example from each of the five major styles. Start with the driest, Manzanilla, and work your way to the sweet end of the spectrum.

Five Sherries compared:
1. Manzanilla
2. Fino
3. Amontillado
4. Oloroso
5. Cream

FOOD PAIRINGS

"Very old and rare **Sherry** should be served with cheese. **Fino** and **Manzanilla** can be served as an apéritif or with light grilled or fried fish or even smoked salmon. You get the taste of the smoke better than if you have it with a white wine. **Amontillado** should be served with light cheese, chorizo, ham, or shish kebab. It is a perfect complement to turtle soup or consommé. With **Cream Sherry**, cookies, pastries, and cakes. **Pedro Ximénez**, however, is better as a topping for vanilla ice cream or as a dessert wine before coffee and brandy."   —*José Ignacio Domecq*

"**Fino** should always be served well chilled. I enjoy having Fino as an apéritif with tapas, but I also like to complement practically any fish meal with the wine—clams, shellfish, lobster, prawns, langoustines, fish soup, or a light fish, such as salmon."   —*Mauricio González*

To clarify the Sherry and remove the sediment, winemakers add **BEATEN EGG WHITES** to the wine. The sediment attaches to the egg whites and drops to the bottom of the barrel. But what do they do with all the yolks? Ever hear of flan? It's the quintessential Spanish custard dessert made from all the yolks. In Jerez, it's called *tocino de cielo*, "the fat of heaven."

——— **FURTHER READING** ———

Sherry by Julian Jeffs

Sherry by Talia Baiocchi

PORT PRODUCTION PER YEAR

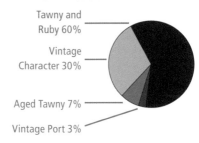

Tawny and Ruby 60%

Vintage Character 30%

Aged Tawny 7%

Vintage Port 3%

IT'S NOT JUST ABOUT PORT. Over the last ten years, Portugal has shifted its focus to dry reds and whites. My favorites include Douro—Real Companhia Velha, Quinta Castro, Quinta du Passadouro, Rozes, and Durum—and Alentejo: Luis Duarte Vinhos and Susana Esteban.

PORT

Port comes from the Douro region in northern Portugal. In recent years, to avoid misuse of the name, authentic Port wine has been renamed Porto, after Oporto, the city from which it ships. Remember, winemakers add neutral brandy to Port during fermentation, which halts the process and leaves from 9 to 11 percent residual sugar. This is why Port tastes sweet.

These are the two types of Port and their various styles:

CASK-AGED	
RUBY PORT	DARK AND FRUITY, BLENDED FROM YOUNG NONVINTAGE WINES. COST: $.
TAWNY PORT	LIGHTER AND MORE DELICATE, BLENDED FROM MANY VINTAGES. COST: $$.
AGED TAWNY	AGED IN CASKS, SOMETIMES FOR FORTY YEARS OR MORE. COST: $$–$$$.
COLHEITA	FROM A SINGLE VINTAGE AND WOOD-AGED AT LEAST SEVEN YEARS. COST: $$–$$$$.

BOTTLE-AGED	
LATE BOTTLED VINTAGE (LBV)	FROM A SINGLE VINTAGE, BOTTLED FOUR TO SIX YEARS AFTER HARVEST, AND SIMILAR TO VINTAGE PORT BUT LIGHTER AND READY TO DRINK ON RELEASE WITH NO DECANTING. COST: $$$
VINTAGE CHARACTER	SIMILAR TO LBV BUT MADE FROM A BLEND OF THE BETTER VINTAGES. COST: $$.
QUINTA	FROM A SINGLE VINEYARD. COST: $$$–$$$$.
VINTAGE PORT	AGED TWO YEARS IN WOOD AND WILL MATURE IN THE BOTTLE OVER TIME. COST: $$$$.

Cask-aged Ports are ready to drink as soon as they're bottled and won't improve with age. Bottle-aged Ports improve as they mature in the bottle. As with Champagne houses, Port vintages vary from shipper to shipper. For example, in 2003, 2007, and 2011, most producers declared a vintage, but many didn't in the intervening years. Depending on the quality of the vintage, a great Vintage Port will be ready to drink 15 to 30 years after the vintage year! See below for the best vintages.

CHOOSING A PORT

As with Sherry, the grape variety shouldn't dictate your choice. Determine the style and the blend you prefer, and look for the most reliable producers. The most important that are available in America include:

A. A. Ferreira	Fonseca	Ramos Pinto
C. da Silva	Harveys of Bristol	Robertson's
Churchill	Kopke	Sandeman
Cockburn	Niepoort & Co., Ltd.	Taylor Fladgate
Croft	Quinta do Noval	W. & J. Graham
Dow	Quinto Do Vesuvio	Warre's & Co.

ENJOYING PORT

Because a bottle of Port likely contains sediment, decant the wine before serving, which will enhance your enjoyment of it (page 340). As with Sherry, an opened bottle of Port also lasts longer than table wine because of its higher alcohol content. To drink Port at its prime, consume the contents of an opened bottle within one week.

THE BRITISH LOVE PORT. Traditionally, on the birth of a baby, parents buy bottles of Port to put away until the child's 21st birthday—the age of maturity for a child and also a fine Port!

THE FIRST VINTAGE PORT was recorded in 1765.

– BEST VINTAGES OF PORT –

1963** 1966* 1970** 1977** 1983* 1985* 1991*
1992* 1994** 1995* 1997** 2000** 2003**
2007** 2011** 2014 2015** 2016

* EXCEPTIONAL VINTAGE   ** EXTRAORDINARY VINTAGE

GUIDED TASTING

As with Sherry, the higher alcohol content in Port means that we're going to taste fewer representative examples than in the other classes. Move from youngest to oldest, and remember as you're tasting that Colheita Port comes from a single vintage and Quinta Port comes from a single vineyard.

Three cask-aged Ports compared:
1. Ruby Port
2. Tawny Port, 10+ years old
3. Colheita

Three bottle-aged Ports compared:
4. Late Bottle Vintage
5. Quinta
6. Vintage Port

FOOD PAIRINGS

"The sweetness of **Port** might deceive you, but it's a particularly versatile wine for pairing with food. The French drink it as an aperitif to stimulate the appetite before a meal. The sweetness of Port aligns nicely with other sweets, such as poached pears, but that same sweetness helps balance foods with more bitterness or saltiness in them, such as cheese—especially a good Stilton—dark chocolate, or walnuts. I like it best after a meal, as a dessert wine, so that it can shine all on its own.

OTHER FORTIFIED WINES

Other fortified wines that you might know include Vermouth, from Italy and France, Marsala from Italy, Pineau de Charentes from France, and Madeira from Portugal. Not as popular as it once was, Madeira wine was probably the first wine imported into America. The colonists, including George Washington, had a taste for it and used it to toast the signing of the Declaration of Independence.

TEST YOUR KNOWLEDGE of fortified wines by trying the quiz on page 391.

—— **FURTHER READING** ——

The Port Companion by Godfrey Spence

Vintage Port by James Suckling

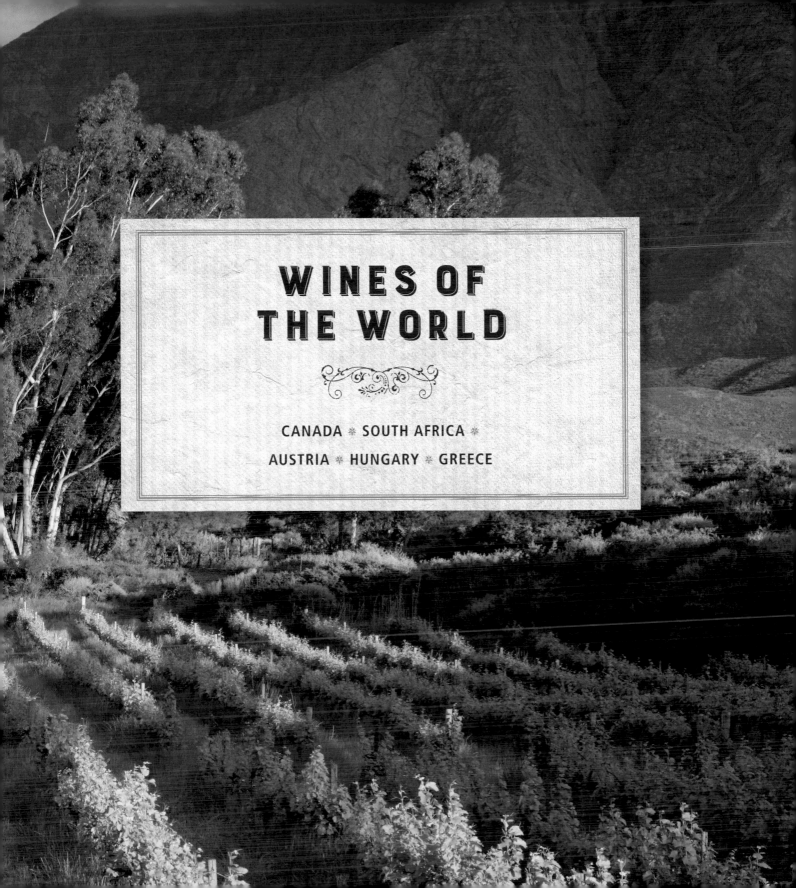

WINES OF
THE WORLD

CANADA ❋ SOUTH AFRICA ❋
AUSTRIA ❋ HUNGARY ❋ GREECE

THE WINES OF CANADA

Commercial winemaking in Canada began in the early 1800s, and its wine history closely follows that of New York. Both began by growing the winter-hardy *labrusca* grapes (Catawba, Concord, Niagara). Like New York, many of Canada's wineries specialized in producing fortified wines often labeled with borrowed European names, such as Port and Sherry. Like America, Canada also had a period of national prohibition, 1916–1927. The first major change in Canadian viticulture occurred during the 1970s, when several small producers began experimenting with French hybrid grapes. Over the last 40 years, the best Canadian wines have come from European *vinifera* grapes.

Canada has two major wine-producing regions: British Columbia on the Pacific Coast and Ontario in the eastern Great Lakes region, and each makes a grab bag of different wines:

REGION	VARIETIES
BRITISH COLUMBIA / OKANAGAN VALLEY	CHARDONNAY, PINOT GRIS, MERLOT, CABERNET CABERNET SAUVIGNON, SYRAH, GEWÜRTZTRAMINER, PINOT NOIR, RIESLING, VIOGNIER, MALBEC
ONTARIO / NIAGARA PENINSULA	CHARDONNAY, RIESLING, PINOT NOIR, VIDAL, CABERNET FRANC

ONTARIO

15,074 acres   130 wineries

BRITISH COLUMBIA

9,500 acres   212 wineries

Many people think that Canada sits too far north to make great wine. Just as in other cool-climate wine regions, such as Germany, most of **THE BEST VINEYARDS LIE NEAR WATER,** which tempers the climate. Ontario has Lake Ontario and Lake Erie, and British Columbia has Okanagan Lake.

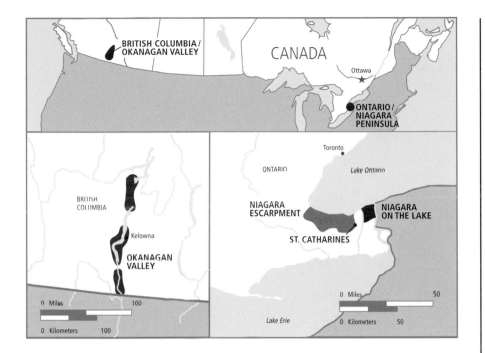

The major white grapes are:

Chardonnay	Pinot Gris	Vidal
Gewürztraminer	Riesling	

The major red grapes are:

Cabernet Franc	Merlot	Syrah
Cabernet Sauvignon	Pinot Noir	

The Vintners Quality Alliance (VQA) formed to regulate the wines of Ontario in 1988 and British Columbia in 1990. A VQA designation stipulates that the wine comes from 100 percent vinifera varieties, and it also controls varietal percentages. If a label lists the grape variety, the wine must contain at least 85 percent of that variety. If the label names a Designated Viticultural Area (DVA), 95 percent of the grapes must come from that area. If a vineyard appears, 100 percent of the wine must come from that vineyard. More than 100 wineries produce VQA wines.

QUEBEC AND NOVA SCOTIA also grow grapes, primarily hybrids.

60 percent of VQA WINES come from white grapes.

Canadians DAN AYKROYD and WAYNE GRETZKY have invested in Canadian wineries.

MY FAVORITE CANADIAN WINERIES

Amisfield	Jackson-Triggs
Château des Charmes	Le Clos Jordanne
Greywacke	Mission Hill
Henry of Pelham	(the largest winery)
Inniskillin	Sumac Ridge

CANADIAN ICE WINE

The first new winery in Ontario since 1927, Inniskillin was founded in 1975 and produced its first ice wine in 1984 after an unseasonably cold winter.

To make ice wine, grapes are allowed to freeze on the vine before being picked by hand. They're pressed carefully while still frozen, yielding a small amount of concentrated juice high in sugar and other components. Canadian law requires that ice wine come only from *vinifera* grapes, usually Riesling and the French hybrid Vidal. It also must contain at least 125 grams of residual sugar per liter. Most ice wines are expensive and sold in half bottles.

- BEST RECENT VINTAGES OF CANADIAN WINES -
ONTARIO: 2010* 2011 2012* 2013* 2014* 2015 2016* 2017
BRITISH COLUMBIA: 2010 2011 2012 2013 2014*
2015* 2015* 2016*
* EXCEPTIONAL VINTAGE

TEST YOUR KNOWLEDGE of the wines of Canada by trying the quiz on page 393.

——— FURTHER READING ———

Canadian Wine for Dummies by Tony Aspler

Vintage Canada by Tony Aspler

The Wine Atlas of Canada by Tony Aspler

SOUTH AFRICA, PAST AND PRESENT

1970: 88,770 hectares

270 million liters

2016: 110,041 hectares

958 million liters

SOUTH AFRICA WINE PRODUCTION

50% white   50% red

Most Western Cape wine regions lie within a two-hour drive of **CAPE TOWN.**

THE WINES OF SOUTH AFRICA

South Africa has the world's oldest wine-growing geology. Dutch settlers founded Cape Town in 1652, and the first grape harvest took place here seven years later. Their descendants and those of the Huguenots who also settled here have grown grapes and made wine for some 350 years, establishing the world-renowned Constantia wine estate in 1685. Until recently, most of the country's wine sold domestically or in Europe and wasn't available in America. Before 1990, a few producers made good wine, but for the most part large cooperatives focused on fortified wines and brandy, basing output on a quota system that valued quantity over quality. In 1994, the dismantling of apartheid and the democratic election of Nelson Mandela as president ended South Africa's economic isolation, allowing its wines to reach the world's markets.

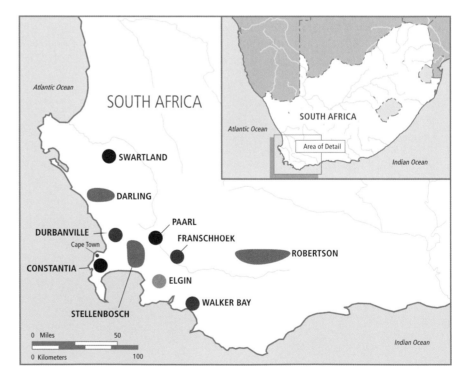

The country has a wide diversity of terrain and weather conditions. Vineyards lie at altitudes from 300 feet above sea level to 1,300. Some vineyards have cool, coastal climates, while in others summer days exceed 100 degrees Fahrenheit. It's a land of contrast, alive with possibilities.

South Africa consists of two main geographic areas, the Western Cape, which produces 97 percent of the country's wine, and the Northern Cape. These break down further into regions, districts, and wards. The most important region is the Coastal Region. The three most historically important Wines of Origin (WO) within the Coastal Region and the best varietals of each are:

WINES OF ORIGIN (WO)	GRAPE VARIETIES
COASTAL REGION	
CONSTANTIA	SAUVIGNON BLANC, MUSCAT
STELLENBOSCH	CHARDONNAY, CABERNET SAUVIGNON, PINOTAGE, BORDEAUX BLENDS
PAARL	CHARDONNAY, SYRAH, CHENIN BLANC

The country's other important areas and their best wines include:

REGION	GRAPE VARIETIES
DARLING	SAUVIGNON BLANC
DURBANVILLE	SAUVIGNON BLANC, MERLOT
ELGIN	RIESLING, SAUVIGNON BLANC, PINOT NOIR
FRANSCHHOEK	CABERNET SAUVIGNON, SYRAH, SEMILLON
ROBERTSON	CHARDONNAY, SHIRAZ
SWARTLAND	SHIRAZ, PINOTAGE, RHÔNE-STYLE BLENDS
WALKER BAY	CHARDONNAY, PINOT NOIR

The major white grape varieties that grow here are:

Chardonnay   Chenin Blanc (Steen)   Sauvignon Blanc

It remains unclear whether Chenin Blanc or Sauvignon Blanc will become South Africa's benchmark white wine. Historically Chenin Blanc has held that position, and some of those vines are more than 100 years old. Some producers age it in oak, others age it unoaked, and several winemakers employ both methods.

The world's **BEST CHENIN BLANCS** come from either South Africa or the Loire Valley in France.

The major red varieties are:

Bordeaux blends   **Shiraz / Syrah**   **Cabernet Sauvignon**   **Pinotage**
(Cabernet Sauvignon,
Merlot, Cabernet Franc)

FOREIGN INVESTMENT

INVESTOR	FOREIGN WINERY	REGION / COUNTRY	SOUTH AFRICAN WINERY
ANNE COINTREAU-HUCHON		FRANCE	MORGENHOF
BRUNO PRATS	CHÂTEAU COS D'ESTOURNEL	BORDEAUX	ANWILKA
DONALD HESS		CALIFORNIA, ARGENTINA, AUSTRALIA	GLEN CARLOU
HUBERT DE BOÜARD	CHÂTEAU ANGÉLUS	BORDEAUX	ANWILKA
MAY DE LENCQUESAING	CHÂTEAU PICHON-LALANDE	BORDEAUX	GLENELLY
MICHEL LAROCHE		CHABLIS	L'AVENIR
PHIL FREESE	FORMERLY MONDAVI	CALIFORNIA	VILAFONTÉ
PIERRE LURTON	CHÂTEAU CHEVAL BLANC	BORDEAUX	MORGENSTER
ZELMA LONG	FORMERLY SIMI	CALIFORNIA	VILAFONTÉ

Over the last 20 years, South African wines have improved dramatically. Many now share center stage with some of the world's best. Winemakers are making up for lost time, and the best is yet to come. South Africa now has more than 600 wineries, and a third of the country's vineyards have been replanted since 1994—a key point to know, given that vine age plays a decisive role in the quality of the wine produced.

Implemented in 1973, WO regulations strictly control labeling. If a region, district, or ward appears on the label, 100 percent of the grapes must come from that place of origin. If a wine label specifies that it is estate-bottled, 100 percent of the grapes must come from that estate. A vintage designation means that 85 percent of the grapes come from the stated vintage,

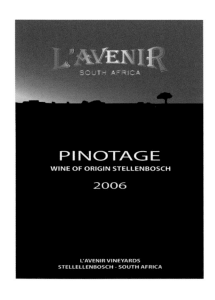

and a varietal designation means that the wine contains at least 85 percent of the named varietal. The WO doesn't control yield per hectare or irrigation.

My favorite South African Chenin Blancs include:

Cederberg	Groote Post	Kanu
De Trafford	Iona	Rudera

PINOTAGE

A viticulturist from Stellenbosch University created this variety in 1925 by crossing Pinot Noir and Cinsault. Unfortunately, it never has had a single taste profile. Pinotage can produce a light, somewhat insipid wine smelling of acetate, banana, or spray paint, with a strong, acrid aftertaste. It also can make a big, full-bodied, luscious, well-balanced wine with tremendous fruit extraction and a long graceful finish, capable of aging for 20 or more years. The best producers of Pinotage follow a similar formula:

- Vines planted in cooler climates and at least 15 years old
- Low per-acre crop yield
- Long skin contact and maceration in open fermentors
- At least two years of oak aging
- Blending with Cabernet Sauvignon
- At least ten years of bottle aging

My favorite producers of Pinotage include:

Fairview	L'Avenir	Simonsig
Kanonkop		

SOUTH AFRICAN DESSERT WINES

Long before vintners in Bordeaux were producing Sauternes or wine-makers in Germany were making Trockenbeerenauslese, South Africa produced one of the world's greatest sweet wines. Constantia has been producing fragrant, aromatic wines from the Muscat grape since the 1700s. The Klein Constantia estate still produces wines in this original style, raisinating the grapes rather than botrytizing them.

MY FAVORITE SOUTH AFRICAN WINE PRODUCERS

STELLENBOSCH

Anwilka	Ken Forrester	Rudera
Cirrus	L'Avenir	Rust en Vrede
De Toren	Meerlust	Rustenberg
De Trafford	Morgenhof	Simonsig
Ernie Els	Morgenster	Thelema
Glenelly	Mulderbosch	Vergelegen
Jordan (Jardin	Neil Ellis	Vriesenhof
in the USA)	Raats Family	Waterford
Kanonkop		

PAARL

Fairview	Nederburg	Vilafonté
Glen Carlou	Veenwouden	

FRANSCHHOEK

Antonij Rupert	Boschendal	Graham Beck
Boekenhoutskloof		

SWARTLAND

A. A. Badenhorst Family	Porseleinberg	Sadie Family
Mullineux		

WALKER BAY

Ashbourne	Bouchard-Finlayson	Hamilton Russell

CONSTANTIA

Constantia Uitsig	Klein Constantia	Steenberg

ELGIN

Paul Cluver

5 BEST VALUE SOUTH AFRICA WINES WINES UNDER $30

Doolhof Dark Lady of the Labyrinth Pinotage • Ken Forrester Sauvignon Blanc •
Rustenberg 1682 Red Blend • Thelema Cabernet Sauvignon •
Tokara Chardonnay Reserve Collection •

See page 364 for a complete list

In 2016, South Africa experienced the **DRIEST WEATHER** on record.

TEST YOUR KNOWLEDGE of the wines of South Africa by trying the quiz on page 393.

――― **FURTHER READING** ―――

Wines of the New South Africa by Tim James

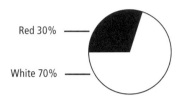

AUSTRIAN WINE PRODUCTION

Red 30%

White 70%

Visit the village of Klosterneuburg on the Danube River to see a monastery that dates from 1114. While there, taste the Grüner Veltliner of Donauland. Also visit **THE KLOSTERNEUBURG SCHOOL OF ENOLOGY,** the oldest in the world, founded in 1860.

THE WINES OF AUSTRIA

Grape growing and winemaking in what is now Austria date back to the fourth century B.C., but only in the past quarter century has the country earned a reputation for producing quality wines, specifically some of Europe's most elegant and best-tasting white wines, both dry and sweet. Its Grüner Veltliners and Rieslings pair beautifully with food, which accounts in part for the recent success of Austrian wines in America. Both chefs and sommeliers agree that these wines work well with nearly any dish, from fish and poultry to most meats. Austria's wines also hold their own when paired with Asian spices.

The country contains four wine regions: Lower Austria, Vienna, Burgenland, and Styria, all located along its eastern borders. The Danube River and the fertile valley that surrounds it define the northern wine regions,

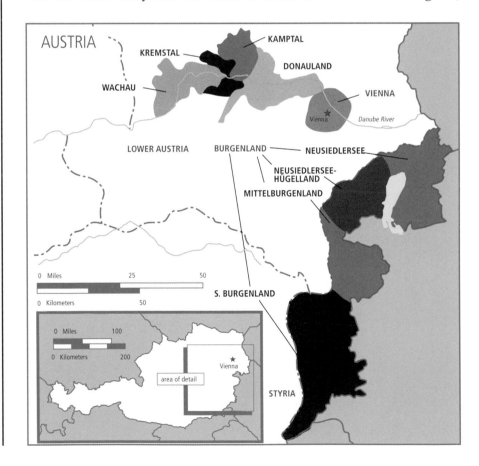

including Lower Austria—which produces 60 percent of the country's wine—and Vienna, one of the world's most beautiful cities and the only major city to be a wine region. The two most important of these regions, their wine districts, and specialties are:

Burgenland: (red and dessert wines) Neusiedlersee, Mittelburgenland, Neusiedlersee-Hügelland

Lower Austria: (white wines) Wachau, Kamptal, Kremstal, Donauland

The main white varieties are:

Grüner Veltliner   Sauvignon Blanc   Riesling   Chardonnay (Morillon)

and the main red varieties are:

Blaufränkisch (Lemberger)   St. Laurent   Pinot Noir

Austria largely follows the same criteria used in other European countries, specifically Germany, with regard to wine labeling, although it maintains even stricter control. Grape ripeness and the sugar content of the fermenting must determines quality levels, the three broadest being:

Tafelwein   Qualitätswein   Prädikatswein

The Austrian wine board tastes and chemically analyzes Qualitätswein and higher levels of wine, giving consumers a guarantee of taste, style, and quality. If a label lists a specific grape, the wine must contain at least 85 percent of that grape. If a label indicates a vintage, the wine must contain a minimum of 85 percent of that vintage. If the label names a wine region, 100 percent of the wine must come from that region.

WACHAU WINES

STEINFEDER: maximum alcohol 10.7%

FEDERSPIEL: maximum alcohol 12.5%

SMARAGD: minimum alcohol 12.5%

(*Sommelier Journal*)

Grüner Veltliner accounts for **MORE THAN ONE-THIRD** of Austrian grape plantings.

TRY BLAUFRÄNKISCH blended with Cabernet Sauvignon.

The **ZWEIGELT** grape is a cross between Blaufränkisch and St. Laurent.

PRAGER

ACHLEITEN
RIESLING
SMARAGD 2007

WACHAU AUSTRIA

TEST YOUR KNOWLEDGE of the wines of Austria by trying the quiz on page 393.

———— **FURTHER READING** ————

The Ultimate Austrian Wine Guide by Peter Moser

The Wines of Austria by Philipp Blom

As with German wines, most Austrian wines are white, but, unlike German wines, most of Austria's wines are dry, with higher alcohol and more body, resembling the wines of Alsace. Gradation of ripeness indicates the amount of residual sugar left in the wine after fermentation. In Austrian wines, it ranges from the very dry Trocken to the very sweet Trockenbeerenauslese.

GRADATIONS OF RIPENESS

DRY	SWEET	VERY SWEET
TROCKEN	TAFELWEIN	AUSLESE
HALBTROCKEN	LANDWEIN	EISWEIN
LIEBLICH	QUALITÄTSWEIN	BEERENAUSLESE
	KABINETT	AUSBRUCH
	PRÄDIKATSWEIN	TROCKENBEERENAUSLESE
	SPÄTLESE	

Ausbruch, one of the world's great dessert wines, comes from the village of Rust in Burgenland and has a history that dates back as far as 1617. On par with French Sauternes, German Beerenauslese, and Hungarian Tokay, it's made with botrytized grapes, primarily Furmint.

MY FAVORITE AUSTRIAN WINE PRODUCERS INCLUDE:

Alzinger	Hirtzberger	Nikolaihof
Bründlmayer	Knoll	Rudy Pichler
F. X. Pichler	Kracher	Prager l
Hirsch	Nigl	Schloss Gobelsburg

– BEST RECENT VINTAGES OF AUSTRIAN WINES –
2006** 2007* 2008** 2009* 2011*
2012 2013* 2015** 2016
*EXCEPTIONAL VINTAGE **EXTRAORDINARY VINTAGE*

5 BEST VALUE AUSTRIAN WINES WINES UNDER $30
Alois Kracher Pinot Gris Trocken • Hirsch "Veltliner #1" • Nigl Grüner Veltliner Kremser Freiheit • Schloss Gobelsburg • Sepp Moser Sepp Zweigelt •

See page 357 for a complete list

THE WINES OF HUNGARY

The wine industry of Hungary dates back as far as the Roman Empire, and it has thrived culturally and economically for nearly 1,000 years. Tokay, its most famous wine, has been produced continuously since the sixteenth century, and Tokaj received the world's first vineyard classification in 1700. The reputation of Hungarian wine suffered a major decline under Communist rule from 1949 to 1989. In that time, a state monopoly shifted production to bulk wine with little regard to maintaining or improving existing quality wines.

Since the fall of Communism, however, emphasis has returned to quality wines, with an influx of capital from Italian, French, and German winemakers. The introduction of Sauvignon Blanc, Chardonnay, and Pinot Gris grapes, new vineyard techniques, and modern equipment have helped rebuild Hungary's wine industry. The famous vineyards of Tokaj received the first wave of attention, but investment has expanded throughout the country.

THE HUNGARIAN LANGUAGE can prove difficult for anyone—especially after a glass of wine! This table will help you understand the style of the wine behind the name.

Hungarian Name	AKA
Kékfrankos	Blaufränkisch
Tramini	Gewürztraminer
Szürkebarát	Pinot Gris
Zöld Veltlini	Grüner Veltliner

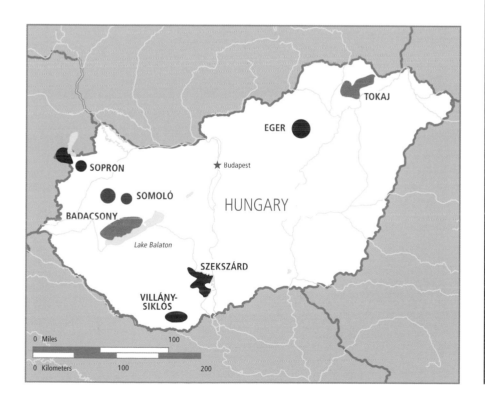

The country has 22 wine regions, seven of which you should know along with their most important grapes:

Badacsony: Olaszrizling
Eger Kékfrankos: Pinot Noir
Somoló: Furmint
Sopron: Kékfrankos
Szekszárd: Kadarka, Merlot, Cabernet Sauvignon
Tokaj: Furmint, Hárslevelü
Villány-Siklós: Cabernet Sauvignon, Kékfrankos

The major grapes are:

	NATIVE TO HUNGARY	INTERNATIONAL
WHITE	FURMINT HÁRSLEVELÜ OLASZRIZLING	CHARDONNAY PINOT GRIS (SZÜRKEBARÁT) SAUVIGNON BLANC
RED	KADARKA KÉKFRANKOS PORTUGIESER	CABERNET SAUVIGNON MERLOT PINOT NOIR

TOKAJ: The name of the village
TOKAJI: From the region
TOKAY: English version of Tokaji

A Sauternes has 90 **GRAMS OF SUGAR,** and a Trockenbeerenauslese has 150 grams of sugar.

TOKAY

This "liquid gold" wine—on par with French Sauternes and German Trocken-beerenauslese—comes from Tokaj, a village in Hungary's northeastern corner and one of the oldest wine regions in the world.

Tokaji Aszú, as it's known in Hungarian, usually blends four native grapes, primarily Furmint. Throughout the fall harvest season, the grapes affected by the Botrytis cinerea mold—or *aszú*—are picked, lightly crushed, and made into a paste. Unaffected grapes ferment into the base wine. Workers collect the *aszú* paste in baskets, called *puttonyos*, then blend those into the base wine according to the desired sweetness, measured in *puttonyos* on the label of all Tokay. The more paste buckets that go into the base wine, the sweeter the outcome.

Puttonyos wine has four levels:

3 Puttonyos	4 Puttonyos	5 Puttonyos	6 Puttonyos
60 grams of sugar per liter	90 grams of sugar per liter	120 grams of sugar per liter	150 grams of sugar per liter

The sweetest Tokaj wines—called "Essencia" or "Eszencia"—contain a whopping 180 grams of sugar. Due to its high concentration of sugar, Essencia may take years to finish fermentation, and even then it will have an alcohol content of only 2–5 percent. It's one of the most unique wines in the world!

MY FAVORITE TOKAY PRODUCERS INCLUDE:

Chateau Dereszla   Hétszölö   Royal Tokaji Wine

Chateau Pajzos   Oremus   Company

Disznókö   Szepsy

- BEST VINTAGES OF TOKAY -

2000** 2001* 2002 2003* 2005 2006* 2007*
2008 2013* 2014 2015* 2017

* EXCEPTIONAL VINTAGE

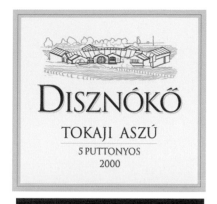

SZAMORODNI is another style of wine made in Tokaj. It ranges from semidry to semisweet but has fewer grams of sugar than three *puttonyos*.

The traditional squat Tokaji Aszú bottles contain **500 MILLILITERS** versus the normal 750 milliliters.

TEST YOUR KNOWLEDGE of the wines of Hungary by trying the quiz on page 393.

—— **FURTHER READING** ——

Wine Guide Hungary by Gabriella Rohaly and Gabor Meszaros

THE WINES OF GREECE

Wine production in the Peloponnese began 7,000 years ago, and wine has played an important role in Greek culture and life since at least the seventh century B.C. It always has ranked as one of the most traded commodities throughout Greece and other Mediterranean countries.

Prior to 1985, most Greek wines were somewhat ordinary. Large bulk-wine producers exported them mainly to Greek communities abroad. Greece joined the European Union in 1981, prompting tremendous investment in winemaking technology and the vineyards there. As a result, especially over the last 25 years, the Greek wine industry has been concentrating on making quality wines. EU subsidies, along with winemakers' dedication, have helped finance state-of-the-art wineries throughout the country.

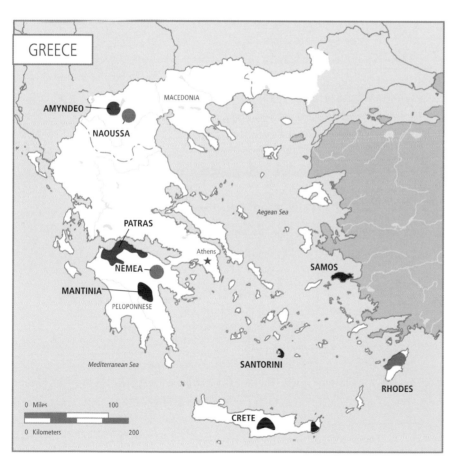

GREEK WINE WORDS

LIBATION: from *leibein*, to pour
SYMPOSIUM: from *symposion*, to drink together
ENOLOGY: from *oinos*, wine, and *logos*, study or speech

"The wine urges me on, the bewitching wine, which sets even a wise man to singing and laughing gently and rouses him up to dance and brings forth words which were better unspoken."

—Odysseus, *The Odyssey*
(14.463–466)

"Shall we not pass a law that, in the first place, no children under 18 may touch wine at all, teaching that it is wrong to pour fire upon fire either in body or in soul . . . and thus guarding against the excitable disposition of the young? And next, we shall rule that the young man under 30 may take wine in moderation, but that he must entirely abstain from intoxication and heavy drinking. But when a man has reached the age of 40, he may join in the convivial gatherings and invoke Dionysus, above all other gods, inviting his presence at the rite (which is also the recreation) of the elders, which he bestowed on mankind as a medicine potent against the crabbedness of Old Age, that thereby we men may renew our youth, and that, through forgetfulness of care, the temper of our souls may lose its hardness and become softer and more ductile."

— Plato, *Laws* 666b

Of Greece's more than 3,000 islands, only **63 ARE INHABITED.**

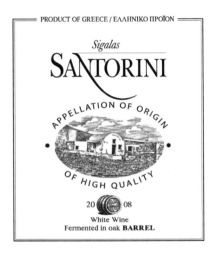

These are best Greek wine-growing regions and their districts

NORTHERN GREECE	SOUTHERN GREECE	AEGEAN SEA
MACEDONIA: AMYNDEO NAOUSSA	PELOPONNESE: MANTINIA NEMEA PATRAS	THE ISLANDS: CRETE SAMOS SANTORINI RHODES

Describing a typical Greek wine poses no easy task. Look at a map of the country and note its many islands and mountains and proximity to the Aegean and Ionian seas of the Mediterranean. It's the third most mountainous country in Europe, and most of its vineyards lie on the slopes of mountains or on remote islands. A typical vineyard here covers less than one hectare (2.471 acres).

Enormous diversity characterizes Greece's wine regions. Some of the climate is distinctly Mediterranean (hot summers; long autumns; short, mild winters), but the mountain regions feature a more typically continental climate: lots of sunshine, cool evenings, dry summers, and mild winters. Some of the islands' volcanic soils make a very different style of wine depending on whether the vineyards lie on flatlands or on steep mountain slopes. Some vineyard owners harvest in August, others in October. According to myth, Dionysus gave wine to the Greeks in Attica, the region containing Athens. Known today for its Retsina and Salvatiano, Attica fosters some of the most exciting experimentation.

The major white grapes are:

Assyrtiko	Moschofilero	Roditis

and the major red grapes are:

Agiorgitiko	Mavrodafni	Xinomavro

Many of the better wines fall into the two governmental categories: OPAP (Wines of Appellation of Origin of Superior Quality, mostly dry) and OPE (Wines of Appellation of Controlled Origin, only sweet). Both designations indicate wines that come from viticultural areas defined in 1971. Nemea is an OPAP wine, and Muscat of Patras an OPE wine. Look for the red stripe at the top of the bottle for an OPAP wine and a blue stripe for an OPE wine. The Greek equivalent to table wine, Epitrapezios Oenos (EO) doesn't include an appellation of origin and may blend wines from

many different regions. Exports of Greek wine to America have increased by 30 percent over the last five years, and the next ten years will define the broader future of the new Greek wines.

RETSINA

Adding pine resin as a flavoring agent to wine creates Retsina. In ancient times, winemakers used pine resin to create an airtight seal on amphorae—large ceramic wine vessels—to prevent wine from oxidizing during transportation and storage. The resin sometimes leaked into the wine, and eventually the Greeks developed a taste for the distinctive flavor. A friend describes its pungent aroma as an "acquired taste." (Think turpentine!)

MY FAVORITE GREEK WINE PRODUCERS

Alpha Estate	Kir Yianni	Samos Cooperative
Boutari	Oenoforos	Semeli
Driopi	Pavlidis	Sigalas
Gaia Estate	Manoussakis	Skouras
Gerovassiliou	Mercouri	Tselepos

TEST YOUR KNOWLEDGE of the wines of Greece by trying the quiz on page 393.

——— **FURTHER READING** ———

The Illustrated Greek Wine Book by Nico Manessis

The Wines of Greece by Konstantinos Lazarakis

BEST RECENT VINTAGES OF WINES FROM GREECE

2008*   2012   2013   2015*   2016*   2017**

* EXCEPTIONAL VINTAGE   ** EXTRAORDINARY VINTAGE

THE GREATER WORLD OF WINE

WINE AND FOOD PAIRINGS * FREQUENTLY ASKED
QUESTIONS ABOUT WINE * THE BEST OF THE BEST *
THE WORLD'S BEST VALUE WINES UNDER $30 *
WINE RESOURCES

ANDREA ROBINSON worked at Windows on the World and is one of only 15 women in the world to hold the title of master sommelier, awarded by the Court of Master Sommeliers. She has written several books on wine and food, and the James Beard Foundation named her Outstanding Wine & Spirits Professional in 2002.

In 2013, the *New England Journal of Medicine* reaffirmed that a Mediterranean diet rich in olive oil, nuts, beans, fish, fruit, vegetables, **AND WINE IS GOOD FOR YOU.**

I cook with wine; sometimes I even add it to food.

—Attributed to W. C. Fields

Are you a menu maven or a wine-list junkie? I look at the wine list first, choose my wine, and then make **MY MEAL SELECTION,** as follows:

• What kind of wine do I like?
• Texture of food (heavy or light)
• Preparation (grilled, sautéed, baked, etc.)
• Sauce (cream, tomato, wine, etc.)

WINE AND FOOD PAIRINGS

BY KEVIN ZRALY AND ANDREA ROBINSON

YOU'VE TASTED YOUR way through 12 classes, more than 100 wines, and discovered a whole shopping cart's worth of bottles that you enjoy. Why? Food! The final stop on our wine odyssey—and really the whole point of the trip—is the dining table. Wine and food were meant for each other. Just look at the dining habits of the world's best eaters, the French, Italians, and Spanish. The American table always features salt and pepper shakers, but in Europe it's the wine bottle because wine enlivens even everyday dishes.

THE BASICS

Forget everything you've ever heard about pairing food and wine. Only one rule applies when it comes to matching the two: The best wine to pair with your meal is whatever wine you like. No matter what! If you know what you want, drink it. Worried that Chardonnay with sirloin isn't "right"? The only palate you must please is your own.

When cooking with wine, try to use the same wine or style that you're going to serve.

HOW MUCH?

Allow one bottle for every five people—that is, one five-ounce glass per person—for each food selection.

SYNERGY

Sounds like a gourmet computer game or a management meeting, right? But it's really not that complicated. If until now you haven't often had wine with dinner, a great adventure awaits you. Remember, the European tradition of wine with meals didn't result from a shortage of milk or iced tea. It developed from the synergy of wine and food. Pairing the two makes both taste better.

How does this concept work? The same way that combining certain foods improves their overall taste. For example, you squeeze fresh lemon juice onto oysters or sprinkle grated Parmesan cheese over spaghetti marinara because that combination of flavors improves the overall dish. It's really that simple. Different foods and wines have different aromas, textures, and flavors. Pairing them provokes more interesting tastes than if you drank just water with dinner. You need only some basic information about wine and food styles to pick wines that will enhance your meals. The first rule of thumb: The more flavorful the food, the more flavorful the wine you should drink.

The addition of **SALT** to food highlights both the tannins and the alcohol in wine.

ACIDITY

Acid turbo-charges flavor. You probably have seen TV chefs using lemons and limes—high-acid ingredients—in many dishes. Even dishes that you wouldn't call sour have a touch of acidity to amp up their flavor. Drink a high-acid wine with dishes featuring cream or cheese sauces to enhance and lengthen the flavor of the dish.

TEXTURE

As we've seen with tannins, wine has a definite texture. It also has taste nuances that can make it adequate, outstanding, or unforgettable with a meal. Full-bodied wines have a mouth-filling texture and bold, rich tastes that you notice on your palate. But when it comes to food, these wines overwhelm delicate dishes and clash with boldly flavored ones. Remember, you want harmony and balance. The sturdier the food or fuller in flavor, the more full-bodied the wine should be. Pair milder foods with wines that have a medium or light body. Once you understand wine texture, food pairings are easy. You'll find two lists (one for red, one for white) on pages 333–334 with suggestions based on texture and the foods that the wines can match.

BITTERNESS in wine comes from the combination of high tannin and high alcohol, and these wines are best served with grilled, charcoaled, or blackened food.

Do you drink your tea with milk or lemon? The milk coats your mouth with **SWEETNESS**, whereas the lemon leaves your tongue with a **DRY CRISPNESS**.

WINE AND CHEESE

As in all matters of taste, the topic of wine and cheese comes with its share of controversy and debate. Wine and cheese naturally go together. For a good cheese and wine, each enhances the tastes and complexities of the other. Also, the protein in cheese softens the tannins in a red wine. The key here lies in carefully selecting the cheese, and now you see the controversy. Some chefs and culinary experts caution that some of the most popular

One of the reasons that classic **FRENCH CUISINE IS NOTED FOR ITS SUBTLETY** is probably because the French want to let their wines "show off." This is an especially good idea if the wine is a special or splurge bottle.

cheeses pair badly with wine because they overpower it. Ripe Brie offers a classic example. So let's keep it simple. The best cheeses for wine are:

Cheddar	Manchego	Parmigiano-Reggiano
Chèvre	Monterey Jack	Pecorino
Fontina	Montrachet	Taleggio
Gouda	Mozzarella	Tomme
Gruyère		

These are my favorite cheese-and-wine pairings:

Chèvre with Sancerre or Sauvignon Blanc

Manchego with Rioja or Brunello di Montalcino

Montrachet or aged (dry) Monterey Jack with Bordeaux or Cabernet Sauvignon

Pecorino or Parmigiano-Reggiano with Chianti Classico Riserva, Brunello di Montalcino, Cabernet Sauvignon, Bordeaux, Barolo, or Amarone

What to drink with Brie? Champagne or sparkling wine. Blue cheeses, because of their strong flavor, overpower most wines except—get ready for this—dessert wines! The classic and truly delicious pairings are:

Roquefort with Sauternes

Stilton with Port

HORS D'OEUVRES AND APPETIZERS

Champagne and sparkling wine have a magical effect. Whether served at a wedding or at home, Champagne remains a symbol of celebration, prosperity, romance, and fun, but don't forget about Cava, Prosecco, and other sparkling wines.

RED WINE PAIRINGS

LIGHT BODY	MEDIUM BODY	FULL BODY
BARDOLINO	BARBERA	BARBARESCO
BEAUJOLAIS	BORDEAUX	BAROLO
BEAUJOLAIS	(CRUS BOURGEOIS)	BORDEAUX
-VILLAGES	BURGUNDY PREMIERS	(GREAT CHÂTEAUX)
BORDEAUX	AND GRANDS CRUS	CABERNET SAUVIGNON
(PROPRIETARY)	CABERNET	CHÂTEAUNEUF-DU-PAPE
BURGUNDY	SAUVIGNON	HERMITAGE
(VILLAGE)	CHIANTI CLASSICO	MALBEC
PINOT NOIR	RISERVA	MERLOT
RIOJA CRIANZA	CÔTES DU RHÔNE	SYRAH / SHIRAZ
VALPOLICELLA	CROZES-HERMITAGE	ZINFANDEL
	CRU BEAUJOLAIS	
	DOLCETTO	
	MALBEC	
	MERLOT	
	PINOT NOIR	
	RIOJA RESERVA AND	
	GRAN RESERVA	
	SYRAH / SHIRAZ	
	ZINFANDEL	

FOOD PAIRINGS		
BELL PEPPERS	EGGPLANT	BEEFSTEAK (SIRLOIN)
CORN	GAME BIRDS	GAME MEATS
DUCK	GREEN BEANS	LAMB CHOPS
EDAMAME	LEEKS	LEEKS
PEAS	MUSHROOMS	LEG OF LAMB
SALMON	SQUASH	MUSHROOMS
SWORDFISH	PORK CHOPS	POTATOES
TUNA	POTATOES	SWEET POTATOES
TOMATOES	ROAST CHICKEN	VEAL CHOP
ZUCCHINI	SWEET POTATOES	

* *Some of these wines come in a range of styles, from light to full, depending on the producer.*
If you don't know a winery's particular style, ask the sommelier or wine merchant for help.

My favorite **RED WINE FOR PICNICS** is Beaujolais. A great Beaujolais is the essence of fresh fruit without the tannins, and its higher acidity blends nicely with all picnic fare.

Most Pinot Noirs are white wines **MASQUERADING AS RED WINES**, which makes them perfect wines for fish and fowl.

YOUNG RED WINES with a lot of tannin taste better when paired with foods that have high fat content. The fat softens the tannins.

Eat your greens, but I don't recommend having them with wine. Artichokes, asparagus, kale, spinach, and other green or leafy vegetables all contain a compound that will make the wine you drink with them **TASTE BITTER**.

My favorite **WHITE WINE FOR PICNICS** is a chilled German Riesling Kabinett / Spätlese. On a hot summer day, I can think of no better white wine. The balance of fruit, acid, and sweetness as well as the lightness (low alcohol) makes these wines a perfect match for salads, fruits, and cheese. If you prefer a drier-style Riesling, try one from Alsace, Washington, or the Finger Lakes region of New York.

Many Chardonnays (especially from California) are red wines masquerading as white wines, which, in my opinion, makes them a **PERFECT MATCH FOR STEAK.**

VEGETABLES ARE VERY VERSATILE both on their own and when included as an ingredient in a larger recipe, so keep that in mind when considering your pairings.

WHITE WINE PAIRINGS

LIGHT BODY	MEDIUM BODY	FULL BODY
ALBARIÑO	CHABLIS PREMIER CRU	CHABLIS GRAND CRU
ALSACE PINOT BLANC	CHARDONNAY	CHARDONNAY
ALSACE RIESLING	GAVI	CHASSAGNE-MONTRACHET
CHABLIS	GEWÜRZTRAMINER	MEURSAULT
FRASCATI	GRÜNER VELTLINER	PULIGNY-MONTRACHET
GERMAN KABINETT AND SPÄTLESE	MÂCON-VILLAGES	VIOGNIER
MUSCADET	MONTAGNY	
ORVIETO	POUILLY-FUISSÉ	
PINOT GRIGIO	POUILLY-FUMÉ	
PINOT GRIS	SANCERRE	
SAUVIGNON BLANC	SAUVIGNON BLANC / FUMÉ BLANC	
SOAVE	ST-VÉRAN	
VERDEJO	WHITE GRAVES	
VERDICCHIO		

FOOD PAIRINGS		
CLAMS	BASS	BELL PEPPERS
CORN	BELL PEPPERS	CAULIFLOWER
CUCUMBERS	CAULIFLOWER	DUCK
EDAMAME	GREEN BEANS	EGGPLANT
FLOUNDER	EGGPLANT	LOBSTER
OYSTERS	PEAS	PEAS
SALAD	SCALLOPS	ROAST CHICKEN
SOLE	SIRLOIN STEAK	SALMON
VEAL PAILLARD	SNAPPER	SQUASH
	SQUASH	SWORDFISH
	TOMATOES	TOMATOES
	ZUCCHINI	TUNA
		ZUCCHINI

* Some of these wines come in a range of styles, from light to full, depending on the producer. If you don't know a winery's particular style, ask the sommelier or wine merchant for help.

NO-FAULT WINE INSURANCE

Drinking wine with food should add enjoyment, not stress, to your meal, but the latter happens all too often. Faced with so many choices, you might choose something familiar—even if the wine doesn't pair well with what you're eating. But it's just as easy to choose the right wine. These user-friendly wines go well with virtually any dish. They all have a light-to-medium body and feature ample fruit, acidity, and low tannins. Which means that you'll taste a harmonious balance of tastes from both the wine and the food. Neither will overwhelm the other. Also, if you want the food to play center stage, these wines are your best bets. They work well for what I call restaurant roulette—where one person orders fish, another orders meat, and so on. They also match well with distinctively spiced foods that otherwise might clash with a full-flavored wine. (It goes without saying that they're enjoyable on their own!)

USER-FRIENDLY WINES

ROSÉ	WHITE	RED
VIRTUALLY ANY ROSÉ OR WHITE ZINFANDEL	CHAMPAGNE AND SPARKLING WINES GERMAN RIESLING, KABINETT, AND SPÄTLESE MÂCON-VILLAGES PINOT GRIGIO POUILLY-FUMÉ AND SANCERRE SAUVIGNON BLANC/ FUMÉ BLANC	BEAUJOLAIS VILLAGES CHIANTI CLASSICO CÔTES DU RHÔNE MERLOT PINOT NOIR RIOJA CRIANZA

FAIL-SAFE FOOD: When in doubt, order roast chicken or tofu, which acts as a blank canvas for almost any wine style—light-, medium-, or full-bodied.

SAUCES

Subtly flavored foods allow the wine to play the starring role, but sauces are game-changers. They can alter the entire taste and texture of a dish. Is the sauce acidic, heavy, spicy? Dishes with bold, spicy ingredients can over-power the nuances and complexity that distinguish a great wine. Consider the chicken breast. A simply prepared chicken paillard might match well with a light-bodied white wine, but if you add a cream or cheese sauce, you

For food with **SPICY SAUCES,** try something with carbon dioxide, such as a Champagne or a sparkling wine.

might prefer a high-acid, medium-bodied, or even full-bodied white wine. A tomato sauce calls for a light-bodied red. Always consider the sauce!

DESSERT WINES

Beerenauslese, Port, Sauternes, Tokay—all very different wines—have sweetness in common. They count as dessert wines because their sweetness closes your palate and makes you feel satisfied after a good meal. But dessert holds only one part of the story. In America, coffee is more common with dessert, but more restaurants are adding by-the-glass dessert wines to their menus. (A full bottle of a rich dessert wine isn't practical unless the whole table shares it. For dinner at home, go for dessert wines in half-bottles.) Try a dessert wine a few minutes before the dessert itself to prepare your palate and recalibrate it. These are some of my favorite wine-and-dessert combinations:

Asti Spumante with fresh fruit or biscotti

Beerenauslese and late harvest Riesling with fruit tarts, crème brûlée, or almond cookies

Madeira with milk chocolate, nut tarts, crème caramel, or coffee or mocha desserts

Muscat Beaumes-de-Venise with crème brûlée, fresh fruit, fruit sorbets, or lemon tart

Port with dark chocolate desserts, walnuts, poached pears, or Stilton

Sherry (Pedro Ximénez) on top of vanilla ice cream and with raisin-nut cakes or other desserts containing figs or dried fruit

Sauternes or Tokay with fruit tarts, poached fruits, crème brûlée, caramel and hazelnut desserts, or Roquefort.

Vin Santo with biscotti (dipped in the wine)

Vouvray with fruit tarts or fresh fruit

Try serving a dessert wine as the dessert itself. That way you can concentrate on savoring the complex and delicious flavors with a clear palate. It's especially convenient at home. All you have to do is pull a cork! Also, one glass of dessert wine affords the satisfying sweetness of a dessert with zero fat!

—— FURTHER READING ——

Great Wine & Food Made Simple by Andrea Robinson

Perfect Pairings by Evan Goldstein

FREQUENTLY ASKED QUESTIONS ABOUT WINE

DOES CALIFORNIA OR FRANCE MAKE THE BEST WINES?

Nice try! California and France both make great wines. The French make the best French wines, and California makes the best California wines. Each region has a distinct profile. Both California and France grow many of the same grape varieties. They also have many differences, including climate, soil, and tradition.

The French regard their soil with reverence and believe that the best wines come only from the greatest soil. When vineyard owners planted California's original grapes, soil didn't determine which grapes grew where. Over recent decades, however, vineyard owners have given this consideration much more importance. Today winemakers cite their best Cabernet Sauvignons as coming from a specific vineyard or even area. As far as weather, temperatures in Napa and Sonoma obviously differ from Bordeaux and Burgundy. European vintners grow gray hair over cold snaps and rainstorms in the growing season, but Californians can count on nearly abundant sunshine and warm daytime temperatures.

Tradition separates the two. Vineyard and winery practices in Europe have remained virtually unchanged for generations, and these age-old techniques—some written into law—define each region's style. In California, where few traditions exist, winemakers can experiment and create new products based on consumer demand. If you've ever had a wine called Two Buck Chuck, you know what I mean. Burgundy has been making white wines for more than 1,500 years, but the California wine renaissance only just reached its fiftieth anniversary.

Buy how you feel on a given day: Do you want to end up in Bordeaux or Napa Valley?

DOES VINE AGE AFFECT WINE QUALITY?

As a vine ages, especially beyond 30 years, it starts losing its production value. In commercial vineyards, vine production slows at about 20 years, so most vines are replanted by their fiftieth birthday. French wine labels sometimes use the term *vieilles vignes* ("old vines"). In California, many Zinfandels come from vines more than 75 years old. Many wine tasters, including me, believe that these old vines create a different complexity and taste than younger vines. In many countries, grapes from younger vines don't go into a winery's top wine. In Bordeaux for example, Château Lafite-Rothschild produces a second wine, Carruades de Lafite-Rothschild, from the youngest vines (fewer than 15 years old).

WHO HAS THE BEST WINE SERVICE?

The James Beard Foundation recognizes the following restaurants with the Outstanding Wine Service Award:

1994   Valentino, Santa Monica
1999   Union Square Café, New York City
2001   French Laundry, Yountville, California
2002   Gramercy Tavern, New York City
2003   Daniel, New York City
2004   Babbo, New York City
2006   Aureole, Las Vegas
2007   Citronelle, Washington, D.C.
2008   Eleven Madison Park, New York City
2009   Le Bernardin, New York City
2010   Jean Georges, New York City
2011   The Modern, New York City
2012   No. 9 Park, Boston
2013   Frasca Food and Wine, Boulder, Colorado
2014   The Barn at Blackberry Farm, Walland, Tennessee
2015   A16, San Francisco
2016   Bern's Steakhouse, Tampa, Florida
2017   Canlis, Seattle, Washington
2018   FIG, Charleston, South Carolina

Winners of the James Beard Award for Wine and Spirits Professional of the Year include:

1991   Robert Mondavi, Robert Mondavi Winery
1992   Andre Tchelistcheff, Beaulieu Winery
1993   Kevin Zraly, Windows on the World
1994   Randall Grahm, Bonny Doon Vineyard
1995   Marvin Shanken, *Wine Spectator*
1996   Jack and Jaimie Davies, Schramsberg Vineyards
1997   Zelma Long, Simi Winery
1998   Robert M. Parker Jr., *Wine Advocate*
1999   Frank Prial, *New York Times*
2000   Kermit Lynch, writer and importer
2001   Gerald Asher, writer
2002   Andrea Robinson, author
2003   Fritz Maytag, Anchor Brewing Co.
2004   Karen MacNeil, author
2005   Joseph Bastianich, Italian Wine Merchants
2006   Daniel Johnnes, The Dinex Group
2007   Paul Draper, Ridge Vineyards
2008   Terry Theise, importer, Terry Theise Estate Selection
2009   Dale DeGroff, author and master mixologist
2010   John Shafer and Doug Shafer, Shafer Vineyards
2011   Julian P. van Winkle III, Old Rip van Winkle Distillery
2012   Paul Grieco, Terroir
2013   Merry Edwards, Merry Edwards Winery
2014   Garrett Oliver, Brooklyn Brewery
2015   Rajat Parr, Mina Group
2016   Ron Cooper, Del Maguey Single Village Mezcal, Ranchos de Taos
2017   Sam Calagione, Dogfish Head Craft Brewery
2018   Miljenko Grgich, Grgich Hills Estate

WHAT ARE THE HOT AREAS IN WINE?

These areas in particular have seen major growth and improvement in quality, over the last 20 years:

Argentina: Malbec
Austria: Grüner Veltliner
Chile: Cabernet Sauvignon
France: Rosé
Italy: Prosecco
Hungary: Tokay
New Zealand: Sauvignon Blanc, Pinot Noir
South Africa: Sauvignon Blanc, Pinot Noir, Syrah

HOW LONG SHOULD I AGE MY WINE?

The *Wall Street Journal* reported that most people have one or two bottles of wine that they've been saving for years for a special occasion. Not a good idea! More than 90 percent of all wine—red, white, rosé—is made to be consumed within a year. Some wines—dry Riesling, Sauvignon Blanc, Pinot Grigio, Beaujolais—are ready to drink immediately. But keep in mind the following guidelines for aging wine from the best producers in the best years:

WHITE	
CALIFORNIA CHARDONNAY	2–10+ YEARS
FRENCH WHITE BURGUNDY	3–8+ YEARS
GERMAN RIESLING (AUSLESE, BEERENAUSLESE, AND TROCKENBEERENAUSLESE)	3–30+ YEARS
FRENCH SAUTERNES	3–30+ YEARS
RED	
CALIFORNIA / OREGON PINOT NOIR	2–5+ YEARS
CALIFORNIA MERLOT	2–10+ YEARS
FRENCH RED BURGUNDY	3–8+ YEARS
CHIANTI CLASSICO RISERVA	3–10+ YEARS
ARGENTINEAN MALBEC	3–15+ YEARS
BRUNELLO DI MONTALCINO	3–15+ YEARS
CALIFORNIA CABERNET SAUVIGNON	3–15+ YEARS
CALIFORNIA ZINFANDEL	5–15+ YEARS
SPANISH RIOJA (GRAN RESERVA)	5–20+ YEARS
BAROLO AND BARBARESCO	5–25+ YEARS
HERMITAGE / SYRAH	5–25+ YEARS
BORDEAUX CHÂTEAUX	5–30+ YEARS
VINTAGE PORTS	10–40+ YEARS

Exceptions to the rules always apply, particularly when it comes to generalizing about aging wine (especially with variations in vintages). I've had Bordeaux wines more than a century old that were still going strong, and you're not likely to find a great Sauternes or Port that couldn't do with more age after 50 years. But these age spans represent more than 95 percent of the wines in their categories.

The oldest bottle of wine still aging in Bordeaux is a 1797 Château Lafite-Rothschild!

DO ALL WINES NEED CORKS?

Most corks come from oak trees in Portugal and Spain, but only tradition calls for corks to seal wine bottles. Most wines don't need them. Since you should drink 90 percent of all wines within one year, a screw cap works just as well if not better. Think about what that means: no need for a corkscrew, no broken corks, and no more wine ruined by contaminated cork. Certain wines—those that age for more than five years—benefit from corks, but also keep in mind that a cork's life span lasts approximately 25 to 30 years. After that, drink the wine, or find somebody to recork it!

Many wineries around the world use the Stelvin screw cap, especially in California (Bonny Doon, Sonoma-Cutrer, etc.), Australia, New Zealand, and Austria. Screw-cap wines represent less than 10 percent of all bottled wine, but 93 percent of New Zealand's bottles use them as do 75 percent of Australia's.

WHAT'S A "CORKED" WINE?

This is a serious problem for wine lovers. Some estimates indicate that faulty corks contaminate between 3 and 5 percent of all wines. The culprit? TCA or 2,4,6-trichloranisole. If you've ever encountered a corked wine, it's a smell you won't soon forget! It's dank, wet, and moldy; some describe it as reminiscent of wet cardboard. It overpowers the fruit in the wine and makes it undrinkable, and it can happen to a $10 bottle or a $1,000 bottle.

DECANTING AND AERATING

A good rule to follow: Do as the Romans do—or in this case, the French. For example, in Burgundy, they never decant their Beaujolais or other delicate wines, but in Bordeaux they decant their Cabernet Sauvignon and Merlot most of the time, especially when young. Decant a Vintage Port but not a Ruby or Tawny Port.

To decant:

1. Remove the entire capsule, or protective sleeve, from the neck of the bottle so you can see the wine clearly as it passes through the neck.
2. Light a candle. Most red wines come in dark green glass bottles, making it difficult to see the wine pass through the neck of the bottle. A candle gives the extra illumination you need and also adds a theatrical touch. (If you don't have a candle handy, a flashlight will suffice.)
3. Grasp the decanter—which can be a carafe or glass pitcher—firmly in hand.
4. With the bottle in your other hand, gently pour the wine into the decanter. Hold both over the candle so that you can see the wine pass through the neck of the bottle.
5. Keep pouring until you see the first signs of sediment. Stop decanting as soon as you see sediment!
6. If there's still wine left, let it stand until the sediment settles. Then decant the rest.

WHAT'S THAT ON THE BOTTOM OF THE CORK?

Tartaric acid, or tartrate, sometimes appears on the bottom of a cork or wine bottle. This harmless crystalline deposit looks like glass or rock candy. These crystals take on a rusty, reddish-brown color from the tannins in red wines. Wineries remove most tartrates by lowering the temperature of the wine before bottling, but this strategy doesn't work with all wines. If you keep your wine at a very cold temperature for a long period of time (for example, in your refrigerator), you can end up with this deposit on your cork. Cool-climate regions, such as Germany, have a greater chance of producing this crystallization.

WHY DO I GET A HEADACHE AFTER DRINKING WINE?

Probably overconsumption! In all seriousness, though, more than 10 percent of my students over the years have been medical doctors, and none has been able to give me the definitive answer to this question. Some people get headaches from white wine, others from red, but dehydration always plays a role in how you feel the next day. For every glass of wine you consume, drink *two* glasses of water to stay hydrated.

Many factors influence how your system metabolizes alcohol. The top three are your health, genetics, and gender. Red wines have differing levels of histamines, which can affect you if you have allergies, causing discomfort and headaches. I myself have a slight allergy to red wine, and I "suffer" every day. Doctors have told me that food additives also contribute to headaches. Research also increasingly points to genetics as a cause for chronic headaches. As for gender, because of certain enzymes, women absorb more alcohol into their bloodstream than men. For women, one glass of wine a day represents a safe limit, but equally healthy men can drink two glasses safely.

WHAT IF I CAN'T FINISH THE BOTTLE?

This was one of the most frequently asked questions in the Wine School—although I've never had this problem! If you still have wine left over, whether red or white, recork the bottle and refrigerate it. Don't leave it on your counter. Bacteria grow in warm temperatures, and a room-temperature kitchen will spoil wine very quickly. If refrigerated, most wines won't lose their taste over a 48-hour period. (Some swear that the wine tastes better, but I'm not among their number.)

Eventually the wine—any wine with an alcohol content between 8 and 14 percent—will oxidize. Ports, sherries, and other wines with an alcohol content between 17 and 21 percent will last longer, but don't keep them longer than two weeks. Remember, the less contact with oxygen, the longer a wine will last. Consider buying an affordable wine bottle air pump. Some wine collectors even introduce an inert gas into the bottle, such as argon or nitrogen, which has no odor or taste but which preserves the wine from oxygen.

If all else fails, you have a great cooking wine!

WHAT COUNTRIES OR REGIONS WILL YOU BE WRITING ABOUT IN 2025?

America, Argentina, Australia, China, and Eastern Europe, specifically Bulgaria and Romania

WHAT ARE THE MOST IMPORTANT BOOKS FOR YOUR WINE LIBRARY?

First, thank you for buying my wine book, which I hope you have found useful. As with any passion, people always thirst for more. At the end of each section or chapter of this book, I recommend specific books. Beyond those, these are more suggestions for further reading:

> *Great Wine Made Simple* by Andrea Robinson
> *Hugh Johnson's Modern Encyclopedia of Wine*
> *The Oxford Companion to Wine* edited by Jancis Robinson
> *Oz Clarke's New Encyclopedia of Wine*
> *Oz Clarke's New Essential Wine Book*
> *Oz Clarke's Wine Atlas*
> *Parker's Wine Buyers Guide* by Robert M. Parker Jr.
> *Sotheby's Wine Encyclopedia* by Tom Stevenson
> *The Widow Clicquot* by Tilar Mazzeo
> *The Wine Bible* by Karen MacNeil
> *Wine Folly* by Madeline Puckette and Justin Hammock
> *Wine for Dummies* by Ed McCarthy and Mary Ewing-Mulligan
> *The World Atlas of Wine* by Hugh Johnson and Jancis Robinson

If you find the above too encyclopedic, try one of these two pocket guides:

> *Hugh Johnson's Pocket Encyclopedia of Wine*
> *Oz Clarke's Pocket Wine Guide*

THE BEST OF THE BEST

I have spent more than 40 years traveling, tasting, and studying wine, more than 40 years reading, writing, lecturing, and teaching about wine. I have seen it all: the wines, publications, writers, "experts," lists, controversies, and events. The wine world has changed. From the select wine drinkers of yore to today's great international wines, the following are the best of the best, based on credibility, creativity, experience, impact, and longevity. As with a favorite wine, these are all *personal* selections.

THE WINES

BEST CABERNET SAUVIGNON

Bordeaux, France (Médoc)
Runner-up: California; Best value: Chile

The greatest wines of the world come from the châteaux of Bordeaux, and with 7,000 of them there's plenty to choose at all different price points!

The best Cabernet Sauvignon from California comes from the North Coast counties, especially Napa and Sonoma. Napa Cabernets usually have more intensity of fruit and body; Sonoma Cabernets generally taste softer and more elegant.

The price of a vineyard acre in Chile is so far below that of Napa Valley and Bordeaux that you will find tremendous quality and value in Chilean Cabernets.

BEST MERLOT

Bordeaux, France (St-Émilion, Pomerol)
Runner-up: California

The great châteaux of St-Émilion and Pomerol primarily produce wines made from Merlot, which is the number-one red grape planted in Bordeaux. The major differences between the two regions are availability and price. Pomerol has 1,986 acres, but St-Émilion has more than 23,000. For the better value, go with St-Émilion.

Napa Valley in California produces some superb Merlots as well.

BEST PINOT NOIR

Burgundy, France
Runners-up: Oregon and California

The wine history and tradition of Burgundy run deep. Vines have been growing there for more than 1,000 years, and, aside from Beaujolais, French law allows only the sensuous Pinot Noir to grow there. The only problem with a great Pinot Noir from Burgundy is availability and price. Oregon makes America's best Pinot Noirs and also great Chardonnays, so many people call Oregon the Burgundy of America. In California, the best Pinot Noirs also grow in cooler climates.

BEST CHARDONNAY

Burgundy, France
Runner-up: California

As much as I like the best producers of California Chardonnay, nothing else in the world matches the elegance and balance of fruit and acidity of a white Burgundy. Non-oaked Chablis; Montrachets fermented and aged in barrels; the light, easy-drinking Mâcons; and the world-famous Pouilly-Fuissé—there are a style and a price for everyone.

As with Sauvignon Blanc, the best California Chardonnays come from cooler climates, such as Carneros and Santa Barbara. I'm not a fan of high-alcohol, overly oaked Chardonnays.

BEST SAUVIGNON BLANC

Loire Valley, France
Runners-up: New Zealand and California

Sauvignon Blanc produced in the Loire Valley is best known by regional names, Sancerre and Pouilly-Fumé. The best of the New Zealand Sauvignon Blancs are sold under the producer's name. The stylistic differences between the two are striking. Both have light to medium body and high acidity and work well with fish and poultry, but New Zealand Sauvignon Blancs have what some call a very tropical aroma, which you either like or don't. (I like it!) After Chardonnay, Sauvignon Blanc is the second-highest quality white grape grown in California. The best Sauvignon Blancs come from cooler climates, have no oak, and are lower in alcohol content.

BEST RIESLING

Germany
Runners-up: Alsace, France; and Finger Lakes, New York

Many professionals and wine connoisseurs consider Riesling the best white wine in the world. The German diversity of style—dry, off-dry, semisweet, or very sweet—is why I rank German Rieslings as the world's best. 95 percent of all Alsace Rieslings are dry. Finger Lakes producers make dry, semidry, and sweet Rieslings.

BEST FLYING WINEMAKER

Michel Rolland

Over the last 30 years, the demand for high-quality wine around the world has exploded. Like many other businesses, winemakers often hire consultants. Known as the flying wine consultant, Michel Rolland, a Bordeaux native, works with more than 100 wineries on four continents. His influence on the quality and style of wine produced all over the world is enormous.

BEST WINE TASTER

Robert M. Parker Jr.

Bob and I started studying wine around the same time, but we each took different paths. His scoring system has changed the way people taste and rate wine. No other human being has tasted more wines. Until a few years ago, he tasted *10,000 wines a year*—more than 25 every day on average! Recently he told me that he scaled down to 5,000 per year, still a prodigious number. *Wine Advocate* publishes all of his reviews as does his website, eRobertParker.com. Regardless of whether you agree with his assessments, you have to admire his stamina, perseverance, and red tongue!

Through Christie's wine department, Michael Broadbent, another admirable wine taster, possibly has tasted more older wines than Parker. He doesn't use a numbering system but describes wines in his own British, poetic fashion. Also look for Stephen Tanzer, who has his own publication, *International Wine Cellar*. Many writers and tasters around the world have developed an expertise on specific wines—Bordeaux, Burgundy, California, Tuscany, and so on—and I recommend them throughout this book.

BEST CORK

Frog's Leap Winery, Napa, California

John Williams—owner and winemaker of Frog's Leap and one of California's premier winemakers—adds humor to drinking wine with the inscription "Ribbit" on every Frog's Leap cork.

STORING AND AGING

BEST INVESTMENT

The great châteaux of Bordeaux and California Cabernet Sauvignons

For the last 40 years, I've invested in wine. I have never sold any of my collection, but if I did I'd realize a better return than any money market fund. Even if the market for wine tanks, I can still drink it! From 2000 to 2010, Bordeaux produced the best wine ever, with great vintages in 2000, 2003, 2005, 2009, and 2010 and excellent vintages in 2001 and 2006. The other four vintages were quite good, too, and 2015 also was exceptional.

It's getting harder to buy California's best Cabernet Sauvignons, specifically Napa Valley, where Cabernet Sauvignon thrives. Napa also has had great vintages recently, especially 2012, 2013, 2014, and 2015. You can still buy many of these for less than $50.

BEST WINE TO CELLAR FOR YOUR CHILD'S 21st BIRTHDAY OR YOUR 25th WEDDING ANNIVERSARY

Few wines age well beyond 20 years, but sharing these aged wines makes for one of the greatest joys of collecting wine.

1990 Bordeaux, California Cabernet Sauvignon, Rhône, Burgundy, Tuscany, Piedmont, Sauternes, Champagne, Germany (Auslese and above)

1991 Rhône (North), Port, California Cabernet Sauvignon

1992 Port, California Cabernet Sauvignon and Zinfandel

1993 California Cabernet Sauvignon and Zinfandel

1994 Port, California Cabernet Sauvignon and Zinfandel, Rioja

1995 Bordeaux, Rhône, Rioja, California Cabernet Sauvignon

1996 Burgundy, Piedmont, Bordeaux (Médoc), Burgundy, Germany (Auslese and above)

1997 California Cabernet Sauvignons, Tuscany (Chianti, Brunello, etc.), Piedmont, Port, Australia Shiraz

1998 Bordeaux (St-Émilion / Pomerol), Rhône (South), Piedmont

1999 Piedmont, Rhône (North), California Zinfandel

2000 Bordeaux

2001 Napa Cabernet Sauvignon, Sauternes, Germany (Auslese and above), Rioja, Ribera del Duero

2002 Napa Cabernet Sauvignon, Germany (Auslese and above), Burgundy (Grand Cru), Sauternes

2003 Northern and Southern Rhône, Sauternes, Bordeaux, Port

2004 Napa Cabernet Sauvignon, Piedmont

2005 Bordeaux, Sauternes, Burgundy, Rhône (South), Piedmont, Tuscany, Germany, Rioja, Ribera del Duero, Southern Australia, Napa Cabernet Sauvignon, Washington Cabernet Sauvignon

2006 Bordeaux (Pomerol), Rhône (North), Barolo, Barbaresco, Brunello di Montalcino, Germany (Auslese and above), Argentina Malbec

2007 Sauternes, Rhône (South), Napa Cabernet Sauvignon, Port

2008 Bordeaux, Napa Valley Cabernet Sauvignon

2009 California Cabernet Sauvignon

2010 Bordeaux, Rhône Valley, Brunello

2011 Port

2012 Napa Cabernet Sauvignon

2013 Napa Cabernet Sauvignon

2014 Napa Cabernet Sauvignon

2015 Bordeaux, Rhône (North and South), Napa Cabernet Sauvignon, Vintage Port

2016 Napa Cabernet, Bordeaux, Rhône (North and South)

BEST WINE TO AGE

The great châteaux of Bordeaux

Many great wine regions produce red wines that will age for 30 years or more, but no other region produces both red and white wines that you can drink a *century* later!

BEST BOTTLE FOR AGING

Magnum

My winemaker and wine collector friends say that their best wines will last longer and mature more slowly in a magnum than in a standard bottle. One theory for this difference points to the amount of air in the bottle—between the wine and the cork—versus the quantity of wine. It's also more fun to serve a magnum at a dinner party.

BEST TEMPERATURE FOR STORAGE

55 degrees Fahrenheit

If you have a wine collection or are planning on collecting wines, you must protect your investment. All the great wineries store and age their wine at this temperature, and studies have shown that it's the best temperature for long-term storage. The same studies also show that storing wine at 75 degrees ages wine twice as fast. Just as warm temperatures will age the wine prematurely, temperatures too cold can freeze the wine, pushing out the cork and immediately ending the aging process. Buy a wine refrigerator or build your wine cellar with the proper air conditioning.

BEST HUMIDITY FOR STORAGE

75 percent relative humidity

If you're going to age your wines for more than five years, this is important. (If not, don't worry about it.) If the humidity is too low, your corks will dry out and wine will seep out of the bottle. If wine can get out, air can get in. Too much humidity, and you likely will lose your labels. I'd rather lose my labels than my corks!

WITH FOOD

BEST RED WINE WITH LUNCH

Pinot Noir

The light, easy-drinking style of a Pinot Noir won't overpower your usual light fare of soups, salads, and sandwiches.

BEST WHITE WINE WITH LUNCH

Riesling

Depending on what you're having for lunch, you could go with the low-alcohol (8–10 percent) German Riesling Kabinett. Its slight residual sugar blends nicely with food, especially salads. If you prefer a drier style, French Alsace, Washington, Australia, or Finger Lakes Rieslings are also great choices.

BEST CHEESE WITH WINE

Parmigiano-Reggiano

Now we're getting personal! I love Italian food and wine, but Parmigiano-Reggiano also goes extremely well with Bordeaux and California Cabernets.

BEST RED WINE WITH FISH

Pinot Noir
Runners-up: Chianti Classico, Beaujolais, and Rioja

Pinot Noir is light, easy, and not overpowering. Usually it has high acidity and low tannins and blends nicely with different types of food. It's really a white wine masquerading as a red. Pinot Noir is the perfect wine for a dinner of six or eight where everyone is having something different, whether fish, poultry, or meat.

Other choices include Chianti Classico and Riojas (Crianza and Reserva). For barbecued or grilled fish or shrimp in the middle of the summer, try a chilled Beaujolais-Village or Cru.

BEST WHITE WINE WITH MEAT

Chardonnay

Whoever coined the rule of white wine with fish was probably thinking of Riesling, Pinot Grigio, and Sauvignon Blanc because a vast majority of Chardonnays will overpower fish dishes—except possibly tuna, salmon, or swordfish steak. Many Chardonnays are red wines masquerading as whites, especially the big, oaky, high-alcohol Chardonnays from California and Australia. Usually, the more expensive the Chardonnay, the more oaky it will taste. With its flavor, weight, and tannins, the perfect match for Chardonnay is something like a sirloin steak!

BEST WINE WITH CHICKEN

Anything

Chicken itself doesn't have an overpowering flavor, and it can go with almost any wine—red or white, light, medium, or full.

BEST WINE WITH LAMB

Bordeaux or California Cabernet Sauvignon

The people of Bordeaux have lamb with breakfast, lunch, and dinner! Lamb has such a strong flavor that it needs a strong wine, and the big, full-bodied Cabernet Sauvignons from California and Bordeaux pair with it perfectly.

BEST WINE AFTER DINNER

Port

You don't need to drink a lot of Port to enjoy it fully. One glass of this sweet and fortified wine ends a meal with a satisfying taste. I consume most Port—whether Ruby, Tawny, or Vintage—from November until March, the cooler months in the Northeast. The best way to have Port is when the dishes have been washed, your children are tucked away and dreaming, you're sitting in front of your fireplace, with your dog by your side, while it snows outside.

BEST WINE WITH CHOCOLATE

Port

For me, chocolate and Port together signal the end of the meal. They're both rich, sweet, and decadently satisfying together.

BEST WINE TO ORDER BY THE BOTTLE IN A RESTAURANT

Anything under $75

I've worked in the restaurant business most of my life, but it's one of the worst places to experiment with wine tasting. Restaurants are notorious for marking up their wines, sometimes triple what you would pay retail. It's easy for me to choose $100+ bottles of wine, but it's more interesting to find a $25 bottle of wine that tastes like a $50, a $50 bottle that tastes like a $100, and so on.

A few years ago, while working with Tim and Nina Zagat, I reviewed more than 125 restaurant wine lists in New York City. Tim and I discovered that neither of us spends more than $75 for a bottle of wine in a restaurant . . . unless someone else is paying! As I was reviewing these wine lists, I looked at the percentage of wines under $50, under $75, and under $100. To my surprise, most of them had a large percentage of affordable wines. Restaurants with high-priced wines and very few less than $75 don't get my money.

BEST WINE FOR A PARTY OR RECEPTION

Champagne
Runner-up: any sparkling wine

These are some of the world's most versatile wines.

BEST WINE FOR VALENTINE'S DAY

Château Calon-Ségur

At one time the marquis de Ségur owned Château Lafite, Château Latour, and Château Calon-Ségur. He said, "I make my wines at Lafite and Latour, but my heart is at Calon." Hence the label.

BEST WINE FOR THANKSGIVING

?

The problem with Thanksgiving is that it's not just turkey. Everything else served with it—sweet potatoes, cranberries, butternut squash, stuffing—can create havoc with wine. This is also America's big family holiday; do you really want to share your best wines with your relatives? Try more user-friendly wines instead: easy-drinking, inexpensive wines from reliable producers. Look at the Wine and Food Pairings section again (page 330), and check out the lists on pages 333–334 for more specific wines.

At my Thanksgiving family dinner, I serve a Tawny Port after the turkey with a selection of nuts and fruits.

OTHER BESTS

BEST WINE GLASS

Riedel

This Austrian glassmaking family has crusaded for more than 30 years to elevate drinking wine to a new level with their specially designed varietal glassware. They have designed glasses to accentuate the best components of each grape variety following the principle that, because Cabernet Sauvignon and Pinot Noir are different wines, the glasses from which you drink them should also be different. Riedel glasses come in many different styles, and they make wine glasses for both everyday wine usage and special occasions. The top of the line is the handcrafted Sommelier series. Next comes the moderately priced Vinum collection. If you don't want to spend a lot of money on glassware, look for the Ouverture line.

BEST WINE PUBLICATION

Wine Spectator
Runners-up: *Decanter* and *Wine Enthusiast*

Marvin Shanken bought *Wine Spectator*, a worthwhile publication with a few subscribers, in 1979. Over the last 30+ years he has grown the subscription base to 2.8 million. It's a must-read for the articles and ratings.

Decanter magazine has a totally different format and point of view. This British publication includes feature articles by Michael Broadbent, Clive Coates, Hugh Johnson, Linda Murphy, Steven Spurrier, Brian St. Pierre, and others.

Another important read is *Wine Enthusiast*, a magazine created by Adam Strum, whose primary business is selling wine cellars, glassware, and wine accessories.

BEST WINE EVENT

Wine Spectator's **New York Wine Experience**

In 2016, *Wine Spectator* celebrated the 35th anniversary of the New York Wine Experience, and I have to admit a proud bias since I cofounded the event. What makes this event the best is that we established it on three principles: 1) Only the best wineries of the world would be invited, 2) the winemaker or owner had to be present, and 3) proceeds go to scholarships.

BEST WINE REGIONS TO VISIT

Bordeaux, France
Napa Valley, California
Tuscany, Italy

A great vacation for me consists of great wine, fabulous restaurants, pleasant climate, proximity to the ocean, beautiful scenery, and nice people. (Am I asking too much?) These three wine regions fulfill my needs.

BEST WINE LIE

All wines improve with age.

Think of all of the wines that you used to drink in college and your early 20s. Now think about how much you paid for those wines. I'm sure they didn't last very long!—which is exactly the way it should be. You should drink 90 percent of all wines within one year, and the next 9 percent shouldn't age longer than five years. Only that last 1 percent of wines should age more than that.

BEST WINE MYTH

Everyone tastes wine alike.

No one tastes wine or anything else alike! Taste and smell are like fingerprints or snowflakes—no two are alike. The average person has between 5,000 and 10,000 taste buds. It's difficult to measure how many taste buds someone has, so I can trust only my own judgment and no one else's—as you should too.

TOP VALUE WINE REGIONS

Chianti, Italy

Côtes du Rhône, France

Maipo, Chile

Marlborough, New Zealand

Mendoza, Argentina

Rioja, Spain

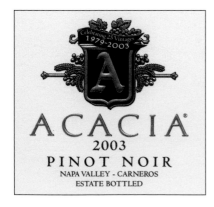

THE WORLD'S BEST VALUE WINES UNDER $30

A few years ago I traveled to 15 countries, 80 regions, and 400 appellations and tasted more than 6,000 wines—all in one year! The experience opened my eyes about the availability of high-quality wines at all price points, which is certainly good news for you. The greatest wines always will remain expensive, and unfortunately only a few people will consume them, but the Great Recession actually benefited the pricing of most wines. It helped change the concept that a good wine has to cost a lot of money. Today, hundreds of wines less than $30 are equal in quality to wines that I've tasted that cost more than $100. Bottom line: This is the best time ever to buy very good wine at reasonable prices.

This list would have included many more of the world's great wine values, but many aren't available in all markets, so I haven't listed them here. Most of the wines below cost $30 or less, but I've also included some that are great values even if they run a little more than $30.

AMERICA

States such as North Carolina, Pennsylvania, Virginia, New York, and many others make great value wines, but unfortunately most of these wines are available only locally. California represents the lion's share of the American market (90 percent) with great Sauvignon Blancs and Chardonnays for the whites and Cabernet Sauvignons, Merlots, Pinot Noirs, Zinfandels, and Syrahs for the reds. Washington, the second largest producer, makes very good value Sauvignon Blancs, Merlots, Chardonnays, and Cabernet Sauvignons. You also can find some Pinot Noirs and Chardonnays from Oregon at reasonable prices. Here are some of my favorite American producers and their value wines:

RED

A to Z Wineworks Pinot Noir	Artesa Pinot Noir
Acacia Carneros Pinot Noir	Atalon Cabernet Sauvignon
Acrobat Pinot Noir	Au Bon Climat "La Bauge" Pinot Noir
Alexander Valley "Sin Zin" Zinfandel	Au Bon Climat Pinot Noir
Andrew Will Cabernet Sauvignon	B. R. Cohn Silver label Cabernet
Argyle Pinot Noir	Sauvignon

Beaulieu Coastal Merlot

Beaulieu Rutherford Cabernet Sauvignon

Bedrock Zinfandel Old Vine

Benton-Lane Pinot Noir

Benziger Merlot

Beringer Knights Valley Cabernet
Sauvignon

Bogle Zinfandel

Bonny Doon "Le Cigare Volant"

Broadside "Margarita Vineyard"
Cabernet Sauvignon

Buena Vista Pinot Noir

Byron Pinot Noir

Calera Pinot Noir

The Calling "Rio Lago Vineyard"
Cabernet Sauvignon

Cambria Julia's Vineyard Pinot Noir

Cartlidge & Browne Pinot Noir

Castle Rock Pinot Noir

Chalone Pinot Noir

Chappellet Mountain "Cuvee Cervantes"
Meritage

Chapter 24 "Two Messengers" Pinot Noir

Charles Krug Merlot

Chateau Ste Michelle "Canoe Ridge"
Merlot

Chateau Ste Michelle "Indian Wells"
Cabernet Sauvignon

Cline Syrah / Shiraz

Cline Zinfandel

Clos du Bois Reserve Merlot

Cloudline Pinot Noir

Columbia Crest Merlot

Cooper Mountain Pinot Noir

De Martino Syrah / Shiraz

Dry Creek Cabernet Sauvignon

Edna Valley Pinot Noir

Elements by Artesa Cabernet Sauvignon

Etude Lyric Pinot Noir

Ex Libris Cabernet Sauvignon

Ferrari-Carano Merlot

Fess Parker Syrah / Shiraz

Fetzer Vineyard Valley Oaks Merlot

Foley Pinot Noir

Folie a Deux Cabernet Sauvignon

Forest Glen Cabernet Sauvignon

Forest Glen Merlot

Forest Glen Syrah / Shiraz

Francis Ford Coppola "Director's Cut"
Pinot Noir

Freemark Abbey Cabernet Sauvignon

Frei Brothers Merlot

Frog's Leap Cabernet Sauvignon

Frog's Leap Merlot

Gallo of Sonoma Cabernet Sauvignon

Garnet Pinot Noir

Gavilan

Geyser Peak Reserve Cabernet Sauvignon

Hess Select Cabernet Sauvignon

Hogue Merlot

Joel Gott Cabernet Sauvignon

Joel Gott Zinfandel

Justin Syrah / Shiraz

Kendall Jackson Merlot

L'Ecole No. 41 Shiraz

La Crema Pinot Noir

Laurel Glen Quintana Cabernet
Sauvignon

Loring Pinot Noir

Louis M. Martini Sonoma Cabernet
Sauvignon

MacMurray Ranch Pinot Noir

Markham Merlot

McManis Cabernet Sauvignon

Meiomi Pinot Noir

Miner Family "Stage Coach" Merlot

Mt. Veeder Winery Cabernet Sauvignon

Napa Ridge Merlot

Neyers Left Bank

Pinot Noir "Sharecropper" Pinot Noir

Ponzi "Tavola" Pinot Noir

Qupe Bien Nacido Vineyard Syrah / Shiraz

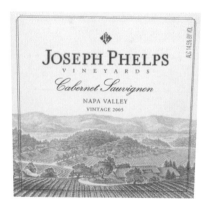

Ravenswood "Belloni" Zinfandel
Red Lava Vineyards Syrah / Shiraz
Rex Hill Pinot Noir
Ridge Sonoma Zinfandel
Robert Mondavi Merlot
Robert Mondavi Napa Cabernet
   Sauvignon
Route Stock Cabernet Sauvignon
Rodney Strong Cabernet Sauvignon
Rutherford Vintners Cabernet Sauvignon
Saint Francis Cabernet Sauvignon
Saint Francis Merlot
Sean Minor Cabernet Sauvignon
Sebastiani Cabernet Sauvignon
Seven Hills Cabernet Sauvignon
Seven Hills Merlot

Siduri Pinot Noir
Silver Palm Cabernet Sauvignon
Souverain Merlot
Stag's Leap Wine Cellars "Hands of Time"
   Cabernet Sauvignon
Swanson Merlot
Trefethen Eshcol Cabernet Sauvignon
Turley Juvenile
Volpaia Chianto Classico
Vista Verde Vineyard Pinot Noir
Waterbrook Merlot
Wild Horse Pinot Noir
Willamette Valley Vineyards Pinot Noir
Wolffer Estate Merlot
Wyatt Pinot Noir
Zaca Mesa Syrah / Shiraz

WHITE

Acacia Chardonnay
Argyle Chardonnay
Arrowood Grand Archer Chardonnay
Beaulieu Coastal Sauvignon Blanc
Benziger Chardonnay
Bergström "Old Stones" Chardonnay
Beringer Chardonnay
Beringer Sauvignon Blanc
Boundary Breaks "Ovid Line North"
   Riesling
Buena Vista Sauvignon Blanc
Calera Central Coast Chardonnay
Cambria "Katherine's Vineyard"
   Chardonnay
Channing Daughters "Scuttlehole"
   Chardonnay
Chateau Montelena Sauvignon Blanc
Chateau St. Jean Chardonnay
Chateau St. Jean Sauvignon Blanc
Chateau Ste Michelle Chardonnay
Chateau Ste Michelle "Eroica"
   Riesling

Clos Pegase Mitsuko's Vineyard
   Chardonnay
Columbia Crest Sémillon-Chardonnay
Covey Run Chardonnay
Covey Run Fumé Blanc
Cristom Vineyard Pinot Blanc / Gris
Cuvée Daniel (Au Bon Climat)
   Chardonnay
Dr. Konstantin Frank Riesling
Elk Cove Vineyards Pinot Blanc/Gris
Estancia Chardonnay
Ferrari-Carano Fumé Blanc
Fetzer Vineyard Valley Oaks Chardonnay
Francis Ford Coppola "Director's Cut"
   Chardonnay
Frog's Leap Sauvignon Blanc
Geyser Peak Sauvignon Blanc
Girard Sauvignon Blanc
Grgich Hills Fumé Blanc
Groth Sauvignon Blanc
Hall Winery Sauvignon Blanc
Heitz Cellars Chardonnay
Hermann J. Wiemer Riesling

Hess Select Chardonnay
High Hook Vineyards Pinot Blanc/Gris
Hogue Columbia Valley Chardonnay
Hogue Fumé Blanc
Honig Sauvignon Blanc
Joel Gott Chardonnay
Joel Gott Sauvignon Blanc
Kendall-Jackson Vintner's Reserve
    Chardonnay
Kendall-Jackson Vintner's Reserve
    Sauvignon Blanc
Kenwood Sauvignon Blanc
King Estate "Signature Collection" Pinot
    Blanc/Gris
La Crema Chardonnay
La Crema Pinot Blanc/Gris

Landmark "Overlook" Chardonnay
Mason Sauvignon Blanc
Matanzas Creek Sauvignon Blanc
Mer Soleil "Silver" (unoaked)
    Chardonnay
Merryvale Starmont Chardonnay
Morgan Chardonnay
Ponzi Pinot Blanc/Gris
Provenance Sauvignon Blanc
Ravines Riesling
Rodney Strong Sauvignon Blanc
Rutherford Ranch Chardonnay
Sbragia Family Sauvignon Blanc
Silverado Sauvignon Blanc
Simi Chardonnay
Truchard Chardonnay

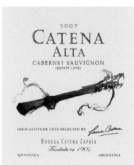

ARGENTINA

Argentina's reputation rests on the Mendoza region and the Malbec grape, but the country makes other wines, such as Bonarda, Cabernet Sauvignon, and Chardonnay, that also are great values. Here are some of my favorite Argentinean producers and their value wines:

RED
Achaval-Ferrer Malbec
Alamos Malbec
Alta Vista Malbec Grand Reserva
Bodega Norton Malbec
Bodegas Esmeralda Malbec
Bodegas Renacer "Enamore"
Bodegas Weinert Carrascal
Catena Malbec
Catena Zapata Cabernet Sauvignon
Clos de los Siete Malbec
Cuvelier Los Andes "Coleccion"

Domaine Jean Bousquet Malbec
Kaiken Cabernet Sauvignon Ultra
Miguel Mendoza Malbec Reserva
Perdriel Malbec
Salentein Malbec
Susana Balboa Cabernet Sauvignon
Susana Balboa Malbec
Terrazas Malbec Reserva
Tikal Patriota
Trapiche Oak Cask Malbec
Valentin Bianchi Malbec

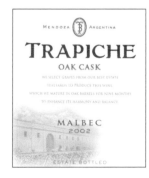

WHITE
Alamos Chardonnay
Alta Vista Torrontes Premium
Bodegas Diamandes de Uco Chardonnay

Catena Chardonnay
Michel Torino Torrontés Don David
Michel Torino Torrontés Don David Reserve

AUSTRALIA

Thirty years ago, Australia took the world by storm with great wines at great prices, and that still holds true today. The most famous red grape, Shiraz, often blends with Cabernet Sauvignon, but this huge country has so many other wine regions that it's easy to find great Cabernet Sauvignons, Chardonnays, and Sauvignon Blancs at unbelievable prices. Here are some of my favorite Australian producers and their value wines:

RED

Alice White Cabernet Sauvignon
Banrock Station Shiraz
Black Opal Cabernet Sauvignon or Shiraz
Chapel Hill Grenache "Bushvine"
Chapel Hill Shiraz "Parson's Nose"
d'Arenberg "The Footbolt" Shiraz
d'Arenberg Grenache The Derelict
    Vineyard
d'Arenberg "The Stump Jump" Red
Jacob's Creek Cabernet Sauvignon
Jacob's Creek Shiraz Cabernet
Jamshead Syrah
Jim Barry Shiraz "The Lodge Hill"
Jim Barry Cabernet Sauvignon
    "The Cover Drive"
Kilikanoon "Killerman's Run" Shiraz
Langmeil Winery "Three Gardens" Shiraz /
    Grenache / Mourvèdre

Leeuwin Estate Siblings Shiraz
Lindeman's Shiraz Bin 50
Marquis Philips Sarah's Blend
McWilliam's Shiraz
Mollydooker "The Boxer" Shiraz
Nine Stones Shiraz
Penfolds "Bin 28 Kalimna" Shiraz
Peter Lehmann Barossa Shiraz
Rosemount Estate Shiraz Cabernet
    (Diamond Label)
Salomon Estate "Finnis River" Shiraz
Schild Shiraz
St. Hallett Shiraz
Taltarni T Series Shiraz
Two Hands Shiraz "Gnarly Dudes"
Yalumba Y Series Shiraz Viognier
Yangarra Shiraz Single Vineyard

WHITE

Banrock Station Chardonnay
Bogle Sauvignon Blanc
Cape Mentelle Sauvignon Blanc-Sémillon
Grant Burge Chardonnay
Heggies Vineyard Chardonnay
Jim Barry Riesling
Lindeman's Chardonnay Bin 65
Matua Valley Sauvignon Blanc
Oxford Landing Sauvignon Blanc

Pewsey Vale Dry Riesling
Rolf Binder Riesling "Highness"
Rosemount Estate Chardonnay
Saint Clair "Pioneer Block 3" Sauvignon
    Blanc
Saint Hallett "Poacher's Blend" White
Trevor Jones Virgin Chardonnay
Yalumba Y Series Unwooded Chardonnay

AUSTRIA

The two major white grapes are Grüner Veltliner and Riesling, perfect wines to serve with all kinds of foods, easy to drink, and readily available. Here are some of my favorite Austrian producers and their value wines:

RED

Glatzer Zweigelt

Sepp Moser Sepp Zweigelt

WHITE

Albert Neumeister Morillon Steirsche
    Klassik
Alois Kracher Pinot Gris Trocken
Brundlmayer Grüner Veltliner Kamptaler
    Terrassen
Forstreiter "Grand Reserve" Grüner
    Veltliner
Franz Etz Grüner Veltliner (Liter)
Hirsch Grüner Veltliner Heiligenstein

Hirsch "Veltliner #1"
Knoll Grüner Veltliner Federspiel Trocken
    Wachau Loibner
Nigl Grüner Veltliner Kremser Freiheit
Salomon Grüner Veltliner
Salomon Riesling Steinterrassen
Schloss Gobelsburg
Walter Glatzer Grüner Veltliner
    "Dornenvogel"

CHILE

The best value in the world for Cabernet Sauvignon is Chile. Also look for their Merlots, Carménères, and Sauvignon Blancs. Here are some of my favorite Chilean producers and their value wines:

RED

Arboleda Carmenère
Caliterra Cabernet Sauvignon or Merlot
Carmen Carménère
Casa Lapostolle "Cuvée Alexandre"
    Merlot
Concha y Toro Puente Alto Cabernet
    Sauvignon
Cono Sur 20 Barrels Cabernet Sauvignon
Cousiño-Macul Antiguas Reserva
Errazuriz Cabernet Sauvignon

Los Vascos Reserve Cabernet Sauvignon
Montes Alpha Merlot Apalta Vineyard
Montes Cabernet Sauvignon
Santa Carolina Cabernet Sauvignon
Veramonte Primus "The Blend"
Veranda Pinot Noir Ritua
Viña Aquitania Lazuli Cabernet
    Sauvignon
Viña San Pedro Cabernet Sauvignon

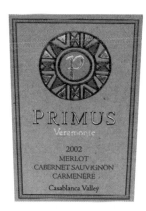

WHITE

Casa Lapostolle Cuvee Alexander
    Chardonnay
Casa Lapostolle Cuvee Alexander Valley
    Sauvignon Blanc

Cono Sur "Bicycle Series" Viognier
Veramonte Sauvignon Blanc
Vina Aquitania "Sol del Sol" Chardonnay
    "Traiguen" 2008

FRANCE

France sometimes has a reputation for very expensive wines (great châteaux of Bordeaux, domaines of Burgundy, etc.), but it always has offered great values. From Alsace: Rieslings, Pinot Blancs, and Pinot Gris; from the Loire Valley: Muscadet, Sancerre, and Pouilly-Fumé; from Burgundy: Beaujolais, Mâcons, Chablis, and Bourgogne Blanc and Rouge; from the Rhône Valley: Côtes du Rhône and Crozes-Hermitage; from Bordeaux: Petit Château and Cru Bourgeois; and the wines from Provence, Languedoc, and Roussillon. Here are some of my favorite French producers and their value wines:

RED

"A" d'Aussières Rouge Corbières
Baron de Brane
Brunier Le Pigeoulet Rouge VDP Vaucluse
Brunier "Megaphone" Ventoux Rouge
Chapelle-St-Arnoux Châteauneuf-du-Pape Vieilles Vignes
Château Bel Air
Château Cabrières Côtes du Rhône
Château Cantemerle
Château Cap de Faugeres
Château Caronne-Sainte-Gemme
Château Chantegrive
Château d'Escurac "Pepin"
Château de Maison Neuve
Château de Mercey Mercurey Rouge
Château de Trignon Gigondas
Château de Villambis
Château Graville Lacoste
Château Greysac
Château Haut du Peyrat
Château Labat
Château La Cardonne
Château La Grangère
Château Lanessan
Château Larose-Trintaudon
Château Le Bonnat
Château Le Sartre
Château Malmaison
Château Malromè
Château Maris La Touge Syrah

Château Pey La Tour Reserve du Château
Château Peyrabon
Château Pontensac
Château Puy-Blanquet
Château Puynard
Château St-Julian
Château Segondignac
Château Senejac
Château Thébot
Château Tour Leognan
Cheval Noir
Clos Siguier Cahors
Confidences de Prieure-Lichine
Côte-de-Nuits-Village, Joseph Drouhin
Croix Mouton
Cuvée Daniel Côtes de Castillon
Domaine André Brunel Côtes-du-Rhône Cuvée Sommelongue
Domaine Bouchard Pinot Noir
Domaine d'Andezon Côtes-du-Rhône
Domaine de la Coume du Roy Côtes du Roussillon-Villages "Le Desir"
Domaine de Lagrézette Cahors
Domaine de'Obrieu Côtes du Rhône Villages "Cuvée les Antonins"
Domaine de Villemajou "Boutenac"
Domaine Michel Poinard Crozes-Hermitage
Domaine Roches Neuves Saumur-Champigny
Georges Duboeuf Beaujolais-Villages

Georges Duboeuf Morgon "Caves Jean-
Ernest Descombes"
Gérard Bertrand Domaine de L'Aigle
Pinot Noir
Gérard Bertrand Grand Terroir Tautavel
Gilles Ferran "Les Antimagnes"
Guigal Côtes du Rhône
J. Vidal-Fleury Côtes du Rhône
Jaboulet Côtes du Rhône Parallèle 45
Jaboulet Crozes-Hermitage Les Jalets
Jean-Maurice Raffault Chinon
Joseph Drouhin Côte de Beaune-Villages
La Baronne Rouge "Montagne d'Alaric"
La Vieille Ferme Côtes du Ventoux
Lafite Réserve Spéciale
Laplace Madiran
Le Médoc de Cos
Louis Jadot Château des Jacques Moulin-
à-Vent

M. Chapoutier Bila-Haut Côtes de
Rousillon Villages
Maison Champy Pinot Noir Signature
Marc Rougeot Bourgogne Rouge "Les
Lameroses"
Marjosse Réserve du Château
Mas de Gourgonnier Les Baux de
Provence Rouge
Michel Poinard Crozes-Hermitage
Montirius Gigondas Terres des Aînés
Nicolas Thienpont Selection St-Emilion
Grand Cru
Perrin & Fils Côtes du Rhône
René Lequin-Colin Santenay "Vieilles
Vignes"
Thierry Germain Saumur-Champigny
Villa Ponciago Fleurie La Réserve
Beaujolais

WHITE

Ballot-Millot et Fils Bourgogne Chardonnay
Barton & Guestier Sauternes
Bertranon Bordeaux Blanc
Bouzeron Domaine Gagey
Château Bonnet Blanc
Château de Maligny Petit Chablis
Château de Mercey Mercurey Blanc
Château de Rully Blanc "La Pucelle"
Château de Sancerre
Château du Mayne Blanc
Château du Trignon Côtes du Rhône Blanc
Château Fuissé
Château Graville-Lacoste Blanc
Château Jeanguillon Blanc
Château Larrivet Haut-Brion
Château Loumelat
Château Martinon Blanc
Clarendelle
Claude Lafond Reuilly
Domaine de Montcy Cheverny

Domaine Delaye St-Véran "Les Pierres
Grises"
Domaine des Baumard Savennières
Domaine Jean Chartron Bourgogne
Aligoté
Domaine les Hautes Cances Cairanne
Domaine Mardon Quincy "Très Vieilles
Vignes"
Domaine Paul Pillot Bourgogne
Chardonnay
Domaine St-Barbe Mâcon Clesse "Les
Tilles"
Faiveley Bourgogne Blanc
Francis Blanchet Pouilly Fumé "Cuvée
Silice"
Georges Duboeuf Pouilly-Fuissé
Helfrich Riesling
Hugel & Fils Gentil
Hugel & Fils Riesling
Hugel Pinot Gris

J. J. Vincent Pouilly-Fuissé "Marie
    Antoinette"
Jonathon Pabiot Pouilly-Fumé
Joseph Drouhin St-Véran
Laroche Petit Chablis
Louis Jadot Mâcon
Louis Jadot St-Véran
Louis Latour Montagny
Louis Latour Pouilly-Vinzelles
Maison Bleue Chardonnay
Marjosse Blanc Réserve du Château
Mas Karolina Côtes Catalanes Blanc
Michel Bailly Pouilly-Fumé
Olivier Leflaive St-Aubin
Pascal Jolivet Attitude

Pascal Jolivet Sancerre
Robert Klingenfus Pinot Blanc
Sauvion Pouilly-Fumé Les Ombelles
Sauvion Sancerre "Les Fondettes"
Simonnet-Febvre Chablis
Thierry Germain Saumur Blanc Cuvée
    "Soliterre"
Thierry Pillot Santenay Blanc "Clos Genet"
Trimbach Gewurztraminer
Trimbach Riesling
William Fèvre Chablis
Willm Cuvée Emile Willm Riesling
    Réserve
Zind Humbrecht Pinot Blanc

ROSÉ
Château Miraval Côtes de
    Provence Rosé "Pink Floyd"

GERMANY

You will find the great value white wines of Germany in the Kabinett and Spätlese styles. Here are some of my favorite German producers and their value wines:

WHITE
Dr. Loosen Riesling
J. J. Prüm Wehlener Sonnenuhr Spätlese
Josef Leitz Rüdesheimer Klosterlay
    Riesling Kabinett
Kerpen Wehlener Sonnenuhr Kabinett
Kurt Darting Dürkheimer Hochbenn
    Riesling Kabinett
Leitz "Dragonstone" Riesling
Meulenhof Wehlenuhr Sonnenuhr
    Riesling Spätlese

Saint Urbans-Hof Riesling Kabinett
Schloss Vollrads Riesling Kabinett
Selbach Piesporter Michelsberg Riesling
    Spätlese
Selbach-Oster Zeltinger Sonnenuhr
    Riesling Kabinett
Strub Niersteiner Olberg Kabinett or
    Spätlese
Weingut Max Richter Mülheimer
    Sonnelay Riesling Kabinett

GREECE
Boutari Moschofilero Mantinia
D. Kourtakis Assyrtiko Santorini

ITALY

Italy is making its best wines ever!—and you can find great values all over. From Tuscany: Chianti Classico Riserva, Rosso di Montalcino, and Rosso di Montepulciano; from Piedmont: Barbera and Dolcetto; from Veneto: Valpolicella, Soave, and Prosecco; from Abruzzi: Montepulciano d'Abruzzo; from northern Italy: Pinot Grigio and Pinot Bianco; and from Sicily: Nero d'Avola. Here are some of my favorite Italian producers and their value wines:

RED

Aldo Rainoldi Nebbiolo
Aleramo Barbera
Allegrini Palazzo della Torre
Allegrini Valpolicella Classico
Antinori Badia a Passignano Chianti
    Classico
Altesino Rosso di Altesino
Antinori Santa Cristina Sangiovese
Antinori Tormaresca Trentangeli
Avignonesi Rosso di Montepulciano
Baglia di Pianetto "Ramione"
Braida Barbera d'Asti "Montebruna"
Bruno Giacosa Barbera d'Alba
Cantina del Taburno Aglianico Fidelis
Carpazo Rosso di Montalcino
Caruso e Minini I Sciani Sachia
Casal Thaulero Montepulciano d'Abruzzo
Cascata Monticello Dolcetto d'Asti
Castellare di Castellina Chianti Classico
Castello Banfi Toscana Centine
Castello Monaci Liante Salice Salentino
Col d'Orcia Rosso di Montalcino
Di Majo Norante Sangiovese Terre degli
    Osci
Einaudi Dolcetto di Dogliani
Fattoria di Felsina Chianti Classico
    Riserva
Francesco Rinaldi Dolcetto d'Alba
Guado al Tasso-Antinori Il Bruciato
La Mozza Morellino di Scansano
    "I Perazzi"

Le Rote Vernaccia di San Gimignano
Librandi Ciro Riserva "Duca San Felice"
Lungarotti Rubesco
Manzone Nebbiolo Langhe "Crutin"
Marchesi de' Frescobaldi Chianti Rúfina
Marchesi di Barolo Barbera d'Alba
Masi "Campofiorin"
Melini Chianti Classico Riserva
    "La Selvanella"
Melini Chianti Classico Terrarossa
Michele Chiarlo Barbera d'Asti
Mocali Rosso di Montalcino
Monchiero Carbone Barbera d'Alba
Morellino di Scansano
Morgante Nero d'Avola
Montesotto Chianti Classico
Podere Ciona "Montegrossoli"
Poggio al Casone La Cattura
Poggio al Tesoro Mediterra
Poggio Il Castellare Rosso di Montalcino
Principe Corsini Chianti Classico
    "Le Corti"
Regaleali (Tasca d'Almerita) Rosso
Ruffino Chianti Classico "Riserva Ducale"
    (Tan label)
Ruffino "Modus"
San Polo "Rubio"
Sandrone Nebbiolo d'Alba Valmaggiore
Santa Cristina Chianti Superiore
Silvio Nardi Rosso di Montalcino
Taurino Salice Salentino

Tenuta dell'Ornellaia Le Volte
Tenuta di Arceno Arcanum Il Fauno
Tolaini "Valdisanti"
Tormaresca "Torcicoda"
Travaglini Gattinara
Valle Reale Montepulciano d'Abruzzo

Volpaia Chianti Classico
Zaccagnini Montepulciano d'Abruzzo
    Riserva
Zenato Valpolicella
Zeni Amarone della Valpolicella

WHITE

Abbazia di Novacella Kerner
Alois Lageder Pinot Bianco
Alois Lageder Pinot Grigio
Anselmi Soave
Antinori Chardonnay della Sala Bramito
    del Cervo
Antinori Vermentino Guado al Tasso
Bolla Soave Classico
Bollini Trentino Pinot Grigio
Boscaini Pinot Grigio
Botromagno Gravina Bianco
Cantina Andriano Pinot Bianco
Caruso e Minini Terre di Giumara Inzolia
Ceretto "Blange" Langhe Arneis
Clelia Romano Fiano di Avellino "Colli di
    Lapio"
Coppo Gavi "La Rocca"
Eugenio Collavini Pinot Grigio
    "Canlungo"
Jermann Pinot Grigio
Kellerei Cantina Terlan Pinot Bianco

La Carraia Orvieto Classico
Le Rote Vernaccia di San Gimignano
Maculan "Pino & Toi"
Malabaila Roero Arneis
Marchetti Verdicchio dei Castelli di Jesi
    Classico
Marco Felluga Collio Pinot Grigio
Mastroberardino Falanghina
Paolo Scavino Bianco
Peter Zemmer Pinot Grigio
Pieropan Soave
Pighin Pinot Grigio
Sergio Mottura Grechetto "Poggio della
    Costa"
Sergio Mottura Orvieto
Soave Classico Pra
Terenzuola Vermentino Colli di Luni
Teruzzi & Puthod "Terre di Tufi"
Terredora Greco di Tufo (Loggia della
    Serra)

ROSÉ

Antinori Guado al Tasso
    Scalabrone Rosato

PROSECCO

Adami
Bortolomiol
La Tordera

Le Colture
Mionetto
Zardetto

NEW ZEALAND

The two most important grapes of New Zealand are Sauvignon Blanc and Pinot Noir. The former—with their tropical aromas and taste with a crisp, citrus finish—have become world famous, but also look for the latter for quality wines. Here are some of my favorite New Zealand producers and their value wines:

RED

Babich Pinot Noir	Oyster Bay Pinot Noir
Brancott Estate Pinot Noir Reserve	Peregrine Pinot Noir
Coopers Creek Pinot Noir	Sacred Hill Pinot Noir
Crown Range Pinot Noir	Saint Clair Pinot Noir "Vicar's Choice"
Jules Taylor Pinot Noir	Salomon & Andrew Pinot Noir
Kim Crawford Pinot Noir	Stoneleigh Pinot Noir
Man o' War Syrah	Te Awa Syrah
Mt. Beautiful Pinot Noir Cheviot Hills	The Crossings Pinot Noir
Mt. Difficulty Pinot Noir	Trinity Hill Pinot Noir
Mud House Pinot Noir	Yealands Pinot Noir
Neudorf Vineyards Pinot Noir	
"Tom's Block" (Nelson)	

WHITE

Ata Rangi Sauvignon Blanc	Mt. Nelson Sauvignon Blanc
Babich Sauvignon Blanc	Mt. Difficulty Pinot Gris
Babich Unwooded Chardonnay	Neudorf Chardonnay
Brancott Estate Sauvignon Blanc	Neudorf Sauvignon Blanc
Cloudy Bay "Te Koko" Sauvignon Blanc	Nobilo Sauvignon Blanc
Coopers Creek Sauvignon Blanc	Oyster Bay Sauvignon Blanc
Cru Vin Dogs "Greyhound" Sauvignon	Pegasus Bay Chardonnay
Blanc	Peregrine Pinot Gris
Giesen Sauvignon Blanc	Saint Clair Sauvignon Blanc
Glazebrook Sauvignon Blanc	Salomon & Andrew Sauvignon Blanc
Isabel Estate Sauvignon Blanc	Seresin Sauvignon Blanc
Kim Crawford Sauvignon Blanc	Stoneleigh Chardonnay
Kono Sauvignon Blanc	Stoneleigh Sauvignon Blanc
Kumeu River Village Chardonnay	Te Awa Chardonnay
Man o' War Sauvignon Blanc	Te Mata "Woodthorpe"
Mohua Pinot Gris	Villa Maria "Cellar Selection" Sauvignon
Mohua Sauvignon Blanc	Blanc

PORTUGAL

Duorum Tons Red
Quinta de Cabriz

Quinta do Crasto
Real Companhia Velha

SOUTH AFRICA

The diversity of South African wines, from Chenin Blanc and Sauvignon Blanc to Cabernet Sauvignon and Pinotage, offers a lot of different choices at great value. Here are some of my favorite South African producers and their value wines:

RED

Boekenhoutskloof "Chocolate Block" Meritage
Doolhof Dark Lady of the Labyrinth Pinotage
Jardin Syrah
Groot Constantia Shiraz
Kanonkop Pinotage

Mount Rozier "Myrtle Grove" Cabernet Sauvignon
Mulderbosch Faithful Hound
Kanonkop Kadette Red
Rupert & Rothschild Classique
Rustenberg 1682 Red Blend
Thelema Cabernet Sauvignon

WHITE

Boschendal Chardonnay
Buitenverwachting Sauvignon Blanc
Ken Forrester Sauvignon Blanc
Groot Constantia Sauvignon Blanc
Glenelly Chardonnay

Raats Family Chenin Blanc
Stellenbosch Vineyards Chenin Blanc
Thelema Sauvignon Blanc
Tokara Chardonnay Reserve Collection

SPAIN

From the time I started studying wine more than 40 years ago, the wines of Rioja have represented great value, especially the Crianzas and Reservas. The Tempranillo grape also shines in Ribera del Duero. Rías Baixas makes good Albariños, and from Penedès we have the great Cavas. Here are some of my favorite Spanish producers and their value wines:

RED

Alvaro Palacios Camins del Priorat
Algueira Ribiera Sacra
Antidoto Ribera del Duero Cepas Viejas
Baron de Ley Reserva
Bernabeleva Camino de Navaherreros
Beronia Rioja Reserva
Bodega Numanthia Termes
Bodegas Beronia Reserva
Bodegas Emilio Moro "Emilio Moro"
Bodegas La Cartuja Priorat
Bodegas Lan Rioja Crianza
Bodegas Leda Mas de Leda
Bodegas Marañones 30 Mil Maravedies
Bodegas Montecillo Crianza or Reserva
Bodegas Muga Reserva
Bodegas Ontañón Crianza or Reserva
Bodegas Palacios Remondo Crianza
Bodegas Señorío de Barahonda "Carro"
   Tinto
Bodegas Urbina Rioja Gran Reserva
Campo Viejo Reserva

Clos Galena Galena
Condado de Haza Ribera del Duero
Conde de Valdemar Crianza
CVNE Rioja Crianza "Viña Real"
Descendientes de José Palacios Bierzo
   Pétalos
Dinastía Vivanco Selección de Familia
El Coto Crianza and Reserva
Ermita San Felices Reserva Rioja Alta
Finca Torremilanos Ribera del Duero
Joan d'Anguera Montsant Garnatxa
La Rioja Alta Reserva Viña Alberdi
Marqués de Cáceres Crianza or Reserva
Marqués de Riscal Proximo Rioja
Onix Priorat
Pago de Valdoneje Bierzo
Pesquera Tinto Crianza
Rotllan Torra Priorat Crianza
Scala Dei Priorat "Negre"
Torres Gran Coronas Reserva

WHITE

Albariño Don Olegario
Bodegas Ostatu Blanco
Burgáns Albariño Rías Baixas
Castro Brey Albariño "Sin Palabras"
Condes de Albarei "Condes do Ferreiro
   Albariño de Albarei"

Legaris Verdejo Rueda
Licia Galicia Albariño
Martin Codax Albariño
Pazo de Senorans Albariño
Terras Guada Albariño
   "O Rosal"

CAVA

Codorníu Brut Classico
Cristalino Brut

Freixenet
Segura Viudas

WINE RESOURCES

BUYING AND STORING WINE

RATINGS AND PRICES

Beverage Tasting Institute, tastings.com

Parker's *Wine Buying Guide*

Snooth.com

Wine Price File

wine-searcher.com

Wine Spectator's Ultimate Buying Guide

SELLERS AND AUCTIONEERS

Aulden Cellars–Sotheby's
  Auction House
sothebys.com/wine

Hart Davis Hart
hdhwine.com

Bonhams & Butterfields
bonhams.com

Morrell & Company
Morrellwineauctions.com

Chicago Wine Company
tcwc.com

Wally's Wine Auction
wallysauction.com

Christie's Auction House
christies.com

Zachy's
zachys.com/auctions

Other online wine auction houses:

auctionvine.com

spectrumwine.com

brentwoodwine.com

winebid.com

munichwinecompany.com

winecommune.com

STORAGE AND EQUIPMENT

International Wine
  Accessories
iwawine.com

Western Carriers, Inc. Wine
  Cellar Transportation
westerncarriers.com

Sub Zero Freezer Company
subzero-wolf.com

Wine Enthusiast Catalog
wineenthusiast.com

WINE PUBLICATIONS

BOOKS

These books are required reading if you want to delve further into the fascinating subject of wine:

The Essential Wine Book by Oz Clarke

Exploring Wine by Steven Kolpan, Brian H. Smith, and Michael A. Weiss

The Food Lover's Guide to Wine by Karen Page and Andrew Dornenburg

Grapes & Wines by Oz Clarke

Great Tastes Made Simple and *Great Wine Made Simple* by Andrea Immer

Hugh Johnson's Modern Encyclopedia of Wine

The Oxford Companion to Wine by Jancis Robinson

Perfect Pairings and *Daring Pairings* by Evan Goldstein

The Ultimate Wine Companion by Kevin Zraly

Vino Italiano by Joseph Bastianich and David Lynch

The Wine Bible by Karen MacNeil

Wine for Dummies by Ed McCarthy and Mary Ewing-Mulligan

The Wine Lover's Guide to the Wine Country by Lori Lyn Narlock and Nancy Garfinkel

World Atlas of Wine by Hugh Johnson and Jancis Robinson

The above are encyclopedic, so I always carry with me one of these three pocket guides:

Food & Wine Pocket Guide

Hugh Johnson's Pocket Encyclopedia of Wine

Oz Clarke's Pocket Wine Guide

MAGAZINES

Decanter
decanter.com

Food & Wine
foodandwine.com

Tasting Panel
tastingpanelmag.com

Wine Advocate
erobertparker.com

Wine & Spirits
wineandspiritsmagazine.com

Wine Business Monthly
winebusiness.com

Wine Enthusiast
wineenthusiast.com

Wine Spectator
winespectator.com

BLOGGERS

For lists of wine bloggers worth following, see:
wineblogawards.org
winebusiness.com
dinersjournal.blogs.nytimes.com

WINE EDUCATION

For a complete list of wine schools, visit the Society of Wine Educators website, societyofwineeducators.org.

WINE CERTIFICATION PROGRAMS

For the professional or those wishing to become sommeliers:

American Sommelier Association
americansommelier.com

International Wine Center
internationalwinecenter.com

Society of Wine Educators
societyofwineeducators.org

Sommelier Society of America
sommeliersocietyofamerica.org

Wine & Spirit Education Trust
wsetglobal.com

Wine Spectator Wine School
winespectator.com/school

CONSUMER EDUCATION

Sherry-Lehmann / Kevin Zraly Master Classes
kevinzraly.com
845-255-1456 or
kevin@kevinzraly.com

WINE EVENTS

SELECT CONSUMER EVENTS

Check localwineevents.com for events in your area.

Auction Napa Valley
napavintners.com/anv/

Boston Wine Expo, winter
wine-expos.com

Charlotte Wine & Food Weekend, every other year in the spring
charlottewineandfood.com

Epcot Food & Wine Festival
disneyworld.disney.go.com/parks/epcot

Finger Lakes Wine Festival
flwinefest.com

Florida Winefest & Auction
floridawinefest.com

Food & Wine Classic in Aspen
foodandwine.com/classic

Grand Wine and Food Affair (Texas)
fortbendwineandfoodaffair.com

Naples Winter Wine Festival
napleswinefestival.com

New York Wine Experience
212-684-4224

New York Wine Expo
wine-expos.com

Newport Mansions Wine & Food Festival
newportmansions.org

Saratoga Wine and Food Festival
spac.org

South Beach Wine & Food Fest
sobewineandfoodfest.com

Washington International Wine & Food Festival
wine-expos.com

Westchester Magazine Wine and Food Festival
winefood.westchestermagazine.com

TRADE EVENTS

American Wine Society National Conference
americanwinesociety.org

Society of Wine Educators Conference
societyofwineeducators.org/conference.php

SMELL AND TASTE

The Emperor of Scent: A True Story of Perfume and Obsession by Chandler Burr

Jacobson's Organ and the Remarkable Nature of Smell by Lyall Watson

Life's a Smelling Success: Using Scent to Empower Your Memory and Learning by Alan Hirsch, M.D.

Monell Chemical Senses Center,
www.monell.org

National Institutes of Health,
www.nidcd.nih.gov/health/smelltaste

A Natural History of the Senses by Diane Ackerman

Professional Friends of Wine: A Sensory User's Manual,
www.winepros.org/wine101/sensory_guide.htm

Sense of Smell Institute,
www.senseofsmell.org

The Senses Bureau,
www.thesensesbureau.com

Sensonics, www.sensonics.com

Smell & Taste Treatment and Research Foundation,
www.scienceofsmell.com

Tim Jacob Smell Research Laboratory,
www.cf.ac.uk/biosi/staff/jacob

University of California San Diego
Nasal Dysfunction Clinic, health.ucsd.edu/specialties/surgery/otolaryngology/nasal

Wine Aroma Wheel, by Ann Noble,
www.winearomawheel.com

LOOKING BACK WITH GRATITUDE

I always will remember:

- Working with and learning from John Novi at the Depuy Canal House, 1970–76
- My first visit to a winery, Benmarl, in 1970
- My first wine classes in 1971, one where I was a student and the other where I was the teacher
- Hitchhiking to California to visit wine country in 1972
- Teaching a two-credit course as a junior in college (open only to seniors) in 1973
- Father Sam Matarazzo, my early and now spiritual leader
- Living and studying wine in Europe, 1974–75
- Planting my own vineyard (four-time failure) in 1974, 1981, 1992, 2014 and making my own wine in 1984 (so-so)
- The excitement of opening Windows on the World in 1976
- The support and friendship of Jules Roinnel, going back to our earliest days together at Windows
- Wine tastings with Alexis Bespaloff and friends
- Mohonk Mountain House in New Paltz, New York, where ideas come easy
- Evening, late-night, and early-morning wine discussions with Alexis Lichine in Bordeaux
- Adviser and great listener Peter Sichel, whose generosity of spirit inspired the way I teach and share my wine knowledge
- Sharing great old vintages with Peter Bienstock
- Jules Epstein, for his advice and for sharing his wine collection
- Touring the world with wine expert Robin Kelley O'Connor
- Creating and directing the New York Wine Experience, 1981–91
- Those no longer here to share a glass of wine: Craig Claiborne, Joseph Baum, Alan Lewis, Raymond Wellington, and my father, Charles
- Witnessing the success of Michael Skurnik, who worked with me at Windows in the late 1970s and quickly rose to fame as a great importer
- Watching my former student Andrea Robinson turn into a superstar wine-and-food personality and author
- The Food Network's *Wines A to Z*—together with Alan Richman
- Reading and enjoying the observations of the great wine writers and tasters (listed throughout the book)
- Having the opportunity to meet all the passionate winemakers, vineyardists, and owners of the great wineries of the world
- The wine events, wine dinners, and tastings around the country that I have had the privilege of attending
- All the groups that have invited me to entertain and educate them about wine
- Writing the first chapter of this book with Kathleen Talbert in 1983
- The original Sterling Publishing team of Burton Hobson, Lincoln Boehm, and Charles Nurnberg
- Marcus Leaver, former CEO of Sterling Publishing, for his tremendous support on all of my books
- To all my editors over the last three decades, especially Felicia Sherbert, Stephen Topping, Keith Schiffman, Steve Magnuson, Hannah Reich, Becky Maines, Mary Hern, Diane Abrams, Carlo DeVito, and James Jayo

- The Sterling team for this edition: James Jayo, Rich Hazelton, Kevin Ullrich, Ashley Prine, Linda Liang, Elizabeth Lindy, Hannah Reich, Katherine Furman, Fred Pagan, Betsy Beier, Chris Bain, Rodman Neumann, Maha Khalil, Nicole Vines Verlin, and Chris Vaccari as well as Rose Fox, Jay Kreider, Maria Mann, Marilyn Kretzer, and Toula Ballas.
- Karen Nelson for 25 years of beautiful cover designs
- Jim Anderson, who designed the original edition, and Richard Oriolo for capturing my spirit in subsequent editions
- Barnes & Noble for always supporting my books and ideas
- Carmen Bissell, Raymond DePaul, Faye Friedman, Jennifer Redmond, and Maria Battaglia for their help with the Wine School
- All my pourers at the school over the last 40 years
- Having a great relationship with my New York City wine-school peers, especially Harriet Lembeck (Beverage Program) and Mary Ewing-Mulligan (International Wine Center)
- The Baum-Emil team, who recreated Windows on the World in 1996
- Conducting the Sherry-Lehmann / Kevin Zraly Master Wine Class with Michael Aaron, Michael Yurch, Chris Adams, Shyda Gilmer, and Matt Wong
- Michael Stengel and Joe Cozza at the Marriott Marquis Hotel NYC for their advice and support since September 11, 2001
- My continuing grief at the loss of those friends and coworkers who lost their lives on September 11th
- Robert M. Parker Jr., who so generously donated his time and talents to aid the families of September 11th
- Alan Stillman, founder, chairman, and CEO of the Smith & Wollensky Restaurant Group
- Being honored for "loving wine" and receiving the 2011 Lifetime Achievement Award from the James Beard Foundation.
- Teaching at Cornell University and the Culinary Institute of America
- Serving as a member of the Culinary Institute's Board of Trustees
- All the special wine friends who have helped deplete my wine cellar over the years, especially Harvey
- Those who have tried to keep me organized in my business life: Ellen Kerr, Claire Josephs, Lois Arrighi, Sara Hutton, Andrea Immer, Dawn Lamendola, Catherine Fallis, Rebecca Chapa, Gina D'Angelo-Mullen, Michelle Woodruff, and Judy Cohen.
- My four best vintages: Anthony (1991), Nicolas (1993), Harrison (1997), and Adriana (1999)
- My mom, Kathleen
- My sisters, Sharon and Kathy
- The 20,000 students who attended the Windows on the World Wine School, which celebrated its 40th anniversary and final semester in 2016
- Everyone who worked at Windows on the World, especially my colleagues in the wine department

SPECIAL REMEMBRANCE

Morley Safer for his wonderful segments on wine for *60 Minutes*, especially the French Paradox (see page 76).

A FINAL NOTE

If this were an award-acceptance speech, the music probably would have drowned me out after the first ten bullets above. No doubt I've forgotten to name at least one or two folks—an occupational hazard of consuming so much wine! To everyone I've ever met or known, from grammar school on: *May all your vintages be great!*

WINE QUIZZES

PRELUDE TO WINE

1. What are the three flavors in wine?
2. What are three sources that can affect a wine's taste?
3. What species of grape makes the most wine?
4. Name three grapes that have high tannin.
5. What is terroir?
6. What is Brix?
7. What is phylloxera?
8. What is Noble Rot?
9. Sugar + _____ = _____ + Carbon Dioxide
10. What are the percentage ranges of alcohol in sparkling wine, table wine, and fortified wine?
11. What is must?
12. How do red grapes make white wine?
13. What is maceration?
14. What is chaptalization?
15. What is residual sugar?
16. Where does tannin come from?
17. What does a vintage on a bottle indicate?
18. What are two factors that affect whether a wine will last more than five years?
19. What is a "corked" wine?
20. Why do vintners use sulfur dioxide in the winemaking process?
21. What is vertical tasting?
22. What happens to the color of white wines as they age?
23. What happens to the color of red wines as they age?
24. What is the difference between aroma and bouquet?
25. Why should you swirl a wine before smelling it?

Turn the page for the answer key.

PRELUDE TO WINE
ANSWERS

1. Sweet, sour, and bitter

2. Grapes, fermentation, and maturation and aging

3. *Vitis vinifera* makes the most wine.

4. Nebbiolo, Cabernet Sauvignon, Syrah/Shiraz

5. Terroir is how the "somewhereness" of a particular region or vineyard tastes, including soil, geography, sunlight, weather, climate, surrounding plant life, and other elements.

6. The winemaker's measure of sugar in grapes

7. A grape louse that can kill the entire plant

8. *Botrytis cinera*, a mold that slowly pierces grape skins, allowing their water content to evaporate and giving the wine a more intense flavor.

9. Sugar + Yeast = Alcohol + Carbon Dioxide

10. Sparkling wine: 8–12 percent; table wine: 8–15 percent; fortified wine: 17–22 percent.

11. The mixture of grape juice and skins

12. Winemakers remove the skins of red grapes to make white wine from the pulp.

13. Soaking the skins to extract aromas, tannins, and color

14. The process of adding sugar to the must so the yeast generates more alcohol in the final wine

15. When some of the natural sugars in the must remain unfermented by yeast

16. Tannin comes from the skins, pits, and stems of the grapes.

17. A vintage indicates the year that growers harvested the grapes.

18. The grape, the vintage, where the wine comes from, how the wine was made, and storage conditions

19. Corked wine is when trichloroanisole (TCA) from the cork has spoiled a wine.

20. As an antioxidant, preservative, and disinfectant to prevent unwanted oxidation and to inhibit the action of bacteria or wild yeast

21. Comparing wines from different vintages

22. As they age, white wines gain color.

23. Red wines lose color as they age.

24. Aroma represents the smell of the grapes in the wine; bouquet describes the total smell of the wine (usually found in older wines).

25. To allow oxygen to aerate the wine, releasing the esters and aldehydes that combine with oxygen to yield the wine's aroma or bouquet.

CLASS ONE

AMERICAN WINE AND
THE RED WINES OF CALIFORNIA
QUIZ

1. What percentage of wine consumed in America comes from the United States?

2. Approximately how many wineries are there in the United States?

3. How many states have wineries?

4. What is the name of a wine-grape species native to America?

5. When did phylloxera first destroy the vineyards of California?

6. In what year did Prohibition begin?

7. In what year did Prohibition end?

8. What is an American Viticultural Area (AVA)?

9. Approximately how many AVAs does America have?

10. If an AVA appears on a wine label, what percentage of the grapes must come from that region?

11. Name the top five states in wine production.

12. Name the top ten states in wine consumption.

13. What are the main viticultural areas of California?

14. What are the top grapes planted in Napa

15. What are the top grapes planted in Sonoma?

16. Are Americans drinking more red wine or white wine?

17. Does California grow more red grapes or white?

18. What are the three most planted red grapes in California?

19. What does the word "Reserve" mean on a California wine label?

20. In which French wine region do you find great Cabernet Sauvignon?

21. What is the most planted red grape in the Napa Valley?

22. In which two French wine regions do you find great Pinot Noir?

23. Which county in California has the most plantings of Pinot Noir?

24. What California grape has the same DNA as the Italian grape Primitivo?

25. In which French wine region do you find great Syrah?

26. Which California counties have the most Syrah planted?

27. What was the most planted red grape in California in 1970?

28. What is a Meritage wine?

29. Name two Meritage wines.

Turn the page for the answer key.

AMERICAN WINE AND
THE RED WINES OF CALIFORNIA
ANSWERS

1. More than 75 percent

2. More than 7,700

3. All fifty

4. Wine grape species native to America include *Vitis labrusca* and *Vitis rotundifolia*.

5. 1876

6. 1920

7. 1933

8. A specific grape-growing area within a state or region recognized by and registered with the federal government

9. More than 230

10. At least 85 percent

11. California, Washington, New York, Oregon, and Texas

12. Washington, DC; New Hampshire; Vermont; Massachusetts; New Jersey; Nevada; Connecticut; California; Rhode Island; and Delaware

13. North Coast, North Central Coast, South Central Coast, and San Joaquin Valley

14. Cabernet Sauvignon, Chardonnay, and Merlot

15. Chardonnay, Pinot Noir, and Cabernet Sauvignon

16. Red

17. Red grapes

18. Cabernet Sauvignon, Zinfandel, and Merlot

19. The word has no legal meaning. Each winery that uses it defines the term individually.

20. Bordeaux

21. Cabernet Sauvignon

22. Burgundy and Champagne

23. Sonoma

24. Zinfandel

25. The Rhône Valley

26. San Luis Obispo and Sonoma

27. Zinfandel

28. A red or white wine made in America from a blend of the classic Bordeaux grape varieties

29. Examples include: Cain Five, Dominus, Insignia, Magnificat, Opus One, and Trefethen Halo.

CLASS TWO
THE WHITE WINES OF CALIFORNIA
AND OTHER AMERICAN WINES
QUIZ

1. What's the most important white-wine grape grown in California?

2. Name three other major white-wine grapes grown in California.

3. What is the difference between Sauvignon Blanc and Fumé Blanc?

4. What are the major grapes grown in Washington?

5. Does Washington produce more red wine or more white?

6. How many AVAs does Oregon have?

7. What grape does Oregon grow most?

8. Name the three main wine regions of New York.

9. Which Native American varieties of grapes are grown in New York?

Turn the page for the answer key.

AMERICAN WINE AND THE
WHITE WINES OF CALIFORNIA
ANSWERS

1. Chardonnay

2. Sauvignon Blanc, Chenin Blanc, and Viognier

3. Trick question! There's no official difference between Sauvignon Blanc and Fumé Blanc. Robert Mondavi invented the latter name to increase sales.

4. Chardonnay, Riesling, Cabernet Sauvignon, and Merlot

5. Another trick question! Washington produces 50 percent white wine and 50 percent red.

6. 18 AVAs

7. Pinot Noir

8. Finger Lakes, Hudson Valley, and Long Island

9. Concord, Catawba, and Delaware

FRENCH WINE AND
THE RED WINES OF BORDEAUX
‹› QUIZ ‹›

1. Match grape variety with wine region

   a. Riesling   _____ Champagne

   b. Sauvignon Blanc   _____ Loire Valley

   c. Chardonnay   _____ Alsace

   d. Sémillon   _____ Burgundy

   e. Gewürztraminer   _____ Bordeaux

   f. Grenache   _____ Côtes du Rhône

   g. Pinot Noir

   h. Cabernet Sauvignon

   i. Chenin Blanc

   j. Syrah

   k. Merlot

2. When were the Appellation d'Origine Contrôlée (AOC) laws first established?

3. How many acres are in a hectare?

4. How many gallons are in a hectoliter?

5. What is the English word for red Bordeaux wine?

6. How many appellations does Bordeaux have?

7. What approximate percentage of red wine does Bordeaux produce?

8. What are the three major red grapes that grow in Bordeaux?

9. What red grape grows primarily on the left bank of the Garonne River?

10. What red grape grows primarily on the right bank of the Dordogne River?

11. Name the three quality levels of Bordeaux wine.

12. Approximately how many wine-producing châteaux does Bordeaux have?

13. What percentage of Bordeaux wine costs between $8 and $25 retail?

14. In what year did wine brokers classify the best châteaux of the Médoc?

15. How many châteaux did they classify?

16. What percentage do the Grands Crus Classés Châteaux represent of the total volume of Bordeaux?

17. Name one château from each of the five growths.

18. In what year were the wines of Graves first classified?

19. In what year were the wines of St-Émilion first classified?

20. What's the primary red grape used in St-Émilion wine?

21. Name three great recent vintages from the left bank of the Garonne River.

22. Name three great recent vintages from the right bank of the Dordogne River.

23. Name two second-label wines of classified châteaux.

Turn the page for the answer key.

CLASS THREE
FRENCH WINE AND
THE RED WINES OF BORDEAUX
ANSWERS

1. Grape variety and wine region

   Champagne: Pinot Noir & Chardonnay

   Loire Valley: Sauvignon Blanc & Chenin Blanc

   Alsace: Riesling & Gewürztraminer

   Burgundy: Pinot Noir & Chardonnay

   Bordeaux: Cabernet Sauvignon, Merlot, Sauvignon Blanc & Sémillon

   Côtes du Rhône: Syrah & Grenache

2. 1930s

3. 1 hectare = 2.471 acres

4. 1 hectoliter = 26.42 gallons

5. Claret

6. 57

7. 85 percent of Bordeaux wine is red, and 15 percent is white.

8. Merlot, Cabernet Sauvignon, and Cabernet Franc

9. Cabernet Sauvignon

10. Merlot

11. The three quality levels are Bordeaux Appellation, Appellation Region, and Region + Chateau.

12. 7,000

13. 80 percent

14. 1855

15. 61

16. Less than 5 percent

17. See pages 124–125 for the complete list.

18. 1959

19. 1955

20. Merlot

21. 1990, 1995, 1996, 2000, 2003, 2005, 2009, 2010, 2015

22. 1990, 1998, 2000, 2001, 2005, 2009, 2010, 2015

23. Alter Ego, Carruades de Lafite, Le Clarence de Haut-Brion, Echo de Lynch Bages, L'Espirit de Chevalier, Les Forts de Latour, Pavillon Rouge du Château Margaux, Le Petit Lion, Le Petit Mouton, Réserve de la Comtesse, La Réserve Léoville-Barton, Les Tourelles de Longueville

THE RED WINES OF BURGUNDY
AND THE RHÔNE VALLEY

QUIZ

1. What are the main red wine–producing regions in Burgundy?

2. What are the two grape varieties used in making red Burgundy wine?

3. How did the Napoleonic Code affect the vineyards of Burgundy?

4. What grape variety is Beaujolais made from?

5. What are the three quality levels of Beaujolais?

6. How many Cru Beaujolais are there?

7. Name three Cru Beaujolais villages.

8. When does Beaujolais Nouveau release?

9. Name two wine villages of the Côte Châlonnaise.

10. What are the four quality levels of the Côte d'Or?

11. Name the two regions within the Côte d'Or.

12. How many Grand Cru vineyards does the Côte d'Or have?

13. Name two wine villages from the Côte de Beaune known for producing red wine.

14. Name two red Grand Cru vineyards of the Côte de Beaune.

15. Name two wine villages from the Côte de Nuits known for making red wine.

16. Name two red Grand Cru vineyards from the Côte de Nuits.

17. Where in France does the Rhône Valley lie?

18. What are the three major quality levels of the Rhône Valley?

19. What percentage of Côtes du Rhône wines come from grapes grown in the southern region?

20. How many Crus does the Rhône Valley have?

21. Name two Crus from the Northern Rhône.

22. Name two Crus from the Southern Rhône.

23. What two main red grape varieties grow in the Rhône Valley?

24. What's the primary red grape used in the Northern Rhône?

25. What is Tavel?

26. How many different grape varieties can go into Châteauneuf-du-Pape?

27. Name the four most important grapes used to make Châteauneuf-du-Pape.

28. What's one difference between a Côtes du Rhône and a Beaujolais?

29. Which wine will age longer, a Côtes du Rhône Villages or a Hermitage?

30. Name two white wines from the Rhône.

Turn the page for the answer key.

THE RED WINES OF BURGUNDY
AND THE RHONE VALLEY
ANSWERS

1. The Côte d'Or (Côte de Nuits, Côte de Beaune), Beaujolais, and Côte Châlonnaise

2. Pinot Noir and Gamay

3. It instituted equal inheritance laws for heirs, thereby fragmenting the vineyards of Burgundy.

4. 100 percent Gamay grapes

5. Beaujolais, Beaujolais-Villages, and Cru

6. Ten Crus

7. Brouilly, Chénas, Chiroubles, Côte de Brouilly, Fleurie, Juliénas, Morgon, Moulin-à-Vent, Régnié, and St-Amour

8. The third Thursday of November

9. Mercurey, Givry, and Rully

10. Regional (Bourgogne), Village, Premier Cru, and Grand Cru.

11. The Côte de Beaune and Côte de Nuits

12. 32 Grand Cru vineyards

13. Aloxe-Corton, Beaune, Pommard, and Volnay

14. Corton, Corton Bressandes, Corton Clos de Roi, Corton Maréchaude, and Corton Renardes

15. Chambolle-Musigny, Flagey-Échézeaux, Gevrey-Chambertin, Morey-St-Denis, Nuits-St-Georges, Vosne-Romanée, and Vougeot

16. Bonnes Mares, Musigny, Échézeaux, Grands-Échézeaux, Chambertin, Chambertin Close de Bèze, Chapelle-Chambertin, Charmes-Chambertin, Griotte-Chambertin, Latricières-Chambertin, Mazis-Chambertin, Mazoyères-Chambertin, Ruchottes-Chambertin, Clos de la Roche, Clos des Lambrays, Clos de Tart, Clos St-Denis, La Grande-Rue, La Romanée, La Tâche, Malconsorts, Richebourg, Romanée-Conti, Romanée-St-Vivant, and Clos de Vougeout

17. Southeastern France, south of Burgundy

18. Côte du Rhône, Côte du Rhône Villages, and Côte du Rhône Crus (Northern and Southern)

19. More than 90 percent

20. 13 Crus

21. Château-Grillet, Condrieu, Cornas, Côte-Rôtie, Crozes-Hermitage, Hermitage, St-Joseph, and St-Peray

22. Châteauneuf-de-Pape, Gigondas, Lirac, Tavel, and Vacqueyras

23. Grenache and Syrah

24. Syrah

25. A dry rosé made primarily from the Grenache grape.

26. 13 different grapes

27. Grenache, Syrah, Mourvèdre, and Cinsault

28. Côtes du Rhône has more body and alcohol than Beaujolais.

29. Hermitage

30. Condrieu and Chateau Grillet

THE WHITE WINES OF FRANCE
⊰ QUIZ ⊱

1. Name one difference in style between a Riesling from Alsace and one from Germany.

2. What's the most planted grape in Alsace?

3. Name two important shippers of Alsace wine.

4. What's the grape variety for Sancerre and Pouilly-Fumé wines?

5. What's the grape variety for Vouvray wine?

6. Define the term "sur lie."

7. What does the word "Graves" mean in English?

8. The majority of the white Bordeaux wines use which two grape varieties?

9. Name two classified châteaux of Graves.

10. What's the primary grape used for Sauternes?

11. What are the three classification levels of the châteaux in Sauternes?

12. Name the main regions of Burgundy.

13. Which region of Burgundy produces only white wine?

14. Which region of Burgundy produces the most red wine?

15. Does the Côte d'Or produce more white wine or more red?

16. Name three quality levels of Burgundy.

17. For Chablis, name two Grand Cru vineyards and two Premier Cru vineyards.

18. Which are the three most important white wine villages in the Côte de Beaune?

19. Name three white Grand Cru vineyards from the Côte de Beaune.

20. From which region in Burgundy does Pouilly-Fuissé come?

21. In Burgundy, what does "estate-bottled" wine mean?

Turn the page for the answer key.

THE WHITE WINES OF FRANCE
ANSWERS

1. Rieslings from Alsace are dry, while most German Rieslings have some residual sugar. Also the alcohol content is lower in German wines.

2. Riesling

3. Domaine Dopff au Moulin, Domaine F. E. Trimbach, Domaine Hugel & Fils, Domaine Léon Beyer, Domaine Marcel Deiss, Domaine Weinbach, Domaine Zind-Humbrecht.

4. Sauvignon Blanc

5. Chenin Blanc

6. Wine aged on its "lees" (sediment)

7. Gravel

8. Sauvignon Blanc and Sémillon

9. Château Bouscaut, Château Carbonnieux, Château Couhins-Lurton, Domaine de Chevalier, Château Haut-Brion, Château La Louvière, Château La Tour-Matillac, Château Laville-Haut-Brion, Château Malartic-Lagravière, Château Olivier, Château Smith-Haut-Lafitte

10. Sémillon

11. Grand Premier Cru, Premiers Crus, Deuxièmes Crus

12. Chablis, Côte Chalonnaise, Côte d'Or (Côte de Nuits, Côte de Beaune), Mâconnais, Beaujolais

13. Chablis

14. Beaujolais

15. More red

16. Regional Appellations, Village wine, Premier Cru, and Grand Cru

17. Grand Cru vineyards of Chablis: Blanchots, Bougros, Grenouilles, Les Clos, Preuses, Valmur, and Vaudésir. Premier Cru vineyards of Chablis: Côte de Vaulorent, Fourchaume, Lechet, Montée de Tonnerre, Montmains, Monts de Milieu, and Vaillon

18. Meursault, Puligny-Montrachet, and Chassagne-Montrachet

19. Corton-Charlemagne, Charlemagne, Bâtard-Montrachet, Montrachet, Bienvenue-Bâtard-Montrachet, Chevalier-Montrachet, Criots-Bâtard-Montrachet

20. Mâconnais

21. The owner of the vineyard makes, produces, and bottles the wine.

❧ CLASS SIX ❧
THE WINES OF SPAIN
❧ QUIZ ❧

1. Name three of Spain's major winemaking regions.
2. What does *cosecha* mean in English?
3. Name two Spanish wine regions that historically make high-quality wine?
4. What two primary red grapes make Rioja wines?
5. What percentage of Rioja grapes are red?
6. What does *vinos de pagos* indicate about a wine?
7. What are the three levels for aging Rioja wines?
8. In which wine region would you find Bodegas Montecillo, CVNE, and Marqués de Cáceres?
9. In which wine region would you find Vega Sicilia and Pesquera?
10. What major red grapes go into the wines of Ribera del Duero?
11. What is Spanish sparkling wine called, and which region produces most of it?
12. What major grapes make the wines of Priorat?
13. In which region would you find the wines of Alvaro Palacios, Mas Igneus, and Pasanau?
14. Where in Spain does Rueda lie?
15. What major grape makes the majority of wine from the Rías Baixas region?

Turn the page for the answer key.

❧ CLASS SEVEN ❧
THE WINES OF ITALY
❧ QUIZ ❧

1. How many wine regions does Italy have?
2. Historically what are Italy's top three wine-producing regions?
3. According to Italian wine laws, what's the highest quality level?
4. Name the three different quality levels of Chianti.
5. In which Italian wine region do you find Chianti, Vino Nobile di Montepulciano, and Brunello di Montalcino, and what primary grape makes these wines?
6. What's the minimum amount of time that a Brunello di Montalcino must age in oak?
7. What is a "Super Tuscan" wine?
8. What are the three major red grapes of Piedmont?
9. What's the biggest difference between France's AOC laws and the DOC wine laws of Italy?
10. What's the only grape that can produce Barolo and Barbaresco wines?
11. Under DOCG wine laws, which must age longer, a Barolo or Barbaresco?
12. From which Italian wine region do Valpolicella, Bardolino, Soave, and Amarone come?
13. Define the following terms: Ripasso, Classico, Superiore.
14. What are three different ways that Italian wines are named?
15. What are some other important regions in Italy?

Turn the page for the answer key.

THE WINES OF SPAIN
ANSWERS

1. Rioja, Ribera del Duero, Penedès, Priorat, Rueda, Rías Baixas, Jerez

2. Harvest or vintage

3. Rioja and Priorat

4. Tempranillo and Garnacha

5. Red grapes account for 90 percent of Rioja grape production.

6. The wine comes from a single estate.

7. Crianza, Reserva, and Gran Reserva

8. The Rioja region

9. The Ribera del Duero region

10. Tempranillo, Cabernet Sauvignon, Merlot, Malbec, and Garnacha

11. The Penedès region produces Cava.

12. Garnacha, Cariñena, Cabernet Sauvignon, Merlot, and Syrah

13. Priorat

14. North-central

15. Albariño

THE WINES OF ITALY
ANSWERS

1. 20

2. Veneto, Piedmont, and Tuscany

3. DOCG / Denominazione di Origine Controllata Garantita

4. Chianti, Chianti Classico, and Chianti Classico Riserva

5. Tuscany, and the primary grape is Sangiovese.

6. Two years

7. Super Tuscan wines are high-quality table wines from Tuscany that include previously DOC-forbidden grapes, such as Cabernet Sauvignon.

8. Barbera, Dolcetto, Nebbiolo

9. Italy's DOC mandates aging requirements.

10. Nebbiolo

11. Barolo

12. The Veneto

13. Ripasso is the adding back of grape skins from Amarone wine to Valpolicella, giving it extra alcohol and more flavor. Classico means the vineyards lie in the historical part of the region. Superiore means higher levels of alcohol and longer aging.

14. Italian wines are named by grape variety, village or district, or a proprietary designation.

15. Some other important wine regions in Italy are Abruzzo, Fruili-Veneza Giulia, Trentino-Alto Adige, Lombardy, Umbria, Campania, and Sicily.

 CLASS EIGHT  CLASS NINE

THE WINES OF AUSTRALIA AND NEW ZEALAND
✧ QUIZ ✧

1. Name the two top red grapes and the two top white grapes grown in Australia.

2. Name the four Australian states known for wine production and one wine district from each state.

3. What Australian wine region is known for its sparkling wines?

4. If a label specifies a wine growing district, what percentage of the wine must originate from that district?

5. What are some recent good vintages for Australian wine?

6. When did New Zealand record its first vintage?

7. Name New Zealand's three main grape varieties.

8. Name three of the most important winemaking regions of New Zealand.

9. Does New Zealand produce more red wines or white?

10. What are the flavor characteristics of a Marlborough Sauvignon Blanc?

Turn the page for the answer key.

THE WINES OF SOUTH AMERICA
✧ QUIZ ✧

1. Name the two major white grapes and the four major red grapes that grow in Chile.

2. What percentage of Chile's total grape acreage does Cabernet Sauvignon represent?

3. Name Chile's three most important winemaking regions.

4. What Chilean grape was mistaken for Merlot?

5. If a grape name appears on a Chilean wine label, what minimum percentage of that grape must the wine contain?

6. Where does Argentina rank in worldwide wine production?

7. When were the first grapes planted in Argentina?

8. Name two major white grapes and two major red grapes that grow in Argentina.

9. Name Argentina's three main wine regions.

10. If a grape name appears on an Argentinean wine label, how much of that grape must the wine contain?

Turn the page for the answer key.

THE WINES OF AUSTRALIA AND NEW ZEALAND
ANSWERS

1. Red: Shiraz and Cabernet Sauvignon; white: Sauvignon Blanc and Chardonnay

2. South Australia: Adelaide Hills, Clare Valley, Coonawarra, Barossa Valley, McLaren Vale; New South Wales: Hunter Valley; Victoria: Yarra Valley; Western Australia: Margaret River.

3. Tasmania

4. 85 percent

5. 2010, 2012, and 2013

6. 1836

7. Sauvignon Blanc, Pinot Noir, and Chardonnay

8. Gisborne, Hawke's Bay, Martinborough / Wairarapa, Marlborough, and Central Otago

9. White

10. Crisp, mineral, acidic flavors of grapefruit, lime, or other tropical fruit

THE WINES OF SOUTH AMERICA
ANSWERS

1. White: Chardonnay, Sauvignon Blanc; red: Cabernet Sauvignon, Carménère, Merlot, and Syrah

2. 32 percent

3. Casablanca Valley, Maipo Valley, and Rapel Valley / Colchagua

4. Carménère

5. 85 percent of the grape variety

6. Fifth

7. 1544

8. White: Torrontés Riojano and Sauvignon Blanc; red: Malbec and Cabernet Sauvignon

9. North, Cuyo, and Patagonia

10. 100 percent

CLASS TEN
THE WINES OF GERMANY
QUIZ

1. What percentage of German wines are white?

2. If a German wine has the name of a grape variety on a label, what's the minimum percentage of that grape in the wine?

3. What percentage of the grapes planted in Germany are Riesling?

4. What German grape is a cross betwen Riesling and Chasselas?

5. If a German wine lists a vintage on the label, what's the minimum percentage of that year in the wine?

6. How many winemaking regions are there in Germany?

7. Name Germany's four most important wine regions.

8. Describe the overall style of German wines.

9. Name the three basic styles of German wine.

10. What does the word "Trocken" say about the style of the wine?

11. What's the average alcohol range for German wines?

12. What are the two main categories of Qualitätswein?

13. Name the levels of ripeness of Prädikatswein.

14. What does "Spätlese" mean in English?

15. What is Eiswein?

16. What is Süssreserve?

17. Match the region to the village:

    a. Rheingau   _____ Oppenheim

    b. Mosel   _____ Rüdesheim

    c. Rheinhessen   _____ Bernkastel

    d. Pfalz   _____ Piesport

                             _____ Johannisberg

                             _____ Deidesheim

                             _____ Nierstein

18. What does "Gutsabfüllung" indicate?

19. What is *Edelfäule*?

Turn the page for the answer key.

CLASS TEN
THE WINES OF GERMANY
ANSWERS

1. 65 percent
2. At least 85 percent
3. 21 percent
4. Müller-Thurgau
5. 85 percent
6. 13 regions
7. Rheinhessen, Rheingau, Mosel, and Pfalz
8. A balance of sweetness with acidity and low alcohol
9. Trocken, halbtrocken, and fruity
10. It's dry.
11. Between 8 percent and 10 percent.
12. Qualitätswein bestimmter Anbaugebiete and Prädikatswein.
13. Kabinett, Spätlese, Auslese, Beerenauslese, Trockenbeerenauslese, and Eiswein
14. "Late picking"

15. A sweet, concentrated wine made from grapes pressed while still frozen
16. When winemakers reserve grape juice and add it to the wine after fermentation
17. Oppenheim: Rheinhessen

    Rüdesheim: Rheingau

    Bernkastel: Mosel

    Piesport: Mosel

    Johannisberg: Rheingau

    Deidesheim: Pfalz

    Nierstein: Rheinhessen
18. Estate-bottled
19. The German word for *Botrytis cinerea.*

CLASS ELEVEN
SPARKLING WINES
QUIZ

1. Where in France does the Champagne region lie?
2. What are the four main areas of the Champagne region?
3. What three grapes go into making Champagne?
4. What are the three major types of Champagne?
5. What's the Champagne making process called?
6. What's the minimum amount of time that a nonvintage Champagne and a vintage Champagne must age in the bottle?
7. What is *liqueur de tirage*?
8. Define the following terms: riddling, disgorging, dosage.
9. What are the seven levels of dryness/sweetness in Champagne?
10. What is a Blanc de Blanc Champagne? A Blanc de Noir?
11. Roughly how many pounds per square inch of pressure does a Champagne bottle contain?
12. What are the names for sparkling wine from Spain, Italy, and Germany?
13. Which region in Italy does Prosecco come from?

Turn the page for the answer key.

CLASS TWELVE
FORTIFIED WINES
QUIZ

1. What is a fortified wine?
2. What's the alcohol range in a fortified wine?
3. Name the three towns in Spain that form the Sherry triangle.
4. What two grapes make Sherry?
5. Name the five types of Sherry.
6. Which wine did George Washington serve at the signing of the Declaration of Independence?
7. In the context of Sherry, what's a *bodega*?
8. What percentage of Sherry is lost to evaporation each year?
9. What's the Solera Method?
10. Sherry usually is aged in what type of oak?
11. Where does true Port come from?
12. When is the neutral brandy added to Port wine?
13. Name the two main categories of Port.
14. What kind of Ports are Late Bottled Vintage, Vintage Character, Quinta, and Vintage?
15. What kind of Ports are Ruby, Tawny, and Colheita?
16. How long does Vintage Port age in wood?
17. What's the approximate alcohol content of Port?
18. What percentage of all Port does Vintage Port represent?

Turn the page for the answer key.

CLASS ELEVEN
SPARKLING WINES
ANSWERS

1. Northeast of Paris

2. Marne Valley, Côte des Blancs, Reims Mountain, and Aube

3. Pinot Noir, Pinot Meunier, and Chardonnay

4. Nonvintage/multiple vintage, vintage, and "prestige" cuvée

5. Méthode Champenoise

6. Nonvintage Champagne: 15 months; vintage Champagne: 3 years

7. A mixture of sugar and yeast added to the base wine after the blending process to begin the second fermentation.

8. Riddling: gradually turning Champagne bottles while slowly tipping them upside down. Disgorging: freezing and removing the sediment in the neck of a Champagne bottle. Dosage: A mixture of wine and sugar that replaces the wine lost during disgorging.

9. Brut nature, extra brut, brut, extra sec / dry, sec, demi-sec, and doux

10. Blanc de Blanc Champagne comes from 100 percent Chardonnay, Blanc de Noir from 100 percent Pinot Noir.

11. 90 PSI

12. Cava, Spumante, and Sekt

13. The Veneto

CLASS TWELVE
FORTIFIED WINES
ANSWERS

1. A wine that contains added neutral brandy to raise the wine's alcohol content

2. 15–20 percent

3. Jerez de la Frontera, Puerto de Santa María, and Sanlúcar de Barrameda

4. Palomino and Pedro Ximénez

5. Manzanilla, Fino, Amontillado, Oloroso, and Cream

6. Madeira

7. An aboveground structure used to store wine

8. At least 3 percent

9. Fractional blending or the continuous blending of several vintages to maintain the house style

10. American oak

11. The Douro region in northern Portugal

12. During fermentation

13. Cask-aged and bottle-aged

14. Bottle-aged

15. Cask-aged

16. Two years

17. Around 20 percent

18. Only 3 percent

WINES OF THE WORLD

QUIZ

CANADA

1. When did Canadian commercial winemaking begin?
2. Name three major white grapes and three major red grapes grown in Canada.
3. What are Canada's two major wine-producing regions?
4. In a Canadian varietal wine, what minimum percentage must the wine contain of a specific grape?
5. How is ice wine made?

Turn the page for the answer key.

SOUTH AFRICA

1. Describe the South African winemaking terrain.
2. Name the three major white grapes and three major red grapes grown in South Africa.
3. Name the three WOs within the Coastal Region.
4. What are some of the ways to make a great Pinotage?
5. In a South African vintage or varietal wine, what minimum percentage must a wine contain of a specific year or grape?

Turn the page for the answer key.

AUSTRIA

1. What are Austria's four main wine regions?
2. Name three major white grapes and three major red grapes that grow in Austria.
3. What are the three major quality levels of Austrian wine?
4. What is Austria's great dessert wine?
5. What qualities of wine do Riedel glasses enhance?

Turn the page for the answer key.

HUNGARY

1. Name the three major white grapes and three major red grapes native to Hungary.
2. Name three major wine regions of Hungary.
3. How is Tokaji Aszú made?
4. What are the four levels of Puttonyos wine?
5. What is the name of the sweetest of the Tokaji wines?

Turn the page for the answer key.

GREECE

1. Roughly when did Greek winemaking begin?
2. What are the characteristics of the Mediterranean climate?
3. Name the three major white grapes and three major red grapes that grow in Greece.
4. Name two of the most important winemaking regions of Greece.
5. What is the winemaking terrain of Greece?

Turn the page for the answer key.

WINES OF THE WORLD
ANSWERS

CANADA

1. The early 1800s

2. White: Chardonnay, Pinot Gris, Riesling, Gewürztraminer, Vidal; red: Pinot Noir, Cabernet Sauvignon, Merlot, Cabernet Franc, and Syrah

3. Ontario / Niagara Peninsula and British Columbia / Okanagan Valley

4. 85 percent

5. By pressing naturally frozen, hand-picked grapes

SOUTH AFRICA

1. Vineyards lie at altitudes from 300 feet above sea level to 1,300. Some have cool, coastal climates, and in others summer days exceed 100 degrees Fahrenheit.

2. Chenin Blanc (Steen), Sauvignon Blanc, Chardonnay; red: Cabernet Sauvignon, Shiraz, Pinotage

3. Constantia, Stellenbosch, and Paarl

4. Vines planted in cooler climates, at least fifteen years old, low per-acre crop yield, long skin contact, maceration in open fermenters, at least two years of oak aging, blending with Cabernet Sauvignon, at least ten years of bottle aging

5. 85 percent

AUSTRIA

1. Lower Austria, Vienna, Burgenland, and Styria

2. White: Grüner Veltliner, Riesling, Sauvignon Blanc, and Chardonnay (Morillon); red: Blaufränkisch (Lemberger), St. Laurent, Pinot Noir

3. Tafelwein, Qualitätswein, and Prädikatswein

4. Ausbruch

5. Aroma, bouquet, and taste

HUNGARY

1. White: Furmint, Hárslevelü, and Olaszrizling; red: Kadarka, Kékfrankos, and Portugieser

2. The major wine regions of Hungary include: Badacsony, Eger, Somoló, Sopron, Szekszárd, Tokaj, and Villány-Siklós.

3. Grapes affected with *Botrytis cinerea* are made into a paste. Unaffected grapes ferment into the base wine, and workers blend in baskets of the noble rot paste according to the desired sweetness level.

4. 3 baskets, (60g sugar / liter), 4 baskets (90g), 5 baskets (120g), and 6 baskets (150g)

5. Essencia

GREECE

1. 5000 B.C.

2. Hot summers; long autumns; and short, mild winters

3. White: Assyrtiko, Moschofilero, and Roditis; red: Agiorgitiko, Xinomavro, Mavrodafni

4. The most important wine-making regions in Greece include: Macedonia, Peloponnese, and the Islands.

5. Most vineyards lie on the slopes of steep mountains or remote islands.

IMAGE CREDITS

ABOUT THE AUTHOR

Kevin Zraly is the founder and teacher of the Windows on the World Wine School, which has graduated more than 20,000 students in 40 years, as well as the Sherry-Lehmann/Kevin Zraly Wine Club and master classes. His Windows on the World Complete Wine Course has sold more than three million copies worldwide, making him the world's best-selling wine author. He has received the James Beard Lifetime Achievement Award and the European Wine Council's Lifetime Achievement Award, among numerous other awards, and has been featured in *GQ*, the *New York Times*, *Newsweek*, *People*, *USA Today*, *Wall Street Journal*, and other publications. He lives in New York.

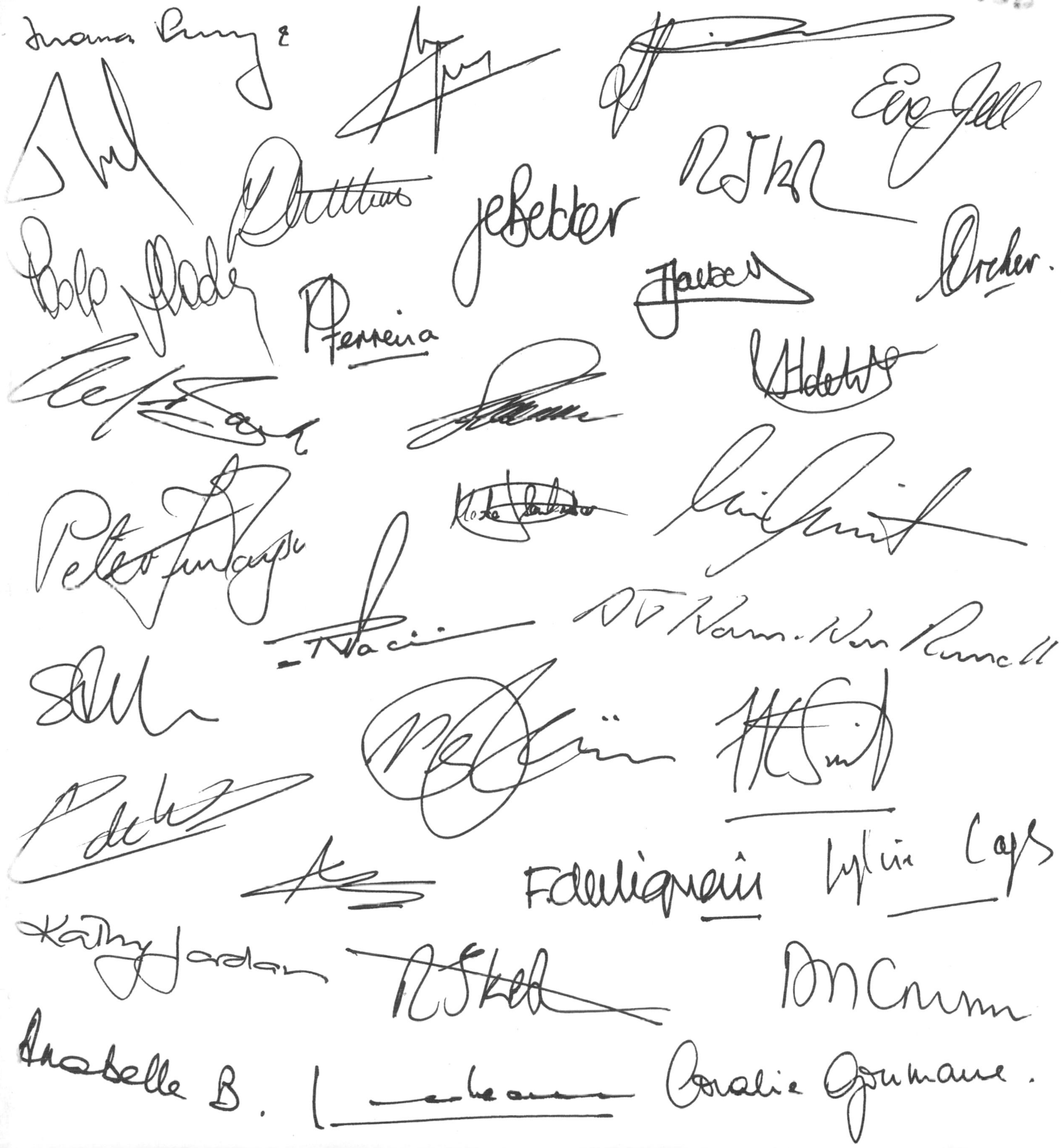

Ferreira
Kathy Jordan
Anabelle B.

JCP

P. PHILIPPE

Sofia Perpera

David Strada

Fiona Donald

Rory Callaha

Jana Stravitz

Rod McDonald.

David Slingsby Smith

Louisa Rose

Chris Burdin

Rute Monteiro